AN ACCOUNT OF AN ELIZABETHAN FAMILY

AN ACCOUNT OF AN ELIZABETHAN FAMILY

THE WILLOUGHBYS OF WOLLATON BY CASSANDRA WILLOUGHBY (1670–1735)

edited by
Jo Ann Hoeppner Moran Cruz

with the assistance of
Kate Sampsell

CAMDEN FIFTH SERIES
Volume 55

CAMBRIDGE
UNIVERSITY PRESS

FOR THE ROYAL HISTORICAL SOCIETY
University College London, Gower Street, London WC1 6BT
2018

Published by the Press Syndicate of the University of Cambridge
University Printing House, Shaftesbury Road, Cambridge CB2 8BS, United Kingdom
One Liberty Plaza, Floor 20, New York, NY 10006, USA
477 Williamstown Road, Port Melbourne, VIC 3207, Australia
C/Orense, 4, Planta 13, 28020 Madrid, Spain
Lower Ground Floor, Nautica Building, The Water Club,
Beach Road, Granger Bay, 8005 Cape Town, South Africa

© Royal Historical Society 2018

First published 2018

A catalogue record for this book is available from the British Library

ISBN 9781108492515 hardback

SUBSCRIPTIONS. The serial publications of the Royal Historical Society, *Royal Historical Society Transactions* (ISSN 0080-4401) and Camden Fifth Series (ISSN 0960-1163) volumes, may be purchased together on annual subscription. The 2018 subscription price, which includes print and electronic access (but not VAT), is £195 (US $325 in the USA, Canada, and Mexico) and includes Camden Fifth Series, Volumes 54 and 55 and Transactions Sixth Series, Volume 28 (published in December). The electroniconly price available to institutional subscribes is £163 (US $272 in the USA, Canada, and Mexico). Japanese prices are available from Kinokuniya Company Ltd, P.O. Box 55, Chitose, Tokyo 156, Japan. EU subscribers (outside the UK) who are not registered for VAT should add VAT at their country's rate. VAT registered subscribers should provide their VAT registration number. Prices include delivery by air.

Subscription orders, which must be accompanied by payment, may be sent to a bookseller, subscription agent, or direct to the publisher: Cambridge University Press, University Printing House, Shaftesbury Road, Cambridge CB2 8BS, UK; or in the USA, Canada, and Mexico: Cambridge University Press, Journals Fulfillment Department, One Liberty Plaza, Floor 20, New York, NY 10006, USA.

SINGLE VOLUMES AND BACK VOLUMES. A list of Royal Historical Society volumes available from Cambridge University Press may be obtained from the Humanities Marketing Department at the address above.

Printed in the UK by Bell & Bain Ltd.

CONTENTS

ACKNOWLEDGEMENTS	vii
LIST OF FIGURES	ix
LIST OF TABLES	xi
LIST OF ABBREVIATIONS	xiii
INTRODUCTION	1
EDITORIAL CONVENTIONS	64
ACCOUNT OF AN ELIZABETHAN FAMILY: THE WILLOUGHBYS OF WOLLATON BY CASSANDRA WILLOUGHBY (1670–1735)	67
SELECT BIBLIOGRAPHY	259
INDEX	269

ACKNOWLEDGEMENTS

I am deeply grateful to Lord Middleton for giving me permission to introduce, edit, and comment on this manuscript and to the Willoughby family for having maintained over the centuries such a rich collection of archival sources that allows scholars to explore, in this case, the Elizabethan period in depth. I am also grateful to the staff of the University of Nottingham's Department of Manuscripts and Special Collections for their unfailing help throughout the research and writing process. I particularly want to thank Linda Shaw, Senior Archivist, and Dorothy Johnston, previous Keeper of the Manuscripts, at the University of Nottingham Manuscripts Collection, for their assistance. The staff at Nottingham as well as the staff at the Huntington Library in San Marino, California, have been enormously helpful. I would particularly like to thank Andrew Spicer, Literary Director of the Royal Historical Society, and Miranda Bethell, my copy-editor for Cambridge University Press, both of whom, at the editing stage, have devoted much time to this text and have made numerous improvements, and Melanie Howe and Daniel Pearce and all the team at Cambridge University Press. I thank them for their time and attention. Georgetown University has provided summer research support, without which this edition could not have completed.

Norman Jones and Dorothy Johnston have read the introduction to the manuscript and provided suggestions and corrections. Dr Kate Sampsell has provided valuable research assistance and has carefully checked my transcription against the manuscript; this book is, in part, hers. Many years back, as graduate students, Melinda Zook and Kathleen Colquhoun Halm, contributed to the transcription. I also value the suggestions provided by my colleagues in the History Department at Georgetown University, Jim Collins, David Collins SJ, Dagomar Degroot, Alison Games, John McNeill, Susan Pinkard, and Jim Shedel, and by the two outside reviewers of this manuscript project. All these people have helped to make this a better book. Alice Friedman originally suggested the need for this edition, and I have depended on her previous work on the Willoughbys; I am sure that she did not expect this to take so long.

This edition is dedicated to my husband, Fernando Cruz-Villalba, whose willingness to provide the space and time I have needed to complete this work was exemplary. It is also dedicated to the memory of my mother, Maurine Hoeppner, who read most of what I have published and was looking forward to reading this.

LIST OF FIGURES

Figure 1. Jan Siberbrechts, Wollaton Hall and Park, Nottinghamshire (1697), Yale Center for British Art, New Haven, CT   6

Figure 2. Francis Willoughby, age 26 (1573). Reproduced by permission of Lord Middleton and the University of Nottingham Library Manuscripts Collection   34

Figure 3. Elizabeth Willoughby, age 27 (1573). Reproduced by permission of Lord Middleton and the University of Nottingham Library Manuscripts Collection   35

Figures 4 and 5. Letter from Lady Elizabeth Willoughby to Sir Francis Willoughby (1585). Reproduced by permission of the British Library   59–60

Figures 6 and 7. Letter from Dorothy Willoughby to her sister Bridget Willoughby (c.1597). Reproduced by permission of Lord Middleton and the University of Nottingham Library Manuscripts Collection   214–215

LIST OF TABLES

Table 1. Genealogy of the Willoughby Family.   5

ABBREVIATIONS

Account/Mi, LM 26	Cassandra Willoughby, 'An Account of the Willughby's of Wollaton', 1
Mi, LM 27	Cassandra Willoughby, 'An Account of the Willughby's of Wollaton', 2
BL	British Library
C	Chancery
CPR	*Calendar of Patent Rolls*
CSP Dom	*Calendar of State Papers, Domestic*
DNB	Leslie Stephen and Sidney Lee (eds), *The Dictionary of National Biography: From the Earliest Times to 1900*, 22 vols (London, 1921–1922)
HMC Middleton	W.H. Stevenson (ed.), *Historical Manuscript Collection Report on the Manuscripts of Lord Middleton preserved at Wollaton Hall, Nottinghamshire* (London, 1911).
Mi	Manuscripts and Special Collections in the University of Nottingham Library, The Family and Estate Papers of the Willoughby Family, Lords Middleton, of Wollaton, Nottinghamshire, Middleton, Warwickshire and Birdsall, Yorkshire
ODNB	H.C.G. Matthew, Brian Harrison, et al. (eds), *The Oxford Dictionary of National Biography* (Oxford, 2004–)
OED	*Oxford English Dictionary*
PROB	Probate Registers

SBTRO	Shakespeare Birthplace Trust Record Office
STAC	Star Chamber
STB	Huntington Library, Stowe Temple Brydges Collection
TNA	The National Archives
TSRS	Thoroton Society Record Series
TTS	*Transactions of the Thoroton Society*
VCH	Victoria County History

INTRODUCTION

Background

In the 1980s, while completing a book on education and literacy in late medieval England, I ran across a manuscript housed at the University of Nottingham containing fair copies, synopses, and selections of letters and household accounts from the family of Sir Francis Willoughby (1546/7–1596) of Wollaton Hall outside Nottingham. A descendant, Cassandra Willoughby (1670–1735), composed this 'Account of the Willoughbys of Wollaton' between 1695 and 1721. In 1687 she had moved into Wollaton Hall, a family residence that had been mostly deserted since a fire in 1642. There she took it upon herself to investigate the library. In the process she copied down (partially or fully or in summary form) in two volumes a cache of family letters and household accounts dating from the 1540s until 1690. The second volume of her 'Account', hereafter *The Continuation of the History of the Willoughby Family*, which picks up the family history with Percival Willoughby (c.1560–1643), Francis's son-in-law, was edited and published in 1958 by A.C. Wood.[1] The first volume of Cassandra's 'Account' (hereafter Account), which includes letters, accounts, and genealogical materials prior to the 1630s and comprises nearly 200 folio pages, provides one of the most extensive and intimate portraits of an Elizabethan family that survives. It has never been published in full, although it has recently garnered attention particularly in regard to a growing interest in letter writing in Elizabethan England.[2] Cassandra concentrated her

---

[1] Cassandra, Duchess of Chandos, *The Continuation of the History of the Willoughby Family*, being Vol. II of the Manuscript, ed. A.C. Wood (Eton, 1958), hereafter *The Continuation of the History*.

[2] Extensive excerpts were published in W.H. Stevenson (ed.), *Historical Manuscripts Commission Report on the Manuscripts of Lord Middleton* (London, 1911), 504–610, hereafter *HMC Middleton*. Among more recent uses of Cassandra's 'Account' (hereafter Account) is an article by Alice Friedman, 'Portrait of a marriage: The Willoughby letters of 1585–1586', *Signs*, 11 (1986), 542–555, and her *House and Household in Elizabethan England: Wollaton Hall and the Willoughby Family* (Chicago, 1989); references to the Willoughbys in James Daybell, *Women Letter-Writers in Tudor England* (Oxford, 2006), esp. 78–79; and an extended analysis of one of the vituperative letters from the Willoughbys in Michelle

efforts on recording personal letters between Sir Francis, his wife, his sister, his father-in-law, his six daughters, and various sons-in-law and prospective sons-in-law. The letters describe events, relate casual gossip, and record opinions on such varied themes as love and marriage, household management, social expectations, and the everyday concerns (including intrigues) of servants, relatives, neighbours, and members of the Elizabethan court. The collection especially sheds light on the experiences of the Willoughby women (eight of the main correspondents are women). Overall the letters provide portraits of a range of romances and marital experiences, and of private concerns and personal struggles within an upper-gentry family with significant connections to the court.

The marriage between Francis Willoughby and Elizabeth Lyttleton, which began in 1564 when they were 17 and 18 years of age respectively, was stormy and unstable, and the couple was given to impassioned confrontations and accusations.[3] A dominant thread running through the letters is the refusal of Elizabeth Lyttleton Willoughby to obey her husband and his efforts to force her obedience through appeals to her father, public shaming, imprisonment within the household, and, finally, banishment from the house and family. Remarkably, these letters reproduce a number of quotations from their conversations written to provide correspondents with detailed evidence of indignities suffered at the hands of their spouse or other household members. By contrast, the marriage of their daughter Bridget to a cousin, Sir Percival Willoughby, was a solid, even happy one; their early letters reflect this in delightful expressions of love, while their mature correspondence reveals trust and respect despite difficult financial situations. Other daughters had more problematic marriages, also detailed to some degree in this Account. Overall, the letters describe a range of marital experiences in the Elizabethan context from companionable, such as that between Bridget and Percival, to troubled, such as that of Bridget's

---

O'Callaghan, ' "An Uncivill Scurrilous Letter", "Womanish Brabb[l]es", and the Letter of Affront', in James Daybell and Andrew Gordon (eds), *Cultures of Correspondence in Early Modern Britain* (Philadelphia, PA, 2016), 174–177. There is also a brief mention in Norman Jones, *The Birth of the Elizabethan* Age (Oxford, 1993), 112–114. Rosemary O'Day's *Women's Agency in Early Modern Britain and the American Colonies* (Abingdon, 2007) uses Cassandra Willoughby's notebooks, currently housed at the Huntington Library, San Marino, CA, which include an earlier draft of the Account. The materials in the Huntington Library, Stowe Brydges Collection are referenced herein as STB. STB 1 is Box 1, in which each document is catalogued in a separate folder. STB Box 2, folders 1 and 2 contain far more material. STB 2 (1) holds three notebooks of material, the first two of which are relevant to the present project.

[3] Copies of original portraits of Francis and Elizabeth (Figures 2 and 3), dated 1573, now hang in Wollaton Hall. Francis is described as 26 years of age and Elizabeth as 27.

parents and several of their other daughters. They afford us rare and detailed insights into the social and emotional dynamics of a long-standing, wealthy, and well-connected household during the reigns of Queen Elizabeth I, her predecessors and successors.

The letters enrich our knowledge of early modern childhood, education, marriage and marriage settlements, the roles of wives, daughters, husbands, and fathers, and the activities of servants. They provide insights into Queen Elizabeth's role in supporting disadvantaged women, the social dynamics of Elizabethan marriage, and the functions of a large Elizabethan household with an extended social network. They also offer a rich source for studying the culture of letter writing and of literacy (especially female literacy). Less discernible are the religious dynamics of this extended family in the wake of the Reformation. It is possible that the various correspondents purposefully avoided mention of religious issues at a time when Catholics and Catholic sympathizers (for example, the Lyttleton family, and certainly one of the prospective sons-in-law) were in retreat and those with Calvinist tendencies (such as, apparently, Sir Francis) were not in accord with the Elizabethan settlement of the Church.

In the first part of the introduction I look at Cassandra Willoughby (her life and her role in preserving the letter collection) and follow with a brief investigation into the rise of the Willoughby family in Nottinghamshire, concluding with the context for the Elizabethan Willoughbys and a description of the edited text.

Cassandra Willoughby as Transcriber and Editor

Without Cassandra Willoughby, the letters that passed between Francis Willoughby, his wife, their daughters, sons-in-laws and acquaintances, would have been lost to time. With one exception the original letters have not survived,[4] apparently thrown away in about 1832 when the sixth Baron Middleton, Henry Willoughby, built a new strongroom for his personal papers.[5] We can, however, reconstruct the process Cassandra followed in her compilation and

---

[4] See Friedman, 'Portrait of a marriage', which includes four letters that have survived as part of the Burghley archives (BL, Lansdowne MS 46/30–33), a copy of only one of which, however, Cassandra seems to have seen and copied into her Account. The circumstances of the survival of this letter collection are similar to those attending the letters of John Holles which were copied down by his son. As in the Willoughby case, only one original letter of all the copied Holles letters has survived. P.R. Seddon (ed.), *Letters of John Holles 1587–1637*, I, Thoroton Society Record Series (TSRS), XXXI (Nottingham, 1975), xi.

[5] Pamela Marshall, *Wollaton Hall and the Willoughby Family* (Nottingham, 1999), 11; in Chandos, *The Continuation of the History*, xvii n. 1, Wood gives the date as 1835.

judge the extent to which we can use her account in reconstructing the lives of her great-great-grandparents and great-grandparents/aunts/uncles.

Cassandra Willoughby was the only daughter of Francis Willoughby (the naturalist) (1635–1672), and the great-great granddaughter of Sir Francis Willoughby (known as the builder) and his wife Elizabeth Lyttleton.[6] (See Table 1.) Cassandra was an educated, well-travelled, one might say scholarly woman.[7] Her upbringing, interrupted by the death of her father when she was two years of age, was in a household that included John Ray, her father's collaborator and her brothers' tutor. Then, in 1676, when Cassandra was six years of age, her life was interrupted again when her mother, Emma Barnard, married Sir Josiah Child, moving with her children (but not with Ray) from the family home in Middleton, Warwickshire, to Essex.[8] By all accounts the relationship between the children (Cassandra and her two brothers Francis and Thomas) and their stepfather was strained.

In large part due to these strains, Cassandra's brothers and soon Cassandra herself moved from Essex, settling at Wollaton Hall in Nottinghamshire (Figure 1), the other Willoughby family home, which had not been kept up, had been partially burnt down in 1642, and had been used to house Parliamentary forces during the

---

[6] Contemporary references to the Willoughbys of Wollaton generally follow the spelling that was common in the day: 'Willoughby' rather than the more modern form of the family name 'Willughby'. This edition uses Willoughby throughout except where the primary sources use 'Willughby'. Cassandra differentiated between the two branches of the family – those at Bore Place and those at Wollaton – by using different spellings; thus, when Bridget Willughby married Percival Willoughby, Cassandra changed her name to Bridget Willoughby. The names of the Wollaton family are doubled as 'Willoughby (Willughby)' in the index for ease of reference.

[7] Information on the life of Cassandra Willoughby comes from Joan Johnson, *Excellent Cassandra: The Life and Times of the Duchess of Chandos* (Gloucester, 1981); Rosemary O'Day (ed.), *Cassandra Brydges (1670–1735), First Duchess of Chandos: Life and Letters* (Woodbridge, 2007); and Huntington Library, Stowe Temple Brydges Collection, STB, Boxes 1 and 2.

[8] Emma Barnard was the third wife of Sir Josiah Child (*c.*1633–1699). Famous as a merchant and mercantile thinker, Child was a member of Parliament on and off from 1658 to 1685, a founding member of the Royal African Company, owner of over 1,000 acres in Jamaica and, due to his purchases of stock in the East India Company, a controlling presence in the East India Company in the 1680s and 1690s. 'Contemporary notices of him are generally unfavourable', as he was considered to be 'vain, covetous and [...] cunning', *The History of Parliament Online:* http://www.historyofparliamentonline.org/search/site/Josiah%20Child. Perhaps Cassandra was drawn to the story of Francis Willoughby, as she and her brothers had also lost a parent very young and were forced to move. Her brothers were named Francis and Thomas, just as Margaret Willoughby's brothers were. Cassandra lost one of her brothers young, just as Margaret had. See Table 1. I thank Miranda Bethell for this insight.

Table 1. Genealogy of the Willoughby Family.

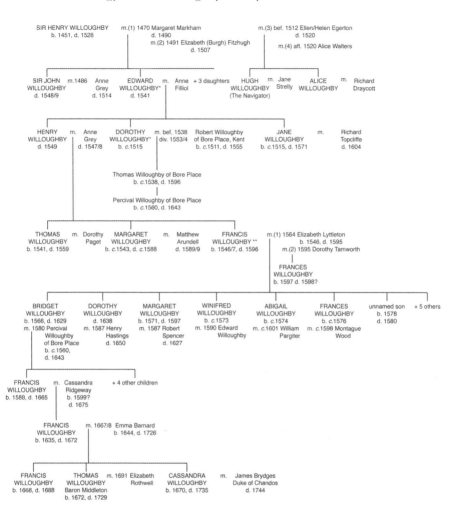

Figure 1. Jan Siberbrechets, Wollaton Hall and Park, Nottinghamshire (1697), oil on canvas, in colour online, Yale Center for British Art, New Haven, CT. This painting illustrates Wollaton Hall at the time when Cassandra and her brother Thomas were in residence.

Civil War.⁹ It was in 1687, when Cassandra was not more than 17 years of age, that her older brother Francis asked her to join him at Wollaton to preside over its rehabilitation. She went, 'thinking it would be no small pleasure to me to be Mistress of Wollaton and to doe whatever I had a mind to'.¹⁰ They proceeded to repair, renovate, redecorate, rebuild, and restore order to the estate.¹¹ Francis died in 1688; Cassandra, however, remained at Wollaton and was joined by her younger brother, Thomas, and his tutor Thomas Man (c.1655–1690), who was a physician.¹² Dr Man, with whom Cassandra shared an interest in gardens – especially the physic garden kept at Wollaton for Dr Man's use – continued at Wollaton and seems to have been the third part in the family nucleus.¹³ Cassandra, Thomas, and Dr Man restored and labelled her father's cabinet of specimens, both honouring and continuing his work.¹⁴ When Man died in 1690, he left his books to Thomas and a writing desk to Cassandra.¹⁵ Cassandra continued (on and off) at Wollaton, helping to oversee the house and estate, run the household and, after his marriage in 1691, raise her brother's family and continue to advise him. Cassandra also travelled with her brother 'to visit the family estates and check on their condition', suggesting that she played a role in managing the Willoughby estates.¹⁶

---

⁹ For information relating to this fire and the damage to Wollaton Hall, see Cassandra Willoughby, 'An Account of the Willughby's of Wollaton', 2, Nottingham University Library MSS Collection, Middleton Collection (hereafter Mi), LM 27, fos 70–72; Chandos, *The Continuation of the History*, 66–68, and 'The Wollaton Estate and the Civil War, 1643–1647', in J.H. Hobson, P.A. Kennedy, and V.W. Walker (eds), *A Nottinghamshire Miscellany*, TSRS, XXI (Nottingham, 1962), 3–4. Sir Percival Willoughby, Cassandra's great-grandfather, made only essential repairs, and the Hall remained virtually unoccupied by the family until Cassandra and her brother moved in. Percival Willoughby died at Wollaton in 1643.
¹⁰ Chandos, *The Continuation of the History*, 125; Mi, LM 27, fo. 137; Johnson, *Excellent Cassandra*, 34.
¹¹ Johnson, *Excellent Cassandra*, 36.
¹² Isabelle Charmantier, Dorothy Johnston, and Paul J. Smith, 'The Legacies of Francis Willughby', in Tim Birkhead (ed.), *Virtuoso by Nature: The Scientific Worlds of Francis Willughby, FRS (1635–1672)* (Leiden, 2016), 369–372.
¹³ Johnson, *Excellent Cassandra*, 38–40; Chandos, *The Continuation of the History*, 129–135, 137–138; Mi, LM 27, fos 142–149, 152–153.
¹⁴ Charmantier et al., 'Legacies', 366–368, 371. With Dr Thomas Man, Thomas continued the insect studies his father's death left unfinished (p. 371).
¹⁵ For his will, see TNA, PROB 11/414/320, fos 295–295v: 'those Effects, the income of my Chambers etc which I have in Colledge, my books which have a place amongst Sir Thomas Willoughbys, I leave to Sir Thomas Willoughby; and those written books or papers I desire may be read by him and what he thinks not for his vse be burnt'. Man's will also mentions the pupils he was teaching.
¹⁶ Johnson, *Excellent Cassandra*, 52–55.

Cassandra also spent time in the old family library and among its neglected family papers. There she found deeds, wills, marriage settlements, and other, mostly legal, papers dating back to the twelfth century, sixteenth- and seventeenth-century family letters, copies of orders for running the household from the sixteenth century, and sixteenth- and seventeenth-century household accounts and inventories.[17] Cassandra then proceeded to copy down some of these materials. Cassandra also kept a journal from 1692 to 1718.[18] She wrote poems and essays, and produced at least two letter books with copies of outgoing and some incoming letters from 1713 to 1735.[19] In 1713, at the age of 43, Cassandra married her first cousin, James Brydges, who, by 1720, had been made duke of Chandos. Moving from Wollaton to her husband's house in Stanmore, Middlesex in 1713, Cassandra took on numerous social obligations and ongoing financial concerns as well as responsibilities for her husband's children from a previous marriage, his extended family and a household of upwards of ninety members, including a chaplain and a librarian. James Brydges was a notable patron and collector of art, and Cassandra herself was an 'amateur but expert' artist, particularly involved with painting portraits of family members.[20] Together, they patronized a number of artists, including the women artists, Maria and Adriana Verelst.[21] Rosemary O'Day describes the emergence of several elite 'crazes' of the time: 'for family history, genealogy, and

---

[17] Although Cassandra consistently refers to these papers as papers found at Wollaton, she may also have copied papers brought to Wollaton, along with the family library, from Middleton Hall where her father and mother had primarily lived. Many of the documents she saw had descriptions written by her father on them.

[18] Cited in O'Day, *Cassandra Brydges*, 2 and n. 3. It is in two sections and focuses mainly on her travels. See Huntington Library STB, Box 2 (2), misc. uncatalogued papers and notebooks, and the Stoneleigh MSS, Gloucestershire Papers 20–21 at the SBTRO (DR 18/20/21/1).

[19] The letter books are edited in O'Day, *Cassandra Brydges*; letter book I is in the Stoneleigh MSS collection at the SBTRO (DR 18/20/21/2). Letter book II is owned by the Governors of North London Collegiate School. The Huntington Library has a collection of letters to Cassandra and two poems written by her in the Stowe Temple Brydges Collection, STB 1 (file nos 1-47) and STB (2). Uncatalogued misc. papers; compiled family genealogies are in BL, Stowe MS 656 and in Huntington Library STB 2 (1) book 3, a genealogical notebook. Additional genealogical material is in Mi, LM 13.

[20] Rosemary O'Day, 'Family galleries: Women and art in the seventeenth and eighteenth centuries', *Huntington Library Quarterly*, 71 (2008), 323–349. The 'amateur but expert' assessment is on p. 323. Many of the paintings in the homes of James Brydges and Cassandra were unattributed and, according to their inventories, had no value. Most of them were quite likely done by Cassandra, whom Horace Walpole once called 'a great artist'. See STB 1, no. 45, for a signed but undated and unfinished graphite drawing by Cassandra of Thoresby Hall. The sketch suggests that she lacked instruction in perspective drawing. O'Day, *Cassandra Brydges*, 342, fig. 13.

[21] *Ibid.* 273, fig. 11.

for likenesses of living family women and art [...] for collecting, classifying, and recording, and for touring and topography [... and] gardening'.[22] Cassandra was accomplished in all of these, but for the most part used her talents toward serving the needs and memorialization of her family.

As duchess of Chandos, Cassandra lived a socially active life; her correspondence, which was largely but not exclusively with women, shows Cassandra involved in matchmaking, acting as a godparent, shielding her husband from importunate relatives, discussing her health (which was often problematic) and that of her correspondents, attending to properties, handling requests regarding stocks (for example, the stock of the South Sea Company) and positions, and coping with her husband's debts. Her interests ranged from finance to medicine, to patronage, to painting and architecture, to parliamentary elections. Cassandra took particular care to keep in touch with relatives and also friends, for, as she says in one of her early letters, 'I take too much sattisfaction in hearing from my friends, to lose it by a neglect of my own.'[23]

Cassandra was, to a very great degree, self-effacing. One must examine minutely everything she touched to find her imprint. She managed and consulted on properties and stock purchases; she planned and executed architectural renovations, based on knowledge acquired through her travels surveying English architecture and gardens. She managed her own finances with care but also took on advising members of her family and sometimes helping to support them. She was a noted musician, textile artist, and portrait painter, who, however, seems to have put everyone else's interests first and desired, above all, to be useful. As Cassandra herself put it, when explaining her reasons for marrying, 'I had no concern so much at my heart as what might tend to the good of the family.'[24] When she died in 1735, James Brydges wrote to his nephew that it was 'a loss whereby I am deprived of one of the most excellent persons of the age'.[25]

Despite these many activities, and despite bouts of ill health, Cassandra continued to work on her Account, or at least on the second volume, until the 1720s.[26] In preparing it she was working with a very large cache of letters and accounts, some of which were in poor shape and difficult to read. She praises the letters

---

[22] O'Day, 'Family galleries', 331–332.
[23] O'Day, *Cassandra Brydges*, 334.
[24] *Ibid.* 12.
[25] *Ibid.* 324.
[26] Chandos, *The Continuation of the History*, xi.

written by Bridget Willoughby Peckham (c.1600), half-sister of Percival Willoughby, to Bridget Willoughby as:

> well writ, the hand fine, and the manner of expression so agreeable to the present stile and mode of writing, that I should not have thought a letter of hers had been writ more days then it had been years. And indeed many of those letters which are above a hundred years old, are expressed in very much the same manner, that the way of writing letters now is, and much more like the present English than some of those letters which are in the Library at Wollaton, which are of a later date.[27]

With or without regard to the quality of older handwritings, Cassandra's accuracy in copying letters and overall believability must be assessed.

Nearly all the materials transcribed by Cassandra in her preparatory notes or in her final family history have been lost. In the interest of time, perhaps, and certainly in the face of some difficulty in reading the materials, Cassandra paraphrased, provided a précis or truncated her sources.[28] Regarding this practice, for example, while introducing letters relating to Margaret Willoughby, Lady Arundell, Francis Willoughby's older sister, Cassandra wrote, 'I shall shew by copying part of a letter from her to her Brother'.[29] Concerning the description of a conversation between Lady Arundell and Squire, one of Elizabeth Willoughby's servants, Cassandra wrote, 'There is a very long dialogue writ down by Squire, too much to copy'.[30]

Looking to what she does include, we can judge how accurate Cassandra's transcriptions are by examining the surviving original letter.[31] (See Appendix to this Introduction.) Elizabeth Willoughby wrote this particular letter toward the end of 1585, at a time in the lives of Elizabeth and Francis when they had been separated for a number of years and she was appealing to return to the marriage and his house. The final transcription by Cassandra, while accurately paraphrasing some of the letter and, at times, copying it word for word, omits significant portions.[32] Cassandra softens Elizabeth's

---

[27] Chandos, *The Continuation of the History*, 22; Mi, LM 27, fos 17–18.
[28] On Cassandra's practice in preparing the family history, see O'Day, *Cassandra Brydges*, 49, where O'Day notes that she edited and re-edited her history, searched out facts (e.g. in parish registers), and talked about her work with her brother and others. See the untidy early draft of her family history in the Huntington Library, STB 2 (1), 3 notebooks.
[29] Cassandra Willoughby, Account, Mi, LM 26, fo. 58 (hereafter Mi, LM 26, or the Account): see p. 91 below.
[30] Mi, LM 26, fo. 70: see pp. 103–104 below.
[31] BL, Lansdowne MS 46/31; Friedman, in 'Portrait of a marriage', edits the letter on pp. 550–552.
[32] Mi, LM 26, fos 126–127: see pp. 59–63, 157–158 below.

accusation that Francis was spying on her or believing slanders being bruited around about her. Cassandra also excludes a segment of the letter that relates to Lady Willoughby's expenses while in London and her reluctance to return to Francis for fear she would lose the small living she was currently allowed. In the original letter, but not in the copy, Lady Willoughby writes that she was warned that Francis had determined and vowed, should she return, to lock her in a chamber and not allow her to go out, even into the garden, without his leave and licence. She mentions 'her old yeares' and her body now subject to sickness and her mind disquieted with her former troubles, none of which is in the copy letter. She then promises to:

> study to conforme all my wordes as I may best content & please yow, as also to performe all good duties that do become a loving & obedient wife towards her husband. So on the other side my assured hope & truste is that yow having buryed & blotted out of yor remembrance all former unkyndnesses contryved againste me, will both repute of me as of yor honest & lawfull wife, & requite me wth all like love & offices of a good & kynd husband

most of which is not included in Cassandra's copy letter. While copying accurately the material she includes, Cassandra excludes materials that describe a deeper chasm and greater suspicion between Elizabeth and Francis than is evident from what she repeats or retells. It may be that her sensitivity as a descendant moved her to exclude some of the more emotionally difficult or dramatic passages. As she notes in her account for 1578, when copying down a heated (and public) conversation between Francis and Elizabeth: 'Many more spitefull disrespectfull speeches she [Elizabeth] made which are there copied, but this I think is sufficient to shew the nature of their uneasiness, and too much to be noted down by a Granddaughter in the fourth descent from this Lady.'[33]

There are also occasional differences between the draft notes for Cassandra's Account, held in the Huntington Library, and her fair copy, edited here.[34] In her earlier notes, when describing a letter from Francis Willoughby to his father-in-law, Sir John Lyttleton, she wrote:

> In this letter he writes that being to goe to London he [Sir Francis] set down directions for his Men to observe in ordering his family in his Absence [...] viz That Joahn should look to the ordering of the Children, to which she [Elizabeth] said who ever should take upon them to order her Children in her Presence she would Mischief, she said Joahn was his Whore and that

---

[33] Mi, LM 26, fo. 90: see p. 123 below.
[34] STB Box 2 (1), books 1 and 2.

she would not be left amongst such Villains, but would goe into the Town [...] which Sr F:W: denying her she fell into very pashonate expression and sitting down called for a Knife threatning to make away with herself, and the Knife being denied her she would have struck her Self in the Belly with her Scisors if she had not been prevented, ^then she^ said she would never eat or drink more, but with the same Knife she was next to eat with would Kill herself[35]

The fair copy omits the comment about Joahn being Francis's whore as well as the passage where Elizabeth says she will never eat or drink again but would use the knife to kill herself.[36] Throughout this edition any differences between the draft notes and the fair copy of Cassandra's Account are referenced in the footnotes or, for longer passages, included in brackets and italics in the text itself.

There is also a problem of dating in Cassandra's Account. Cassandra clearly tried to copy the letters in chronological order, although at one point she skips from 1575 back to 1572. There are letters, however, that are undated, or only partially dated. In particular, the letters from Lady Margaret Arundell, sister to Francis Willoughby, are mostly dated by month and day, but not by year, although they do mention where she is at the time of writing.[37] Cassandra has had to contextualize Lady Arundell's letters in terms of what she knows of her interactions with her brother, her travels and the world around her in order to guess how to place her letters.

Despite dating difficulties and Cassandra's practice of excluding information or paraphrasing her materials, she is remarkably accurate in what she reports and never manufactures content.[38] Her accuracy is evident in a letter that she copied from Queen Jane to Edward Willoughby in 1537, which is a near duplicate of an original letter from Jane Seymour to Edward's brother John Willoughby.[39]

---

[35] STB Box 2 (1), book 1, fo. 22v.

[36] Mi, LM 26, fo. 92: see p. 125 below.

[37] Mi, LM 26, fo. 63: see p. 94 below. Cassandra notes that 'The date of the year, is not writ to any of these letters from Lady Arundell.' See also Mi, LM 26, fo. 106: see p. 137 below.

[38] See her transcriptions of her father's paper volume of memoirs and observations taken out of old muniments, which are also accurately done, with only an occasional omission, addition, or correction. Mi, LM 13, summarized in small part in *HMC Middleton*, 269–271. See Mi, LM 26, fos 4–6 and 8–13, where she transcribes fos 47–61 of her father's account of the Marmion family in the period after the Conquest and his account of the Montforts and the Barons' revolt of 1264–1267. She gives credit to her father's MS 'which gives an account of some Antiquities of our Family'.

[39] Mi, LM 26, fo. 35v: see p. 68 below; *HMC Middleton*, 517–518. Mi, C 10; Mary A. Welch (ed.), 'Willoughby letters of the first half of the sixteenth century', TSRS, XXIV (Nottingham, 1967), 4. As Welch notes, in editing the letter to John Willoughby,

INTRODUCTION 13

In addition, toward the beginning of her two volume account of the Willoughby family, Cassandra includes many pages of descriptions of the account books of George Medley, gentleman, brother-in-law, and executor of Henry Willoughby, father of Francis Willoughby, covering legal and other expenses as guardian of Sir Henry Willoughby's children from 1549 to 1562.[40] Cassandra's account echoes very exactly the surviving account books.[41] For example, when Cassandra notes 'by a book of Medeleys accounts for the childrens cloaths etc. [...] I find that his Nephew Francis Willughby and his Neece Margaret removed to Tyltey April the 21th 1550', she is quoting exactly from Medley's book of accounts for 1550 where there is a memorandum 'that my Nepveu Fraunces Willoughbye and my nece Margarett Wylloughbye his syster came to Tyltey the xxith of Apryll'.[42] When Cassandra notes on folio 46 that the cost of Francis Willoughby's board at St Anthony's School in London was £2 16s 0d, she had correctly added the boarding expenses listed in the Medley Account book dating from 18 January to 13 June, 3 Mary [1554/5], although she does not mention Master Lyse, the name of the schoolmaster.[43] Similarly accurate is her calculation of the boarding expenses for Margaret Willoughby at Tilty from 9 May to 11 July 1555.[44]

In a second surviving account book in George Medley's hand, Cassandra's excerpts on fo. 52 of her Account once again accurately reflect the original, including the final summation of expenses at the very end of the manuscript.[45] Where this account book notes, in 1553: 'To the Clarke of the Signett for the chargez of Wryting and the Seale of Lycence for my coosyn Thomas Wylloughbye to goe over the seaez to the universitye of Parys to studye [...] vi s viii d' Cassandra copies: 'After this there is set down 6^s 8^d paid to the Clerk of the Signet for the writing, seal and lycence for his Cousin Thomas Willughby to goe beyond sea to the University of Paris to

---

'The wording of this letter is almost identical with that copied by Cassandra apart from the variation in a phrase and the omission of another word.' Welch concludes that these were identical letters sent to the Willoughby brothers with scribal variants from a master draft.
[40] Thomas, Margaret, and Francis: see below, pp. 27–28.
[41] Mi, Medley Account books A 31, 32; Mi, LM 26, fos 40–55. (Mi, A 32 has duplicate pagination. Initially the folios were numbered; at some later time page numbers were added.) W.H. Stevenson also copied down extracts from these account books. *HMC Middleton*, 397–414.
[42] Mi, LM 26, fo. 40: see pp. 70–71 below; Mi, A 32, fo. 1, p. 1; also quoted in *HMC Middleton*, 399. On Tilty, located in Essex, see the edited text (hereafter 'Text'), Text n. 12.
[43] Mi, A 32, fo. 25, p. 47; *HMC Middleton*, 409.
[44] Mi, A 32, fos 25–25v, pp. 47–48.
[45] Mi, A 31; some of the expenses are transcribed in *HMC Middleton*, 397–399.

study.'[46] With regard to a third household account book, copied down in part by W.H. Stevenson and dated 1587, Cassandra, who excerpts the same account book on folios 127v, 129–129v and 130v, includes nearly identical information with minor discrepancies.[47] Finally, for the years 1596–1599, Cassandra transcribed coal accounts, including coal receipts. There is a single surviving summary account for eleven months ending 27 August 1596 that supports her figures.[48]

If further evidence is needed to confirm the accuracy of her reporting, we find that Cassandra describes a letter:

> from Edward Willoughby to his Brother Sir Percivall [the son-in-law of Francis] dated November 1588, in which he [...] tells this story of Alderman Catcher and Alderman Skinner, that they were both by order of the Privie Counsel committed to the fleet, for whiping two Gentlewomen in Bridewell as common whores, and it was supposed it would cost them 2000^{li} before they got out, the Queen taking the matter hardly against them, their fine was like to be the greater. One of these Gentlewomen was Wife to him that sue'd to be Lord Latimer, the other was Captain Nunames Wife.[49]

This same episode is described in another letter, not copied by Cassandra, sent from John Adams to his brother-in-law Percival Willoughby in the same year:

> I am more sory that Mr. Catcher the Friday next after this terme was fined for the whipping of Mrs. Newnam and Mrs. Nevill in Bridewell[50] to the Queene CCCCC^{li} and CC^{li} to the ii gentleweomen, on hundred^{li} apeec, and his fellow Skinner to on thowsand markes to the Queene, and CCCC^{li} to the two gentleweomen [...]They have besydes as parte of theyre judgment iii

---

[46] Mi, LM 26, fo. 50: see p. 82 below; Mi, A 31, fo. 11, p. 21; *HMC Middleton*, 398. The date for this account is 1553. Another example of her accuracy is evident in Text n. 67, where she transcribed information from Mi, A 31, fo. 10. Further, she also reports correctly the sum total of expenses calculated at the very end of Mi, A 31, fo. 26v. See Text n. 76. For further references to her accuracy in transcribing information from the Account Books, see pp. 70–73, 74–85 (esp. nn. 40, 54–55, 78) and 162 (esp. n. 284), 168 (esp. n. 313). of the edited text below.

[47] *HMC Middleton*, 452–456; Mi, A 69/1–2, fos 1–13v, 19.

[48] Chandos, *The Continuation of the History*, 30–32; Richard S. Smith, 'The Willoughbys of Wollaton 1500–1643 with special reference to early mining in Nottinghamshire, 1500–1643', PhD thesis, University of Nottingham, 1964, 96. See Mi, Ac 49: 'A note of all the changes of the Cole booke since Jo. Speed entred that is from the ii of October tell the xxviith of Auguste 1597. List of various expenses add up to 915^{li}—4^{s}—5^{d}. The whole gets from the daye abovesaid to the daye aforesaid is 6631 rookes of coles the value of them is: 1105^{li}—3^{s}—4^{d}.'

[49] Mi, LM 26, fos 133–133v: see p. 172 below.

[50] 'being ga' crossed out.

monthes imprisonment, and to aske the gent[lewomen's] forgivenes at theyre house at the Counter and at Bridewell.⁵¹

Finally, there is a surviving draft letter transcribed by W.H. Stevenson from Percival Willoughby to Lord Burghley dated 1597 and a companion letter from Percival to Burghley, described by Cassandra in her Account and dated October 1597 regarding the wardship of the daughter of Sir Francis Willoughby by Dorothy Tamworth, Lady Wharton, his second wife, whose daughter had been born on 3 May of that year. They echo one another in their concerns for the overreaching of Lady Wharton, her machinations through her stepfather Sir Mychell Molins, and Percival's own poor estate, although Cassandra truncates her copy:

> There is the copy of a letter from Sir Percivall Willoughby dated October 1597 to the Lord Burghley, then Lord high Treasurer of England, who had given the wardship of that child [the youngest daughter of Sir Francis Willoughby] to his Son the Secretary. In this letter Sir Percivall desired the Lord Burghley that for the avoiding of the malice of his adversaries, and the better establishing of his perplexed estate he would vouchsafe so far to recomend his humble sute to his Son, that he might have the wardship of the child, for the land only, for such considerations as should seem good to his Honour. And that he might the better judg of the value of it, Sir Percivall writ that he had inclosed the particular of those lands, and by that particular, he would also see what lands this Lady the widow of Sir Francis Willughby, by the help of Sir Micheal Molyns, and the rest of their accomplices, had got for herself and her heirs, though her usages of Sir Francis had been such, that she had ill deserved it.⁵²

---

⁵¹ Mi, C 18/1; *HMC Middleton*, 158–159. The date of this letter is 21 Aug. 1588. John Adams goes on to write that the two women were pregnant, and that one of them miscarried ten weeks later as a consequence of her mistreatment: 'the cyrcumstances did aggravat the offence, first the punishment without any fault in specially the hasty proceeding, the whipping of weomen, maryed gent[elweomen] with child, crying on there knees for mercy, wipte by a man, in the sight of men, and rejoyseing, whereby proceeded untymely chyld birthe (and the chyld as they sayd borne a live, died) and this chanced within x weekes after'.

⁵² Mi, LM 26, fo. 157: see pp. 198–199 below. The draft original, copied down by Stevenson, reads: 'R[ight] ho[nourable] my humble dutie remembred; I make myself ᵇᵒˡᵈᵉ (humbly craving pardon) to implore the honourable contynuaunce of your Lordship's favour in recommending my former suite to Mr. Secretarie, towching the wardship of the landes of Sir Fraunces Wyllughbyes yongest daughter; being the rather incited thereunto, for that I finde the nowe Ladie Wharton, the mother thereof, to be my ernest competitour therein, suggesting many thinges alltogether untrue, to withholde the same from me, and thereby to procure it unto herself; which if your honourable Lordship doo not helpe to prevente, ~~my estate is farre more miserable then ever it was~~, I shall hardlye be able ever to free my poore estate, or to make any dewe satisfaction to Sir Fra[ncis's] many creditors. For she, which was so unkynde a wyfe, to so over loving a husbande, as

In this particular case and in much of the other material she copied and paraphrased, Cassandra included sufficient material for the reader to conclude that, while sometimes excluding material that she regarded as superfluous, too much to copy, or too damaging to the reputation of her ancestors, she is a trustworthy witness who was not averse to describing the dramas and difficulties between Elizabeth and Francis or between other members of the family, including the servants, all of which make her Account so interesting. Rather than setting this correspondence aside because of its transmission through Cassandra's pen, it is best to study the materials we have while recognizing the problems associated with their second-hand survival.

Cassandra was also willing to draw conclusions. Her assessment of Sir Francis Willoughby's character is a sympathetic one. She notes that he appears to have been of a very mild, sweet disposition, and a lover of hospitality, but a little too apt to be imposed on by stories from his servants.[53] This portrait is somewhat belied by what appears to have been an overly suspicious character and one who not only fell out with his wife but also with his children and his son-in-law and heir, Percival Willoughby. In addition, there was at least one illegitimate child by Sir Francis, baptized in 1584/5 in the West Riding of Yorkshire,[54] while a draft will of Sir Francis in 1579, although perhaps

having absolutely contryved and gotten to herself and [her] heires the greatest parte of his landes, colde not afforde his dead corps the leaste parte of those ~~duties~~ rightes and obsequies which weare due to suche a man; and hath bin so harde a stepmother to his children, as firste to withdrawe his fatherly affeccion from theim in his lyfe tyme, to be a straunger, or rather an enemy, unto theim since his deathe, and nowe of late [by Sir My[c]hell Molins meanes] to invegle the yongest of them with faire promises of advauncement to come up to London, and within theis iiii[or] or fyve dayes to bestowe her in marriage upon an apprentice or petti merchant of lytle worthe; she that hath in so many thinges (not unknowen to the worlde) since her firste meeting with Sir Fraunces soughte the subvercion and overthrowe of his howse and name: What I may then looke for att her handes (if I be [should be any waye] subjecte to her [malice] [~~whom whe holdeth her professed enemy~~] your Lordship in your honourable wysdome and consideracion may easily conjecture. And therefore humbly craving your Lordship's honourable care of my [word crossed out] releise herein, doo still rest your Lordship's in all dutie and devocion and so righte humbly take my leave.' Mi, F 10/32; *HMC Middleton*, 620–621.

[53] Mi, LM 26, fo. 87: see p. 119 below. This assessment is echoed by comments made by Thomas Stanhope, a close associate of the Willoughbys and one of the leading gentry in Nottinghamshire: 'he [Sir Francis] is [...] a very sweet-natured man and not greatly followed, yet easily governed'. Centre for Kentish Studies U 1590 C 2/3, cited in Beryl Cobbing and Pamela Priestland, *Sir Thomas Stanhope of Shelford: Local Life in Elizabethan Times* (Radcliffe-on-Trent, 2003), 188.

[54] STB (2) 2, Uncatalogued half-sheet of paper signed 'Rob[t] Barnard Vic[r]': see below, Introduction n. 202.

patterned after other puritanically inclined wills, exhibits an extreme sense of sinfulness.[55] Finally, in a household where family, servants, and other hangers-on jockeyed for influence, it is telling that Sir Francis left them all in a state of limbo, having written at least four drafts of his will but dying intestate, for, as Percival Willoughby wrote to his wife in 1588, '[Francis] was every day in a thousand minds what to doe with his estate.'[56]

Cassandra concludes that Lady Willoughby seems to have been a woman of wit and virtue but of a turbulent spirit and ungovernable passions. In support of her assessment of Elizabeth, she copies down a number of letters and dialogues, one of which, to the London Alderman Catcher, in the early 1590s, certainly bears out Cassandra's description:

> You causlessly condemn me of unkindness to Percivall Willoughby. I will forbear to repeat his unfriendly behaviours, because I will not disclose his faults to a babling fool. Expecting no better than the worst you can practice, I stay my own trouble, and stay you your tongue for al = be = it, I am Fatherless, I am not Husbandless nor friendless, but
>
> A Dispiser of vain Fools
> Elizabeth Willughby.[57]

It is probable that Elizabeth used this same sharp reproachful tone with her daughters as several of them, as we will see later, accused her of misusing them. Cassandra, however, does not copy down some of those letters that might offer more insight into her troubled relationships with her daughters. On the other hand, one must keep in mind that Elizabeth, who was often ill, had had at least twelve pregnancies between 1565 and 1579, with six surviving daughters and a son (her last child) who lived to approximately two years of age.

The information in the letters that Cassandra provides offers sufficient material for the reader to conclude that issues of obedience were central to the difficulties between not only Elizabeth and Francis, but also in the lives of their daughters. Cassandra, reading these letters over a century removed, appears not to have reacted negatively to Francis's expectations of obedience from his wife and his actions and threats to curtail her freedom. Indeed, in a 1730 letter, written to a newly married niece, Cassandra advises, 'I think the best way for a wife to secure her own happiness is by striving to render her husband's life as happy as is in her power.'[58] A reader today, however,

---

[55] Mi, 7/180/5/1, fo. 2.
[56] Mi, LM 26, fo. 135: see p. 174 below.
[57] Mi, LM 26, fo. 133v: see p. 173 below.
[58] O'Day, *Cassandra Brydges*, 243.

might find herself more sympathetic to Elizabeth, despite the sharpness of her language, and less inclined to view Francis as mild in his demands of her, particularly in the face of her many reported illnesses, recurrent pregnancies, and our knowledge (which Cassandra knew and Elizabeth must have known) of his infidelity in the marriage. Similarly, the control over their daughters that both Francis and Elizabeth exercised, while perhaps unremarkable for the period, produced some very unfortunate results, and issues of abusive husbands, and obedient or disobedient wives and children continue to surface in the correspondence of the next generation.

The reader of these letters must also realize that he or she may be getting only one side of the story, perhaps deliberately constructed to produce a certain response from recipients; in addition, the letters, while ostensibly private, could be expected to be read, and commented on, by others.[59] An instructive example of the problem is the description Cassandra gives, based on her reading of many family letters, of the relationship between Frances, the youngest daughter of Sir Francis and Elizabeth, and her husband Montague Wood. Cassandra notes,

> By many other letters one may believe that this Mountague Wood of Lamley was a very ill man, as well as a very ill Husband to this Frances Willughby [...] I believe very soon after they married, he began to use his Wife very ill and continued to doe so as long as she lived. There are many letters from her to her Sisters which give an account of his barbarity to her viz: that he turned her out of doors, beat her, and made her suffer the want of the necessarys for life, and other of her letters complain of the unkindness of his relations to her. So that upon the whole, one may judg that she had a very miserable life.[60]

In letters not copied down by Cassandra, however, Montague Wood, writing in 1600 to Abigail Willoughby, one of Frances's sisters, offers a different side of the story:

> Good Sister I had thought not to have written unto you, untill I had sent you sum good news, but sutche occasions have happned of late, that I am forced to send you as ill news, as ever you herde and worst to me then to all the worlde besides. Soo it is that foure my last goinge to London, your sister Fraunces, by the evill perswationes of sum dishonest people hathe acquainted

---

[59] For an analysis of women's letter writing that elaborates on these points, see Laura E. Thomason, *The Matrimonial Trap* (Lewisburg, PA, 2014), 12–14, although her focus is on English women letter-writers in the 18th century. See also Daybell and Gordon (eds), *Cultures of Correspondence in Early Modern Britain*.

[60] Mi, LM 26, fo. 194v: see p. 251 below.

herselfe, withe a coople of gentlemen bothe strangers to her before nowe and to me, bothe unmaried men and of notorious fame, and hathe yelded soo mutche to her pleasures as she hathe not refused to goe to taverns, to foll withe them, I knowe not howe often, and to staye at the taverne, whole nights withe them, she hathe ridden, to one of there howses, and hathe sent awaye her servaunte for the space of three dayes not sufferinge soo mutche as her mayde to staye withe her.[61]

Clearly, both partners in this marriage were using letters to construct a case against each other and were expecting a sympathetic response from their correspondents. One also notes, since it is entirely likely that Cassandra had access to the letters of both Montague and Frances, that Cassandra may have chosen to present Frances's complaints but not those of her husband. She appears to be similarly one-sided regarding the correspondence from Dorothy Willoughby complaining about her husband Henry Hastings, although Henry appears to have tried, at least at the beginning of the marriage, to justify himself to Francis Willoughby.[62]

Generally, Cassandra seems concerned to detail cases in which the women about whom she writes were constrained or troubled in some ways, as she continues to do in the second volume of her Account, copying down Frediswith (Phridelwide/Frediswide) Willoughby Adams's complaints of not being allowed to travel,[63] detailing the financial and familial struggles of Bridget Willoughby, the problems Bridget's daughter Lettice had with an unwanted suitor, extended letters regarding arrangements and concerns about the wedding of Cassandra's grandparents (Francis Willoughby and Cassandra Ridgeway), a fall and illnesses of her grandmother Cassandra, the financial difficulties, widowhood and illnesses of her aunts, the marital explorations of her father, the pity she felt for her mother's troubles between her children and their stepfather with the jointure in her mother's remarriage, Cassandra's own trauma in losing her older brother, and her strangely strained reaction to her younger brother's marriage, at which point she abruptly ended her account.[64]

---

[61] Mi, C 29; The remainder of this letter and a second letter from Montague Wood full of similar complaints, are included as part of the edited text below, pp. 251–253. These letters are included by the kind permission of Lord Middleton.

[62] Mi, LM 26, fo. 168: see 211–212 below.

[63] Mi, LM 27, fos 21–22; Chandos, *The Continuation of the History*, 26. In a letter to Bridget Willoughby she wrote, 'her Husband does not care she should goe journeys from him [...] but must sit mopeing at home by her fire side, turning apples – and may goe to Church to pray for her friends'.

[64] Chandos, *The Continuation of the History*, 26–29, 46–47, 62, 69–86, 89–92, and *passim*; Mi, LM 27, fos 21–24, 42–43, 64, 74–95v, 99–101, and *passim*. She ends her account with her first sight of her brother's wife: 'The first sight which I had of that Lady which my

Cassandra, for the most part, ignored the political, financial, economic, and material aspects of the Elizabethan Willoughbys. A.C. Wood, who edited and published Volume II of Cassandra's Account in 1958, was dismissive of her perspective:

> It cannot be claimed that her narrative throws any light on the general history of the period it covers [...] The explanation of so much omission must surely lie in the fact that she was a woman; a man would hardly have turned his back on the dramatic political scene in this way. We can only conclude that her sex, and the conditions of life in which women lived in the seventeenth century, narrowed her world and vision.[65]

While Cassandra did include some household accounts and a few political references, but in no systematic fashion, it is clear that she was primarily concerned with the family archive of personal letters and that she was keenly interested in the family's genealogical history and extended family ties. Rosemary O'Day has described Cassandra as being 'obsessed with ancestry, descent and connection'.[66] This genealogical interest is evident in the first 38 folio pages of her Account where she mistakenly begins with one William Willoughby, *temp.* Edward I.[67] Here she partly attempts to contextualize the early history of the family in relationship to some of the more dramatic moments in medieval English history, viz. the Baronial Revolt of the thirteenth century, some of the military excursions to the continent, the Wars of the Roses, and the revolt of Lambert Simnel under Henry VII. In these cases she largely relied, sometimes verbatim, on the published chronicles of William Dugdale, William Camden, and Richard Baker, as well as on the manuscript mentioned above written by her father.[68] These first 38 folio pages are largely derivative and not included in this edition, although it is noteworthy that she spends time detailing the marriages, not only of the sons of her Willoughby ancestors, but also the daughters who, for the most part, drop out of the standard genealogies of the time. As she moves forward in her Account, however, and begins to focus on family letters, she does not attempt to contextualize her notes in terms of national politics, nor does she try to follow the financial vagaries of Francis Willoughby's ill-conceived schemes for

---

Brother was to marry, struck me with such a lively impression of my eldest Brothers face (who had been dead two years and a half) that it was very hard for me to recover the great surprise which it gave me.' Chandos, *The Continuation of the History*, 141; Mi, LM 27, fo. 156.

[65] Chandos, *Continuation*, xvii–xviii.

[66] O'Day, *Cassandra Brydges*, 14.

[67] See other genealogical writings in BL, Stowe MS 656 and STB 2 (1) book 3.

[68] Mi, LM 13, a volume of memoirs and observations taken out of old muniments. See Introduction n. 38.

manufacturing woad, glass, or iron;[69] she does not focus her attention on the building of Wollaton Hall, a project that has interested a number of scholars;[70] nor does she dwell on the declining profits of the Willoughby coal mines by the 1590s,[71] although she must, perforce, mention the financial difficulties that seep into the personal letters of Francis and Elizabeth and dominate the lives of Bridget and Percival. Instead, she organized her Account around the personalities involved, beginning with the marriage of Francis and Elizabeth and then systematically collecting information and copying letters relating to each daughter in turn. She saves, however, much of what she has to report about Bridget, the oldest daughter, and her husband Percival Willoughby, for the second volume where she continues the Account through her grandparents, parents and her own generation.

Cassandra's interest in the interpersonal relations of her ancestors has fortunately left us with a rich portrait of a family dominated by the discourse of women intersecting with the demands of husbands and would-be husbands who were at times and by turns affectionate and controlling. In the final analysis, however, they were not often capable of understanding or coping with the strong-willed Willoughby women – women who sometimes chose what, in patriarchal Elizabethan society, could only be destructive behaviour and ended up leading, as Cassandra put it, 'very unhappy lives'.

Willoughby Family Background

The Nottinghamshire Willoughbys of Wollaton would have been aware, in the seventeenth century, that their family could be traced

---

[69] Richard S. Smith, 'A woad growing project at Wollaton in the 1580s', *TTS*, 65 (1961), 27–46; R.S. Smith, 'Sir Francis Willoughby's ironworks, 1570–1610', *Renaissance and Modern Studies*, 11 (1967), 90–140; R.A. Pelham, 'The establishment of the Willoughby ironworks in north Warwickshire in the sixteenth century', *University of Birmingham Historical Journal*, 4 (1953–1954), 18–29. Francis was also trying to expand coal production and the market for coal, and he was considering funding a paper mill.

[70] M. Airs, *The Tudor and Jacobean Country House: A Building History* (Stroud, 1995); Friedman, *House and Household*; Mark Girouard, *Robert Smythson and the Elizabethan Country House* (London, 1983); Sheila M. Strauss, *Wollaton and Wollaton Hall: A Short History* (Nottingham, 1989); Marshall, *Wollaton Hall and the Willoughby Family*; Nikolaus Pevsner, 'Double profile: A reconsideration of the Elizabethan style as seen at Wollaton', *The Architectural Review*, 107 (1950), 147–158; and a number of articles in *TTS*, Vols 6, 72, and 76. See also John Kelly Hayden, 'Sir Francis Willoughby of Wollaton, 1547–1596', PhD thesis, University of Virginia, 1991.

[71] Smith, 'Willoughbys of Wollaton', chs 7–11; Richard S. Smith, *Early Coal-Mining around Nottingham 1500–1650* (Nottingham, 1989), 22–23. Cassandra does include some receipts from coal for 1596–1599 in the 2nd vol. of her Account, Chandos, *Continuation*, 30–32.

to one Ralph Bugge (d. c.1250), a wealthy Nottingham wool merchant and Derbyshire lead mine owner who flourished in the early thirteenth century and is first mentioned in Nottingham records c.1209.[72] Modern research has so far been unable to push the lineage further back. Ralph Bugge built up a landed estate in Willoughby-on-the-Wolds in Nottinghamshire and left it to his youngest son Richard.[73] Within three generations the heirs of Ralph Bugge through Richard had climbed through land acquisitions and fishing rights on the Trent, profits from mining, military experience, legal careers, wealth-building marriages, and local office holding into the ranks of the upper gentry and had taken as part of their name the place name of Willoughby (spelled variously Willughby, Wylughby, Wilubee and so forth).[74]

At the time of the 1362/3 death of Sir Richard de Willoughby, chief justice and the fifth in descent from Ralph Bugge, Richard held manors in Nottinghamshire, Lincolnshire, Derbyshire, Leicestershire, and four other counties, overall holding lands in nineteen counties worth between £500 and £700 annually.[75] This placed the Willoughby wealth somewhere between that enjoyed by the lay barons and the

[72] Sir William Dugdale, *The Antiquities of Warwickshire* (London, 1656), only carried the family's origins back to Sir Hugh Willoughby *temp.* Henry VI (p. 757b), but Robert Thoroton, *The Antiquities of Nottinghamshire* (London, 1677), 35, traced the family back to Ralph Bugge, his son Richard Bugge and grandson Richard de Willoughby, knight. Cassandra traces the Willoughby origins to William Willoughby in the reign of Edward I. This is due to a mistake in the family pedigree at Birdsall House drawn up in 1573. *HMC Middleton*, 504 n. 2. Cassandra's father Francis Willoughby's genealogical notes frequently mention Richard and Ralph Bugge, references that Cassandra did not pursue. Mi, LM 13, 39, 44, 69, 85, 97, 133, 134. The Birdsall House genealogy was probably taken from William Flower, *The Visitations of the County of Nottingham in the Years 1569 and 1614*, Harleian Society, IV (London, 1871), 145, where he begins with William Willoughby *temp.* Edward I.

[73] The earliest evidence of Ralph Bugge owning property in Willoughby is from a charter dated sometime between 1209 and 1233 in which he bought a mill and two acres of land in Willoughby-on-the-Wolds. See J.C. Holt, 'Willoughby Deeds', in Patricia M. Barnes and C.F. Slade (eds), *A Medieval Miscellany for Doris Mary Stenton*, Pipe Roll Society, NS XXXVI (London, 1962), 181; and Michael R. Bloom, 'The careers of Sir Richard II de Wiloughby and Sir Richard III de Willoughby, chief justice of the king's bench (1338–1340); and the rise of the Willoughbys of Nottinghamshire', DPhil thesis, University of Oxford, 1985, ch. 1, for further information on Ralph Bugge's accumulated holdings.

[74] See *HMC Middleton*, 735, for over 30 different spellings of the name.

[75] For the lands of Richard Willoughby d.1362/3 (Mar. 14), see the *Inquisitiones Post Mortem relating to Nottinghamshire*, II, TSRS, IV (Nottingham, 1914), 256, taken at the time of his death in 1362/3. H.L. Gray has calculated, from the income tax returns for 1436, that the average income for lay barons was £882, while that of the greater knights was £208. This places Richard de Willoughby's income at the high end of the greater knights. H.L. Gray, 'Incomes from land in England in 1436', *English Historical Review*, 49 (1934), 630. *HMC Middleton*, 99; Hayden, 'Sir Francis Willoughby of Wollaton', 59 n. 21; the information regarding the lands in nineteen counties comes from Simon Payling, 'Sir Richard Willoughby (c.1290–1362), justice', *ODNB*.

greater knights of the shire.[76] Richard also appears to have been the first of the family to exploit coal mining at Cossall and Wollaton and perhaps elsewhere. Subsequently coal, in addition to rents, agricultural profits, benefits deriving from local and national positions of responsibility, and profitable marriages undergirded the family's wealth.[77]

The Willoughbys were unusually fortunate throughout the fourteenth and fifteenth centuries. During a time of recurrent plague, wars with France, and internal conflicts, they nonetheless managed to secure their inheritance intact through male descent from the time of Ralph Bugge until the generation with which this book is concerned.[78] Regarding the final failure of the Willoughby family line in the male line at the end of the sixteenth century, Simon Payling notes that out of 45 knightly families in Nottinghamshire in 1325, 13 had failed in the male line by 1400, another 18 in the fifteenth century, and 8 in the sixteenth century. By 1700 there were only three knightly families in the shire that still continued in the male line.[79]

By the end of the fifteenth century, the Willoughbys were poised to move into the higher ranks of the aristocracy. Why they did not do so rests, in part, on the careers of two of the sixteenth-century Willoughby heirs – Henry (1451–1528) and Francis himself, as well as the involvement of the family in the ill-fated effort to place Lady Jane Grey on the English throne in 1553 and the subsequent conservatism of Queen Elizabeth, who raised only a small handful of her closest advisers to the peerage.[80]

Henry Willoughby inherited substantial lands, including the manor of Middleton in Warwickshire from his father's estates in 1474, and, with his mother's death in 1490/1, Wollaton. He also married four times; at least two of his wives were sole heiresses.[81] He came

---

[76] Simon Payling, *Political Society in Lancastrian England: The Greater Gentry of Nottinghamshire* (Oxford, 1991), 2, table 1.1.

[77] This editor is preparing an extended article on the rise of the Willoughbys from the 13th into the 16th century.

[78] The family survived several minorities, such as that of Richard de Willoughby the senior at the end of the 13th century, and that of Sir Francis Willoughby himself in the 1550s. On several occasions the inheritance descended to a younger brother or half-brother.

[79] Payling, *Political Society*, 66.

[80] On Sir Henry Willoughby, see Hayden, 'Sir Francis Willoughby of Wollaton', 26–36; and Alan Cameron, 'Sir Henry Willoughby of Wollaton', *TTS*, LXXIV (1970), 10–21.

[81] By his first wife Margaret, the daughter of Sir Robert Markham, he had two sons and three daughters, and by his third wife, Helen, the daughter of John Egerton, he had another son and daughter.

to maturity in the confusing political period of the Wars of the Roses and survived serving under Lord Hastings and then the duke of Buckingham, both of whom were executed by Richard III.[82] After Richard's defeat at Bosworth Field in 1485, Henry Willoughby supported Henry VII, serving him well throughout his reign, moving in the highest circles, and benefiting from his close relationship to the Crown; Henry VIII may not have valued him, however, to the extent that his father did.

Locally and regionally, Henry Willoughby was high sheriff of Lincolnshire (1491, 1501/2), high sheriff of Nottinghamshire and Derbyshire (1495/6), high sheriff of Warwickshire (1505/6; 1519-1520, 1526), and justice of the peace in Lincolnshire and Warwickshire, and, for more than thirty years in Nottinghamshire (1492-1528), among other offices and responsibilities.[83] Alan Cameron points out how important a personage Henry was with several examples, perhaps the most telling of which is that the Nottingham Borough took care to present Sir Henry with a suitable gift (usually wine) when he attended quarter sessions.[84]

Henry was an enthusiastic if somewhat conventional Catholic[85] who could afford to pay for a chantry at Wollaton church and many additional indulgences and engage in lavish almsgiving to scholars, friars, anchorites, players, poor men, and others.[86] Already by 1497/8, his income 'was comparable with that of most contemporary noblemen'.[87] Henry was the beneficiary of dowries from his marriages, from a variety of land purchases and perhaps from some foreclosures and some possibly illegal seizures of land.[88] His income from the coal

---

[82] See W.H. Dunham, *Lord Hastings Indenture Retainers, 1461-1483* (New Haven, CT, 1955), 129.

[83] *Calendar of the Fine Rolls*, Vol. XXII: *Henry VII, 1485-1509* (London, 1962), sub nomine; *Calendar of the Patent Rolls: Henry VII, 1485-1509*, 2 vols (London, 1914-1916), sub nomine. See also *HMC Middleton*, 123, 131, 141, 508, 512, 514; Cameron, 'Sir Henry Willoughby of Wollaton', 18.

[84] *Ibid.* 17.

[85] *HMC Middleton*, 124, 137-140. See Mi, F 1/4 for a letter of fraternity from the Cistercian Abbey of Chalons for Henry Willoughby and his wife Elizabeth, at the intercession of the abbot of Fountains Abbey, York, offering all the privileges of the order, dated c.1500. See also Mi, F 1/7, dated 1512, for a letter of fraternity from Frater Robert, provincial prior, from the Carmelite order at Coventry for Henry 'Willolowz' and his wife Helena.

[86] *HMC Middleton*, 124, 127, 137, 330-387; Cameron, 'Sir Henry Willoughby of Wollaton', 19. He was also granted participation in the prayers of the Observant Friars.

[87] *Ibid.* 11.

[88] Henry engaged in enclosing his lands on a significant scale. 'The Domesday of inclosures for Nottinghamshire, 1517', TSRS, II (Nottingham, 1904), 39.

pits at Wollaton, receipts from which rose steadily up to 1510, was substantial.[89]

With all this, however, Sir Henry never rose to noble status. The reasons are not entirely clear. It would appear, from scattered references, that Henry Willoughby could be quarrelsome and had certainly fought with the Stanhope and Plumpton families, as well as with Lord Grey of Codnor, and even with his own mother.[90] In 1518, however, Sir Henry received, by letters signet from King Henry VIII, an appointment as captain to raise and equip soldiers, notwithstanding the Statute of Retainers. Toward the end of his life, in 1525, he also received a commission under the signet ring to repress riot in Coventry.[91] Henry Willoughby died in 1528, by which time he had rewritten his will numerous times.[92]

Henry Willoughby married off his children with great care,[93] and the alliances contracted had the potential to raise the Willoughbys into the very highest ranks of the nobility, had it not been for the damning involvement of the Grey family in the politics of royal succession and the too rapid deaths of Henry's heirs – his three sons (Edward Willoughby in 1541, Sir John Willoughby in 1548/9, and Sir Hugh Willoughby the navigator in 1554), his grandson Henry Willoughby in 1549 and his great grandson Thomas in 1559[94] – three generations within the space of eighteen years. In 1559 the inheritance was left in the hands of Henry's great-grandson Francis (the last remaining heir in the male line), who was between twelve and thirteen years old at the time, and those who held his wardship.[95]

John Willoughby, Sir Henry's eldest son and heir, had married Anne Grey, eldest daughter of Edward Grey, Viscount Lisle.[96] This marriage placed the Willoughbys close to Sir Edward Seymour, later duke of Somerset and protector of King Edward VI, as Anne

---

[89] Cameron, 'Sir Henry Willoughby of Wollaton', 11–12, 20; see table 1 in Cameron. Smith, 'The Willoughbys of Wollaton', 11, estimates that Henry's income from the coalfields in 1515–1516 and 1520–1521 was at least £325 annually.

[90] *HMC Middleton*, 115–120; Cameron, 'Sir Henry Willoughby of Wollaton', 14–16.

[91] *HMC Middleton*, 131, 141.

[92] Mi, F 6/5 (1489), 6/22 (1497), 6/2 (1512), 6/24 (1508), 6/25 (1513), 6/28 (1528); *HMC Middleton*, 121–122, 123, 126, 128, 130. See *North Country Wills: Being Abstracts of Wills Relating to York, Nottingham, Northumberland, Cumberland, and Westmoreland 1383 to 1558*, Surtees Society, CXVI (London and Durham, 1908), 121–123, for his 1528 will.

[93] An example of the care that Sir Henry took over marriage arrangements can be seen in a letter relating to negotiations in 1515 over the marriage of Thomas Gresley. *HMC Middleton*, 513 and Mi, 5/168/46.

[94] For the exact date of Thomas Willoughby's death, see p. 30 below.

[95] Initially Sir Francis Knollys held the wardship of Francis Willoughby. See below, pp. 32–33, for the negotiations concerning this wardship.

[96] *HMC Middleton*, 121. Anne's dowry was a modest 700 marks. Mi, D 4804.

was co-heiress with her sister, who married Edward Seymour. Alan Cameron characterizes Sir John Willoughby as 'Undoubtedly the wealthiest layman resident in the county [of Nottinghamshire]', with a gross income 'of the order of £1,800 per annum',[97] an estimated £600 to £750 coming from coal receipts.[98] He was the protector and seneschal of two monastic houses – Lenton and Beauvale – with which the Willoughbys had had long-standing connections. In 1505 John and his wife Anne received a letter of fraternity from the hospital of Holy Trinity, Wolsoken (Walsingham?) in the diocese of Norwich, and in 1521 John was made a Knight of the Holy Sepulchre.[99] Sir John Willoughby's religious beliefs seem to have been, like those of his father, strongly Catholic; he was associated with his father in several of their religious affiliations and there is evidence that he went on two pilgrimages – one to Saint James of Compostela (Santiago de Compostela) and the other to Rome.[100] Post-Reformation, however, John Willoughby apparently accommodated to the changes,[101] although, in the wake of the dissolution of the monasteries, the Willoughbys profited very little.[102]

John was 47 when his father died in 1528; he then died on 10 January 1548/9 without heirs.[103] Since his younger brother and heir, Edward, had died in 1541, the Willoughby estates descended to Edward's son and John's nephew Henry. This Henry had married Anne (another Anne Grey) daughter of the second marquis of Dorset, once again strengthening Willoughby ties with the Grey family.[104] At the beginning of Cassandra's Account, she writes,

> This was the fourth time that the Willughbys had matched with this family of the Greys, which had made a very great intimacy between the two families, as appears by many of the old papers. In the books of accounts there is often mention made of Sir Henry Willughby's being at Bradgate [the home of Henry Grey, 3rd marquis of Dorset, later duke of Suffolk and also Henry Willoughby's brother-in-law] for severall days together, and in the account

---

[97] Alan Cameron, 'Some social consequences of the dissolution of the monasteries in Nottinghamshire', *TTS*, 79 (1975), 50–59.
[98] Smith, 'The Willoughbys of Wollaton', 18, citing Mi, M 145/6.
[99] Mi, F 1/5 1505; Mi, C 8/2.
[100] *HMC Middleton*, 132, 136; see Mi, F 10/13 for the signet letter from Henry VIII for a safe conduct for his pilgrimage to St James of Compostela, dated 22 Feb. 9 Henry VIII.
[101] See a letter to John from Henry VIII raging against Rome. *HMC Middleton*, 509.
[102] Cameron, 'Some social consequences', 50–59, esp. 53–54.
[103] For his will of 20 Dec. 1548, see Mi, 6/179/30–31; *North Country Wills, 1383 to 1558*, 201–203.
[104] The marquis was a frequent guest at the house of Henry Willoughby in late 1524 to 1525. *HMC Middleton*, 377–380, 384, 141, 514; Welch, 'Willoughby Letters', 51–53, 76–77; Mi, 7/180/30–31; Mi, C 11/2. For the 1528 marriage settlement, see Mi, 6/170/146–148.

book of bills of fair for [the] Wollaton family (which shews what company daily came to Wollaton) I often find some of the family from Bradgate set down.'[105]

The Children of Henry (c.1510–1549) and Anne Grey Willoughby (c.1519–1547/8) and the Childhood of Francis Willoughby

Henry was a young husband with three small children when he was killed in the 1549 commotion of Kett's rebellion. The rebellion was brutally suppressed by an armed force under the leadership of the earl of Warwick, and one of the casualties in the earl's forces was Henry. At this point Cassandra's Account provides a great deal of information, mostly drawn from old papers, a few letters, and account books. She notes: 'This Sir Henry Willughby was one of those gentlemen that went to appease the rebels in Norfolk who had got together under Robert Ket, a tanner, upon a grievance on account of inclosures, and was killed at Norwich, August the 27th, 1548 [*sic*]. He and his lady both lye buried in the Church at Wollaton, where there is a monument for them.'[106] Henry had enjoyed his inheritance for less than a year. He and his wife Anne Grey, who had died the year previously (3 January, probably 1547/8), left two sons and one daughter, all very young. Thomas, the eldest (b.1541), was eight years of age and Francis, the youngest (b.1546/7), only two years old; Margaret Willoughby, the daughter, was apparently about three years older than Francis (b.1543?). Cassandra notes that, 'It appears by some of the old papers that Sir Henry Willughby left these three children to the Marquis of Dorsets care, and that the three executors of his will were George Medley and Gabriell Barwyke, esquires, and John Hall, gent:.'[107] The children were put in the care of Anne's brother Henry, 3rd marquis of Dorset and duke of Suffolk, at

---

[105] *HMC Middleton*, 519; Mi, LM 26, fos 37–38.
[106] Mi, LM 26, fo. 39: see p. 69 below. There is an epitaph of Henry Willoughby in Francis Willoughby's handwriting in Hebrew, English, Latin, and Greek, estimated written c.1575. Mi, F 10/2; *HMC Middleton*, 155–156.
[107] Mi, LM 26, fo. 39: see p. 69 below. John Hall was the bailiff at Middleton; George Medley was half-brother to Anne Grey and her brother Henry Grey. His mother, Margaret Wotton, was the second wife of Thomas Grey, 2nd marquis of Dorset. As a result, George Medley was an uncle [or a half-uncle] to Thomas, Margaret, and Francis Willoughby. The other executors were Gabriel Barwyke and Henry Marmion, servants to the Willoughbys. The supervisors of Henry's will were Henry Grey and Sir John Markham. Mi, 6/179/35/1–2; *HMC Middleton*, 149, 396.

Bradgate[108] but were soon transferred to the guardianship of George Medley, who owned or leased a house in Tilty, in Essex, and partially owned a London house in the Minories.[109]

> There is a letter from George Medeleye dated from London in February 1549 [1549/50], in which he writes that the Marquis of Dorset, being now daily to attend the King, he intended to remove his family from Bradgate to London, and therefore ordered that 12 horses should be sent for from Wollaton and a cart and horses from Middleton to come up to London with Mrs.[110] Margaret and little Mr. Francis Willughby. Attended thus, a servant to carry Master Francis before him, another servant to carry Mrs. Margaret, and another servant to carry little Whytneye, a horse for Mrs. Lenton [the governess], another horse for the maid, and 4 for the four men to wait upon them, a man to lead a horse to carry the male [a travelling bag], and two more servants to take care of the horses. It does not appear where these children were after this journey, till by a book of Medeleys accounts for the childrens cloaths etc. from the 4th of Edward the 6th to the 1st of Elizabeth [1550–1558], I find that his Nephew Francis Willughby and his Neece Margaret removed to Tyltey, April the 21th, 1550 [...] I don't find where Mr. Thomas Willughby was when his Brother and Sister removed to Tiltey, but in Mr. Medeleys account book there is set down 20^{sh} for Mr. Thomas Willughby's board with him from May the 27th to June the 11th that year and 10^{s} for Mr. Thomas Willughbys mans board the same time. And again the same sume is set down for his and his mans board with Mr. Medeley from November the 3^{d} to the 18th, which day I find by the book of houshold expences for the family at Tyltey Mr. Thomas Willughby went to Cambridg.[111]

Thomas Willoughby, by then no more than nine or ten years of age, must have boarded at one of the several grammar schools in Cambridge, preparatory to attending the University.[112] This absence

---

[108] *CPR 1550*, Edward VI, iv, 11 gives to Henry Grey the wardship and marriage of Thomas Willoughby with an annuity of £40. According to the will, Francis was to receive £10 a year. At 16 Margaret was to receive 600 marks and Francis was to have £20 per year for clothing and learning until he came of age.

[109] The name is derived from the precinct in London that had housed the abbey of the Minoresses of St Mary of the Order of St Clare.

[110] 'Mrs.' was the abbreviation for Mistress.

[111] Mi, LM 26, fos 39–40: see pp. 70–71 below; Mi, A 32, fos 1, 4, pp. 1, 7; *HMC Middleton*, 399, 402. Thomas was in Cambridge by 1550. He then boarded at Tilty for 20 weeks (23 May to 10 Oct.) in 1551 'when the greate swett was in Cambrydge and other placez'. Mi, A 32, fo. 5, p. 9; *HMC Middleton*, 404.

[112] See *HMC Middleton*, 474–477, for excerpts from a 1550 inventory of things at Wollaton Hall in George Medley's hand, including 'Naperier and Lynen, with other stuffe sent to my cousin Maister Thomas Willoughbye at Cambridge'. See J.A. Venn, *Alumni Cantabrigienses*, IV (Cambridge, 1922), 423, who places Thomas at Magdalene College in 1551. He places him at Lincoln's Inn in 1558.

of his older brother (particularly after 1551 during which year Thomas had returned for twenty weeks because of the 'swett' at Cambridge) and the rapid change of residences, in addition to the deaths of his father and mother, must have impacted Francis's life dramatically at a very early age. It is also clear from the notes that Cassandra took, that life at Tilty was something of a social whirlwind, with visits from Lady Jane Grey, first cousin to the Willoughby children, and the princess Mary Tudor, among others. All of this was cut suddenly short by the elevation of Lady Jane Grey to queen for nine days and, in the wake of Wyatt's Rebellion in January 1553/4, her execution, along with the execution of her husband, Lord Guildford Dudley, and her father, Henry Grey, who was also the maternal uncle to Thomas, Margaret and Francis. In the wake of this tragedy, the older son Thomas's wardship, which had been given to the marquis of Dorset, was transferred to William, Lord Paget, and Thomas joined his household.[113] There was discussion of sending Thomas to school at Paris, but by 1558, at the age of seventeen, he was admitted to Lincoln's Inn. More importantly, George Medley, who now had wardship of Francis and Margaret, was, as the half-brother of Henry Grey and half-uncle to Lady Jane Grey, suspected of involvement in the plot to bring Lady Jane Grey to the throne and in Wyatt's Rebellion. In addition, his brother-in-law, Thomas Dannett, may have conspired with Henry Grey, perhaps agreeing to bring 400 men to his aid at Leicester. Although Dannett, in the end, did not supply the expected troops, he was nonetheless suspected, captured, and placed in the Tower for a month before being released and going into exile on the continent.[114] As Cassandra writes, 'I believe about this time [1553–1554] Mr. Medeley and the whol familie at Tyltey were involved in great troubles upon the Duke of Suffolks account, who was beheaded upon the 23rd of February [1553/4] following. Mr. Francis and Mrs. Margaret were removed to the Minoryes, [just outside Aldgate near the Tower of London] with their servants, I believe a house where Mr. Medeley used to live.'[115] As a result, George Medley also spent time in the Tower, and his lodgings in the Minories were searched by Bishop Gardiner.[116] From February and into April executions of large numbers of the rebels took place, with bodies publicly displayed

---

[113] *CPR 1554*, Philip and Mary I, i. 238–239. Lord Paget received an annuity of £100 in addition to custody and the marriage of Thomas until he reached full age or Lord Paget obtained the effect of his marriage.

[114] James D. Taylor Jr., *Sir Thomas Wyatt the Younger c.1521–1554 and Wyatt's Rebellion* (New York, 2013), 92.

[115] *HMC Middleton*, 521; Mi, LM 26, fo. 45: see pp. 75–76 below.

[116] *HMC Middleton*, 521 n. 1.

throughout London. Thus, by the time that Francis Willoughby was eight years of age, he had lost his mother and his father; his cousin, Lady Jane Grey; and his uncle Henry Grey (as well as one other of the Grey uncles) had been executed;[117] he and his sister and their household had been moved about several times, and his guardian, foster father and uncle, George Medley, was under suspicion and briefly imprisoned, as was Medley's brother-in-law. In addition, the children may have been traumatized by the numbers and brutality of the executions taking place throughout the city. Then, when Francis was between twelve and thirteen, his older brother Thomas died, and Francis became heir to the Willoughby name and estates.[118]

Francis had received the kind of education that would stand him in good stead as heir to the Willoughby estates. Beginning in 1550, when Francis was three years old, his governors spent 20d for a 'pounde of sugere plate and greate comffetes to make hym larne his booke'. They also purchased two ABCs for 1d. Later in 1550 additional ABCs were purchased for 2d.[119] In 1552 the accounts mention costs of a Greek and a Hebrew grammar book for Francis; in 1553 the accounts list two French books for Margaret[120] and other books for Francis as well as moneys 'to Mystris Lenton for teaching and lokyng to' Francis and Margaret for a year and a half.[121] The 1554 accounts of George Medley record the purchase, for 3 pennies, of Evaldus Gallus's *Pueriles Confabulatiunculae*, a book of Latin dialogues.[122] In 1555, Francis was going to school at Saffron Walden in Essex[123] but by early 1556 he was boarding at St Anthony's grammar school

---

[117] The only uncle on the Grey side to survive in the wake of Wyatt's Rebellion was John Grey, the youngest son in the family. Although imprisoned, he was ultimately released and regained land and reputation under Queen Elizabeth. Francis Willoughby was to consult John, Lord Grey of Pirgo, when he engaged himself in marriage to Elizabeth Lyttleton (see below, p. 37).

[118] Mi, 6/171/10 is a parchment document that describes the estate and wardship of Francis Willoughby, dated 1 July 1560. It notes that Thomas Willoughby esquire was deceased 'the xvith day of August anno primo Elizabeth Queen'. It continues by noting that, at Thomas's death, Francis Willoughby was 12 years 30 weeks and 2 days old. This would put his birth date at about 17 Jan. 1546/7.

[119] *HMC Middleton*, 400–402; Mi, A 32, fos 2, 3, pp. 3, 5.

[120] *HMC Middleton*, 406–407; Mi, A 32, fos 8,10, pp. 15, 19. This last bill, dated 1553, was written up by Margaret 'wrytten with her owne hande' when she was presumably about ten years of age. The subsequent bills were also written up by Margaret, as she mentions 'Mystris Lenton for teaching and lokyng to my brother Fraunces and me [...] to Clarke for teaching me to playe upon the virginalles'. She was apparently keeping a book of her bills.

[121] *HMC Middleton*, 406; Mi, A 32, fos 8, 10–10v, pp. 15, 19–19b.

[122] *HMC Middleton*, 408; Mi, A 32, fo. 17v, p. 32b.

[123] Mi, A 32, fo. 22, p. 41; *HMC Middleton*, 409.

INTRODUCTION   31

in London where he remained through the first half of the year.[124] By summer 1556 he had transferred back to Saffron Walden.[125] There Francis received a thoroughly humanist and elitist education that was gradually becoming part of the grammar school curriculum in England's best schools. His studies involved learning Cato's *Disticha*, a first reading text of Latin moral sayings, *Cicero's Letters*, Vives's *Colloquies*, and a Latin–Greek dictionary by Ambrose Calepin (printed in Strasburg in 1537), a dictionary in English (probably the dictionary of Thomas Elyot), Erasmus's *De Copia* and his *Adages*, Lorenzo Valla's *De Elegantia Linguae Latinae*, Ceporinus's Greek grammar, the *Acts of the Apostles* in English and with notes to sing and play, Mathurin Cordier's *Libellus de Corrupti Sermonis Emendacione*, the *Floures for Latine Spekynge* perhaps by Nicholas Udall, and Richard Sherry's *Treatise of the Figures of Grammar and Rhetorick*.[126] The accounts record payments to a writing master teaching Francis to write, as well as the cost of a 'Terence' and a Latin psalter.[127] By 1557 Francis was learning to write the Italian hand; he was also being taught 'arethmetick' by Master Horseley.[128] There are numerous notations in George Medley's account book of costs for teaching Francis and Margaret to play upon the virginals.[129] An entry of 1557 is particularly interesting in that it concerns a book which was purchased for the young Francis to notate his musical studies.[130] A much later surviving shelf list of books includes a 1552 copy of Galigai's *Practica d'arithmetica* which may also have been one of

---

[124] Mi, A 32, fo. 25, p. 47; *HMC Middleton*, 409.

[125] Mi, A 32, fos 22, 25, 28v–29, pp. 41, 47, 54–55; also cited in Friedman, *House and Household*, 19. The account book includes payments for schooling at St Anthony's from January to mid June 1556. On 15 Sept. 1556 Medley's account book records 3s 4d to the schoolmaster at Saffron Walden for teaching Francis for one quarter (fo. 28v, p. 54). *HMC Middleton*, 409–411.

[126] *HMC Middleton*, 406–414; Mi, A 32, fos 28v–30, 34, pp. 54–57, 65. For Francis Willoughby's schooling, see T.W. Baldwin, *William Shakespeare's small Latine and lesse Greeke*, 1 (Urbana, IL, 1944), 375–379. See also Kenneth Charlton, *Education in Renaissance England* (London, 1965), 93 ff.; and more recently Ian Green, *Humanism and Protestantism in Early Modern English Education* (Farnham, 2009), *passim*, although he does not cite specific school curricula or Sir Francis. See also Friedman, *House and Household*, 19.

[127] Mi, A 32, fo. 28v, p. 54; *HMC Middleton*, 411.

[128] Mi, A 32, fos 34–34v, pp. 65–66; *HMC Middleton*, 413. Stevenson dates this 1557, but the very next entry mentions 16 Apr. 1558.

[129] Mi, A 32, fos 12, 18, 18v, 20; pp. 22, 33, 34, 37; see *HMC Middleton*, 407–408, 412–413, for more notations on Francis's musical education. We know very little about the education Margaret received beyond the two French books mentioned earlier, that Mrs Lenton was teaching her along with Francis, that she was writing up bills at the age of ten, and that she shared, with Francis, their musical education. That it was advanced is suggested by a reference in Cassandra's account of Margaret discussing astronomical texts in Italian with a family servant. Mi, LM 26, fo. 70.

[130] Mi, A 32, fos 32v, 34v, pp. 62, 66; *HMC Middleton*, 412–413.

Francis's school texts.[131] Instructed in Greek, Latin and Hebrew grammar, writing, arithmetic, Latin rhetoric, and music, Francis was sufficiently educated to be considered a cultured man. In 1558 he went 'to Cambridge to schole wyth docketer Carre'.[132] But with his brother's death in 1559, Francis Willoughby's wardship became valuable, and in 1560/1 it was formally assigned to Sir Francis Knollys,[133] with the proviso that an annuity of £100 was to be set aside for Francis's education.[134]

Knollys was a committed Protestant who was married to the daughter of Mary Boleyn, Queen Elizabeth's cousin and reputed by some to be her half-sister. Knollys was vice-chamberlain of the royal household and a member of Elizabeth's Privy Council; as a result, Francis would have spent time with the Knollys family at court. In June 1564, at the request of Francis Willoughby himself (now 17 years old), however, the wardship was reassigned from Sir Francis Knollys to Henry Medley, Gabriel Barwick, and John Hall, the original executors of Henry Willoughby's estate, or, in the case of George Medley, to his son after Medley's death in 1562/63.[135] The cost of this transaction was £1,500. Among other reasons for this transfer, Francis had refused to marry Elizabeth Knollys,[136] the daughter of his guardian, who was, at the time, about 15 years of

---

[131] Friedman, *House and Household*, 32.

[132] Mi, A 32, fo. 35v, p. 68; *HMC Middleton*, 413–414. In 1559 he was still 'at docketer Carrez in Cambridge'. Mi, A 32, fo. 37, p. 71; *HMC Middleton*, 414. This was perhaps Dr Nicholas Carr at Trinity College, although Francis Willoughby's later close associations were with Jesus College. Francis was perhaps 13 years of age at the time.

[133] See Mi, 6/171/10 for the grant of custody, wardship and marriage of Francis Willoughby to Sir Francis Knollys, dated 1 July 1560. It describes a list of all the 'extent and clere yerelye value of all the mannors landes and hereditaments' of Thomas Willoughby who died 16 Aug. 1559. See Mi, A 31, fo. 24v for the costs (£10) of delivering Francis to Sir Francis Knollys at London and for staying there to conclude the agreement in 1560. Friedman, *House and Household*, 20. On Sir Francis Knollys, see Alexandra F. Johnston, 'Sir Francis Knollys and His Progeny: Court and Country in the Thames Valley', in Norman L. Jones and Daniel Woolf (eds), *Local Identities in Late Medieval and Early Modern England* (New York, 2007), 131–155. For George Medley's will and codicil in 1562, see Mi, 7/183/12.

[134] Mi, 6/171/10. See also 6/171/11–12, 14; *CPR 1560–1563*, Elizabeth I, ii, 180, dated 28 Feb. 1560/1.

[135] See Mi, 6/178/49 for the indenture of the release, signed by Knollys, Francis Willoughby, Matthew Arundell, and Margaret Arundell, and also Mi, 6/171/15, 17–18, for a licence to assign custody of the ward. The estate had to reimburse Knollys £1,500 for the losses he would sustain as a result of this transfer. Some of this £1,500 was paid by Margaret, his sister, and her husband Matthew Arundell, a point that Margaret makes in a letter to Francis about the time of Francis's marriage with Elizabeth Lyttleton. See also Friedman, *House and Household*, 21.

[136] Elizabeth Knollys did not marry until she was 29 years of age – a late age at the time – at which time (1578) she married Sir Thomas Leighton of Feckenham, Worcs. He served as Governor of Jersey and Guernsey.

age. One also wonders whether Francis shared the strongly Protestant beliefs of the Knollys family that had sent them into continental exile under Queen Mary. As an adult Francis does seem to have been a committed Protestant. Alice Friedman speculates that Francis was not comfortable with the court life into which he had been thrust through Knollys.[137] Perhaps the traumas of his early childhood experiences led him to be wary of the court.[138] On the other hand, perhaps he already had another marriage in mind.

The Willoughby Letters: Sir Francis Willoughby, his Marriages, and the Next Generation

Most of the information about the Willoughbys thus far, Cassandra had copied from old papers, a few letters and account books she had found. Although Cassandra continued to draw from these account books, at this juncture she moved on to the family letter collection at the point where Francis Willoughby decided to marry.

Very shortly after Francis Willougby's release from his wardship with the Knollys family he began negotiations for a marriage with Elizabeth Lyttleton of the Lyttleton family of Frankley.[139] At the time (1564) Francis was 17 years of age (Figure 2). Elizabeth

---

[137] Friedman, *House and Household*, 21. Court life 'required him to enter a world which thwarted his independence and ambition'. One also needs to keep in mind that, by then, he had lost his elder brother and George Medley, his uncle, who died in 1562 and who had taken care of him since his parents' death. It may not have been independence, so much as stability and perhaps family that he desired. R.S. Smith states, 'There is only one record of his ever having visited Court.' R.S. Smith, *Sir Francis Willoughby of Wollaton Hall* (Nottingham, 1988), 16.

[138] There may have been other reasons for his lack of interest in the life at court. Many years later (in 1626), one of Francis's sons-in-law, Montague Wood, writing to his brother-in-law Percival Willoughby, recalled that 'olde Sir Francis when he came of yeares and had been brede a greate scholler, his officers [...] bringinge in ther severall accomptes both of mony and landes he sawe that it was too muche for him to manage himselfe, he wished he had bene lefte one hundrethe powndes by the yeare and his bookes'. Mi, 2/76/3–16, cited in Friedman, *House and Household*, 37; and in Smith, 'The Willoughbys of Wollaton', 69.

[139] The Lytteltons were an established Worcestershire family whose prominence was due, in large part, to the family fortunes founded by Sir Thomas Lyttleton (1422–1481), Judge of the Common Pleas and author of 'Lyttleton's Tenures'. Lyttleton is the spelling used by the senior (Frankley) branch of the family. John Lyttleton II, the father of Elizabeth, inherited a substantial estate that was widely scattered. Between 1531 and 1565 he enlarged and consolidated his holdings and from then until his death in 1590, he concentrated on managing his estate and establishing a political name for himself among the north Worcestershire gentry, becoming an MP in 1553, justice of the peace and, by 1556, high sheriff of Worcestershire. J.M.J. Tonks, 'The Lytteltons of Frankley and their Estates', MLitt thesis, University of Oxford, 1978, 7, 15–22, 39–41.

Figure 2. Francis Willoughby, age 26 (1573), in colour online. Reproduced by permission of Lord Middleton and the University of Nottingham Library Manuscripts Collection.

Figure 3. Elizabeth Willoughby, age 27 (1573), in colour online. Reproduced by permission of Lord Middleton and the University of Nottingham Library Manuscripts Collection.

Lyttleton was born in 1546 and was 18 years of age (Figure 3).[140] Francis was attracted to Elizabeth in part because she was the daughter of a neighbouring family with estates in Worcestershire not far from Middleton in Warwickshire. Although Francis does not say so, the fact that the Lyttletons owned coal and limestone on their estate at Halesowen may have attracted him.[141] There were strong family connections; the dowry promised (£1,500) was unusually substantial and was complemented with an offer to board the couple, their horses and six servants for three years.[142] Francis was to promise his wife a 'very reasonable' jointure and settlement of 'but one-third' of his estate on heirs male by her.[143] As Francis put it in a letter to his

---

[140] According to a portrait copy that now hangs in Wollaton Hall, originally painted in 1573, Elizabeth Willoughby was then 27 years of age. This suggests that she was 18 years of age in 1564, at the date of their marriage. If, as has been suggested above, Introduction n. 118, Francis Willoughby was born Jan. 1546/7, he was a year younger. His portrait copy in Wollaton Hall, painted at the same time, lists his age as 26; he was probably 17 when they married.

In her study of courtship patterns in Kent, Diana O'Hara finds that 'restraints upon too early marriages were internalized by the parties themselves'. Diana O'Hara, *Courtship and Constraint: Rethinking the Making of Marriage in Tudor England* (Manchester, 2000), 159. She cites Martin Ingram, who found, in Wiltshire court cases, some antagonism towards the marriage plans of inexperienced adolescents. These studies, however, focus on ecclesiastical court records and village families. See Alan Macfarlane, *Marriage and Love in England: Modes of Reproduction, 1300–1840* (Oxford, 1986), 211–216, for evidence that it was commonly assumed that men matured only after 25 and women only after 20. Ann Jennalie Cook, *Making a Match: Courtship in Shakespeare and his Society* (Princeton, NJ, 1991), 17–38, cites marital ages of 17–22 for women and 20–25 for men. Reconstitutive evidence supports the theory that early modern England fits the north-west European demographic formation pattern of later marriages between partners of similar ages, although early marriage was more common in the aristocracy and squirearchy. O'Hara, *Courtship and Constraint*, 165. Women were often given their portion of parental bequests at the age of 18 or 21, although sometimes the age of 16 or at the time of marriage was stipulated. According to the data from wills compiled by O'Hara, expectations of 'age of marriage' 'being of age' or 'lawful age' – the age at which property transfers were defined – increased significantly from the late 15th century to 1575–1599, with 80.6% of all wills giving the age for men as 20–24 and 64.2% specifying age 21, while the age of women fell largely between 15 and 24. O'Hara, *Courtship and Constraint*, 175–177. Based on this, while Elizabeth Lyttleton may have been considered of age to marry, Francis was on the young side. See Mi, 5/167/154 for Francis's coming of age and an indenture from Robert Penruddoke detailing records of his estates in 1568.

[141] See Tonks, 'The Lyttletons of Frankley', 33–34, for information on the mineral holdings and investments of the Lyttletons.

[142] Mi, LM 26, fos 55v and 60: see pp. 88, 91–92 below; for the settlement documents, see Mi, 7/ 183/19–25, dated Nov. 1564. The arrangements would appear to have been extraordinarily generous on the bride's side. In wealthy families, settlements would sometimes include the maintenance of the couple for a period of years; normally this was an offer made by the groom's family rather than the bride's. Amy Louise Erickson, *Women and Property in Early Modern England* (London and New York, 1993), 93.

[143] Mi, LM 26, fo. 60, p. 92 below.

uncle the Lord John Grey of Pirgo, 'After good deliberation it had pleased God to give him a liking to the young Gentlewoman, who had had a good education and was descended from a house of great antiquity, well friended and alyed, dwelling near his house of Middleton. And Mr. Lyttleton's offers with his Daughter being reasonable, could he have his Lordships favour he was fully minded to match himself to her'.[144]

Francis entered into this negotiation with the support of some of his advisers but without consulting his sister Margaret and her husband, Matthew Arundell.[145] Francis consulted, instead, Lord Dudley, earl of Leicester,[146] and others; he also received approval from Lord Grey.[147] His sister accused him of following the advice of George Willoughby, an illegitimate uncle,[148] who had ties to the Lyttleton family.[149] It is possible that George Willoughby, perhaps in

---

[144] Mi, LM 26, fo. 55v, p. 88 below.

[145] In 1558 Margaret had married Matthew Arundell, of Wardour Castle, Wilts. (knighted in 1574). Her dowry was a modest one of £300. Earlier, from 1450 to 1550, the median dowry for knights' daughters was 200 to 300 marks, a pound being 20 shillings and a mark 13s 4d or ⅔ of a pound. Barbara J. Harris, *English Aristocratic Women 1450–1550* (Oxford, 2002), 46–47.

[146] He was the surviving son of the duke of Northumberland who had been executed in the wake of the Jane Grey debacle.

[147] Mi, LM 26, fos 55v, 59–60: see pp. 87–88, 91–92 below. John, Lord Grey of Pirgo, died 19 Nov. 1564, one day prior to the date of the marriage settlement.

[148] George was the illegitimate half-brother of the father of Margaret and Francis and, apparently, a recusant at the end of his life. See Mi, LM 26, fo. 43 and Text n. 27. In a letter dated, most probably, in the early 1540s, Henry Grey, 3rd marquis of Dorset writes to Sir John Willoughby, noting that Henry Willoughby was willing to send his illegitimate half-brother George to study abroad: 'I understand that my Brother Wyllughbye [Henry] is wyllyng to send George your kynsman, a yonge man in my opinion moche desyrous of learnyng, to some universytye beyonde the seas ther tarme [to arm] hym sylfe as well wyth good learnyng as the knoledge of foran cuntryes: yow wyll, and that the rather at my requeste, helpe the yonge man in thys hys honeste and godlye travayle wyth some monye yerlye towardes hys exhybytyon, for the tyme he shall ther tarrye, wherunto I truste, (my requeste sett aparte) verye naturall love and the vertuous desyre of the yonge man, wyth consideratyon had how the habylytye of my brother Wyllughbye wyll not stretche suffycyentlye wythout your helpe and others to fynd hym ther wull be a suffycyent spure to prycke yow, besides that ther can be no more godlye thynge done than to helpe forwarde those that be studyous'. Welch, 'Willoughby Letters', 66–67, no. 42; Mi, 7/180/1. In 1546/7 Sir John was giving George Willoughby an annuity of 20s. Welch, 'Willoughby Letters', 66 n. 3. The will of Henry Willoughby gave the Inne called the Castle in Holborne to George Willoughby alias Fox, his bastard brother, and to the heirs of his body. For the will, see Mi, 6/179/35/1–2. For George Willoughby, see Robert Thoroton, *The Antiquities of Nottinghamshire* (London, 1677), 223. For more on George Willoughby (Fox), see Mi, 6/171/28, a letter dated 1570 between Francis and John Lyttleton regarding land that George held. George Willoughby had two sons and a stepson named Richard Repington, a lawyer employed by Francis (Mi, LM 26, fo. 66 and see Text n. 125).

[149] It is notable that the negotiations conducted around the marriage of Francis and Elizabeth were done by men in the family. Erickson has noted that marriage negotiations

consultation with the Pagets, promoted the Lyttleton arrangement because of the shared Catholic leanings among them.[150] On the other hand, Dudley would not have shared these religious proclivities, and John Grey, at least in 1560, was denouncing the 'Pagetyan' faction at court.[151]

The marriage agreement was drawn up on 20 November 1564. Almost immediately, in 1564, Matthew Arundell made clear his opposition to the marriage, and Lady Arundell 'used her outmost' to break the match.[152] The promise that Sir John Lyttleton made, of a dowry or portion of £1,500,[153] was generous by the standards of the time,[154] and it was backed up by an agreement by Sir John and his son Gilbert to pay £2,000 if they did not perform the covenants agreed upon. Nonetheless, Margaret and Matthew Arundell were suspicious of Sir John's promises, as it turned out for good reason.[155] In 1566 and 1567 it appears that Francis and Elizabeth

in the upper classes in early modern England were largely carried out by women. Erickson, *Women and Property*, 93. Perhaps this was another reason for the negative views that Margaret Arundell held regarding the marriage.

[150] Forty years after Francis's marriage, by which time he was dead, his Lyttleton nephew, Humphrey, was arrested for protecting fugitives implicated in the Gunpowder Plot, while another Lyttleton, probably Humphrey's nephew, Stephen, was the tenant of the only place (Holbeche House in Staffordshire) where any gunpowder exploded. Both of these Lyttletons were executed as co-conspirators in the plot.

[151] Michael C. Questier, *Catholicism and Community in Early Modern England: Politics, Aristocratic Patronage and Religion, c.1550–1640* (Cambridge, 2006).

[152] Cassandra's assessment of this situation was that Lady Arundell was in the habit of governing her younger brother and was highly offended that he had taken the decision to marry Elizabeth Lyttleton without consulting her. 'She writes that she marvels much that his hast should be so great, and his estimation of her so little, as never to consult her in the matter'. Mi, LM 26, fo. 56: see p. 89 below. Margaret rebutted any accusation that she was against his marriage in the expectation that she might enjoy Francis's estate. Mi, LM 26, fos 58–59: see p. 91 below. The marriage was particularly troubled by the poor relationship between Elizabeth and Margaret Arundell, who, herself may have married when she was only 15 while her husband Matthew was perhaps 25–27 years of age.

[153] Mi, LM 26, fo. 60: see p. 92 below; Mi, 7/183/19.

[154] J.P. Cooper's study of knightly families in the 16th century finds an average portion of £286 in the first half of the century and £859 in the latter half. By the early 17th century, in upper gentry families, portions ranged from £1,000 to £5,000. J.P. Cooper, 'Patterns of inheritance and settlement by great landowners from the 15th to the 18th centuries', in J. Goody, J. Thirsk and E.P. Thompson (eds), *Family and Inheritance: Rural Society in Western Europe, 1200–1800* (Cambridge, 1976), 192–327.

[155] The Lyttleton family seems to have been contentious. See a letter from Hugh Willoughby, uncle to Francis Willoughby, regarding all his debts where he states that he owes Edward Lytleton £16 and has no 'grayte trust in hym but that he wyll sowe [sue] his oblygacion'. Mi, 6/135/32; Welch, 'Willoughby Letters', 79–82. There is a complicated marriage settlement in 1564 that appears to be in the Lyttleton favour made between John Lyttleton and Richard Smyth regarding the marriage of William, youngest son of John Lyttleton, with Margaret Smyth, sole heiress of Richard Smyth, in which John Lyttleton agrees to a payment of £1,300 and maintenance of the couple; the couple will receive

were living with her family, per the marriage settlement, since there are letters between Francis and Sir John Lyttleton that seem to have been written while Francis was away from Frankley, but from 1568 forward, when Francis was 21 and had come into control of his estates, they set up an independent household.[156] In 1569 Sir John Lyttleton sent Francis £110, apologizing for not paying the whole sum of money due.[157] By perhaps 1572–1574 Francis writes to his sister that the bargain between his father-in-law and himself is broken off, because he can have no good assurance for the money, and he fears he shall be compelled to sue him.[158]

Elizabeth Willoughby took it amiss from the very beginning that she did not have the favour (but rather the disfavour) of her sister-in-law; this rift was never healed. Indeed, relatively early in the marriage Elizabeth wrote to her brother-in-law Matthew Arundell making it clear that she did not desire her sister-in-law's presence in her home. The language is strong: 'she is resolved never to stay in the house where his Wife is'.[159] While in the beginning, Francis Willoughby defended his wife,[160] eventually he began to blame her.

Marriage, in Elizabethan England, was not normally only (and sometimes not ever) a matter of the heart; it was an economic decision with status implications and normally effected in the midst of consultations and, very commonly, with go-betweens.[161] This upset between brother and sister, which produced a good many letters between them, seems to have set the tone for a destructive and long-lasting antagonism between Margaret Willoughby Arundell and Elizabeth Lyttleton Willoughby. In the event, Francis Willoughby never did receive the full amount of the dowry promised him by Elizabeth's father.[162] This not only confirmed Margaret's suspicions

---

Richard Smyth's estate on the death of Richard and his wife Frances. In default of any issue from William and Margaret, the estate would devolve to William and any other heirs of his body. Mi, 6/176/156 and 6/176/158–159. The estate appears to have conveyed to the Lyttletons in 1575/76. Mi, 6/176/160. See below, pp. 90–91 and Text n. 97.

[156] In 1568, just after coming of age, a 'receipt was made out in the form of an indenture between Francis and Robert Penruddoke, the chief steward for the Dorset estates, detailing the court rolls, accounts and other evidences then being handed over by Penruddoke to Francis'. Welch, 'Willoughby Letters', 6; Mi, 5/167/154. Francis received licence to enter into his inheritance on 10 May 1568. *CPR 1566–1569* Elizabeth I, iv, 150.

[157] Mi, LM 26, fo. 63: see p. 95 below.
[158] Mi, LM 26, fo. 67: see p. 99 below.
[159] Mi, LM 26, fo. 68: see p. 99 below.
[160] Mi, LM 26, fo. 72: see p. 105 below.
[161] O'Hara, *Courtship and Constraint*, ch. 3.
[162] Mi, LM 26, fo. 67: see p. 99 below.

but may have led Francis to value his wife less, as appears to be the case already by c.1570.

The marriage between Francis Willoughby and Elizabeth Lyttleton was not a success, as the letters make clear.[163] The decision to marry seems to have been taken in some haste,[164] and the marriage suffered from the relatively young age at which they wed, a point that Elizabeth Willoughby makes clear later with regard to her own behaviour. A further exacerbation in the marriage was the number of children Elizabeth Willoughby bore, and the toll that it took on her health. While we know of six living children, all female, and one male child who perhaps lived to the age of two,[165] Elizabeth also had a number of miscarriages.[166] In a letter to her husband c.1579, she notes that she had borne him 12 children.[167] Whether it was on account of her constant pregnancies, on account of Francis's constant 'dealing' with her (as she put it),[168] or due to reasons that we cannot now access, Elizabeth seems to have become easily angered.

By c.1572 Lady Arundell was recommending that the next time Elizabeth Willoughby fell into one of her rages Francis and Elizabeth should repair to Elizabeth's father's house 'till such time as she should have lost her willfullness, and would apply herself to please him'. Another solution she suggested would be for Francis to leave his wife and spend time at her household.[169] By March 1573 the letters report that Elizabeth Willoughby was very ill and in London for help. Since Francis could not accompany her, he appealed to Thomas Willoughby (father of Sir Percival, their future son-in-law), living apparently in Kent, to help his wife in London.[170] At about the same time letters detail a plot on the part of at least six of Francis Willoughby's servants to defame Lady Willoughby.[171] Meanwhile Lady Arundell did her best to question the servants in

---

[163] A pamphlet written for Middleton Hall describes the marriage as 'one of the worst marriages ever recorded in any detail'.

[164] Mi, LM 26, fo. 59: see p. 91 below where Margaret writes that they were marrying 'more in hast then they needed'.

[165] Francis, d. Dec. 1580; in Feb. 1578 Elizabeth reported that she was pregnant. In Dec. 1579 she was in need of a nurse for her son. It is likely that Francis was born in the late summer or early fall of the year in 1578. He was therefore perhaps two years old when he died.

[166] Mi, LM 26, fo. 67: see p. 99 below.

[167] Mi, LM 26, fo. 98: see p. 130 below.

[168] Mi, LM 26, fo. 67: see p. 99 below.

[169] Mi, LM 26, fo. 68: see p. 100 below.

[170] Mi, LM 26, fos 72–73: see pp. 105–106 below.

[171] Mi, LM 26, fo. 69: see pp. 101–102 below. These 'servants' were often younger, unlanded sons of gentry families who served in the household.

order to pick up information she could use against Lady Willoughby. One particular defamatory piece of information that Cassandra records is Elizabeth's friendship with a Mistress Haddam [Juliana Stanhope, wife of John Hotham].[172] She is represented by Margaret together with the 'cabal' of servants as 'a vile woman' and, a little later on, as a dishonest person.[173]

During the 1570s Francis and Elizabeth lived handsomely, with their wealth coming from rents and fines,[174] coal receipts,[175] wood sales, and interest on loans to others including a loan of £1,900 to the earl of Huntingdon. They were also buying land, making charitable gifts (e.g. to the poor, to prisoners and to widows) and maintaining a lavish style of living and hospitality.[176] They most likely hosted Queen Elizabeth at Middleton in 1575, and they regularly dined with thirty to forty friends and neighbours, including the earls of Rutland and Huntingdon. Cassandra lists forty-eight servants at this time; she also records one account of household expenditures of approximately £1,400 over fourteen months, costs that were recorded by only one of their household accountants. One such account book provides extremely detailed expenses paid by Thomas Shawe between November 1572 and February 1575. Included, for example, are necessities for the children, payments to Elizabeth Willoughby (for example, £40 in November 1572), payments for doctors' visits and various medical and herbal concoctions, alms to the poor, payments for everyday things like reeds, horsemeat and the shoeing of horses, for musicians, supplies for the dogs, books and paper, wages for the servants, etc.[177] The totals for the month of November 1572 were £111 3s 2d, while the weekly sums for November 1574 were between £30–£40.[178] Francis lived the life of a country aristocrat, despite belonging to the upper gentry, spending

somewhere in the region of £1,200 per annum on household expenses [...] In November 1572 a bill paid to a London grocer amounted to £22 8s 10d, with

---

[172] Mi, LM 26, fos 70–72: see pp. 103–105 below and Text n. 141.

[173] Mi, LM 26, fos 71–72: p. 105 below.

[174] In a 'Liber Concessionum', dated 1573/4 there is a list of leases up for renewal; the fines listed as paid were £2,600. Smith, *Sir Francis Willoughby*, 17. Smith notes that the rents were unrealistically low. Therefore any profits derived from the lands came from fines which, if land was lent out for three lives, would have been levied after decades rather than years.

[175] *Ibid.* 15, where he mentions the rise in coal revenues in the 1560s and 1570s, 'though the need to install horse-driven pumps in the Wollaton coalfield for the first time in 1573 foreshadowed the difficulties to come'. See also Richard S. Smith, *Early Coal-Mining around Nottingham 1500–1650* (Nottingham, 1989).

[176] *Ibid.* 12; Smith, 'The Willoughbys of Wollaton', 36–37.

[177] Mi, A 57, fos 8–93; excerpts in *HMC Middleton*, 421–451

[178] No monthly tallies were given in 1574.

an extra 6d paid out in tolls for the three horses which carried the goods to Nottingham. The order contained luxury spices including pepper, nutmegs, ginger, cinnamon, mace, cloves, dates, prunes, raisins, currants, liquorice, aniseed, almonds, and rice as well as 190 pounds of sugar of varying quality [...] Fish and wine were brought in from Hull, but much of the produce which ended up on Sir Francis's table would have come from his own lands [...] Sir Francis spent at least £20 a year on musicians' wages and occasionally had companies of visiting players under noble patronage perform at Wollaton Old Hall.[179]

Letters between Francis and Elizabeth do not appear in this collection until 1574, at which time Elizabeth was in London in poor health and Francis had remained behind to attend to 'earnest business'. The very first letter we have from Elizabeth is a dramatic notice of her health, where she states that she would prefer death to living continually sick. Shortly thereafter, Cassandra notes that these and many more letters in the library show that Sir Francis and his Lady lived very unhappily together, a conclusion she repeats concerning their correspondence in the summer of 1575.[180]

By 1575 Elizabeth Willoughby was increasingly not at home, neither at Wollaton, at their property in Middleton, nor wherever else they owned houses. Francis, while concerned for her health, was also concerned with his expenses maintaining her journeys and separate stays 'in other mens houses'.[181] He was also considering an alteration in their marriage settlement.[182] By now George Willoughby, who had helped arrange the marriage, was recommending that Francis banish Elizabeth.[183] In very many letters at this time, Francis writes of his wife's wilfulness.[184] In a letter to John Lyttleton, Francis says that he expects to meet his wife at Middleton, 'where, (if she would goe thither) she should be used as became Sir John Lyttletons Daughter and his Wife, but if she refused, she should have but small maintenance or comfort from him'.[185] The father, intervening, assures Francis that he 'hoped [she] would suffer reason to take place, for she had now faithfully promised that she would be directed by her Husband as duty required, and that she would refer her self and cause to him, to order as he should think well off [of], and that at

---

[179] Marshall, *Wollaton Hall and the Willoughby Family*, 22; see also Mi, A 57; *HMC Middleton*, 421–451.
[180] Mi LM 26, fos 72–72v, 74, 85: see pp. 105–108, 117 below.
[181] Mi, LM 26, fo. 74: see p. 108 below.
[182] Mi, LM 26, fo. 85: see p. 118 below.
[183] Mi, LM 26, fo. 85: see p. 118 below.
[184] See, for example, Mi, LM 26, fos 74, 75: see pp. 108–109 below.
[185] Mi, LM 26, fos 74–75: see p. 108 below.

her return from Buxton[186] she would come to Middleton to him, and remain there, or at any other place, where he should think good, not weighing her health, or life, so much as contenting him'.[187]

In the summer of 1575 Francis Willoughby was knighted. On 20 July 1575 Lord Burghley wrote that the Queen, after her progress to Kenilworth, planned to visit Wollaton; at the same time Sir Francis Knollys wrote to Francis to give him notice of the Queen's coming to Wollaton: 'Her Majesty is determined to tary two days at your house that is to say tomorrow night and Thursday all day, whereof I thought good to advertise you betimes'. Instead she seems to have visited Middleton Hall rather than Wollaton. John Nichols, in his standard work on Queen Elizabeth's progresses, notes that 'whilst the Queen was at Kenilworth, we are told [...] that she had invitations to visit Lichfield, Worcester and Middleton. There are accounts of her being at the two first of these places, but I cannot find that she was at Middleton'.[188] Mary Hill Cole, in a recent study of Elizabeth's progresses, concludes that from 28 to 29 July 1575 Elizabeth did visit Francis at Middleton, where he was knighted.[189] Although Cassandra thinks that, during this interlude in 1575, the marriage returned to relative calm, it did not remain so.

By late 1575 Francis had become extremely disenchanted with his marriage. In a letter to his father-in-law he charges Elizabeth with 'froward humour' and particularly with preventing Lady Arundell from visiting over the past eight years and when she did visit, Elizabeth had called her names and refused to eat, drink or sleep until she was revenged of her.[190] Cassandra writes that, 'There are many letters which shew that towards the end of the summer An.D. 1575 Sir Francis Willughby and his Lady lived very unhappily together.'[191] One letter, in particular, written by Sir Francis to Sir John Lyttleton in 1575 is full of complaints:

> amongst other things he writes that one day at Wollaton, as he was talking with Mary his fool of going to Kinsbury, his Wife answer'd she would not goe thither, upon which he asked her if she would stay at Wollaton, or goe

---

[186] Buxton was a fashionable spa and resort in Derbyshire frequented by Burghley, Leicester, and Mary, Queen of Scots, among others. See fo.74 and Text n. 148.
[187] Mi, LM 26, fo. 75: see pp. 108–109 below.
[188] Mi, LM 26, fo. 76: see p. 110 below. John Nichols, *The Progresses and Public Processions of Queen Elizabeth* (London, 1823), xviii.
[189] Mary Hill Cole, *The Portable Queen: Elizabeth I and the Politics of Ceremony* (Amherst, 1999), 188; see also Text n. 106.
[190] Mi, LM 26, fos 86–87: see p. 119 below.
[191] Mi, LM 26, fo. 85: see p. 117 below.

to Middleton. She answer'd that she would not stay there, and that if she had not been lately very sick; he would not have found her there, for she would have gone before he had returned. He asked her whither, to which she answer'd, her friends would not see her destitute, and she would not bear so much as she had done, and that she would not with her good will tarry any longer with him, who she said kept her but as a fool, to jest, and flout at.[192]

Between 1575 and 1578, it is not clear exactly where Elizabeth Willoughby was, but the letters suggest that she may have gone back to her parents' household part of this time, although her father was, at times, considering disowning her. In early 1578, at Kingsbury Hall, Warwickshire, Francis Willoughby confronted his wife in the Gallery in front of influential friends and servants after a dinner that was originally designed to reconcile them. A long written account of what happened, abbreviated by Cassandra, reported:

after they had supped at Kinsbury Sir Francis Willughby sent to his Lady (who had before refused to come to supper) to requir her to speak with him. She sent word she would speak with him in the Gallery, where they all went. What Sir Francis said at first going into the Gallery was not heard by the company, but his Lady answer'd in great coller, I will blaze your armes and make you better known. Sir Francis pressed her to be reconciled to his Sister, which she refused. He then asked her if in all other things she would be ruled by him, to which she answer'd she would not be ruled by him. Upon which Sir Fowlk Grevell [1st Baron Brooke] said why, Madam, will you refuse to be ruled by your husband. She answer'd she was the Queens sworn servant and knew not but Sir Francis might command her something against her Majesties proceedings, to which Sir Fowlk said that was an evil objection for a Wife to lay to her Husband.[193]

She answered that 'her heart was hardned against Sir Francis, and she could not love him as she had done'.[194]

Matters went from bad to worse as Elizabeth Willoughby became convinced that some of the servants were out to murder her; nor would she stay alone in the house with Joahn, one of the servants,

---

[192] Mi, LM 26, fo. 85: see p. 118 below.

[193] Mi, LM 26, fos 89–90: see pp. 122–123 below. Barbara J. Todd notes that there were two exceptions in the common law to a wife's subservience to her husband. One was with regard to her own soul and the second was 'the acknowledgement that all women, including wives, bore personal allegiance to their sovereign under common law'. Barbara J. Todd, 'Written in her heart: Married women's separate allegiance in English law', in Tim Stretton and Krista J. Kesselring (eds), *Married Women and the Law: Coverture in England and the Common Law World* (London, 2013), 163–191. Todd documents the challenge to this principle in the 17th century and later.

[194] Mi, LM 26, fo. 90: see p. 123 below.

whom she claimed was Francis's whore.[195] In February 1578 she was threatening suicide if she could not leave the house and go to an inn. Francis, as a result, placed her under close watch by the servants; she was not allowed to see her friends or to have anything to do with the children. She could not discharge or receive any servant or send any servant with a message to any place. She could not order any horse for her use or buy anything. Francis further ordered 'That she have no authority to command any thing in the house except necessary diet for herself'.[196] In response, she left the house to confer with her brother and other friends and relatives, was locked out by the servants and forced to move to a house provided for her by the Mayor and Aldermen of Coventry.[197] By her account, she was also pregnant at the time. From this point forward Elizabeth seems to have returned briefly to her father, then to have moved to Berkswell, Warwickshire, the home of Thomas Marrow, her brother-in-law, wandered 'from place to place' and finally settled in London, by which time she had given birth to their son.

Despite very many letters in which Elizabeth Willoughby alternately offers her submission, asks for an allowance and complains about her daughters being taken away from her, Sir Francis was unwilling to help or take her back. Subsequently her cause and a request for allowance from Francis was to be heard by the earl of Leicester and Sir Francis Walsingham and brought to the Queen.[198] Lady Arundell subsequently reported, in an undated letter, that Elizabeth brought witnesses up before the Secretary, Walsingham; she urges Francis to provide a catalogue of his wife's faults to send to Walsingham and Leicester to prevent them from interceding with the Queen on his wife's behalf.[199] In response to

---

[195] This claim was not included in Cassandra's final copy, but it is included in her draft copy. STB Box 2(1), book 1, fo. 22v. On Joahn, see Text n. 200.

[196] Mi, LM 26, fos 92–93, pp. 125–126 below.

[197] Coventry was perhaps 20 miles from Kingsbury, while Middleton was perhaps 4 miles from Kingsbury in the opposite direction.

[198] It is possible that this case came through the court of requests, which functioned as an equity court under the Privy Seal. This court, as did chancery, functioned alongside the common law courts. The power exercised in the court of requests was an extension of the monarch's prerogative right to hear and determine subjects' complaints. Tim Stretton (ed.), *Marital Litigation in the Court of Requests 1542–1642*, Camden 5th ser., 32 (Cambridge, 2008), 8. See also Stretton, *Women Waging Law in Elizabethan England*. A number of disputes between spouses came to this court, which was an important avenue for married women to receive more equitable treatment than they would have received at common law. The records, however, as reported by Tim Stretton in 2008, are in disrepair and difficult to use. The finding aids are also insufficient. The current handwritten catalogue in the National Archives does not list the over 300 bundles of cases chronologically or alphabetically.

[199] Mi, LM 26, fos 103–104: see p. 135 below.

Elizabeth's request for support, Lord Burghley's secretary, Sir Michael Hicks, wrote:

> according to ye ordinance of God and the covenants of your marriage, yow [must] endevor to subdue and submytt yor will to ye plesure of yor hedd, in all honest and lawfull things seking rathr to wynne his good will wth covering his faultes, and bearing with his infirmyties, then to wreste hym to your owne [...] the wch although it may seme hard to fleshe and bloude, yett is it warranted by ye woorde of God, wch byndes all women [...] to yelde due benevolence and obedyence to their husbands.[200]

By 1582, it appears that Queen Elizabeth had responded positively to Elizabeth Willoughby's request, for Francis was obliged to allow her £200 a year for separate maintenance.[201] But already, in December 1580, their young son had died and Lady Willoughby was requesting to return to Francis with the hope that, although approaching forty years of age, she might still bear him a son. It is very likely that by this time Francis was no longer faithful to the marriage. There is evidence for at least one illegitimate child by 1584/5 – a William Deverell alias Willoughby, son of Katharine Deverell.[202] Now that Francis had turned against his wife, she had very little male support during their separation, a serious concern in a patriarchal society. With no sons to buttress her position, a father who was maintaining his distance from her, and no male in-laws in evidence to help her, she was dependent on friends and possibly her brothers, none of whom was sufficient. Elizabeth badly needed to return to Wollaton.

In 1585 an exchange of letters took place between Elizabeth Willoughby and Francis, one of which is copied in its entirety in

---

[200] BL, Lansdowne MS 101/41, quoted in Friedman, *House and Household*, 64.

[201] Mi, LM 26, fo. 104: see p. 136 below. Elizabeth could, potentially, also have requested maintenance from the ecclesiastical courts. In 1610 members of Parliament complained about the Ecclesiastical Commission granting alimony to separated wives 'to the great encouragement of wives to be disobedient and contemptuous against their husbands', E.R. Foster (ed.), *Acts of Proceedings in Parliament 1610*, II (New Haven, CT, 1966), 265, cited in D.M. Palliser, *The Age of Elizabeth: England under the Later Tudors 1547–1603*, 2nd edn (New York, 1992), 74.

[202] STB Box 2(2), Uncatalogued half-sheet of paper signed 'Robt Barnard Vic{r}'. According to this paper, found in Cassandra's notes to her history in the Huntington Library, by 1584/5 Sir Francis had fathered an illegitimate son. The note reads: 'William Deverell alias Willoughby son of Katharine Deverell and as she has confess'd him, the son of Sir Francis Willoughby Knt of Nottinghamshire Baptized the 4th day of March 1584. This is a tru copy taken out of the Register of Laughton in the morthing [Laughton-en-le-Morthen] in the County of York, and attested by Robert Barnard Vicar.' For a William Willoughby recorded in Yorkshire early in the 17th century, see Text n. 281.

the appendix to this introduction. These letters were designed to produce amity between them; but it was not until early in 1588 that Elizabeth finally returned to Francis and to Wollaton Hall.[203] Subsequently, there are far fewer letters between them leading up to her death in 1595.[204]

The subservience Francis expected from a wife with a sharp tongue and strong sense of her own entitlement resulted in a thoroughly unhappy marriage; it was Elizabeth Willoughby, however, who suffered the most as a result. In addition to her twelve pregnancies and the deaths of six of her children, she had an unfaithful husband whose correspondence suggests a too ready willingness to believe the worst of people and a hardness of heart toward his dependents as well as his own children, a meddling and ill-disposed sister-in-law, threats and the actuality of imprisonment in her own home, ten years of banishment with, much of that time, an inadequate allowance, and many years of sickness and separation from her children. During all this time, Elizabeth Willoughby alternately refused obedience and promised submission to her husband.

Cassandra's Account, in addition to detailing the story of a dysfunctional marriage, tells us a great deal about the role that servants played in a large household (including copying down several sets of orders for the servants to follow), a bit about the cultural interests of Sir Francis, and about the relationship of the family to the court; it also provides information, unsystematically, on various detailed land transactions and marriage settlements. What her account does not tell us is about Sir Francis's entrepreneurial efforts,[205] his building of Wollaton Hall or the various local and provincial offices and responsibilities that Francis held.[206]

---

[203] Mi, LM 26, fos 134, 136: see pp. 173–174, 176 of the edited text.

[204] On the date of Elizabeth Willoughby's death, see fo. 141: see Text n. 353.

[205] For this, see Hayden, 'Sir Francis Willoughby of Wollaton', esp. ch. 4; Smith, 'The Willoughbys of Wollaton'; Smith, 'A woad growing project', 27–46.

[206] Sir Francis received commissions relating to musters in the counties of Kent, Warwick and Nottingham, in 1577, 1580, 1589, 1591, and 1594. He was made high sheriff of Nottinghamshire in 1579 and in 1588–1589: see a 1588 letter of John Adams to Percival Willoughby: 'I am sory Sir Frauncis is made shiryf this yeare. Let his under-shiryfe take heed for his yeare to come. All the judges of the Comon Plees have taken order to oversee all the offences of undershirifes to be duely and severely punished and also hathe appointed on to followe the informations against them. Lett him therefore beware.' Mi, C 18/1; *HMC Middleton*, 158. He must have been made sheriff again in 1593/4 as there is an acquittance of the Pipe for him as sheriff of Nottingham. He was also justice of the peace at the Quarter Session in 1580, as his rulings for that year have survived in the Willoughby MS collection. See the range of materials in Mi, O. In 1592 Francis received a commission to administer the oath of supremacy within the county of Nottingham.

Although Francis, in 1575, understood that 'his estate was very well know[n] both to Her Majesty and the whol Cownsel to be nothing inferiour to the best'[207] – to the point that Lord Burghley thought to include him as a possible peer[208] – , he ended his life in serious debt. He ran into financial difficulties in the 1580s in the building of Wollaton Hall, in the costs of some of his entrepreneurial enterprises that failed and generated legal costs, and in paying dowries for three of his daughters in the 1580s.[209] By 1581 he was already beginning to borrow rather than lend money, first £300, then £500, then £2,181, £1,468, and then £2,007 between 1581 and 1585.[210] By 1587–1588 a list of debts to be paid off that year amounted to £11, 956.[211]

Cassandra estimated the cost of building Wollaton Hall (Figure 1) to have been £80,000 – a stupendous figure if anywhere close to accurate.[212] P.E. Rossell, who has studied the annual building expenses from 1581–1588, has figures that add up to £5,763 and estimates that the total may have been as high as £8,000,[213] a far more reasonable estimate although probably too low.[214] Francis also had to consider the cost of having six daughters at a time when there was considerable inflation in the cash dowries required for marriage.[215]

---

[207] *HMC Middleton*, 538; Mi, LM 26, fo. 76: see p. 109 below.

[208] Smith, *Sir Francis Willoughby*, 19.

[209] The best description of the financial difficulties Francis (and subsequently his son-in-law Percival Willoughby) endured is in Smith, 'The Willoughbys of Wollaton', 46–70.

[210] Smith, *Sir Francis Willoughby*, 22 notes that 'One of the mysteries of Sir Francis's ever deeper involvement in debt is that he could not bring himself to sell land on a sufficient scale to clear himself from debt'. See also Smith, 'The Willoughbys of Wollaton', 48.

[211] *Ibid*. 51, citing Mi, 6/170/132.

[212] *HMC Middleton*, 566 and n. 1; Mi, LM 26, fo. 129.

[213] P.E. Rossell, 'The Building of Wollaton Hall, 1580–1588', 2 vols, MA thesis, University of Sheffield, 1957, cited in Hayden, 'Sir Francis Willoughby of Wollaton', 192.

[214] Mi, LM 26, fo. 129: see Text n. 295.

[215] O'Hara, *Courtship and Constraint*, 211. Three of his daughters married in the 1580s. Bridget received a dowry of only 2,000 marks, perhaps because of expectations that the bulk of the estates would be settled on her and Percival. Mi, 5/168/74–76; Mi, 1/7/3, dating between 1581 and Nov. 1584. The wedding expenses in 1580 amounted to £1,213 2s 4d: Mi, A 60/2, fo. 1; see also *HMC Middleton*, 555. Total expenses for 1580–1585 were over £13,400, including £4,737 3s 5d in lands purchased. Mi, A 60/2, fos 2–2v. See a letter written by Francis to Thomas Willoughby (Mi, 2/76/3/4) relating to debts. Francis continued to buy, not selling sufficient lands to pay his debts. Smith, *Sir Francis Willoughby*, 22–26. For the marriage of Dorothy Willoughby with Henry Hastings, Francis agreed to settle land worth £200 per annum on the couple and to give £2,000 with his daughter in 1585. Mi, 6/170/127. Cf. also Mi, 6/170/131.2 and Mi, 2/76/3/7. For Margaret Willoughby's marriage to Robert Spencer in 1587, see M.E. Finch, *The Wealth of Five Northamptonshire Families, 1540–1640*, Northamptonshire Record Society, XIX (1956), 54. For the marriage settlement document, see Mi, 6/178/86. See also Mi, 6/178/88–94. Margaret's dowry was £4,000, and Robert had hopes that Francis would settle part of his estate on them in the future.

Francis compromised his estates even further after Elizabeth's death in June, 1595 when he precipitously married a recent widow, Dorothy Tamworth,[216] by August 1595. In this hasty marriage, performed before any settlement could be drawn up,[217] Francis planned to provide her a jointure of several lordships worth approximately 2,000 marks a year. She, however, 'liking the land tyed for her security better than the joynture which was to have been settled upon her, took care to prevent that settlement from being made'.[218] Sir Francis seems to have leased out (for up to three lives) the greatest part of his estate, the properties at Wollaton, Cossall, Trowell, Middleton and Kingsbury that were to be settled on Sir Percival Willoughby as his heir. The money from these leases, as well as from the sale of other lands and woods, Francis secured for his new wife. The result was a series of bills in chancery between Sir Francis and Sir Percival. In 1595 John Spencer wrote to Sir Francis to remind him that interest was due on £22,000 by All Saints Day.[219] For the year 1596, Cassandra writes, 'thus having charged his estate with as much money as it could bear [...] to raise a great sum of money for his Lady, he fell very sick. There is a tradition in the family that his friends suspected his Lady had given him poyson, but whither that was so, or not, is uncertain'.[220] Francis Willoughby died in November 1596 and was buried quickly and unceremoniously at St Giles Cripplegate, London, on 16 November 1596.[221] Percival and Bridget Willoughby greatly feared that Dorothy Tamworth Willoughby, now widowed but pregnant, would give birth to a male heir. In the end she gave birth to a daughter, Frances, but she nonetheless kept possession of all the revenues from the estates that Sir Francis Willoughby left. Percival and Bridget, thenceforth, were involved in many costly law suits against Dorothy

---

[216] Dorothy Colby Tamworth (1565–5 Apr. 1621) was the daughter of Thomas Colby (c.1530–5 Mar. 1588), of Sherfield-upon-Ludden, Hampshire (Hants), a 'puritan west country lawyer' (http://www.historyofparliamentonline.org/volume/1558-1603/member/colby-thomas-i-1530-88) of Grey's Inn and Elizabeth Gilbert, daughter of Edward Gilbert, alderman of London. She was named her father's heir at an Inquisition *post mortem* held on 11 Dec. 1588. She married her first husband, John Tamworth of Leake, Lancs (1562–18 Feb. 1594), in 1583. He was a squire of the body to Queen Elizabeth. Less than two years after Dorothy was widowed, she received a visit from William Russell, steward in the employ of Sir Francis who was under orders to find Francis Willoughby a new wife.
[217] Mi, LM 26, fo. 145: see pp. 185–186 below.
[218] Mi, LM 26, fos 145–46: see p. 186 below.
[219] Mi, LM 26, fo. 184: see p. 236 below.
[220] Mi, LM 26, fo. 156: see p. 197 below.
[221] See the parish register for St Giles Cripplegate, London Metropolitan Archives A/002/MSO6419/001, under 16 Nov. 1596.

Willoughby, one consequence of which was that Lady Willoughby (very shortly thereafter Lady Wharton because of a third marriage) bribed the Lord Chancellor Francis Bacon to the amount of £310, and this became one of the charges against Lord Bacon that brought him down.[222] Percival was left with debts of £4,000 for the portions of three of Francis's daughters, £1,786 in debts that Sir Francis owed, £3,050 for iron works that Percival was bound to pay, £1,370 of interest due on loans that Sir Francis left, and a debt of £21,000 that Percival was bound for based on Francis's promise to leave to him and his wife the whole remainder of his estate. The cost to Sir Percival to regain his inheritance at court was £3,000. As Cassandra sums it up, 'Thus when Sir Percivall first enjoy'd Sir Francis Willughbys estate he found himself engaged in excessive troubles, for from those 5 Lordships which were settled upon him he could receive but 550li—16sh—0d per annum, and those Lordships were charged with the debt of 35156li'.[223] She aptly describes the estate that Sir Percival received as 'shattered'.

Cassandra's assessment of Francis was that he was a man of great piety and learning. He had a substantial library of the most valuable books of his time, of which only a handful remain, including, among the medieval manuscripts, an Anglo-Norman penitentiary and a book of sermons, several French romances, fragments from the *South English Legendary*, the *Confessio Amantis* of John Gower, and a Middle English *Speculum Vitae* and *The Lay Folks' Catechism*.[224] Cassandra saw many notes and remarks in Francis's books as well as several other small manuscripts and 'pious discourses' written by Francis on theological subjects, some of which 'seem to have been heads of sermons for his chaplains to preach upon'.[225] Francis's surviving lute book includes forty-seven pieces of music, three of them written by Francis;[226] he also translated at least a portion of *De Re Metallica* by Agricola from the Latin into English.[227] The surviving

---

[222] Mi, LM 26, fo. 157v: see p. 199 below.

[223] Mi, LM 26, fos 159–160: see pp. 201–202 below.

[224] Mi LM 4, 6, 7, 8 and 9. Ralph Hanna and Thorlac Turville-Petre (eds), *The Wollaton Medieval Manuscripts: Texts, Owners and Readers* (York, 2010) describe various medieval MSS in the Willoughby archives, a number of which are legal, devotional or liturgical in character.

[225] Mi, LM 26, fo. 160: see p. 202 below. 'This Sir Francis was a man of great piety and learning. There is still remaining a collection which he made of the most valuable books of his time, and many notes and remarks upon them writ with his own hand. There is also in the Library severall other little manuscripts writ by himself upon divine subjects some of which seem to have been heads of sermons for his chaplains to preach upon.'

[226] *The Lute Book of Francis Willoughby, c.1575*, facs. edn, with introduction by Jeffrey Alexander and Robert Spencer (Kilkenny, Ireland, 1978); Mi, LM 16.

[227] Mi, X 2/5. The surviving portion deals with the problem of flooding in the mines and of pumping, an issue for the Wolloughby mines as they dug deeper for coal.

sixteenth-century printed books that Francis owned, and in which he wrote marginal notes are: Elyot's *The boke named the Gouvernour* (1531); John Brentius, *In evangelii quod inscribitur, secundum Lucam, duodecim priora capita Homiliae centum et decem* (1537); *Breviarium seu Portiforium ad usum ecclesie Sarisburiensis* (1561); *Les oeuvres de Clement Marot* (1564); *The works of Thomas Becon* (1564); Raphael Holinshed, *The first volume of the chronicles of England* (1577); Wolfgang Musculus, *Common places of Christian religion* (1578), and three volumes of Richard Hakluyt, *The principall navigations, voiages and discoveries of the England nation* (1589).[228] There may have been a *Romance of Godfrey of Bologne*, printed by Caxton in 1481, also in the library.[229] There are extant notes in Francis Willoughby's hand from John Foxe's *Book of Martyrs*, a copy of which may also have been in the library.[230] Alice Friedman has estimated, based on a c.1690 shelf list and a much later sale catalogue, that Francis had a library of roughly two hundred fifty volumes.[231] The Christie's sale catalogue, from 1925, included a copy of Erasmus's *Apophthegms* (1542) with the signatures of both Francis and Elizabeth,[232] as well as a copy of Foxe's *Ecclesiasticall History* (1570 edition) with the initials FW in it. Friedman remarks 'that a number of Willoughby's speeches before the Quarter Sessions included quotes from this volume'.[233] W.H. Stevenson describes a few additional books that are now not in the Middleton archives, viz. a c.1400 manuscript of John of Trevisa's *Polychronicon* with the signatures of Master Gabryell Barwyke and Alys Jeaycoote, a fifteenth-century manuscript of Lydgate's translation of John Bochas's *Book of Princes*, and a 1520 copy of the *Sarum Antiphonale*, printed in Cologne and given by Henry Willoughby to his chapel of St Thomas.[234]

Drawing upon the late seventeenth-century catalogue from Wollaton Hall and looking for those books with sixteenth-century imprints, Friedman notes the marked emphasis on English language books and a focus on mathematics, geography, natural science, and law, including books on mechanics and experimental science. Among the sixteenth-century imprints were a collection of books on medicine, popular

---

[228] Mi, LP 1–10.
[229] Mi, F 15/1–15. It was sold from the Willoughby collection in 1883.
[230] Mi, O 16/1.
[231] Friedman, *House and Household*, 30; for a description of the late 17th-century shelf list, see William Poole, 'The Willughby Library at the Time of Francis the Naturalist', in Tim Birkhead (ed.), *Virtuoso by Nature: The Scientific Worlds of Francis Willughby FRS (1635–1672)* (Leiden, 2016), 227–243.
[232] STC 10443; printed by Richard Grafton with a preface by William Tyndal, in English; currently at the Folger Library.
[233] Friedman, *House and Household*, 30. See Mi, O 16/7/1, which is a copy, in Francis Willoughby's hand, of excerpts from Foxe.
[234] *HMC Middleton*, 621–622.

works, some twenty or thirty books on religious themes, some Latin works of philosophy and literature, a few advice handbooks, four primers or dictionaries, and, as might be expected from someone who invested in the significant and advanced architectural programme of Wollaton Hall, a number of books on art and architecture.[235] One cannot assume, however, that the sixteenth-century imprints were all collected in the sixteenth century, although one book listed, the *Historie of Man, Sucked from the Sappe of the Most Approved Anathomistes*, written by John Banister, surgeon and physician to the Willoughby household in the 1570s, includes a dedication to Sir Francis in which he praises Sir Francis for his scholarly seclusion 'in Ciceros ocium'.[236]

Sir Francis's papers feature charges by him as justice at the Quarter Sessions, examinations of witnesses and notes on his reading.[237] In one of these papers, Francis addresses Justice: 'Justice is as a magistrate whose office is to give to everye man his owne, to defend the godlye, and to punishe the wicked. The mouth of justice is the true witnes giver, who speaketh nothing but truth itselfe'. Witnesses, according to Francis, sometimes speak too much while others speak too little, '[they] halte betwixt trueth and lyinge: [they] denye God, dissemble with the truth, & deceave men'. Francis goes on to discuss the role of the jury and the magistrate, impediments to the truth, causes for assembly of the Quarter Session, referencing at points Alexander the Great, Solomon and Moses 'the magistrate'.[238] In other notes of charges, Francis cites the example of Numa Pompilius, presumably invoking Livy's *History of Rome*, citing a king who was skilled in both human and divine laws, perhaps, as John Hayden suggests, championing the Elizabethan Settlement with this parallel.[239] In a third document Francis brings in 'good king' John to support the need for law and order.[240]

---

[235] Friedman, *House and Household*, 30–33 provides a much more detailed description of some of these books. She assumes, however, that the 16th-century imprints in the surviving library catalogue of *c.*1690 were included in the 16th-century library. The catalogue is Mi, I 17/1/1. In addition, there is a surviving Forest Book, relating to Sherwood Forest, in the Middleton MSS Collection. Mi, L 3/ 1 & 2. It is the earliest extant version in English of a forest book for Sherwood Forest, written in a late 15th-century hand and, in the latter part, in a late 16th-century hand. See Helen E. Boulton (ed.), *The Sherwood Forest Book*, TSRS, XXIII (Nottingham, 1965), 12–17.

[236] Poole, 'The Willoughby Library', 228.

[237] *HMC Middleton*, 284; Mi, O 16/6, 16/9, 16/14, 2/2/5, all dated *c.*1580; Hayden, 'Sir Francis Willoughby of Wollaton', ch. 5.

[238] Mi, O 16/6; Hayden, 'Sir Francis Willoughby of Wollaton', 160–165.

[239] Mi, O 16/14; Hayden, 'Sir Francis Willoughby of Wollaton', 166.

[240] Mi, O 16/9; Carole Levin, *Propaganda in the English Reformation: Heroic and Villainous Images of King John* (Lewiston, NY, 1988), 107. She describes the 16th-century heroic image of King John used to de-legitimize any idea of rebellion.

One of the tasks of the justices of the peace was to remove recusants from office. On 22 October 1592 the Privy Council wrote to Sir Francis, Thomas Markham,[241] Sir Thomas Stanhope and others to remove, as justices of the peace, anyone refusing an oath to her Majesty's supremacy, not participating in common prayer at divine service and not attending church. The names of those who refused were to be furnished to the Lord Keeper.[242]

Surprisingly, the letters offer very little insight into the religious sensibilities of Francis, his wife or their children.[243] This correspondence suggests that religious differences, for the most part, were of less importance than local and kinship connections.[244] Although religion may have been a positive consideration in the marriage of Margaret Willoughby to Matthew Arundell, a family with strong Catholic connections at the English court,[245] Catholicism would appear to have been a negative consideration a few decades later in the marriage of one of the Willoughby daughters, Margaret, described below.[246]

Elizabeth Lyttleton Willoughby came from a family with Catholic leanings. Her father, John Lyttleton, had enjoyed influence at the court of Mary Tudor, and Gilbert, his heir and her brother, had married into an influential Catholic family (Coningsby of Hampton Court, Hereford).[247] According to one study, John Lyttleton remained a Catholic sympathiser to the end, and seems to have used his position in the county 'to soften the impact of anti-Catholic legislation on his neighbours'.[248] At the same time, in his position as custos rotulorum in 1581, he was involved in

---

[241] On the Catholic sympathies of Thomas Markham's family, particularly his wife and three of his sons, see below, pp. 55–56 and n. 259.

[242] Mi, O 2/2/6; *Acts of the Privy Council*, XXIII (1592), pp. 253–261; Hayden, 'Sir Francis Willoughby of Wollaton', 168–169.

[243] Similarly the Wollaton library catalogue from 1690 is 'almost barren of patristic authors or of any scholarly contributions to the endless confessional polemics of the day', although it did include devotional literature and sermons. Poole, 'The Willoughby Library', 240.

[244] On this issue in Elizabethan England, see Richard Greaves, *Society and Religion in Elizabethan England* (Minneapolis, MN, 1981); Peter S. Bearman, *Relations into Rhetoric: Local Elite Social Structure in Norfolk, 1540–1640* (Rutgers, NJ, 1993); Norman Jones, *Governing by Virtue: Lord Burghley and the Management of Elizabethan England* (Oxford, 2015), 6–7. In Nottinghamshire, as opposed to Monmouthshire, Lancashire, Durham and Warwickshire, there appear to have been few Catholics. And this may help explain the absence of religious concerns.

[245] On the Arundells and their Catholic network, see Questier, *Catholicism and Community in Early Modern England*.

[246] See p. 55 below.

[247] Tonks, 'The Lyttletons of Frankley', 17.

[248] *Ibid.* 41.

proceedings against recusants,[249] and he was on good terms with Bishop Babington of Worcester, including inviting him to hunt.[250] His youngest son George was a Catholic recusant, and his grandson, Humphrey, was executed in 1606 for his participation in the Gunpowder Plot.[251] Francis Willoughby, on the other hand, seems to have been resolutely Protestant, quite likely influenced in this direction by the Grey family and perhaps also during the four years (1560–1564) he spent as a ward of Francis Knollys, whose fervent evangelical Protestantism entailed spending much of the reign of Queen Mary in exile.

While, as noted above, Francis wrote sermons or sermon headings for his chaplains to preach, none of these survive. The best testimony of Francis Willoughby's commitment to Protestantism is the marginalia in his copy of Musculus's *Commonplaces of Christian Religion*, where he shows particular interest in the sections relating to free will, election, and the sacraments (particularly the eucharist or lord's supper). Also, in a separate page glued onto the back cover of a 1542 copy of Erasmus' *Apophthegms*, along with the names of Francis and Elizabeth Willoughby is a fragment 'regarding wealth' with Calvinist language.[252] The preamble of his 1572 will is further suggestive of strong Protestant sensibilities: 'first I bequeath & commend my soule & all that I am & shallbe unto the great mercye of my savior & redeemer Jesus Cryst by whose death & passion I trust to be part taker of the kingdume prepared for god hys elected'.[253] His 1578 draft will has an even more lengthy Protestant preamble, but this seems to have been copied from the will of the earl of Essex.[254] In 1583, and again in 1592, Sir Francis was among the JPs and 'persons of great calling', passing guilty judgments and committed to safekeeping recusants in the shire.[255] And yet, the family had long-lasting ties with Catholic families – the Pagets, Catesbys, Lyttletons, Markhams, Arundells, and also George Willoughby, who is listed from 1593–1595 in the Recusant Rolls.

---

[249] J.W. Willis-Bund and William Page (eds), *A History of the County of Worcester: II*, VCH (London, 1971), 214.

[250] Adrian Morey, *The Catholic Subjects of Elizabeth I* (London and Boston, and Totowa, NJ, 1978), 136.

[251] Tonks, 'The Lytteltons of Frankley', 40, 48; see also H. Bowler (ed.), *Recusant Roll No. 2 (1593–1594)*, Catholic Record Society, 57 (1965), 149–150.

[252] 'that by pryde ye do atribute nothing unto your selves, but do discretely consyder, that the thynge whiche ye have, ye have it by the fre goodnes of God in Jesu Christ, & not by your owne merites & deseruynes, but by fayth whiche ye have for to helpe them which have nede of it'. Folger Library, STC 10443

[253] Mi, 1/13/4–4a.

[254] Mi, 1/13/10–11.

[255] Hayden, 'Sir Francis Willoughby of Wollaton', 168.

There are suggestions of anti-Catholicism in a series of exchanges between the Willoughby and Markham families, when Margaret Willoughby, the third daughter of Francis and Elizabeth, and Griffin Markham, a cousin and suitor to Margaret, were engaged in marriage negotiations. They were kinsfolk as Margaret Markham was the first wife of Henry Willoughby (d.1528) and the great-grandmother of Francis Willoughby. The families had spent time together when the children were young, and Griffin, writing from Gonville & Caius College, Cambridge c.1585/6 had high hopes for and expectations of a marriage with Margaret.[256] His many love letters to her, signed 'Yours to command while life doth last' or 'yours to trust until he be dust', detail his infatuation with and commitment to her. Although there is some suggestion, by Cassandra, that Francis Willoughby did not like the terms of the marriage, a letter from Elizabeth Willoughby to her daughter makes clear that religion was at the bottom of it, and that the Markhams were suspected of popery.[257] From the extended exchange of letters regarding the possible match, it appears that Margaret, while protesting her constant obedience to her father and her commitment not to proceed without his consent, may have given Griffin hope. Elizabeth Willoughby was, however, completely opposed to the marriage, writing,

> I desire the Almighty to bless you, and continue you in that faith which your Father and I carefully desired you should learn from your cradle, and as a Mother I charge and exhort you not to enter into any union which may draw you from the same. Marriage is honourable, but if religion fail on the one party, it is in my opinion a wicked joyning of the faithfull with the ungodly. I write this because I hear of a marriage motion'd to you, which for the religion suspected, or professed, is not to be received. I also hear that to procure your good will tokens have been given you which are markes and signs of popery, I mean crucifixes and such like. Either you must in time go back or God hath lost a servant, and my self a Daughter.[258]

---

[256] Mi, LM 26 fos 174–180: see pp. 220–230 below.

[257] Mi, LM 26, fo. 180: see pp. 229–230 below. Griffin Markham was exiled from England in 1605 for his recusancy and involvement in the Bye and Main Plots against James I. While in the Low Countries he was appointed lieutenant of the English army by Thomas Arundell, the son of Margaret Willoughby and Matthew Arundell. Questier, *Catholicism and Community*, 89. Griffin Markham married Anne Roos, the daughter of Peter Roos, Esq., of Laxton, in 1592. Bridenbaugh notes that 'Lady Markham, wife of Sir Griffin, appeared at [Paul's Cross] in 1618 to do penance for marrying one of her servants while her husband was still alive. She had to stand again at other places and pay a fine of £1000'. Carl Bridenbaugh, *Vexed and Troubled Englishmen, 1580–1642* (Oxford, 1968), 372.

[258] Mi, LM 26, fo. 180v: see p. 230 below.

In the end Griffin's mother Mary, heiress of Rice Griffin of Braybrooke and Dingley, Northamptonshire, also ruled against the match, noting that having Margaret Willoughby in her home would disturb her devotions.[259] Whatever Margaret's feelings, she was constrained by having to show her father any letters between herself and Markham and to divulge any conversation they may have had.[260]

The subsequent marriage of Margaret with Robert Spencer in 1587 seems to have been, as far as Cassandra can judge (and as far as we can see) a happy marriage.[261] The same cannot be said for Dorothy Willoughby, Francis and Elizabeth's second daughter who married Henry Hastings, nephew of his namesake, the third earl of Huntingdon, after negotiations that lasted from 1584 to 1587.[262] Cassandra copies part of a communication from one of Francis Willoughby's friends listing ten considerations against the match.[263] Once they were married, however, Sir Francis was more than a little reluctant to provide a property to Dorothy and Henry, and Henry Hastings, perhaps due in part to their straightened circumstances and Francis's unwillingness, for years, to part with a property called the Woodland, 'used his Wife very ill'.[264] By the period 1615–1628, thirty to forty years into the marriage, Dorothy writes a great many letters to Bridget and Percival Willoughby[265] on business and family matters, but interspersed among these letters she writes at some length that her husband threatens to lock her up and use her like a dog; her children dissemble with her to their own advantage; the people around her, as well as her husband, will poison her before long; they write letters in her hand which she never saw; her husband

---

[259] Mary Markham came from a staunchly Catholic family, although her husband, Thomas Markham, seems to have conformed. Their sons, however, remained Catholic, with Robert fleeing to Rome, Griffin as noted above, and his two brothers, Charles and Thomas, involved in treasonous activities in the 1603 plots. Their daughter married Nicholas Longford, a Derbyshire recusant. 'Markhams' house at Ollerton became a centre for Catholicism for many years.' Cobbing and Priestland, *Sir Thomas Stanhope of Shelford*, 198. See also W.J. Tighe, 'A Nottinghamshire gentleman in court and country: The career of Thomas Markham of Ollerton (1530–1607)', *TTS*, 90 (1986), 30–45; D.F. Markham, *History of the Markham Family* (London, 1854); and Mark Nicholls, 'Treason's reward: The punishment of conspirators in the Bye Plot of 1603', *The Historical Journal*, 38 (1995), 821–842.

[260] See Mi, 5/168/80 – a copy of a draft and undated marriage settlement between Sir Francis Willoughby and Thomas Markham, Esq., 1585/6, 28 Elizabeth.

[261] See the Inquisition *post mortem* for Francis Willoughby, 4 September 1597, that says that Margaret Spencer died prior to the date of the Inquisition. Mi, 1/2/2/1.

[262] Mi, LM 26, fos 162–165, pp. 204–208 below. The marriage took place 9 July 1587.

[263] Mi, LM 26, fo. 164: see pp. 205–206 below.

[264] Mi, LM 26, fo. 168: see p. 211 below.

[265] Mi, LM 26, fos 170–173v: see pp. 214–220 below.

gives her nothing but meat and drink and neither cloths nor money, threatens to lock her up, and refuses to let her use the coach except to go to church on Sunday. Cassandra concludes that 'By some of the old letters one may believe that the first cause of the unhappyness of Mr. Hastings and his Lady might proceed from his desiring to have her estate in land sold, and her unwillingness to part with it.'[266]

Winifrid Willoughby, the fourth daughter, fared equally poorly. Cassandra did not choose to copy the 'many letters which shew that Lady Willughby used her Daughter Winifrid with very great severity'.[267] By 1589 Edward Willoughby, the brother of Percivall, was pursuing a marriage with Winifrid 'his beloved mistris' but could not gain Lady Willoughby's consent. 'And for fear least Winifrid should steal away and marry him privately, she [Lady Willoughby] kept her locked up, by such hands as he could not convey a letter to her, or get one from her.'[268] By 1590 Edward's concern for Winifrid reached such a pitch that he found a way of getting her away and marrying her privately without the consent of either Francis or Elizabeth; the result, however, was that even after Elizabeth Willoughby's death, Sir Francis refused to see his daughter or to admit her to his house, refusing also to provide the £40 yearly support that was due her. By 1600 Edward Willoughby was in debtor's prison.

The fifth daughter, Abigail, took care of her mother during her final illness and managed the household after her death. A few years after her father's death Abigail married William Pargiter, a Northamptonshire gentleman. About this marriage Cassandra seems to have little information. At the end of this volume, her attention turns to Frances, the youngest daughter, who fled Wollaton on the eve of her mother's death and whose marriage with Montague Wood, probably in 1597,[269] was preceded by the cruelty with which she was treated by her mother and an investigation in 1595 by the ecclesiastical High Commission into whether she had had an affair with John Drake,[270] as well as the loss of both parents soon after she left.

---

[266] Mi, LM 26, fo. 173v: see p. 220 below.
[267] Mi, LM 26, fo. 185: see p. 237 below.
[268] Mi, LM 26, fo. 186: see p. 239 below.
[269] Mi, LM 26, fos 193v–194, pp. 249–250 n. 488 below. This marriage of Frances and Montague Wood is mentioned in Percival Willoughby's draft letter to Lord Burghley in 1597 where he accuses Francis Willoughby's second wife of inveigling the youngest daughter to marry an apprentice or 'petti merchant of lytle worthe'. See Introduction n. 52.
[270] John Drake, Esq., of Ashe and Mount Drake, Devon (c.1560–1628), was, in 1595, captain of a militia in Devon. He later became an active member of Parliament from 1614–1626. Drake appears, however, to have been married to Dorothy Button and to already

By far the greatest attention Cassandra paid to the daughters of Francis and Elizabeth Willoughby is to the oldest, Bridget, who married her cousin Sir Percival Willoughby of Kent; these were Cassandra's great-grandparents. Bridget seems to have been a refuge and help to her sisters whenever possible. Cassandra follows the story of Percival and Bridget in great detail in this volume and in the second volume edited by Wood. In addition, there are a number of original letters not copied by Cassandra and still in the Middleton archival collection at Nottingham University Library as well as lost letters that were copied down by W.H. Stevenson. They had, by all accounts, a companionate marriage (a marriage with strong ties of affection),[271] enduring together a long series of law suits, particularly in their attempt to retrieve the Willoughby lands from Sir Francis's second wife. This marriage of equal partners stands out in contrast to the dysfunctional marriage of Francis and Elizabeth and Francis Willoughby's insistence on obedience in the marriage, a sentiment that, however difficult the lives of Bridget and Percival may have been, never enters into the correspondence between them.

Amy Louise Erickson, in her book on *Women and Property in Early Modern England* (1993), concludes that early modern women in England did not write about their own experiences, and the best avenue that one can find to determine their attitudes towards people and property is through legal documents. Cassandra Willoughby's project of telling the story of the Willoughby women who preceded her by copying down or abstracting many of their letters, however, has provided a window into a quite complex marital world where premarital settlements were essential, personal relationships determinative, and propertied or monetary support crucial and fought for tenaciously. The Willoughby marriages resist any particular marriage model, and the women often acted in ways that defied prevailing patriarchal sentiments of female obedience to a husband or father.[272] In the case of Elizabeth Willoughby, however, her unwillingness to any longer obey a husband she no longer loved resulted in years of banishment from her family, harsh treatment by her husband, alienation of her daughters, and a great bitterness of spirit as she aged.

---

have two children in 1595. See Mi, 2/75/2/8/1-4 for the High Commissioner for Ecclesiastical Causes documents.

[271] Lawrence Stone, *Family, Sex and Marriage in England, 1500–1800* (New York, 1977), esp. ch. 8 on 'The Companionate Marriage'.

[272] Although David Underdown has argued that the Elizabethan and Jacobean periods were a time of strained gender relations, Alison Wall has concluded, based on her study of the letters of the sisters Joan and Maria Thynne, that such strained gender relations are more apparent than real and based largely on the greater availability of court records for historians to study. Cited in Palliser, *The Age of Elizabeth*, 75.

APPENDIX

An illustration of how Cassandra calendared the letters from the family archives can be seen by comparing an extant letter in the British Library with her Account. The sections **not included** in her Account are in bold (Figure 4 and 5).[273]

62v: *My Lady Willoughby to Sr. Fr. Sent about ye end of 1585*

61r: *Sr: Albeit in respect of ye manifold wronges & wantes, wch I have endured for the space of theise 7 yeares paste, I have has [sic] iuste cause as ever any had to hate even from my very harte, all those who by their lewde & sclanderous reportes have bene the contryvers and contynuers therof. Yet* **since it hath pleased god now at the lengthe to move yor harte, to make some showe of better inclination towardes me**, *I protest unto yow before god I do not only frely & unfaynedly forgive them, but also do mooste humbly thanke yow for vouchsafing me* **(to my greate comforte)** *both yor company & conference. A happy entraunce I hope to a full & perfett reconciliation betwixt us. To the performance wherof, as there shalbe no wante on my parte in all good & convenient sort to be dyrected by yow. So I truste yow will hold me excused, if by the advise of my good & wise freindes I shall refuse to enter into any hard condicions,* **or be drawne by any action into any danger of ye losse of that litle poore lyving yow allowe me**.
*Wherin as I do not so muche as conceyve any yll opynion of yow towching yor owne disposition & nature, so am I not ignorant of the setled malyce of some, who seke by all driftes & devises they can, to kepe us still asunder.
I could name many, but I will note but one whom yow knowe & I have tryed, who fearing belyke some lykelyhood of our cominge together againe, and fynding yt false reportes tooke not yt effect wth yow wch he expected, like a* ~~conninge~~ *woodman, channges his course, and comminge to me under the coulor of greate freindshipp, declared unto me how yow were mynded to sue a dyvorce betwxt us, and that to this end* **yow had sent fourthe as it were spyes** *certaine* **good fellowes into dyverse corners of ye countrey, who** *had undertaken to fynd out and bring to light this supposed childe.*
The wch **infamous & forged sclaunder as it hath bene to** *my greate* **greif &** *discreditt, bruted* **abroad by them**,[274] **so, hath it bene if I may so say) ever readily beleaved by yow**.
Wheras if it had pleased yow in the begyninge, when it was brought to yow, to have brought me to myne answere, yor mynde might have bene long synce better satisfied, and the reputation of my honest name not so greatly impayred as it is.

---

[273] BL, Lansdowne 46/31, fos 61–62v; Mi, LM 26, fo. 126: see below pp. 157–158; Friedman, 'Portrait of a marriage', 550–551.
[274] Cassandra writes, 'Which suspicion had been bruted, greatly to her discredit'.

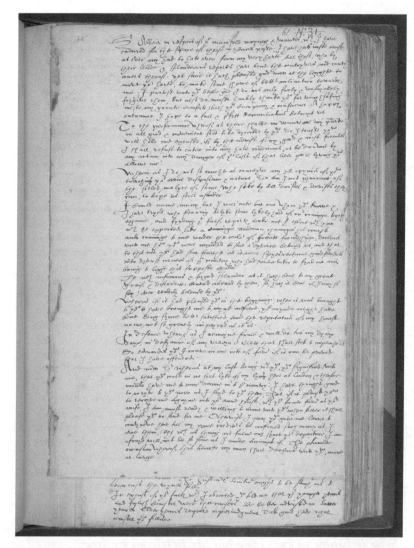

Figure 4. Letter from Lady Elizabeth Willoughby to Sir Francis Willoughby (1585), in colour online. Reproduced by permission of the British Library from Lansdowne MS 46/31, fo. 61r.

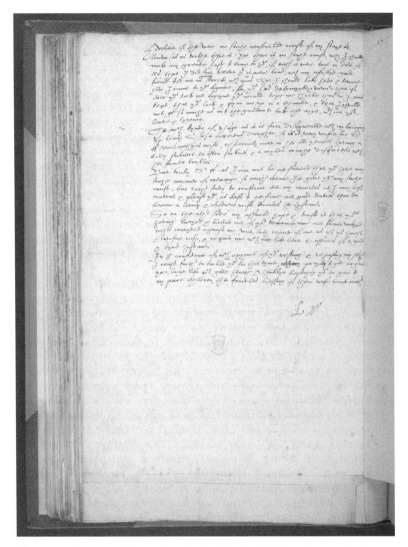

Figure 5. Reverse of letter from Lady Elizabeth Willoughby to Sir Francis Willoughby (1585), in colour online. Reproduced by permission of the British Library from Lansdowne MS 46/31, fo. 6IV.

In defence whereof as I remayne firme & will do till my dying daye, in defyaunce of any villeyn or varlet that shall seek to impeache it. **So towardes yow I crave no one iote of favor if it can be proved that I have offended.**
And now Sr whereas at my last being wth yow, yow signified unto me, that yow could in no sort lyke of my lyving here at London & therfore would have me to come downe in to ye country: I have thought good to wryte to yow now as I sayd to yow than, *that if it please yow to receyve me agayne into yor owne howse, wth yor former favor as yor wife, I am moost ready & willing to come unto yow,* **when soever it shall please yow to send for me. Otherwise I pray yow geve me leave to contynewe here till my pore crediters be answered such mony as I owe them, the wch as thinges are faline out synce yor departure, I am afrayd will not be so sone as I made accompt of. The particuler occasion wherof this bearer my man shall declare unto yow, more at large.**

61v: Howbeit if ther were no suche reasonable cause of my staye at London (as in truthe there is) yet there is no suche cause why I should make any greate haste to come to yow, if eithr it were true in dede, or els that I did but beleve yt it were true, wch my aforsayd good freind told me in great secrete, wch was that I should take hede & beware how I come to yow againe, for yow had determyned & vowed that if ever yow took me agayne, yow would kepe me shorter than ere I was kept, that yow lock and pynn me up in a chamber, & that I should not go so muche as into the garden to take the ayre, wthout yor leave & lycence.
The wch kynde of usage as it is farr desagreable wth my bringing up being Sr John Litteltons daughter, so it is very unfitt for Sr. F Willoughbyes wife, especially now in her old yeares, having a body subiect to often sicknes & a mynde muche disquieted wth her former trobles.
But truly Sr F. as I can not be persuaded that yow have any suche manner of meani[n]ge, so neither meane I to give yow any suche cause, but rather study to conforme all my wordes as I may best content & please yow, as also to performe all good duties that do become a loving & obedient wife towardes her husband.
So on the other side my assured hope & truste is that yow having buryed & blotted out of yor remembrance all former unkyndnesses contryved againste me, will both repute of

me as of yor honest & lawfull wife, & requite me wth all like love & offices of a good & kynd husband.

In ye confidence of wch opyniones of yow resting & reposing my self, I cease further to troble yow for this tyme, [illeg. word crossed out] *praying to god to give yow, longe life wth good health, & humblye besechi[n]g yow to geve to my poore children, the fruitles blessing of their unfortunate mother.*

E.W.

Editorial Conventions

The editorial approach is conservative. The intention is to offer a readable text that is, at the same time, and for scholarly reasons, very close to the original.[275]

Cassandra's spellings have been retained, although most unambiguous abbreviations have been expanded except when it is a familiar form. Mr (Master) and Mrs (Mistress) have been retained as written, although Cassandra will at times spell out Master. In the Account, where Cassandra uses y^e, y^m, y^n and y^t, they have been changed to 'the', 'them', 'then', and 'that' and where she uses an ampersand, &, which she almost invariably uses rather than 'and', I have spelled out 'and' in an effort to ease readability of her text. She also often uses 'off' for 'of' and vice versa. 'Then' is sometimes used for 'than,' mostly in the letters themselves, and this edition will not use *sic* in those cases. Cassandra capitalized a great many words. In this edition most have been changed to correspond to modern practice; exceptions are those words referring to family members (e.g. Uncle, Sister), regional locations (Town, City), dignities (Knight, Major, Aldermen) and rooms or buildings (New House, Wollaton Hall, Library, Gallery). Rather than use full stops, Cassandra regularly used dashes to complete her sentences. In all such cases, the dashes have been changed to points (or omitted in the case of tabular matter). The use of commas is inconsistent, and they have been eliminated or inserted or changed to full stops where the sense of the passage would suggest it. Where necessary all words at the beginning of sentences have been silently capitalized. Cassandra's use of apostrophes, colons and semi-colons has been retained. Any other differences from the original are detailed in the footnotes.

The use of carets (^...^) in the text indicates words that are interlined in the original, although for Cassandra's Account, Volume I, specifically, brief notices of insertions, damage, missing words and other purely textual issues are listed in endnotes Cassandra uses a consistent abbreviation for pounds, which is best approximated by using the Latin abbreviation 'li'.

---

[275] For guidelines on editing 16th- and 17th-century letters, see Giles E. Dawson, 'Problems in editing sixteenth- and seventeenth-century letters', in Dale B.J. Randall (ed.), *Medieval and Renaissance Studies: Proceedings of the Southeastern Institute of Medieval and Renaissance Studies (1974)* (Durham, NC, 1976), 87–103.

Additional materials from Cassandra's notes currently housed at the Huntington Library are inserted either into the main text or into the footnotes, whenever they add information that is not in Cassandra's final, fair Account. These passages are shown in italic and, when placed in the text itself, in square brackets. Additions in square brackets are indicated as coming from the Huntington Library, Stowe Temple Brydges Collection (STB). There are whole letters in italic from the collection of Lord Middleton and from the British Library, in the appendix above, and interpolated in the edited text. In all instances in the transcriptions from the Montague Wood letters (Mi, C 29, see pp. 251–253 below), ellipses in square brackets signal that the word is illegible, otherwise [...] indicates an editorial omission. Square brackets are also used within the text to indicate a modern spelling of a word, a questionable reading, an explanation, or a mistake on Cassandra's part. Since the new year began on 25 March of the English calendar, dates that occur between 1 January and 25 March are, to the extent possible, indicated by the previous and current years, e.g. 1546/7.

ACCOUNT OF AN ELIZABETHAN FAMILY: THE WILLOUGHBYS OF WOLLATON BY CASSANDRA WILLOUGHBY (1670-1735)

THE COLLECTIONS OF CASSANDRA WILLOUGHBY, 1702

[initial, unfoliated page]: Miss Kearney

Honorable John Kearney judge[?][1]
No. 48[?] Somerset Street Portman Square

An Account of the Willughby's of Wollaton taken out of the Pedigree, Old Letters, and Old Books of Accounts in my Brother Sir Thomas Willoughby's Study December A:D: 1702 By Cass: Willoughby

[Folios 1–38 consist largely of family genealogies and national history taken out of Dugdale's *Baronage*, Baker's *Chronicle*, Camden, and Thoroton in addition to a notebook that belonged to Cassandra's father, Francis Willoughby the naturalist. This is followed by a listing of letters mainly associated with Sir Henry Willoughby (d.1528), including a few letters from Henry VIII; one letter from Catherine of Aragon and one from Jane Seymour; and a very few household accounts. The material is largely derivative or, in the case of the letters and accounts, consists of brief notices. Cassandra copied down more substantive materials beginning with the death of Sir Henry Willoughby in 1549. This Sir Henry was the father of Sir Francis Willoughby (d.1596) who was Cassandra's great-great grandfather. The text begins here with folio 39 and the death of Sir Henry Willoughby.]

[1549–1564: The Wardship of the Willoughby Children]

[f. 39] This Sir Henry Willughby was one of those gentlemen that went to appease the rebels in Norfolk who had got together under Robert

---

[1] In 1743, a Dr John Kearney of Kildare married Henrietta Brydges, the niece of Cassandra Willoughby's husband, James Brydges, 1st duke of Chandos. This volume, and Volume II of Cassandra's *Account*, seem to have passed to the Kearney family sometime in the 2nd half of the 18th century and to a Miss Kearney, daughter of John Kearney, Esq. of King Street, Oxmantown, who married the Hon. Randle Plunket in 1778. See their marriage notice in the Dec. 1778 issue of the *Gentleman's and London Magazine*, published in Dublin. Cassandra, Duchess of Chandos, *The Continuation of the History of the Willoughby Family, being Vol. II of the Manuscript*, ed. A.C. Wood (Eton, 1958), xi–xii. About 1885 or 1886 Lord Middleton acquired this first volume.

Ket a tanner upon a grievance on account of inclosures and was killed at Norwich August the 27th 1548 [sic].[2] He and his Lady both lye buried in the Church at Wollaton where there is a monument for them.

They left two Sons and one Daughter all very young. Thomas the eldest Son about eight years and a quarter old and Francis the youngest Son about two years old but the age of Margaret Willughby the Daughter is not mention'd.[3] It appears by some of the old papers that Sir Henry Willughby left these three children to the Marquis of Dorsets [Henry Grey's] care, and that the three executers of his will were George Medley[4] and Gabriell Barwyke[5] Esquires and John Hall Gentleman.[6]

---

[2] Kett's Rebellion, which began in early July 1549, was defeated by 27 Aug. 1549, after the rebels had established several camps across Norfolk and Suffolk. It was part of a wider series of revolts across southern England by people making demands relating to enclosures by lords and others who took common lands and the lands of tenants to graze sheep and cattle and to establish deer parks. Additional demands were to free all bondmen and to lower rents and address other financial injustices. The debasement of the coinage and rising prices in the 1540s contributed to the unrest. The rebels included wealthy manorial tenants as well as the poor and landless. See Jane Whittle, 'Lords and tenants in Kett's Rebellion 1549', *Past & Present*, 207 (2010), 3–52; Stephen K. Land, *Kett's Rebellion: The Norfolk Rising of 1549* (Ipswich, 1977); and Andy Wood, *The 1549 Rebellions and the Making of Early Modern England* (Cambridge, 2007). The death date for Henry Willoughby is therefore 1549 and not 1548, as Cassandra reports. According to a note in the Middleton archives, Henry died on 27 Aug. 3 Edward VI. W.H. Stevenson (ed.), *Report on the Manuscripts of Lord Middleton preserved at Wollaton Hall, Nottinghamshire* (London, 1911), 396 (hereafter *HMC Middleton*).

[3] She may have been born c.1543 and would have been about 6 years old.

[4] George Medley, Esq., was the only surviving child from the 1505 marriage of Margaret Wotton (d.1541) to her first husband, William Medley, Esq. She had 8 known children with her second husband, Thomas Grey, 2nd marquis of Dorset, one of whom, Anne, was the mother of Thomas, Margaret, and Francis Willoughby, and another of whom was Henry Grey, duke of Suffolk and 3rd marquis of Dorset, father of Lady Jane Grey, both of whom were beheaded in the Tower in 1554. Therefore, George Medley was the half-brother of Anne Grey and uncle to Thomas, Margaret, and Francis. See below fo. 40, pp. 70–71. There is a letter to Francis Willoughby from George Medley's widow (fo. 55, p. 87) stating that her husband took charge of Francis for 13 years (viz. 1549–1562). For George Medley's will and codicil in 1562, see Manuscripts and Special Collections in the University of Nottingham Library, Middletons of Wollaton Hall (hereafter Mi) 1/7/183/12. See also TNA, PROB 11/46/75.

[5] Gabriel Barwyke, gentleman, first appears in Willoughby household accounts in 1521–1522. Mi, A 5. From 1549 to 1562 he was one of the executors of the will of Henry Willoughby. *HMC Middleton*, 149, 317, 351, 370, 388, 396, 416. He acquired land in Bulcote, Gunthorpe, and elsewhere in Nottinghamshire and married Elizabeth, daughter of John Marmion of Cotgrave (Mi, 6/176/190). His last appearance in the Willoughby documents is a 1569 letter he wrote reproving Francis Willoughby for marrying 'without the consent of Mr Medley, Mr Haule and me'. (Mi, C 14). Ralph Hanna and Thorlac Turville-Petre (eds), *The Wollaton Medieval Manuscripts* (York, 2010), 15.

[6] John Hall, gentleman, was the bailiff at Middleton Manor in Warwickshire. *HMC Middleton*, 396. For extended excerpts from the Willoughby household accounts relating

There is a letter from George Medeleye dated from London in February 1549, in which he writes that the Marquis of Dorset, being now daily to attend the King, he intended to remove his family from Bradgate[7] to London and therefore ordered that 12 horses should be sent for from Wollaton and a cart and horses from Middleton to come up to London with Mrs.[8] Margaret and little Mr. Francis Willughby. Attended thus, a servant to carry Master Francis before him, another servant to carry Mrs. Margaret, and another servant to carry little Whytneye,[9] a horse for Mrs. Lenton,[10] another horse for the maid, and 4 for the four men to wait upon them, a man to lead a horse to carry the male [mail = a travelling bag], and two more servants to take care of the horses.

It does not appear where these children were after this[11] [f. 40] journey, till by a book of Medeleys accounts for the childrens cloaths etc. from the 4th of Edward the 6th to the 1st of Elizabeth, I find that his Nephew Francis Willughby and his Neece Margaret removed to Tyltey[12]

---

to the 13 years when Hall, Barwyke, and Medley were the executors in charge of Henry Willoughby's estates, see *HMC Middleton*, 396–420. See also Mi, A 31–32. The first mention of Hall (Haull) is as servant to Edward Willoughby c.1528, see Mary A. Welch (ed.), 'Willoughby letters of the first half of the sixteenth century', Thoroton Society Record Series (TSRS), XXIV (Nottingham, 1967), 30.

[7] Bradgate House was the probable birthplace and the childhood home of Lady Jane Grey and had been owned by the Grey family since the mid 15th century. It is located just north-west of Leicester and was one of the earliest brick-built country houses in England, completed c.1520.

[8] Mrs is the standard abbreviation for Mistress, a form of address indicating courtesy or rank but not marital status. See Amy Erickson, 'Mistresses and marriage, or a short history of Mrs.', *History Workshop Journal* 78 (2014), 39–57. Mr is the abbreviation for Master. Although Cassandra will sometimes spell out Master when referring to the young Francis Willoughby, she normally uses Mr.

[9] A Mistress Whytney is mentioned in George Medley's account book for 1550, when she is given cloth to make hose for Margaret and sleeves for Francis. Mi, A 32, fo. 3v, p. 6; *HMC Middleton*, 402.

[10] See below in the edited text (hereafter 'Text'), Text n. 32, for information on Mrs Lenton.

[11] On the verso side of folio 39 is the following note: 'In Trussells Book of Accounts for the 4th of Edward the 6th amongst the wages paid to the servants there is set down paid to four shepherds (one at Worsopp, one at Wollaton, one at Basford and one at Arnolde) these four shepherds were paid ten shillings a year for each of their wages.'

[12] Tilty is in the north-north-west corner of Essex and was originally a Cistercian monastery. On 6 Oct. 1535, the abbot and convent granted the marchioness of Dorset a lease for sixty years 'of the grange, demesne lands, and manor of Tilty, including the house standing against the west end of the church of the monastery of old time called the founder's house, otherwise the Gestes Hall'. 'Such grants made shortly before the dissolution were naturally suspected; but on an inquiry being made afterwards it was found by the jury that the lease was such as used to be granted and in no way fraudulent, and it was consequently allowed by a decree of the Court of Augmentations on 20 Oct. 1538 and confirmed on 4 November.' William Page and J. Horace Round (eds), *A History of the County of*

April the 21th 1550.[13] Mr. Medeley in his letters always calls these children Nephews and Neece which makes me conclude that he was the Son of Margaret Marchioness of Dorset by William Medeley her first Husband, and so half Brother to Lady Anne Willughby.[14]

I don't find where Mr. Thomas Willughby was when his Brother and Sister removed to Tyltey, but in Mr. Medeleys account book there is set down 20[sh] for Mr. Thomas Willughby's board with him from May the 27th to June the 11th that year and 10[s.] for Mr. Thomas Willughbys mans board the same time.[15] And again the same sume is set down for his and his mans board with Mr. Medeley from November the 3[d] to the 18th,[16] which day I find by the book of houshold expences for the family at Tyltey Mr. Thomas Willughby went to Cambridg.

I don't find who was the housekeeper at Tyltey, but believe it might be Lady Anne Willughby's Mother who might also be Mr. Medeleys Mother.[17]

There is a book in my Brother's Library at Wollaton which gives a very particular account of the expences of the family at Tyltey from the 31th of October to the last of February in this 4th year of Edward the 6th, [f. 41] which book[18] shews that there was a very great table kept at Tyltey. This book also gives an account what company came to Tyltey viz. that upon the 31th of October there came my Ladys Grace [Frances Brandon Grey, duchess of Suffolk?] and all her train. But the next day most of her Graces retinue returned home again to Leicestershire. November the 3[d] there came the Lord Thomas [Grey (1526–1554)] and the Lord John [Grey (1523–

Essex: II, VCH (London, 1907), 134–136. British History Online: http://www.british-history.ac.uk/vch/essex/vol2/pp134-136 (accessed 4 Aug. 2015). The monastery signed a deed of surrender in Feb. 1536. On the death of the marchioness in 1541, the lease went to her son, George Medley. The reversion of the lease of the monastery itself, the mansion called 'le Founders Lodging and the Gest Hall', Tilty Grange and the manor of Tilty, the rectory and chapel of Tilty, and some lands, was next granted to Sir Thomas Audley on 24 Apr. 1542 who must then have leased these properties to George Medley. On the Audleys, see Text n. 26.

[13] *HMC Middleton*, 399.

[14] See above, Text n. 4.

[15] *HMC Middleton*, 402; Mi, A 32, fo. 4, p. 7. Medley provides the name of Thomas Willoughby's servant as Dyxon. The dates are actually 30 Oct. to 18 Nov.

[16] *HMC Middleton*, 402; Mi, A, f. 4, p. 7, although the dates given are from 30 Oct. to 18 Nov.

[17] Margaret Wotton. See Text n. 4 above. Margaret Wotton, George Medley's mother, lived in the former guest house of the abbey at Tilty until her death in 1541; she cannot have been the housekeeper (i.e. mistress of the house) in 1550.

[18] 1550. This volume of George Medley's books of accounts is no longer extant, nor is it described in *HMC Middleton*.

1564][19] with 21 servants from London who stayed at Tyltey three days and then returned to London again. That upon November the 16th many honest men of the Country dined there. That upon the 18th the Lord John and others came from Court, which was the same day that Mr. Thomas Willughby, Mr. Henry and Mr. Thomas Medley [two sons of George],[20] Mr. Willughbys man and three more servants went to Cambridg. The Lords and others from Court returned thither again upon the 22th of November. Upon the 23th divers of the Country dined at Tyltey. Upon the 24th ten gentlemen came from London to attend my Ladys Grace to the Lady Marys Grace [Mary Tudor].[21] They stayed at Tyltey till the 26th and then after breakfast my Ladys Grace, with Lady Jane, Lady Catherine and Lady Mary,[22] repaired to Lady Mary's Grace. 'Tis thus enter'd in this book of Tyltey accounts, by which I understand that the Dutches of Suffolk with her three Daughters went to Court to wait upon the Kings Sister, who was, after the Kings death, Queen Mary.

This book says that December the 2^d [1550?] Lady Catherine and Lady Mary with their attendance and a great many gentlemen came to sup at Tyltey. And that December the 16th there came my Lord and Ladys Grace [the duke and duchess of Suffolk], Lord John [Grey], Lady Jane [Grey] and divers attending them from London to Tyltey where they stayed six or seven days [f. 42] December the 25th this book says that divers of the Country dined at Tyltey. And also upon the 26th and the 27th and that that day there came 5 players and a boy, and from that time till January the 9th [1550/1] are set down great numbers that dinned and supped at Tyltey, and that the Lord of Oxfords Players were there.[23] And that from January the 11th to the 20th there was my Lord —, Lord John, Mr.

---

[19] John Grey of Pirgo, Essex, second son of Thomas Grey, 2nd marquis of Dorset and Margaret Wotton, and brother of Henry Grey, 3rd marquis of Dorset and duke of Suffolk. He married Mary Browne of Cowdray, from a prominent Catholic family in Sussex. The Crown's lenient treatment of John Grey in the wake of his brothers Henry's and Thomas's executions after Wyatt's Rebellion may have been due to his wife's influence at the court of Mary Tudor. Michael C. Questier, *Catholicism and Community in Early Modern England: Politics, Aristocratic Patronage and Religion, c.1550–1640* (Cambridge, 2006), 93–94. On Wyatt's Rebellion, see below, Text n. 39.

[20] Henry Medley, son of George Medley, was born in 1533; Thomas Willoughby, heir to Henry Willoughby, was born *c.*1541.

[21] Mary Tudor, the sister of Edward VI and later Queen Mary (r. 1553–1558).

[22] Henry Grey, duke of Suffolk and 3rd marquis of Dorset, and his wife Lady Frances Brandon (daughter of Charles Brandon and Henry VIII's sister Mary) had three daughters: Lady Jane Grey (*c.*1536–1554), Lady Catherine Grey (1540–1568), and Lady Mary Grey (1545–1578). See Leanda de Lisle, *The Sisters Who Would be Queen: Mary, Katherine, and Lady Jane Grey* (New York, 2008).

[23] Also known as the Earl of Oxford's Men, the Players performed at Tilty Abbey, 'the home of George Medley', between 1549 and 1552. Ian Lancashire, *Dramatic Texts and Records*

Treasurer[24] and a greatdeal of other company. And that, that day after dinner, my Lord and Lady's Grace, the Lady Jane, Lady Catherine, Lady Mary, Lady Clare,[25] Lord John and all the gentlemen went from Tyltey to the Lady Audley's at Walden.[26] This book says they all returned again to Tyltey the 22th and that they brought the Lord and Lady Audley to Tyltey with them. And that January the 25th there came Mr. George Willughby[27] and many more strangers. Upon the 26th Lady Audley went to Walden and Lady Catherine went with her, but they both returned again to Tyltey January the 30th where Lord Audley and the rest of the company had stayed all that time. January the 31th there came a gentleman to dinner from the Lady Mary's Grace.

The noting these particulars may seem forein to my story, but they shew the manner of living in England about that time, and this family of the Grey's were the nearest relations the young Willughbys had, and for that reason, I should not pass over the melancholy relation of poor Lady Jane Grey's misfortunes if I had met with any thing in these papers concerning the steps taken for her advancement to the Crown, which cut of [off] her life before she was seventeen years of age. The English history makes her a Lady very extraordinary for piety and learning, and notwithstanding her youth perfectly resigned to dye (which she said she had diserved, not for [f. 43]

---

of Britain: A Chronological Topography to 1558 (Cambridge, 1984), 207, 456; E.K. Chambers, *The Elizabethan Stage*, II (Oxford, 1923), 99–102.

[24] The Lord Treasurer in Jan. 1551 was William Paulet (*c.*1483/85–1572); he was made treasurer in 1550, taking the position after Somerset (Henry Seymour's) fall from grace. In Oct. 1551, Paulet was made marquis of Winchester; he remained Lord Treasurer until his death.

[25] Unidentified.

[26] Elizabeth Grey, daughter of Thomas Grey and Margaret Wotton, married Thomas Audley, 1st Baron Audley (Saffron Walden, Essex) in 1538. Lady Audley was therefore the half-sister of George Medley, sister of Anne, Henry, Thomas, and John Grey, and the aunt of the Willoughby children and Jane, Catherine, and Mary Grey. Walden Abbey, formerly a Benedictine monastery, was granted to Thomas Audley by Henry VIII in 1538. It is currently open to the public and known as Audley End.

[27] George Willoughby (d.1595), alias Fox, was the bastard son of Sir Edward Willoughby and therefore the illegitimate half-brother of Henry Willoughby and uncle to Thomas, Margaret, and Francis. He married Maud Cotton Repington *c.*1550–1553. Henry Willoughby left him an inn called the Castle in Holborne. Regarding this inn, see *Calendar of Patent Rolls* (hereafter *CPR*) 1560–1563, Elizabeth I, ii, 605. Francis Willoughby counterleased Tamworth and Wiginton in Staffordshire to George Willoughby and his two sons Henry and Thomas in 1568 [Mi, 7/183/25]. Inventory dated 1594–1595 INV/86/103, Lincolnshire Archives 057. See also Robert Thoroton, *The Antiquities of Nottinghamshire* (London, 1677), 223. George Willoughby, Esq., is mentioned as recusant in the Recusant Rolls for 1593–1595. H. Bowler (ed.), *Recusant Roll No. 2 (1593–1594)*, Catholic Record Society, 57 (1965), 104–105; *Recusant Rolls Nos 3 and 4 (1594–1595)*, Catholic Record Society, 61 (1970), 56–57, 189.

seeking the Crown, but for not refusing it, when it was offer'd her).[28] When the message was brought her that she must dye the next day, she seemed to rejoyce at it, as a means to set her at liberty. And after when the docter who attended her had obtain'd of Queen Mary that she should live three days longer, she told him[i] he was deceived if he thought she desired life any longer, for it was now tedious to her, and she longed for nothing so much as death. Before she was brought to execution her Husband the Lord Guilford[29] desired some conference with her, but she refused it, saying that would be rather a grief then comfort in death, and she made no doubt, but they should shortly meet in a better place, and in a better condition of society. Thus February the 12th An: D: 1553 being about seven months after she had been proclaimed Queen, her Husband first, and about an hour or two after, she was beheaded within the Tower.

After this digression I must returne to Mr. Medeleys account book and copy that part of it which shews how the young Willughbys were placed.[30]

'Tis before set down that Mr. Thomas Willughby boarded twice a fortnight at a time with Mr. Medeley, and just after that, there is set down for the board of Mr. Francis Willughby from April the 24th to January the 28th [1550–1551] being 40 weeks twenty pounds, which makes me believe they then boarded with Mr. Medeley. There is also set down for Mrs. Margaret Willughby's board the same time 20^{li} and also for Mrs. Lenton's board the same time 20^{li}.[31] This Mrs. Lenton, who I find almost always named [f. 44] after Mrs. Margaret Willughby, I suppose was Mrs. Margarets Governess or

---

[28] Although Lady Jane Grey was imprisoned in the wake of the failed attempt to make her queen, it was the several subsequent rebellions, called Wyatt's Rebellion, in Jan. 1554 that resulted in her execution and the executions of her husband Guildford Dudley, her father Henry Grey, duke of Suffolk, and her uncle Lord Thomas Grey. See Lisle, *The Sisters who would be Queen*, a study of the brief reign of Lady Jane Grey and an examination of the fictions and legends surrounding her; and Eric Ives, *Lady Jane Grey: A Tudor Mystery* (London, 2011).

[29] Guildford Dudley (*c*.1535–12 Feb. 1554), husband of Lady Jane Grey, was the fourth surviving son of John Dudley, 1st duke of Northumberland (1504–1553) and Lady Jane Guildford (d.1555). Married to Jane Grey on 21 May 1553, he and Jane moved into royal apartments in the Tower on 10 June 1553. When Mary Tudor asserted her authority on 19 June 1553, she ordered their arrest. Guildford was tried and sentenced for treason in Nov. 1553 but was not executed until 12 Feb. 1554, following Wyatt's Rebellion. His contemporaries treated his legacy gently, considering him more a victim of his father's and father-in-law's machinations than a true accomplice. G.J. Richardson, entry for 'Dudley, Lord Guildford', *ODNB*.

[30] Mi, A 32.

[31] *HMC Middleton*, 403; Mi, A 32, f. 4, p. 7.

chief servant.[32] There is also set down at the same time for the board of two servants 40 weeks at 5 s. a week for each servant 20^{li}, and twenty pound is set down for the board of one maintained to keep the Willughbys accounts. And for their fewel and washing that 40 weeks five pounds.[33] In the 5th year of Edward the 6th [1551] Mr. Medeley sets down for the board of Master Francis and Mrs. Margaret Willughby, and the same number of servants at Tyltey at the same rate as before from January the 28th to that time the year following being 12 months 121^{li} 13^{sh} 4^{d}.[34]

There is set down for Mr. Thomas Willughbys board at Tyltey 20 weeks the same year to October the 10th ten pounds and for his two men's board the same time ten pounds. In the 6th of Edward the 6th [1552] there is set down for the board of Master Francis Mrs. Margaret Willughby and the same number of servants at Tyltey at the same rate from January the 28th to that time 12 month 121^{li} 13^{sh} 4^{d}.

And for the board of Mr. Thomas Willughby from July the 20th to October the 6th the same year 5^{li} 10^{sh} 0^{d} and for the board of his two men the same time 5^{li} 10^{sh} 0^{d}.[35]

From January the 28th to July the 6th An: D: 1553, being the day King Edward dyed, there is set down for the board of Master Francis Mrs. Margaret Willughby and the same number of servants that are set down before, at Tyltey 48^{li} 10^{sh} 4^{d}. And for all their boards at Tyltey from July the 6th to December the 10th being the 1st of Queen Mary [1553] there is set down 46^{li} 16^{sh} 4^{d}.[36]

Mr. Medeley setts down for the board of Mr. Thomas Willughby at Tyltey this year from July the 8th to November the 25th 10^{li} 0^{sh} 0^{d}. And for the board of his two men the same time also 10^{li} 0^{sh} 0^{d}.[37] [f. 45] I believe about this time Mr. Medeley and the whol familie at

---

[32] Elizabeth Lenton (d. c.1562), possibly the daughter of John Lenton, married John Danet (Dannet/Dannatt/Dannett) in about 1553. Between 1554 and 1562 they were involved in a series of court cases against Richard Mytton in an attempt to claim a grant made to Elizabeth by Queen Mary of the possessions of Lord Thomas Grey at the time of his capture by Mytton in Wyatt's Rebellion. Mytton claimed the right to keep them for himself, since Grey had been captured (in Feb. 1554) in Oswestry in the liberty of the earl of Arundel, whose officer Mytton was. No outcome of the case is recorded. Elizabeth Lenton Danet was probably the sister-in-law of Mary Danet, wife of George Medley, although, since she is still called Mrs Lenton in Feb. 1554 (fos 50–51, p. 82 below), and perhaps also in 1556 (fo. 54, p. 86 below), she may be the mother of Elizabeth Lenton.

[33] Mi, A 32, fo. 4, p. 7; *HMC Middleton*, 403.

[34] The total listed for this year is 147^{li} 18^{s} 1^{d} and includes 10^{li} for the board of Thomas Willughby who stayed at Tylty while the great sweat was in Cambridge and other places. Mi, A 32, fo. 5, p. 9.

[35] Mi, A 32, fos 8–8v, pp. 15–16.

[36] Mi, A 32, fos 9, 13, pp. 17, 24.

[37] Mi, A 32, fo. 12v, p. 23.

Tyltey were involved in great troubles upon the Duke of Suffolks account, who was beheaded upon the 23th of February following.[38]

Mr. Francis and Mrs. Margaret Willughby were removed to the Minoryes,[39] with their servants, I believe a house where Mr. Medeley used to live. While they were there I believe Mrs. Lenton took care for their diet fewel etc. which reckoned by odd weeks from December the 14th to July the 5th came to 34^{li} 0^{sh} 2^{d}.[40]

There is a letter from Mrs. Lenton to John Hall the Baily at Middleton for money, in which letter she says she knows not where to place Master Francis and Mrs. Margaret Willughby, now that Mr. Medleys house was like to be seised etc. Mr. Medeley charges in his account for the diet etc. of Mr. Francis and Mrs. Margaret Willughby and the same number of servants that they used to have

---

[38] Although named after Sir Thomas Wyatt, several notable landholders, including Henry Grey, duke of Suffolk, were also involved in this rebellion against Queen Mary in 1554. They hoped to stop Queen Mary's marriage and perhaps unseat her as queen. A nuanced look at the intentions behind the furor indicates that both religion and the politics of nascent nationalism were at the root. Wyatt raised a substantial force but was ultimately stopped at London Bridge by Sir John Brydges, soon to be Baron Chandos. Mary raised the citizens of London against Wyatt, who was arrested, tortured, and executed along with approximately ninety other rebels. Mary believed her half-sister Elizabeth to be implicated in the plot but found no evidence. See D.M. Loades, *Two Tudor Conspiracies* (Cambridge, 1965); Alan Bryson, 'Order and disorder: John Proctor's history of Wyatt's Rebellion (1554)', in Mike Pincombe and Cathy Shrank (eds), *The Oxford Handbook of Tudor Literature: 1485–1603* (Oxford, 2009), 323–336; and Anthony Fletcher and Diarmaid MacCulloch, *Tudor Rebellions*, 6th edn (London, 2016), ch. 7.

[39] The name is derived from the enclosed precinct where the abbey of the Minoresses of St Mary of the Order of St Clare and the homes of their lay tenants stood. Located at the eastern edge of London, just beyond Aldgate and close by the Tower of London, it was taken by the Crown in 1538 and demised by Edward VI to the Grey family. Henry Grey alienated the property to his younger brothers Thomas and John Grey and his half-brother George Medley. As a result of Wyatt's rebellion, the house was searched, George Medley was imprisoned briefly, and Thomas and John forfeited their shares by attainder. George Medley's brother-in-law, Thomas Danet, as well as his nephew Leonard on his wife's side, were indicted in the wake of the rebellion and committed to the Tower. Both were subsequently released, and Thomas Danet fled to the continent. If Margaret and Francis were staying at the Minories from Dec. 1553 until July 1554, while the whole family was under suspicion, they were also in London at a time when large numbers of those involved with Wyatt's rebellion, including, of course, their uncles, Henry and Thomas Grey, were being executed. For more on the Minories, see A.P. House, 'The City of London and the problem of the liberties, *c.*1540–*c.*1640', DPhil thesis, University of Oxford, 2006; Edward Murray Tomlinson, *History of the Minories* (London, 1907), ch. 7; and H.G. Owen, 'A nursery of Elizabethan nonconformity, 1567–1572', *Journal of Ecclesiastical History* 17 (1966), 65–76.

[40] This is difficult to follow in George Medeley's account book, as the dates for expenses from 6 July to Dec. (1 Mary) (fo. 13) are followed by weekly expenses from Margaret Willughby. Mi, A 32, fo. 13, pp. 24, et seq. Similarly, for the period 6 July forward (2 Mary), expenses are listed weekly (Mi, A 32, fos 22v–25v, pp. 42–48). During much of the fall, Margaret was not boarding at Tylty, as Cassandra notes.

by odd weeks (they being I believe sometimes in one place and sometimes in another) from July the 5th to January the 17th being the 2^d year of Queen Mary [1554–1554/5], the sume off 23^{li} 19^{sh} 0^d. In this time tis often mentioned that Mrs. Margaret was absent with her maid a week at a time. I believe she might then be with the Lady Frances, the Duke of Suffolk's Widow,[41] because there is a letter from Mr. Medeley writ in this year being An: D: 1554 [probably written after the execution of the daughter and husband of Lady Frances in February 1554] in which letter he writes that Mrs. Margaret Willughby was then with Lady Frances.[42]

Mr. Francis Willughby went to St. Antonies School [f. 46] in London.[43] There is set down in Mr. Medeleys account for his board at that School from January the 18th to June the 13th [1555] the sume of 2^{li} 16^{sh} 0^d.[44]

I believe Mrs. Margaret Willughby might stay with Lady Frances till May the 9th. From May the 9th to July the 11th [1555] there is set down in Mr. Medeleys account book for her own and her servants board the sume of 4^{li} 3^{sh} 3^d and for the stewards board who kept the young Willughbys accounts the whole year 10^{li} 0^{sh} 0^d.[45]

From July the 11th to December the 23th [1555] there is no account where Mrs. Margaret Willughby was, but Mr. Medeley's account book shews that December the 23th An: D: 1555, Mrs. Margaret went to the Lady Elizabeth [Elizabeth Tudor, later Queen Elizabeth I] at Hatfield.[46] There is set down for her given to Lady

---

[41] Frances Grey, née Brandon (1517–1559) – see Text n. 22 above – married Henry Grey in the spring of 1533. In the wake of Wyatt's Rebellion, Henry Grey was executed 23 Feb. 1554. Frances then married Adrian Stokes (variously identified as her master of horse, her steward, or a gentleman) on 9 Mar. 1555, although this date is contested. Margaret Willoughby was with Frances, her aunt, during the difficult year of 1554. As the ensuing letters attest, Margaret accompanied Frances to court to attend Queen Mary; there were great expectations of Margaret's preferment at court. Frances Brandon Grey Stokes was also the godmother of Francis Willoughby.

[42] See below, fo. 48, p. 79.

[43] St Anthony's was an endowed grammar and song school in London founded in the 1440s and attached to the hospital of the same name. See Nicholas Orme, *English Schools in the Middle Ages* (London, 1973), 308. It was one of the leading schools in London.

[44] Mi, A 32, fo. 25, p. 47; *HMC Middleton*, 409. Medeley records a cost of 5s 4d for a fortnight of Francis Willoughby's board going to school with Master Lyse at St Anthony's School in London, the cost being 2s 8d per week.

[45] Mi, A 32, fos 21–25v, pp. 39–48.

[46] Mi, A 32, fo 26, p. 49. During most of 1556 Margaret left court and attended Lady Elizabeth at Hatfield. Mi A 32, fos 28–31, pp. 53–59; *HMC Middleton*, 409–412. Margaret, arriving at Hatfield in late Dec. 1555, was with Elizabeth during the period of the abortive Dudley conspiracy. The first half of the year 1556 coincides with the time when Henry Dudley was trying to organize a French-supported invasion of soldiers, English exiles, and malcontents with the aim of placing Elizabeth on the throne. Elizabeth was then 22 years of age. Margaret Willoughby, whose date of birth is unsure but who was probably

Guilfords[47] lackey when he came to fetch Mrs. Margaret Willughby 20 pence.[48]

For money in Mistress Margaret Willughbys pocket	3^{li}	0^{sh}	0^{d}
For money for her expences upon the road from London to Hatfield	3	10	9
Given to the gentleman usher that went with her	0	10	0
February the 8th sent her to Hatfield[49]	2	0	0[50]

September the 27th 1556 there is set down in this account book for Mrs. Margaret Willughbys charges from Hatfield to Tyltey and back again to Hatfield 8^s 6^d. And for her charges from Hatfield to London in Hillary Term 9^s 4½^d and back again to Hatfield 7^s 7^d.[51]

There is also set down in this account book, for Philip's costs[52] when he went to see Mrs. Willughby at Hatfield 2^s 3^d. And for Dick's charges when he went to see[ii] [f. 47] Lady Elizabeth's Grace 9^{sh} 9^d. And for the charges of one sent twice to see Mrs. Willughby 3^s 10^d.[53] There is set down in this book of accounts for Mrs. Margaret Willughby's and her servants board at the Minories from July the 12th 1557 to August the 4th the sume of 1^{li} 13^{sh} 4^d.[54]

And the same year for hers and her servants board at Tyltey the sum of 8^{li} 5^{sh} 0^d.

---

born c.1543 would then have been 12 or 13 when she went to Hatfield to be with Elizabeth. Correspondence suggests that Queen Mary's sending Margaret Willoughby (and also Elizabeth Fitzgerald) into Elizabeth's service in 1556 might have been an attempt to spy on the princess at this conspiratorial time. Joan Greenbaum Goldsmith, 'All the queen's women: The changing place and perception of aristocratic women in Elizabethan England, 1558–1620', PhD thesis, Northwestern University, 1987, 46–47, 225 n. 54. Margaret Willoughby was cousin to Henry Dudley, chief architect of the conspiracy; their mothers were granddaughter and daughter (respectively) of Sir Thomas Grey, 1st marquis of Dorset. It is probably also at this time that John Harington wrote a poem in which he praised Margaret Willoughby as 'worthye willobe' and noted her 'pearcing eye'. Margaret was at the Minories in London by 13 Nov. 1556, having been returned from Elizabeth's household because of the death, from smallpox, of one of her gentlewomen (Mi, A 32, fo. 31, p. 59; *HMC Middleton*, 412; see also fo. 47, p. 79 below).

[47] Mary Wotton Guildford (c.1500–1558), second wife of Sir Henry Guildford (d.1532), comptroller of the royal household of Henry VIII.

[48] Mi, A 32, fo. 26, p. 49; *HMC Middleton*, 409.

[49] By early May 1556 members of Elizabeth's household were arrested on suspicion of involvement in the Dudley conspiracy. Elizabeth herself spent nearly all of 1556 at Hatfield, with the exception of some weeks later in the year. See Text n. 56 below.

[50] Mi, A 32, fo. 28, p. 53.

[51] *Ibid.*

[52] Philip as well as Dick, Hudson, and Kinton were all servants to either George Medley or the Willoughby children.

[53] Mi, A 32, fos 28–28v, pp. 53–54.

[54] Mi, A 32, fo. 30v, p. 58. Cassandra's calculations are accurate, although the final date is 6 Aug. rather than 4 Aug., and the year is 1555.

And for her own and her man Hudsons board at the Minories from October the 24th to the 30th the sum of 10^s 4^d, and for Kinton's board at London who stay'd to attend Mrs. Margaret Willughby to the Lady Elizabeths Grace 3^s 4^d.[55] A servant of the Lady Elizabeth's dying of the Small[pox] Mrs. Willughby removed to the Minories. There is set down in Medeleys account book for her's and her servants board there for 4 weeks at that time 3^{li} 7^{sh} 4^d.[56]

This account book ends here with what relates to Mrs. Margaret Willughby, and to this account of her I shall add part of severall letters that are in the Library at Wollaton, writ by Mr. Medeley concerning her, in the 1st and 2^d years of Queen Mary.

There is a letter from Mr. Medeley to John Hall (who was the baily at Middleton) dated An: D: 1553. This letter is to desire John Hall to send up to the Minories by two trusty servants, all the apparell of gownes and kyrtells and all other things appartaining[iii] to Mrs. Margaret Willughby which remained in his keeping at Middleton, because he intended with my Lord Suffolks help to get her into some honourable place, where my Lords Grace should think most fit for her to be. [f. 48] In this letter he desires woollen blankets may be put between the gownes and kyrtells [kirtles][57] to defend them from fretting and wet.

There is another letter from Mr. Medeley to John Hall dated An: D: 1554 in which he writes that now was the time to prefer Mrs. Margaret Willughby and to put Mr. Francis Willughby to school. [See fos 45–46 above.]

In another letter dated An: D: 1554, he writes that Mrs. Margaret Willughby was now with the Lady Frances [see f. 45 above], who was commanded to attend the Queen, and she had took Mrs. Margaret Willughby with her, who had been very much commended and was so well approved for good behavior etc., that Lady Francis [sic] did not doubt but soon to place her about the Queen so as all her friends would be pleased.[58]

---

[55] Mi, A 32, fo. 30v: see p. 58. Again, her copying of the sum is accurate.

[56] Elizabeth had been summoned to court at the end of November until 3 Dec. 1556 but must have been in London earlier in November. Cassandra's notes say that Margaret was at the Minories 24–30 Oct., then attending Elizabeth in London, but returning to the Minories the week before 20 Nov. Mi, A 32, fos 30v–31, pp. 58–59. 'For one Weekes borde for my cosyn Margarett at the Minorisse ended the xx November is being retorned from my ladye Elizabethes grace because of the deathe of one of her gentellwoemen which dyed of the smallpockes.' Mi, A 32, fo. 31, p. 59; *HMC Middleton*, 412.

[57] Skirts or outer petticoats, *OED*.

[58] Margaret Willoughby became a gentlewoman of the privy chamber, a position that she held until at least 1583. Margaret was present at Lady Mary Grey's secret marriage on 16 July 1565 to Queen Elizabeth I's serjeant porter, Thomas Keyes. Lisle, *The Sisters Who Would be Queen*, 232–233.

There is another letter from Mr. Medeley writ soon after the last to John Hall, in which he says that Mrs. Margaret Willughby had been at court with the Lady Frances's Grace (who had her place in the Privie Chamber). He writes that Mrs. Margaret Willoughby was much commended, and Lady Frances's Grace did not doubt but in a short time so to place her about the Queens Highness so as to content all her friends, and also be to her great preferment.

An: Do: 1555 Mr. Medeley requires the Lord Paget's[59] letter for the payment of a hundred pounds to Mrs. Margaret Willughby.[60]

And in Mr. Medeleys account book for the 1st year of Queen Elizabeth [f. 49] being An: D: 1558 there is set down November the 8th paid [to] Mrs. Margaret Willughby for her marriage money three hundred pounds. By which I believe it was about this time that she married Sir Mathew Arundell.[61]

There is in the Library at Wollaton a large book of the accounts of George Medeley and Gabriell Barwyke Esquires and John Hall Gentleman, the three executers of Sir Henry Willughby, for the 13 years they took care of the estate. This book shews that besides the profits of the land there were large sumes of money received for cole etc., which was brought to account. And yet in conclusion the whole sume raised by them in these 13 years did not amount to more then 3125^{li} 0^{sh} 8^{d}.

In this book there is an account of goods which were valued which Sir Henry Willughby had left at Middleton and Wollaton, amongst which there are set down many vestments, as copes etc. for the Chapel, and many extraordinary armes in the Armory.[62] There are set down by name in this book 42 geldings. And the plate is in this book valued at 447^{li} 10^{sh} 0^{d}. There are amongst the old papers a

---

[59] William, Lord Paget (d.1563), was keeper of the seal and a close adviser to Queen Mary. Lord Paget held the wardship of Thomas Willoughby who then married Lord Paget's daughter, Dorothy.

[60] Mi, A 31, f. 14v; See below, Text n. 73.

[61] Mi, A 31, f. 24. The marriage between Margaret Willoughby and Matthew Arundell took place 20 Dec. 1559. Therefore, this account book may be for 1559, especially since Queen Elizabeth came to the throne only in Nov. 1558. Matthew Arundell's dates are c.1533–1598. He would have been about 26, while Margaret was probably about 16. Matthew Arundell had previously been engaged to Katherine Cornwallis, daughter of Sir Thomas Wriothesley, 1st earl of Southampton. Katherine was to be an uncompromising recusant under Elizabeth. Questier, *Catholicism and Community in Early Modern England*, 514. For an assurance of Margaret's jointure 12 Feb. 1559/60, where she is referred to as his wife, see *CPR 1558–1560*, Elizabeth I, i, 280.

[62] *HMC Middleton*, 474–485. Stevenson describes two inventories of the goods of Henry Willoughby, one in 1549 and the other in 1550. 'Both inventories specify much plate' (p. 474). Mi, I 36 (1549); Mi, I 37 (1550).

great many acquittances for legacies and annuities left by this Sir Henry Willughby.

There is a book of Mr. Medeleys accounts for the 5th year of Edward the 6th being An: D: 1552 in which book he sets down many large sumes of money for his journeys to meet the other executers in order to pay his Brother Willughby's debts. In this book there is set down money paid [to] the Counsel for perusing his Brother Sir Henry Willughby's will.[63] [f. 50]

This book gives an account of much business with Sir Hugh Willughby concerning annuities to be paid out of his land by order of Sir Henry Willughbys will, and of other matters in dispute between Sir Hugh and Mr. Medley. But Sir Hugh promised Mr. Medeley before the Lord Suffolk that he would shew himself conformable to Sir Henry's will.

But after this Mr. Medeley sets down money paid [to] the Counsel for advice upon Sir Hugh Willughbys demands, and money paid for many journeys upon Sir Hugh's account, and for his attendance at the Lord Chancellours. An: D: 1553 Sir Hugh Willughby went into Moscovie,[64] and after that there is an account of Sir Hugh's Lady with her young Son entering upon that estate called Smallwood.[65]

There is a book of Mr. Medeleys accounts for the 1st year of Queen Mary being An: D: 1553. In this book he sets down eight pounds for his costs to London to attend the Lord Suffolk for the redemption of the wardship of his Nephew Thomas Willughby.

There is set down in the book paid the Lord Suffolk 125^{li} in part of payment of a thousand pounds for the redemption of the wardship

---

[63] Mi, A 31, fo. 4. Since Anne Grey, Henry Willoughby's wife, was half-sister to George Medley, Henry Willoughby was his brother-in-law.

[64] Mi, A 31, fos 2–9v; *HMC Middleton*, 397–398. Sir Hugh Willoughby 'the Navigator' (1495–1554) set off north of Russia in 1553 to find a passage to Cathay. Richard Hakluyt, *The Principall Navigations Voiages and Discoveries of the English Nation*, 3, Pt 2 (Edinburgh, 1886), 39–40. He and his crew of seventy died while wintering in the mouth of the river 'Arzina' in Lapland. Russian sailors found the ship and the crew's bodies in the summer of 1554. Although long presumed to have died from cold or some vitamin deficiency such as scurvy, the most up-to-date theory is that the crew perished from carbon monoxide poisoning resulting from over-zealous cold-proofing and burning sea coal. Sir Hugh's will, since lost, was discovered on the ship. Eleanora C. Gordon, 'The fate of Sir Hugh Willoughby and his companions: A new conjecture', *The Geographical Journal*, 152 (July 1986), 243–247. Hugh's wife Joan later married Thomas Shelton. *CPR 1560–1563*, Elizabeth I, ii, 6.

[65] In the 1550s, there was a much-litigated manor house at Smallwood, located in Cheshire near Stoke-on-Trent. See Medley's account books regarding charges relating to matters both before and following the death of Sir Hugh Willoughby. Mi, A 31, fos 9–9v, 14v. For more on Smallwood Manor, see Text n. 439 below.

and marriage of his Nephew Thomas Willughby, which Sir Foulk Grevill[66] would else have bought of the Lord Suffolk.[67]

After this there is set down 6^s 8^d paid to the Clerk of the Signet for the writing, seal and lycence for his Cousin [nephew] Thomas Willughby to goe beyond sea to the University of Paris to study.[68]

But I question whither Mr. Thomas Willughby did goe to Paris, because in a letter from Mrs. Lenton to [f. 51] John Hall dated from the Minories February 1554 she expresses great concern that she knows not where to place Mr. Francis and Mrs. Margaret Willughby now that Mr. Medeleys house was like to be seised and they turned out of doors,[69] but she writ that the Lord Paget would have Mr. Thomas Willughby to be with him. In this letter she desired John Hall would send her some money and writ that Mrs. Medeley [Mary Danet] was constrained to borrow money.

There is a letter from Mr. Thomas Willughby to John Hall for money, not that the Lord Paget denies him any thing (he writ) but he would have some money to spend which he would not always acquaint Lord Paget with.

In another letter from Mr. Thomas Willughby to John Hall for money, he also desired him to send him his Mothers cross=bow.

This Mr. Thomas Willughby married the Lord Pagets Daughter but there is no account when they were married.[70] From some of the old papers there is reason to believe that the Lord Paget suspected Mr. Medeleys honesty, and that therefore after Mr. Thomas Willughby had married his Daughter he was willing to take some care of the Willughbys estate. Mr. Medeley has set down in one of his account books 6^s 8^d for his Counsel when

---

[66] Sir Fulke Greville (1536–1606) was married to Lady Anne Neville (d.1583), daughter of Ralph Neville, earl of Westmoreland. Through his mother Elizabeth Willoughby de Broke, he was 4th Baron Willoughby de Broke. In 1578 Francis and Elizabeth Willoughby received licence to alienate the manors of and lands in Wollaton, Sutton Passeys, and Cossall (Notts.) and also Sellinge manor and lands (Kent) to Fulk Grevyll and his heirs and assigns. *CPR 1575–1578*, Elizabeth I, vii, 468. His son, Fulke Greville (1554–1628), 1st Baron Brooke and 5th Baron Willoughby de Broke, was a councillor and courtier under Elizabeth I and James I. He was a published poet, political writer, and biographer and close friend of Philip Sidney. It is probably the son who appears later in this MS (fos 89–90, pp. 122–123) as a close associate of Sir Francis Willoughby.

[67] For some of the difficulties and expenses related to the negotiations with Lord Paget over Thomas Willoughby's wardship, see Mi, A 31, fos 10, 14–14v. 'Item payde to my Lorde of Suffolke in parte payment of a m^{li} for the redemption of the wardship & marriage of my sayd cosyn [Thomas Willoughby – described above as his nephew] which Sir Foulke Grevyll woolde ells have bought of my sayd lord [Lord Suffolk] – cxxv^{li}.' Mi, A 31, fo. 10.

[68] Mi, A 31, fo. 11; *HMC Middleton*, 398.

[69] Given that Medley's brother-in-law and nephew on his wife's side supported the Grey brothers in Wyatt's rebellion and were imprisoned, it is not surprising that Medley was under suspicion and the Minories possibly to be seized.

[70] Most likely *c.*1557. His wife was Dorothy Paget.

the Lord Paget required the executors to bring in their [f. 52] accounts.

An: D: 1555 Mr. Medeley sets down his expences in going to London to attend the Lord Padget,[71] and carrying him a letter concerning the declaration of the executors accounts made before him at Middleton and Wollaton, and also to declare the doings of Sir Nicholas Streley and Sir Hugh Willughby's Lady, who with her young Son had entered upon that estate called Smallwood. And also to attend the Lord Paget and his Counsel with the books of Peverell Fees[72] and other business relating to the affairs of the Willughbys.[73] In the 1st year of Queen Elizabeth being An:D: 1558 Mr. Medeley sets down in his account book his mans charges when he went to acquaint the Lord John [Grey of Pirgo] of the death of Mr. Thomas Willughby and about the wardship of Mr. Francis Willughby.[74] After this Mr. Medeley sets down his own charges in this book, the 2^{d} year of Queen Elizabeth, for his going to and from London about the causes of the will and what he paid for taking out a letter of administration of Mr. Thomas Willughbys goods.[75]

---

[71] Mi, A 31, fo. 14v. In the same year 1555 he wrote that the Lord Paget had expulsed Thomas Willoughby out of his house and discharged him of his service until he was helped to some 'fermes balywyke' [rents from Willoughby holdings in the Honour of Peverell]. Subsequently Medley lists legal expenses relating to a bill of complaint of Thomas Willoughby.

[72] Mi, A 31, fo. 14v. Peverell refers to lands granted to William Peverell by William I. The Willoughbys held lands in the Honour of Peverell. 'The Conqueror, as a special mark of his royal favour, bestowed on Peverell 162 manors, nine of which were situated in the county of Nottingham [...] Attached to the great honour or barony of Peverel in the counties of Nottingham and Derby, was a jurisdiction or court-leet known as Peverel Court.' Peverell might have been the Conqueror's illegitimate son. Peverell's grandson fled England, and Henry II seized the lands, bestowing most of them on his youngest son John. When John became king, they merged once again with the crown. For more on Peverell, see John Thomas Godfrey, *The Court and the Honour of Peverel: In the Counties of Nottingham and Derby* (Nottingham, 1882), 5–10; and W. Farrer, *Honors and Knights' Fees*, Vols I and II privately published, Vol. III (Manchester University Press, 1923–1925). For Strelley, see John Thoresby (ed.), *Thoroton's History of Nottinghamshire*, 3 vols (Nottingham, 1790), II, 218–222.

[73] For example, Medley wrote that Lord Paget owed a payment of £100 to Margaret Willoughby in 1555. Mi, A 31, fo. 14v; *HMC Middleton*, 522. Further on he noted that on 27 Mar. he had paid Margaret Willoughby £10 owed her from the legacy that Sir John Willoughby gave her. Mi, A 31, fo. 16v.

[74] Mi, A 31, fo. 23v. Thomas Willoughby became the heir at age 8 in 1549 and died 16 Aug. 1559. *HMC Middleton*, 399. See Mi, 6/171/10 for an indenture describing the custody, wardship, and marriage of Francis Willoughby given to Sir Francis Knollys dated 1 July 1560. It includes an attached list of all the lands and manors inherited by Francis Willoughby on his brother's death. The indenture states that at the time of his brother's death, Francis was 12 years, 30 weeks, and 2 days old. This would put his birth date at or about 17 Jan. 1546/47. See Introduction n. 118. See also L.F. Salzman (ed.), *A History of the County of Warwick: IV*, VCH (London, 1947), 157 nn. 46–48.

[75] Mi, A 31, fo. 25. For a partial inventory of the goods of Thomas Willoughby, see Mi, 7/183/7 1559.

In all this book of accounts Mr. Medeley seems to reckon very largely for his own expences, and in conclusion he sets down for the horses bridles and sadles which he had spoyled about the business of his Brother Sir Henry Willughbys will, the sume of 83^{li} 6^{sh} 8^{d}. The sum totall of this book which chiefly relates to Mr. Medeleys own charges and expences comes to 1120^{li} 9^{sh} 3^{d}.[76] In this book Mr. Medley mentions a dispute about the Castle Inn, in Holbourn, which he setts down was intailed by his Brother Sir Henry Willughby.[77]

I could find no farther account of Mr. Thomas Willughby, but that over heating himself with hunting he fell sick and dyed [f. 53] upon the 16th of August An: D: 1558 [*sic*].[78]

By Mr. Medeleys account book Mr. Francis Willughby was removed from St. Antonies School in London and was sent to Walden School[79] in June An: D: 1555. He stayed there till February the 17th. Paid for his board there all that time at 2^s a week 3^{li} 10^{s} 0^{d}. There is set down in this account book paid [to] the Master at severall times for his schooling and in rewards to him severall sumes which altogether amounts to but the sume of 14^{sh} 2^{d}. For his learning to sing while there 5^s and for his learning to wright

---

[76] Mi, A 31, fo. 26v. The total is written iicxx^{li} ix^s iii^d. Many of these expenses are for the costs of horses, boat hire, and food when travelling between London, Wollaton, Middleton, and Tilty. There are also ongoing significant costs for advice of counsel in a number of legal matters.

[77] *HMC Middleton*, 398. W.H. Stevenson has copied down the following extract from George Medley's account book Mi, A 31, fo. 10v: 'This terme I hadde to doe with Gromewell and with Mr. George Wylloughbye, who demaunded all the evidences of the Castell in Holbourne, which is intayled by the last wyll of my brother Willoughbye.' See also Mi, 7/181/7 for proceedings relating to 'le Castell' granted by the King to John Beaumounte and by him to Henry Willoughby, Esq., dated 1544/45. The tenement was located in St Andrew's parish, Holborn. Mi, 7/181/8 is a note of writings delivered by 'Francis Wyllughby' to 'George Wyllughby' relating to 'le Castell' in 1568.

[78] In the extracts from the accounts of George Medley from 1549 to 1562 (Mi, A 31, fo. 23v), W.H. Stevenson copied down under the year 1559 a payment to his servant Philip for 'for his chargez ryding to Horsseley to the corte with Henry Medley, signifying to my Lord John that my nepveu Thomas Wylloughbye was departed'. *HMC Middleton*, 399. Cassandra has mistaken 1558 for 1559. See the inventory of goods of 'Thomas Willughbie' dated 17 Aug. 1559 [Mi, 7/183/7], as well as his Inquisition *Post Mortem* 1 May 1560 [Mi, 7/183/10–11] and the 9 Sept. 1559 grant of administration to George Willoughbie [Mi, 7/183/8]. See Mi, A 31, fo. 25 for a complaint against George Willoughby in 1560. See also Mi, 6/171/10 for the date of death of Thomas Willoughby as 16 Aug. 1 Elizabeth.

[79] *HMC Middleton*, 409–411; Mi, A 32, fos 22, 25, 28v, pp. 41, 47, 54. Most likely Saffron Walden School in Essex, where there was a school as early as 1317 and a grammar school by 1423. In 1525 the grammar school was endowed, becoming a free school. Orme, *English Schools in the Middle Ages*, 314. It appears that Francis first went to Saffron Walden in 1554. He was then at St Anthony's in London for the first half of 1555. He was back at Saffron Walden in June 1555 and into 1556.

one shiling.[80] In the account book for cloaths for Master Francis Willughby some things are remarkably cheap, as seven pence for a hat and three half pence a pair for gloves etc.

This account book shews that Mr. Francis Willughby and his man were at Tyltey from the 17th of February to the 5th day of July in the 4th year of Queen Mary. There is set down for his and his mans board that space of time 15^{li} and for fewel and washing in that time 15^{sh} and for the steward that kept the accounts ten pounds.

And again for his board from the 5th of July to that time twelve= month there is set down 26^{li} and for his man's board 13^{li} and for fewel and washing for them forty shillings. And for the steward that kept the accounts 10^{li}. And again there is set down for his board at Tyltey from that 5th day of July in the 5th year of Queen Mary to the 17th of April twenty pounds, and for his mans board the same time ten pounds, and for fewell 2^{li}. And for his man's board seven weeks at London 6^{li} 5^{sh} 0^{d}. And again for his and his man's board at Tyltey from June the 5th to July the 6th 3^{li} 7^{sh} 6^{d}. [f. 54] And for the servant that kept his accounts the whole year 10^{li}.

And again for Mr. Francis Willoughby's and his man's board at Tyltey in the 6th year of Queen Mary [1558] from July the 6th to October the 17th 11^{li} 5^{sh} 0^{d}, and for Fewill 12^{sh}. And for the servant that kept his accounts 10^{li}. And for his and his man's board at Tyltey from October the 17th to August the 18th (being the first year of Queen Elizabeth and An: D: 1559) there is set down 14^{li} 10^{sh} 0^{d}. And for the servant that kept the accounts 10^{li}.[81]

It may here be observed how large the reckoning for Master Francis Willughbys dyet was at Tyltey, if compared with the two shillings a week paid for him at school, and the severall sumes in reward to his Master and for his schooling all to amount to no more than 14^{sh} 2^{d}.

There are in the Library at Wollaton severall books of Mr. John Hall's accounts for the young Willughby's. In one for the 3^{d} year of Queen Mary, February the 25th he sets down what his charges were to and from London when he was sent for thither by the Lord Privie-Seal[82] who thought Mr. Medeley was at that time gone out of the Realm. There is also set down in Mr. Halls accounts

---

[80] See J.H. Moran, *The Growth of English Schooling 1350–1540* (Princeton, 1985), for an analysis of reading and grammar education in the first half of the 16th century. Learning to sing was often taught separately from reading and grammar. It was also common to employ a separate writing master, as was the case with Francis.

[81] There is another account book of 'The book of charges at Mr. Medleye and Mr. Berwickes being at Wollaton', dated Mar. 1560 [Mi, 7/183/9].

[82] Lord Paget, who held the wardship of Thomas Willoughby and whose daughter Thomas married, was made lord privy seal in Jan. 1556.

many little sumes of money paid to Mrs. Lenton for the children's boards, very often for but a week at a time.

There is a letter from Mr. Medley to [John] Trussell[83] who was the Baily at Wollaton, dated An: D: 1552, to order him to make provision for baking and brewing etc. against the Lord [f. 55] John Grey's coming thither.

There is a letter from Mr. Medeley to John Hall at Middleton, dated from Tyltey August 1553, to desire some of the leveretts[84] bread [bred] at Middleton might be saved for the Lord John.

There is a letter from Mr. Medeley to Trussell about buying Sir Hugh Willughbys estate in Maperley[85] and Basford. He writes that what makes him fear to goe through with it was the recognyzance wherein he stood bound to the Kings Majesty. An: D: 1553

There is an angry letter from Mr. Medeley to Trussell (on April 1562) because he neglected to keep Wollaton in good repair and let the tenants houses goe down; he orders such timber as is needfull to be cut down and the houses to be repaired, and tells him Middleton is otherwise kept, which he may be ashamed off.

There is a letter from Mr. Medeley to Mr. Francis Willughby, dated from Tyltey January 1565,[86] in which he makes heavie complaints of his own debts, but writes that he will not trouble Mr.

---

[83] In 1542 John Trussell is listed as a servant under Sir John Willoughby. *HMC Middleton*, 388. In 1542/3 he is listed as 'gent. and "serviens Domino" ', accounting for various payments, again in 1544/5 accounting for costs and receipts from the coal-pits, and again in 1549/50, in the wake of Henry Willoughby's death accounting for household expenses. *HMC Middleton*, 315–316, 396. Trussell was the bailiff at Wollaton by 1546/7 and still bailiff in 1562, as is clear from Medley's letters to Trussell mentioned here. In 1550 he was one of several who appraised the goods of Henry Willoughby, father of Francis. *HMC Middleton*, 474. Trussell came from a Warwickshire gentry family and was the second son of William Trussell and Cicely Curzon of Billesley Trussell near Stratford-upon-Avon, an estate that was confiscated in the 1580s owing to highway robberies of his great-nephew, Thomas Trussell. Trussell was probably born between 1513 (the possible birth date of his older brother Avery) and 1517, the death date of his father. He married Bridget Marmion, daughter of Henry Marmion. Their son William married Catherine Itell [Ithell?], and a daughter Joane may have married John Squire. All of these names, Ithell, Squire, Trussell, and Marmion (and perhaps even Joane) figure among the servants of the Willoughbys at Wollaton. A Henry Trussell, servant to Elizabeth Willoughby and often mentioned during the time of separation of Francis and Elizabeth, may have been another son of John Trussell. A grandson of John Trussell was John Trussell (1575–1648), poet and historian. On the Trussells, see Robert Frederick William Smith, 'John Trussell: A life (1575–1648)', PhD thesis, University of Southampton, 2013, appendix A.

[84] Young hares less than a year old, *OED*.

[85] In 1507, the property at Mapperley was known as Le Park Halle (today Park Hall in Derbyshire). By 1599, the estate was in the will of Benjamin Smithe. *James v. Smithe*, Chancery (hereafter C), TNA, C 2/Eliz/I1/20.

[86] George Medley died in 1562/3; his will was proved 3 Feb. 1563. TNA, PROB 11/46/75. See also Mi, 1/7/183/12. This must be Henry Medley, the son of George and Mary, although the very next reference, to an account from Mr Medley, clearly refers to George Medley.

Willughby now, because he looks upon him as his chiefest friend, and therefore he reserves him for his greater need. He expresses great concern for his Lady's mishap in her travell and wishes they may both be joyfull Parants of a jolly many Son's.[87]

There is an account which shews that Mr. Medeley demanded 350^{li} for his discharging the trust which Sir Henry Willughby had reposed in him and in this account there is mention made of money which he paid the Duke of Suffolk by Sir Henry Willughby's order.

There are severall letters from Mr. Medeleys widow, to Sir Francis Willoughby An: D: 1568, about her Husbands accounts. In one of the letters she enlarges upon the great care his Uncle Medeley took upon him for 13 years [1549–1562] together to sattisfie the trust which his Father had reposed in him.

[1564–1567: Marriage of Francis Willoughby and Elizabeth Lyttleton: Staying at the Lyttletons]

[f. 55v] There is the copy of a letter from Mr. Francis Willughby to his Uncle the Lord Grey [John Grey of Pirgo] to make him acquainted that he had been invited to many of his friends and kinsmens houses, amongst the rest (as he trusts God did appoint it) he was at Mr. Lyttleton's at Frankley in Worcestershire,[88] sundry times received with great chear and good entertainment, and in the end it was moved to him first by good Lord Dudley[89] and after by Mr.

---

[87] This letter, dated Jan. 1565/6, was written one or two years after the marriage of Francis Willughby to Elizabeth Lyttleton. This letter tells us that Elizabeth was pregnant (possibly with a son) and seems to suggest that she miscarried. There is an irony in the wish for jolly many sons, since Elizabeth was to have at least twelve pregnancies, but the only surviving children were six girls.

[88] See J.M.J. Tonks, 'The Lyttletons of Frankley', MLitt thesis, University of Oxford, 1978. The Lyttletons were an old-established Worcestershire family with lands in the county in the 13th century. They inherited Frankley in 1405 and further established themselves with the career of Sir Thomas Littleton/Lyttleton (1422–1481), who became judge of the common pleas and was famed as author of a *Treatise on Tenure*. Subsequently the family held extensive properties in Shropshire, and two of Thomas Littleton's descendants at Frankley married heiresses. John Lyttleton (1519–1590), the father of Elizabeth, began with substantial properties and throughout his life consolidated his holdings, managing them closely. He was also invested in coal mining and house building, much like his soon-to-be son-in-law. John Lyttleton had been a person of some substance in the court of Queen Mary. Under Elizabeth he reconciled himself to the Elizabethan religious settlement but remained a Catholic sympathizer; as a leader of the north Worcestershire gentry, he joined the county bench, served as high sheriff and MP, and his supporters dominated local and county offices. Tonks, 'Lyttletons', ch. 2.

[89] Robert Dudley, 1st earl of Leicester (1532–1588), Elizabeth's favourite. Dudley had been rehabilitated in 1557 and named earl of Leicester in 1564. The scandal caused by

Lyttleton, a marriage between his Daughter [Elizabeth] and himself. After good deliberation it had pleased God to give him a liking to the young Gentlewoman, who had had a good education and was descended from a house of great antiquity, well friended and alyed, dwelling near his house of Middleton. And Mr. Lyttletons offers with his Daughter being reasonable, could he have his Lordships favour he was fully minded to match himself to her

Mr. Lyttleton offer'd to give with his Daughter 1500^{li}, to apparell her decently, to bear their charges at the time of their marriage, and to give them their table with six persons to attend them, for three years, and the keeping of six geldings.[90] He writes that his Cousin Medley[91] can at large declare to him the manner of his proceeding, and he desires his Lordships favour and good will that he may proceed herein according to his good advice.

There is the copy of a very angry letter from[iv] Mr. Francis Willughby to his Brother Arundell[92] (dated An: D: 1564) for being against his marrying Mrs. Lyttleton, for which he had the advice of his Cousin Medley, the Lord Dudley, the Lord John Grey,[93] and other of his Friends.

---

the death of his wife Amy Robsart in 1560 excluded any possibility of his marrying Elizabeth. Elizabeth banned from court Lettice Knollys, his second wife, who was Elizabeth's cousin and former favourite.

[90] For the 20 Nov. 1564 marriage settlement documents, see Mi, 7/183/19–20. This was a very generous marriage settlement for the time. Tonks calls it 'a massive sum for an upper gentry family' and not surprising that 'Lyttelton was slow in making payment'. Tonks, 'Lyttletons', 44–45. The settlement amount is even more surprising considering that John Lyttleton had to provide for three sons and four daughters.

[91] This must be Henry Medley, son of George Medley and Mary Danet. In 1569, however, Gabriel Berwyke wrote to Francis Willoughby reproving him for marrying 'without the consent of Mr Medley, Mr Haule and me' (Mi, C 14). This seems to contradict the evidence here that Medley, at least, was very much involved in the marriage negotiations.

[92] Matthew Arundell of Wardour Castle in Wiltshire (c.1533–1598/9), also known as Matthew Arundell-Howard, married Francis Willoughby's sister Margaret in 1559. Matthew's father Thomas, favourite of Anne Boleyn, purchased Wardour Castle in 1547 during the monastic dissolutions. Although Arundell was executed for treason in 1551/2, the Crown returned Thomas's lands to his widow Margaret Howard (d.1571), lifting the attainder from the father's treason. The Arundells had been staunchly Roman Catholic. While Matthew's brother was a recusant. Matthew conformed to the Church of England. Matthew's mother was a first cousin of Anne Boleyn, and thus Matthew was second cousin to Queen Elizabeth. For his will, see TNA, PROB 11/93/86, dated 6 Feb. 1598/99.

[93] The fact that Lord John Grey was involved with this negotiation may help to date the marriage. From Aug. 1563 John Grey had taken custody of his niece, Catherine Grey, but that relationship was compromised in Apr. 1564 when a book by John Hales arguing for the validity of Catherine's claim to succession to the throne was published. Lord Grey, as a result, was taken temporarily into custody, and he died in 19 Nov. 1564. It is likely that the marriage between Francis and Elizabeth, then, took place early in 1564, prior to the eruption of further political troubles for the Grey family.

[f. 56] From An: D: 1559 that Mr Francis Willughby was at Tyltey till near the time of his marrying I don't find where he was, but believe he might spend most of that time at the University.

His Sister the Lady Arundell I believe was elder then he, and by being much together when they were children, she had [estimed?] and gain'd to herself such a[v] power of governing[vi] him, that after when he was grown up, she could not leave of [off] the custom she had used in their childhood, but continued to expect that her Brother should advise with her in all his affairs, and therefore when she had heard it was reported that her Brother was going to marry Mr. Lyttleton of Frankeley's Daughter, she was very angry with him for begining such a treaty without first making her acquainted [with] it, and express'd her resentment of it in severall letters.

One she begins with blaming his breach of promise in not coming to London, and then goes on to tell him 'tis reported that he is insured to Mr. Littletons Daughter. She writes that she marvels much that his hast[vii] should be so great, and his estimation of her so little, as never to consult her in the matter, who was always willing to doe anything which might be a pleasure to him[;?] she understood George Willoughby had procured him this marriage, she believed out of some crafty designs of his own, else he would never have perswaded him to proceed so far without consulting any of his friends. She desires him not to trust to George Willoughbys painted words, nor to let his flatery abase him so much as to make him think that he was the only able person to be of his counsel, for he had divers friends that had more care for him, and were better able to advise him. She desires to see him – but writes, if this thing be already past, I pray God to send you as good speed as your hast has been great, which seldom goes [f. 57] together.

There are many more letters in the Library at Wollaton which shew that Lady Arundell was extreamly against her Brother['?]s marrying Mrs. Lyttleton, which he took very unkindly from her and at last began to suspect that Lady Arundell coveted his estate and therefore would be [against his marrying?] any body. Lady Arundell being made acquainted with these thoughts which her Brother had of her, writ him a long letter upon this subject, to justifie her self, and in it gave her reasons why she was against this match, viz: because she thought Mr. John Lyttleton was an ill man, that he was a great dissembler, etc.

There is a story in Dugdales Antiquities of Warwickshire[94] which if true, and of the same Sir John Littleton, would give one reason to

---

[94] Sir William Dugdale, *The Antiquities of Warwickshire* (London, 1656), 37–39.

believe Lady Arundells thoughts that he was an ill man, was but too well grounded.

The story is this.

Sir Walter Smyth of Shirford that was murthered by his Lady, left Richard his Son, his heir. This Richard had but one only Daughter by his first Wife, and doubting of issue male, treated of a match for her with Sir John Littleton of Frankley in Worcestershire for his third Son, and agree'd to settle all his estate, in remainder,[95] after his own decease without other issue upon the said William Littleton and Margaret his Daughter, and their issue, and for want of such issue, to return to his own right heirs. And having the writings drawn he trusted to Sir John Littleton to get them ingrossed, which being done [f. 58] and a day appointed for sealing, Mr. Smyth came over to Frankley where he found very noble entertainment and some of Sir Johns friends to bear him company; in whose presence the writings were brought out and began to be read. But before they came to the uses, there was a plot laid to carry Mr. Smyth a coursing,[96] and Sir John protesting the writings were according to the draughts he had seen, Smyth sealed them, to goe to the park. The children (being about nine years old a piece) were married. About six years after William Littleton dyed. Smyth demanded his Daughter again, but Sir John designing to marry her to his second Son George, refused to deliver her. Upon this dispute the writings were produced, and it appeared by that settlement, so sealed in hast, that for want of issue by this William and Margaret, the estate was to goe to the right heirs of William Littleton, which was Gilbert Littleton his eldest Brother. So William the youngest Son married her, George the second Son enjoy'd her, and Gilbert the eldest Son had her estate, and kept it from Mr. Smyth the true heir, with whom he had great law sutes.[97]

---

[95] A real estate term meaning a future interest given to someone after the expiration of a prior estate, such as a life estate.

[96] 'The sport of chasing hares or other game with greyhounds, by sight,' *OED*.

[97] Cassandra closely follows Dugdale for this portion of the account. It may be, however, that Smith had received £420 from John Lyttleton to allow the reversion to the Lyttletons rather than to any heir he might have. According to Dugdale, Richard Smyth had already experienced substantial tragedy when his aged father Walter married the woman originally intended for Richard; she subsequently, in 1553, had Walter Smyth strangled, as Cassandra notes. The estate of Shirford, gained by the Lyttletons through their negotiations with Richard Smyth, escheated to the Crown when Gilbert Lyttleton's son John participated in Essex's rebellion and died in prison. The son and heir of George and Margaret was Stephen Lyttleton, who, being one of the conspirators of the Gunpowder Plot, lost his life and his estate. Richard Smyth spent the rest of his life pursuing various lawsuits, trying to regain his lost inheritance. This tainted marriage settlement must have been well known at the time, as was the murder of Walter Smyth. For the text of the contested settlement

Lady Arundell not having power enough with her Brother to break the match, though by many letters it appears she used her outmost endeavours, at last sends him her good wishes in the mannor I shall shew by copying part of a letter from her to her Brother which she dates from the Court at St James's. She writes that it well appears [f. 59] that what he writ to her was not his own thoughts but what George Willoughby counseled. She writes that he does her wrong to say she does not like the Gentlewoman. Her saying they were more in hast then they needed, she thought was no dispraise to her. She writes that she can't take it well of him, to burden her with being unwilling that he should marry in hopes she might enjoy his estate; this she writes comes not from himself, who knew that her behaviour to him had deserved a better opinion, himself best knew if she, or any body for her had ever perswaded him not to marry. If she had been against his marrying, she would not have consented to the buying out of his wardship, and he well knew the executors would not have paid the money if she and Mr Arundell had not consented.[98] And if this were all she had to say, she thought this a sufficient proof that she was not against his marrying.

She desires him to make her commendations to her Sister that shall be, with whom she desires to be acquainted, and she wishes them happily to match, and joyfully to live together, and that God may bless them with such increase of children as may be most to both their comforts.

1564 There is the copy of[viii] a letter from Mr. Francis Willughby dated from Frankley, November 1564,[ix] to his Sister the Lady Arundell, in which he tells her that he had then resolved to marry Mrs. Lyttleton, that he was first moved to this marriage by his near Kindsman, the very good Lord Dudley, and divers others who bore him good will; that the Lord Grey (who in duty he thought he ought to advise [f. 60] with) approved of his choice. That Mr. Lyttleton was of a very ancient family and a very good alliance, and had given his Daughter a very good education,[99] and gave her

---

document, confirming Dugdale's (and Cassandra's) account of its contents, see Mi, 7/183/15, dated 15 Mar. 1564, and Mi, 6/176/156, dated 4 Aug. 1566. From other documents, it appears that part of Smyth's estate went from the Lyttletons to Francis Willoughby. See Mi, 7/183/21. On the payment for the reversion, see Tonks, 'Lyttletons', 46 n. 1.

[98] For information on the wardship of Francis Willoughby, which had belonged to Sir Francis Knollys in 1560 but was bought out by the executors of the will of Francis's father in 1564, see Introduction, p. 32. Other than this slight allusion, Cassandra's Account does not address these transactions.

[99] We have no information regarding Elizabeth Lyttleton's education, but it is likely that she learned from a tutor at home and would have been trained to play musical instruments,

a good fortune, and required a very reasonable joynture and the settlement of but one third part of his estate upon heirs male by her etc.[100]

Mr. Lyttleton gave his Daughter 1500^{li} and three years board for themselves their horses and six servants.[101]

There is a friendly letter from Sir Matthew Arundell to Mr. Francis Willughby which gives an account of some things which he had bought for him, and that he had sent him some songs, strings, and three books. And for his Sister[102] some white Flanders work, not so fine as he would have had, but such as was to be had in London, and some combs, and he writes that his Wife had sent a partlet[103] and a pair of sleeves. And if he might know what other things he would have from London he would provide them. He returns thanks to Mr. Littleton and his Lady for his well usage and good cheer. And concludes, I bid you fare as my self, in hast from the Court the 20th of May. Your Brother most lovingly.

There is a letter from Lady Arundell to her Brother Willughby in which she desires to know how his executors had dealt with him and in what condition he had found his land and houses. She writes that she perceives by Mr. Lyttleton, that as yet he has dealt but little in these [f. 61] affairs, and it is her opinion that the sooner he takes them in hand the better it will be both for his experience and profit. She writes that if Sir Matthew Arundell might know when he was to goe into Dorsetshire he would accompany him. She concludes Thus with my hearty commendations to my Sister and you, I bid you fare=well wishing you as I would my self.

There is a letter from Sir John Lyttleton, (who I must now call Sir) to Mr. Willughby, who from this time I will call Sir Francis, not

---

to read and write both English and French, and learned sufficient Latin to read, at a minimum, devotional books and scripture.

[100] 'A Joynture is a competent Livelihood of Freehold Lands or Tenements, etc. for the Wife to take Effect presently in possession or Profit after the natural Death of the Husband, for the Life of the Wife at least, if she herself is not the Cause of the Determination or Forfeiture of it [...] This Definition of a Joynture is made with Respect to the Statute of 27 H. 8 [the Statute of Uses].' Thomas Wood, *An Institute of the Laws of England*, 4th edn (London, 1724), 125. See also John Baker, *The Oxford History of the Laws of England, 1483–1558*, VI (Oxford, 2003), 677, 689. The Lyttletons made generous concessions to the Willoughbys in only requiring a third of the Willoughby estates to be settled on the heirs male of the couple and a 'very reasonable' jointure for Elizabeth. Tonks 'Lyttletons', 44.

[101] See above, fo. 55v, p. 88.

[102] Referring to Elizabeth Lyttleton, who, by the time of this letter, had married Francis Willughby.

[103] Neck and shoulder garment for women, often ruffled.

finding when the Queen knighted him.[104] This letter is dated August the 24th 1566. In it he writes his Son in law word, that if he had not so suddenly departed from Killingworth [Kenilworth] he would have made his Daughter a Lady, for he was sought for but could not be found, within an hour after he was gone, when there were six knights made, viz: Sir William Devereux, Sir George Hastings, Sir John Throgmorton, Sir Foulke Grevile, Sir George Turpin (Sherif of Warwick, and Leicester) and himself.[105] He writes that the Queen went to Mr. Lucyes house, and that the Lord Leicester attended upon her Majesty till her Highness was pass'd Warwick,[106] and then returned to Killingworth, and so much company with him that one would have judged there was nobody wanting but the Queens Highness. And after a days stay at Killingworth he went to the Court.

There is a letter from Sir Matthew Arundell to Sir Francis Willughby to complain of his ill hap not to see his Father in law [sic][107] at the Court, and also complaining that Sir Francis Willughby does not write to him. He hopes being at such a distance will not cause [f. 62] Sir Francis Willoughby to forget him, and writes that it is an evil dog that is not worth regarding.[108]

In another letter Sir Matthew writes Sir Francis Willughby that his Sister will see him at Easter and tarry a month with him, in the mean season use her and me as you judg you may.

In another letter Sir Mathew writes Sir Francis Willoughby that he had been at Woodland[109] to receive the Lord

---

[104] Francis Willoughby was not knighted until 27 July 1575, at his house in Middleton. William Catesby was knighted at the same time. Arthur F. Kinney and Jane A. Lawson (eds), *Titled Elizabethans: A Directory of Elizabethan State and Church Officers and Knights, with Peers of England, Scotland, and Ireland, 1558–1603*, expanded edn (New York, 2014), 199.

[105] *Ibid.* 194. On 20–21 Aug. 1566 John Lyttleton, along with the others named by Cassandra, were knighted by the earl of Leicester at Kenilworth.

[106] Elizabeth visited Kenilworth 19 to 22 Aug. 1566 and went on from there to Warwick Castle and to the house of Sir Thomas Lucy at Charlecote by 24 Aug. Mary Hill Cole, *The Portable Queen: Elizabeth I and the Politics of Ceremony* (Amherst, MA, 1999), app. 2, p. 182. E. Goldring, F. Eales, E. Clarke and J.E. Archer (eds), John Nichols's *The Progresses and Public Processions of Queen Elizabeth I: A New Edition of the Early Modern Sources*, I (Oxford, 2014), 465–466. Other than Cassandra's reference here, there is little surviving description of the 1566 visit to Kenilworth.

[107] Presumably he is referring to Francis Willoughby, although Francis was his brother-in-law.

[108] John Ray, *A Complete Collection of English Proverbs* (1768; rev. edn, London, 1813), 101: 'It is an ill dog that is not worth the whistling'; 'It is an ill dog that deserves not a crust.'

[109] Woodland was an estate in Dorset that had belonged to Sir Edward Willoughby (d.1541). Woodland eventually passed to Francis Willoughby and his heirs, coming to Dorothy Willoughby, Francis's second daughter, and her husband Henry Hastings, but

Herbert[110] who came and killed a buck in the Park with his hounds, of which pack tho he might have commanded, yet he would not send Sir Francis Willoughby any, because he did not like them, nor can he commend the hounds of that Country; but if he hears of any good he will try to get them, or any thing else which he shall have a mind to. He has sent a brace of young dogs apt for game. He writes that he will not fail the Queen at Oxford, where he wishes Sir Francis Willughby would also be. There is like to be great shews of learning, and a notable tragedy[111] there is in hand, and if he would come Sir Matthew promises to be his harbinger. Dated from Wilton. [1566].

There is a letter from Lady Arundell which gives an account of the Earl of Leicesters entertainment of the Court at Kellemyale [Kenilworth] his house; and she also seems to write with pleasure of an entertainment which he gave to Sir Francis Willughby and the rest of his country gentlemen. This letter tells her Brother that she has made enquiry but could not yet hear of one that could play and sing[;?] but she hopes she shall provide him one when she goes to London. She writes that she has seen his house of Woodland, which is very ancient and in great decay. She concludes with thanks for his mare, commendations to his wife, Sir John Lyttleton, and his Lady, with thanks for [f. 63] their courtious entertainment of her.

The date of the year, is not writ to any of these letters from Lady Arundell. But there are many very friendly letters from Sir John Lyttleton to Sir Francis Willughby dated An: D: 1566 and 1567, which seem to have been writ when Sir Francis had gone journeys of business from Frankley. In one Sir John thanks Sir Francis Willughby for a fat buck. In another he wishes Sir Francis Willughbys business were finished that they might soon see him again at Frankley, and sends hearty commendations from his [Francis's] Wife and Mother [Mother-in-law].

---

not without a great deal of trouble, as Cassandra's Account below describes (see fos 166–169, pp. 208–212 below).

[110] William Herbert, 1st earl of Pembroke (1506/7–1570). His landed estates in Wiltshire and Wales made him one of the most powerful men in England. He was named high steward of the royal household in 1568. P. Sil Narasingha, 'Herbert, William, first earl of Pembroke', *ODNB*.

[111] Elizabeth visited Oxford from 31 Aug. to 6 Sept. in 1566. Cole, *The Portable Queen*, app. 2, p. 182; Nichols's *Progresses and Public Processions*, 1, 466–672, for the many orations, disputations, plays, and poems presented to Elizabeth while there. The tragedy was a Latin tragedy called 'Progne' ['Procne'], written by Gregorio Correr *c.*1427; the other play on Palamon and Arcite turned into a tragedy when part of the stage collapsed and several people were killed.

[Established at Wollaton, 1567?][112]

In a letter from Sir John Lyttleton to Sir Francis Willughby dated An: D: 1569 he expresses a kind concern for his Daughter's health, and also a concern for not paying the whol sume of money that was due, at the time he had promised it, but he writ that he had been ill used by his attorney, and therefore could only send now by the bearer 110^li.

There is a letter from Lady Arundell to Sir Francis Willughby dated from the Court. In this letter she writes that tho he has no great matter to write off [of] yet it pleaseth her to hear of his good state, as she had lately done by the Lords that were with him, who had told her they had not seen him look so well of a good time, which made her think he had recover'd his cough. She writes that she here incloses the letter he desired, which was not sent to herself but to Sir Matthew, and in his absence she intersepted it, and intended to have kept it to shew him if he had not sent for it. She desires to know if Sir John Lyttleton had paid the money, or set the day when he would, and [f. 64] wishes him better fortune with the rest that is to come than he has hitherto had etc.

In another letter Lady Arundell writes Sir Francis Willughby that she should have thought Sir John Lyttletons house the best place for him to have been in, had he been such a man as he professed, but in his dealing with him he had verified her opinion of him, that he was a great dissembler, and for that reason it was that she misliked his matching into that house. For his Wife she writes, that ways might be found to deal with her, whose country friends would stand her in but little stead. She writes that she intended to stay at the Court all Sumer.

There is a letter from Lady Arundell to her Brother dated from Shaftesbury[113] in which she hopes business of his side is less

---

[112] Sometime between 1567 and 1569 Elizabeth and Francis moved out of Frankley and into the Willoughby households. On 6 June 1568 Robert Penruddoke of Hale signed an indenture turning over documents relating to the lands, accounts, rentals, drafts of wills, surveys, bills of complaint, leases, lists of feofees, depositions, etc. releasing the Dorset estates to Sir Francis Willoughby, now aged 20 and coming into his inheritance. Mi, 5/167/154. Penruddoke was the chief steward for the Dorset estates. See also Mi, 7/183/22–25, dated 1566–1568.

[113] Shaftesbury Abbey in Dorset was dissolved in 1539 by Thomas Cromwell and purchased by Sir Thomas Arundell, Sir Matthew's father, in 1540. William Herbert, 1st earl of Pembroke, bought the Abbey from the Crown after it was seized in 1552 owing to Thomas Arundell's attainder. Matthew and his mother lost everything and had to flee the country for awhile. It took Matthew at least two decades to recover his properties (he never did get Shaftesbury Abbey back). 'Shaftesbury', in *An Inventory of the Historical*

troublesome than with them, where the great murther[114] has been done and favour procured for the help of them. His cares she guesses is building and setting up of houses. She makes a doubt whither his Wife will like housekeeping, especially when she knows of the company he means to have.[115] She thinks she can't come to him till after Easter [1567?], and believes in the mean time he will not be idle. She desires to know how his last being at the Bath [spa][116] proved with him, and concludes wishing his well doing.

In another letter, which Lady Arundell dates from the Court, she writes her Brother that she thinks the time long since she heard any thing from him, and she is very desirous to know how he likes houskeeping, now, before she can come herself to see. She is sorry she can't now fix the [f. 65] time when that shall be. She writes that the Lord Admirall[117] desires that when he sells his woods he may have them for his money before any other, which will be a conveniency to him, being so near his house and also to himself. She concludes wishing long the well doing of himself and his Wife.

There is another letter from Lady Arundell to her Brother, in which she wishes he had not began his work upon the Treant[118] (the making it navigable) because it would be so chargable. She writes that she thinks his Wife should not be so unreasonable, and if he continues at Middleton that will make a tryal, whither she more desires to enjoy his company or follow her own will. She writes

---

Monuments in Dorset, 4: *North* (London, 1972), 55–76; British History Online, 'Shaftesbury', http://www.british-history.ac.uk/rchme/dorset/vol4/pp55-76 (accessed 31 Mar. 2018).

[114] The most likely reference is to the murder of Lord Darnley (Henry Stuart, duke of Albany, husband of Mary Stuart, and potential successor to the English throne) which took place the night of 10 Feb. 1566/7, which would date this letter to 1567. Darnley and his mother, Margaret Douglas, had been at the English court from 1563 until early 1565, in which case Margaret would have known them.

[115] Elizabeth and Francis had a three-year commitment for room and board at the Lyttletons. In 1567 they were reaching the end of this agreement and should have been moving over to Middelton and/or Wollaton.

[116] Bath is a general term for spa. It could also reference the spa in the town of Bath, although the Willoughbys seem to have frequented the spa at Buxton.

[117] Edward Fiennes de Clinton (between 1512 and 1516–Jan. 1585), 1st earl of Lincoln, lord high admiral 1550–1553 and 1559–1585. Clinton was a privy counsellor under Edward VI and helped subdue Wyatt's Rebellion in 1554. He was sent with Ambrose Dudley, earl of Warwick, to subdue the 1569 Northern Rebellion, in which the Catholic earls Northumberland and Westmorland attempted to depose Elizabeth in favour of Mary, Queen of Scots. Clinton became earl of Lincoln in 1572. Anne Duffin, 'Clinton, Edward Fiennes, first earl of Lincoln (1512–1585)', *ODNB*.

[118] The River Trent, probably for shipping coal. This widening does not appear to have taken place.

that she is uncertain whither her Highness will goe to York, or stay at Kyllingworth.[119]

In a letter dated from Wilton Lady Arundell writes Sir Francis Willughby that she is come from the Court to Lord Pembrokes house in Wiltshire[120] where she intends to stay 3 months, and e're it be long Mr. Arundell will begin to keep house. She writes that before she left the Court she dealt with the Lord Warwick concerning setting forth men towards Scotland,[121] and found him so willing to pleasure Sir Francis that he said he should have consider'd it himself if she had not spoke, and did assure her that he would not be unmindfull of it when occasion should serve. In this letter she writes that she thinks her Aunt Topclyfe[122] is sorry she is come down, and that she has got profers for her Husband, but wishes Sir Francis Willughby would doe something in the matter, for she believed if he perceived [f. 66] that he would take his Aunts part, he would then[x] offer some reasonable provision for her. In this letter she prays to be remember'd to her Sister, and looks daily to hear of her good delivery,

---

[119] This may refer to the visit that Queen Elizabeth made to Kenilworth from 13–16 Aug. 1572. Nichols's *Progresses and Public Processions*, II, 38. The following letters, however, from Margaret Arundell are earlier – from 1569–1570. Elizabeth never did make a journey to York. See Cole, *The Portable Queen*, app. 2.

[120] Wilton House in Wiltshire, near Salisbury, formerly Wilton Abbey. Henry VIII presented the estate to Sir William Herbert, afterwards the 1st earl of Pembroke, in the 1540s.

[121] Ambrose Dudley, 3rd earl of Warwick (*c.*1528–1590), elder brother to Robert Dudley, earl of Leicester, was sent with Clinton to subdue the 1569 Northern Rebellion. This dates Margaret's letter to late 1569/early 1570. The references to Jane Topcliffe in the same and subsequent letters also suggest a date of 1569/1570.

[122] Jane Willoughby Topcliffe (*c.*1525–*c.*1571) was the daughter of Edward Willoughby of Wollaton (1467–1541) and Anne Filliol. She married Richard Topcliffe (1531–1604) of Somersby, Lincs., who later became notorious for the use of torture in interrogating recusants and Catholic priests. They had four sons and two daughters. Jane separated from her husband at some point before her death, which would be before he made a career out of interrogating those who did not conform to the Church of England. The *History of Parliament* places Topcliffe in a house in Westminster in 1571 and states that at some point (no dates given), his personal life was 'clouded' by his 'alleged failure to pay his wife adequate maintenance'. http://www.historyofparliamentonline.org/volume/1558-1603/member/topcliffe-richard-1531-1604 (accessed 20 June 2018). On Topcliffe, see Adrian Morey, *The Catholic Subjects of Elizabeth I* (London and Boston, and Totowa, NJ, 1978), 87, 118, 138, 201; and Questier, *Catholicism and Community in Early Modern England, passim*. Carole Levin calls Topcliffe, 'A man of dubious integrity and strange reputation' and lists, in a footnote, a variety of views by modern historians on Topcliffe. She mentions his interrogation of Thomas Portmort, priest, who claimed that Topcliffe bragged of his intimate personal and physical relationship with the Queen. Levin, *The Heart and Stomach of a King: Elizabeth I and the Politics of Sex and Power* (Philadelphia, PA, 1994), 141–142, 205 n. 45. For more on Topcliffe, see John Guy, *Elizabeth: The Forgotten Years* (New York, 2016), 170–176.

and desires to know what good liking he had of Asplehut,[123] and how long he tary's there.

In another letter Lady Arundell writes that she doubts Topclyfe will not be got to pay his Wives portion[xi], and she pittys her case.

And in another letter she expresses great concern for her Aunt Topclyfes miserable condition, her Husband not performing what he had promised for her maintinance.

And in another letter she writes Sir Francis Willughby that she has got the Bishop of London, and others in comission with him to cause Mr. Topclyfe to appear before them, and if this helps not she knows not what will.

This Topclyf, that Lady Arundell often writes off [of], with much compassion, was Jane the Daughter of Sir Edward Willughby, and Sister to Sir Henry that was killed at Norwich An: D: 1548 [sic].

If George Willughby was a Brother of hers [viz. Jane Willoughby Topcliffe], tis more then the pedigree shews, for there is no mention of any younger Brother George, but by many letters it appears that Sir Francis Willughby called George Willughby Uncle, and that George Willughby was one that Sir Francis often employed in business.[124]

There is a letter from this George Willughby dated February 1574 directed to his Son=in=law Repington,[125] who seems to have been a lawyer employed by Sir Francis Willoughby. In this letter George Willughby writes that there are other lands to pass in the same fine which are not part of the joynture,[126] as namely the manours of Wollaton and Sutton Passis, Cossall, Gunthorp and Lewdham, in the County of Nottingham, Dunsby in Lincolnshire, and Woodland in Dorsetshire, all which he writes are to pass in this manner, viz. to Sir Francis Willughby and his heirs male, and for want of [f. 67] such issue, to his heirs generall, and for want of such issue to the right heirs. There is a letter from Sir Francis Willoughby to his Uncle George Willughby, about buying land of the Earl of Huntington[127] and others.

---

[123] Aspley Hall in the city of Nottingham. Originally belonging to the monks of Lenton Priory, it came into the hands of the Willoughbys after the dissolution of the monasteries.

[124] On George Willoughby, an illegitimate son of Edward Willoughby and therefore a half-brother of Jane Willoughby Topcliffe, see above, Text n. 27.

[125] The wife of George Willoughby was Maud Cotton, widow of Francis Repington. The Repington mentioned here may be her son and therefore a stepson of George Willoughby. There is a letter from Richard Repington in the Middleton file Mi, Da 80/1–37. Repington was a lawyer and steward of the Borough of Sutton Coldfield, Warks., where the Willoughbys owned land and worked coal mines.

[126] The jointure was that part of the estate that would go to Elizabeth Willoughby if Francis were to predecease her. See Text n. 100 above.

[127] Henry Hastings, 3rd earl of Huntingdon (c.1535–1595). See Claire Cross, *The Puritan Earl: The Life of Henry Hastings, Third Earl of Huntingdon* (London, 1966).

There is a letter from Lady Arundell to Sir Francis Willughby to put him in mind of his promise of coming to them which both she and Mr. Arundell (she writes) look for, and desire, and if his Wife like to travell with him she might be wellcom.

Upon the back side of this letter there is writ the copy of a letter from Sir Francis Willughby to his Sister, in answer to hers. He writes that much business relating to his estate prevents his being able to come to her at this time. One thing that hinders, is land purchased lately in Cossall,[128] which he doubts he shall lose, if there be not some friend to move the Queen, and in this he should be glad to use her help, thinking she would be at the Court before he should be compelled to make his direct answer. He writes that the bargain between his Father-in-law and himself is broken off, because he can have no good assurance for the money, and he fears he shall be compelled to sue him. He writes that his Wife is great with child, and that if after her delivery she shall retain her usual trade, he shall be forced to change his mind as her frowardness shall occasion him. She had burden'd him in that by his dealing with her he had been the occasion of the loss of her children, which tho not true he was contented to bear.

There is a letter from Lady Arundell to Sir Francis Willughby in which she writes, that Lady Willughbys dislike of her coming, and writing a letter to Mr. Arundell to stay her, had made her not willing to come, to bring unquietness to any place, and much less to his house, where she prays he may be quiet without her, and then she would content herself with forbearing to come.

[f. 68] The copy of Lady Willughbys letter to Sir Matthew Arundell which still remains in the Library at Wollaton, is to this effect. That she hears his Wife is comming to see her Brother, which she desires he will prevent, for she is resolved never to stay in the house where his Wife is. She believes Sir Matthew is not ignorant what letters his Wife had writ to her Brother Sir Francis Willughby four years before this time, in which she would have represented her a person fitter for Bridewell[129] than to trouble any honest

---

[128] Willughby possession of land in Cossall seems to have been the source of litigation for a number of years, being part of Peverell's Fee. See Thoresby, *Thoroton's History of Nottinghamshire*, II, 215–217. Francis lost Cossall Manor in 1569: 'The mannor of Cossal alias Cossal Marsh, late belonging to the monastery of Newstede, and in the occupation of Francis Willughby, 21 July, 10 Eliz. was granted to Percivall Bowes, and John Moysier, gentlemen'.

[129] Bridewell, given to the City of London by Edward VI in 1553, was a prison for the disorderly, an orphanage, and a training facility for apprentices. Debtors made up the majority of long-term inmates. See Norval Morris and David J. Rothman, *The Oxford History of the Prison: The Practice of Punishment in Western Society* (Oxford, 1998), 73, 75. See

gentlemans house. These letters she had ready to shew, to testifie the ill will which she bore herself and children. And she believed her comming now would tend to no other end but to break the good agreement which there was now between her Husband and self, as she had endeavoured heretofore etc. Dated from Kinsbury April the 5th.[130]

There is a letter from Lady Arundell to her Brother in which she writes that if her comming to his house would stand him in any stead, she shall not refuse to come, tho she had as great dislike to come into his Wives company, as she had to come into hers.

In another letter from Lady Arundell to Sir Francis Willughby she expresses her trouble, that what should be his comfort, is his greatest grief, and writes that she often imagins how this might be help'd, and would advise that the next time she [Elizabeth] falls into those rages, that he should send for her Father to come to her, and that they should both goe with him home and board there with a convenient number of servants, till such time as she should have lost her willfullness, and would apply herself to please him. Or if he would like, since home gave him no content, to come abroad to her, and keep Christmas with them. Mr. Arundell and she should be glad of his company, but if business would not let him come now into these parts, shortly after Christmas she was to goe up to wait and stay half a year,[131] in which space she hoped he would take some good occasion [f. 69] to come up.

In another letter from Lady Arundell to Sir Francis Willughby she writes, that she has spoken to the Lord Keeper,[132] and finds the reason that he was out of the Comission of Peace in Nottinghamshire, was because he was in that for Warwickshire, and it was not allowed

---

William G. Hinckle, *A History of Bridewell Prison, 1553–1700* (London, 2006). Bridewell became an eponym; work houses and debtors' prisons became known as bridewells. For the eponymous nature of Bridewell for houses of correction outside London, see Paul Griffiths and Simon Devereaux (eds), *Penal Practice and Culture, 1500–1900: Punishing the English* (London, 2004); and Joanna Innes, 'Prisons for the poor: English bridewells, 1555–1800', in F. Snyder and D. Hay (eds), *Labour, Law and Crime: An Historical Perspective* (London, 1987), 42–122. In the 16th century, 170 houses of correction, known as bridewells, opened throughout England in response to rising vagrancy.

[130] Kingsbury, Warks. In the draft in the Stowe Brydges Collection, Huntington Library, San Marino, CA (hereafter STB), STB Box 2 (1), fos 20v–21. Cassandra places the date of this letter at about the second half of 1575.

[131] Margaret was very likely talking of going up to London where she was one of the gentlewomen of the bedchamber and of the privy chamber.

[132] The lord keeper was the custodian of the Great Seal and after his status was fixed by the Lord Keeper Act of 1562, he also functioned as lord chancellor. For Bacon, who was lord keeper from 1558–1579, see Robert Tittler, *Nicholas Bacon: The Making of a Tudor Statesman* (Athens, OH, 1976).

that one man should be[xii] of that Comission in two Counties, but he might chuse which County he would be of the Comission in. In this letter she writes that she is glad to hear his Wife behaves herself better.[133]

There is a letter from Sir John Lyttleton to Sir Francis Willughby dated June 1572, in which he makes great complaints of two of Sir Francis Willughbys servants viz: Catesbie,[134] and Marmyon,[135]

---

[133] A Commission of the Peace was a commission from the crown to appoint, under the Great Seal, justices of the peace to keep the peace within each county. According to evidence from the several *Libri pacis* in the National Archives, Francis Willoughby served as a justice of the peace for Warwickshire from 1573 to 1584. Cathryn Enis, 'The Dudleys, Sir Christopher Hatton and the justices of Elizabethan Warwickshire', *Midland History*, 39 (2014), app. 2, which may date this letter to 1573. Francis Willoughby may have been appointed as part of the growing influence and patronage of Christopher Hatton within Warwickshire. On the importance of commissions, see Norman Jones, *Governing by Virtue: Lord Burghley and the Management of Elizabethan England* (Oxford, 2015), 19–22.

[134] Catesby or Catesbie is a Warwickshire name. This Catesbie is probably one of the younger sons (either George or John) of Sir Richard Catesby of Ashby St Ledgers, Warks. (d.1553) and his wife Dorothy Spencer. His aunt would have been Isabel Spencer who married Sir Nicholas Strelley of Nottinghamshire in 1546. For Sir Richard Catesby, see his will, TNA, PROB 11/36/261. It is probably Richard Catesby who is listed over several years from 1521 to 1526 in the Willoughby account books as receiving monies for his schooling at Sutton Coldfield. It is likely that he spent part of his youth in the Willoughby household. (*HMC Middleton*, 363, 369, 383, 385), and his son followed suit. The Catesbys were a mostly Catholic family with declining resources and influence within the county by the 1570s. See Enis, 'The Dudleys, Sir Christopher Hatton and the justices of Elizabethan Warwickshire', 1–35. William Catesby (the oldest son of Richard Catesby) was at Middleton in 1575 when both he and Francis Willoughby were knighted. William Catesby was instrumental in petitioning Queen Elizabeth, unsuccessfully, to withhold her assent from anti-Catholic legislation in 1585; he was also involved in a plan with Francis Walsingham to found a colony for Catholics in America. Morey, *The Catholic Subjects of Queen Elizabeth I*, 66, 136. William Catesby's son by Anne, née Throckmorton, Robert Catesby, was involved in the 1601 Essex Rebellion and was a co-conspirator in the Gunpowder Plot of 1605. 'The Gunpowder Plot', *ODNB*.

[135] Henry Marmion is listed as one of Henry Willoughby's most highly paid servants, 1522–1525. From 1535 to 1543 he is listed as the bailiff for Wollaton, Cossall, and Sutton Passeys (*HMC Middleton*, 313–315, 338, 361, 370). In 1547 he was receiving an annuity of £5 from John Willoughby from the income of Wollaton and Sutton Passeys (*HMC Middleton*, 316–317). Henry Marmyon, gentleman, was one of the executors to the will of Henry Willoughby, father of Francis. This particular Marmion, William, may have been his son. See below, fo. 83, p. 115 (1572), and fo. 101, p. 133, and Text n. 214 where Trussell in 1580 refers to his uncle Marmion, whom Cassandra understands to be one of Francis Willoughby's servants. Since John Trussell, a servant to the Willoughbys since the 1540s married Bridget Marmion, it is likely that this Trussell is the son of John Trussell and is referring to a brother of Bridget Marmion who might well be William Marmion (see fo. 83, p. 115 below in the list of servants). For a history of the Marmions from the perspective of the 17th-century Willoughbys, see Mi, LM 13, pp. 47–51, 73–74; *HMC Middleton*, 271, 506; Mi, LM 26, fos 4–8. The Marmions received, from William I, the castle of Tamworth. The last Marmion lord of Tamworth was Philip de Marmion, who died in 1291/2, leaving an estate divided among female heirs. On the many estates

who he writes spread slanderous reports of his Daughter, the Lady Willughby.

There is in this year An: D: 1572 a long and very particular account in writing of a scene of great vilany laid by Ithel, Catesbie, Marmyon, Pardia, Barthol, and Widdison, all servants of Sir Francis Willughby,[136] who had plotted together to defame their Lady, and thereby make a breach between her and Sir Francis. Amongest these wicked servants Ithel seems by this account to have been the worst. 'Tis there noted down that he took great pains to have drawn Squire, another of Sir Francis Willughbys servants, to have been in their cabal, but they could not prevail with him, who would always assert his Ladys inocency and pitty her misfortunes.

There is a paper writ by Squire in which he says he has often heard his Lady with tears bewaile her unquiet life through Ithel and his companyons dealing against her, and belying her, to her Husband; and that she had told him that being one day with her Husband at Streley, she had heard Sir Anthony Streley[137] say to another Gentleman leaning in a windoe with

---

granted or sold to Philip and, subsequently, his partitioned estate, see *HMC Middleton*, 71–75, 77–83. In 1283 he was proposing to found a Premonstratensian house at Tamworth.

The particular Marmion mentioned above (William), who was to cause so much trouble within the Willoughby household, was a servant at Wollaton from 1572 to 1578. *HMC Middleton*, 152–155, 542, 560. Mi, LM 26, fos 69, 83, 119. This was probably the same Marmion who was a servant of the countess of Shrewsbury (Elizabeth Talbot, known as Bess of Hardwick, *c*.1521/2 or 1527–1608) and wrote to Francis Willoughby *c*.1580 from the household of the earl and countess saying that he was leaving that household to return to Wollaton and that he was implicated in the 'cyvill warres' between the countess and her husband. 'That howse is a hell [...] I tould your worship at your being last at Haddon of a broyle or kynd of tragedy betwixt my Lord and Lady of late, wherin, as alwayes in maner hertofore, my Lord hathe made me playe a parte, so I thinke the tragedy would not hould if I be lefte out.' He writes that Lord Shrewsbury blames Marmion and his wife, Elizabeth [the countess of Shrewsbury], as the sole cause of Queen Elizabeth's reducing the allowance paid for the 'Lady of Skottlandes dyat [...] but he would remove me and shutt her Ladyship up without suffring any sarvauntes about her than of his owne placing.' He states that he will consult with his father [perhaps Henry Marmion], but he hopes to return to Sir Francis's household. 'And thoughe I speake it, methinks Wollaton Howse should not be without a Marmyon.' *HMC Middleton*, 152–155. See also *Bess of Hardwick's Letters: The Complete Correspondence c.1550–1608*, letter 078 (26 June 1580); online at https://www.bessofhardwick.org/home.jsp (accessed 31 Mar. 2018).

[136] There has been relatively little research done on the role of servants in Tudor England. See a general overview by Alison Sim, *Masters and Servants in Tudor England* (Stroud, 2006). It is interesting that there were a number of marriages among the servants, in these cases between the Trussell, Marmion, Ithell, and Squire families. See above, Text n. 83.

[137] Sir Anthony Strelley (1528–*c*.1596) was the son of Nicholas Strelley and Isabel Spencer. Anthony Strelley was a frequent visitor at the Willoughbys. The Strelleys had previously intermarried with the Stanhope, Markham, and Willoughby families, and Sir

him, I am heartily sorry for that poor Gentlewomans miserable case, there being certain verlots [varlets][138] who villanously seek her utter undoing.

[f. 70] Squire writes that Lady Willughby upon telling him this, desired he would stand her friend, and learn what he could of their meaning, but she chiefly fear'd Lady Arundell, and Ithel.[139] He writes that he promised his Lady with an oath that he would deal for her faithfully and truely in all respects.

There is an account, of Squires writing, that one time when he was going from London to Nottingham he went to wait upon the Lady Arundell to know if she would comand him any service to her Brother. She said she had great matters to talk with him about, such as she was loath to commit to writing, expecting to see him shortly in London, which she willed me to tell him, if he was not coming towards London before I came to Nottingham. She willed me to stay a while that she might talk with me, for now she had leasure the Queen being gone to Leicester House. After a little astronomicall talk, and about mathematicall books in the Italian tongue etc.[140] she made a large enquiry after her Sister the Lady Willughby, viz: what company she kept etc. Upon this subject there is a very long dialogue writ down by Squire, too much to copy, but in short it plainly shews that Lady Arundell strove to learn of Squire stories of her Sister, that she might tell her Brother in order to give him ill impressions of his Lady. Squires answers all tend to excuse and comend his Lady. He named some of the Ladys that she most viseted amongst which were the Lady Stanhop, and Mrs. Haddam,[141] to which Lady Arundell answer'd

---

Anthony's nephew Nicolas married Bridget Willoughby, the daughter of Percival and Bridget (1605). The Strelley holdings, which included coal mines and lands in Nottinghamshire, were in decline by the 16th century. From 1608 to 1610 Sir Percivall Willoughby was in court against the Strelleys for owing monies due from coal deposits, perhaps in regard to the marriage settlement between his daughter Bridget and Nicholas Strelley. For the will of Anthony Strelley, see a copy at Borthwick Institute, York, Prob. Reg. 26, fo. 287. Strelley's comment here, sympathizing with Elizabeth's troubles, indicates that Sir Francis's treatment of her was not a secret, so much so that she was gossiped about by men leaning in windows.

[138] According to Peter Mack, *Elizabethan Rhetoric: Theory and Practice* (Cambridge, 2002), 236, a verlet [or varlet] is someone who is proud and impudent.

[139] Ithell is a Welsh surname. A Mary Ithell, born in Wales (c.1518–1612), was baptized in Gloucestershire and married Richard Wardwell (1512–c.1541) of Warwickshire. Mary died in Warwickshire.

[140] This suggests that Margaret Willoughby Arundell had received a fairly high level of learning.

[141] Lady Stanhop is Anne Rawson (1513–1587/8), wife of Sir Michael Stanhope of Shelford and Elvaston (c.1502–1552), mother of Sir Thomas Stanhope of Shelford. Haddam's wife is Lady Stanhope's daughter, Juliana, who married John Hotham of

that woman with her, I heard so before, well, my Sister doth not well, and I marvell my Brother will suffer it.

There are many letters from Lady Arundell to Sir Francis Willughby which as well as this dialogue, writ by Squire, shew that she must have been very much to blame in agrivating Lady Willughbys faults to Sir Francis, and thereby increasing the uneasiness that was [f. 71] between her and her Husband. It appears that she had an inquisitive way of picking up all the little stories that she could of Lady Willughby, and then telling them with advantage to her Brother. There are severall letters from Lady Arundell to her Brother in which she excuses Ithel. And there is the copy of a letter from Sir Francis Willughby to his Sister, which shews that Sir Francis had upon examination found Ithel guilty of telling stories and making lyes of his Wife.

There is a long letter from Lady Arundell in answer to this from her Brother, in which she accuses Squire as the person that had raised ill reports of Ithel, and writes that it was Squire himself that had first told her what company his Wife kept, and that she had a great liking to Haddam's Wife, to which she had answer'd him, that she wished her Sister had chose a better companion, for she was like to get no good by keeping her company. Lady Arundell writes that many stories were bruted about by Squire, and that he would find him to be a desembling knave. She had learnt that he had been with the Countess of Warwick[142] to acquaint her that

---

Scarborough, Yorks. *c*.1560. By early 1569 John Hotham had barred his house to her, and she returned to live with her mother. Scandalous accusations flew between the estranged couple, including the accusation that John Hotham was having an affair 'with a naughty pack' [immoral woman], while accusations against Julian, not detailed in any of the extant correspondence and court cases, appear to have shamed her; her husband slandered her and was, according to Anne Stanhope, 'reporting sundry untruths of her in all places where he comes'. John Hotham seems never to have provided maintenance for his wife after their separation, and she died in Nottingham in 1577. See Beryl Cobbing and Pamela Priestland, *Sir Thomas Stanhope of Shelford: Local Life in Elizabethan Times* (Radcliffe-on-Trent, 2003), ch. 4, and esp. p. 65. BL, Lansdowne MS 12/1, fos 2–3v is a 1569 letter from Anne Stanhope appealing to William Cecil, Lord Burghley, to intercede with John Hotham or, at a minimum, help provide for her daughter who has been 'left penyles to defend her cause'. See also BL, Lansdowne MS 12/76, fo. 170r, an appeal in 1570 to Cecil to bring the business between Hotham and her daughter to some good end. Throughout the 1570s the Willoughbys and Stanhopes visited one another often and exchanged gifts frequently. Mi, A57 fos 21v–86v, cited in Cobbing and Priestland, *Sir Thomas Stanhope*, 74.

[142] The sense of this passage seems to be: Lady Arundell had learnt that Squire had been with the countess of Warwick to acquaint her (the countess of Warwick) that Ithel had told Lady Arundell stories of her Sister (Sir Francis's wife), and to persuade the countess not to believe any thing which Lady Arundell should say of her Sister the Lady Willughby (Sir Francis's wife). The countess of Warwick may have been Anne Seymour (1538–1588), daughter of Edward Seymour, 1st duke of Somerset (executed in 1552), who married

Ithel had told her stories of her Sister, and to perswade the Countess not to believe any thing which she should say of her Sister the Lady Willughby.

There is the copy of a letter dated May 1572 from Squire to Lady Willughby, in which he gives her notice of a great plot laid against her to defame her to her Husband, because she kept company with Haddams Wife who they would represent as a vile Woman, but he had ever thought her to be a good honest Gentlewoman. He prays God to defend Lady Willughby from such enemies.

[f. 72] There is the copy of a long letter writ by Sir Francis Willughby, June 1572, which seems to be an answer to one which Lady Arundell had writ to him full of stories of his Lady, who Sir Francis vindicates, and seems not to credit Lady Arundells reports of her. He writes that he guesses this comes from Catesbies Wife[143] who is scant honest and admit that his Wife should keep company with Haddams Wife, doth it follow, that she must be touch'd with the like spot of dishonesty.

There is a letter from Ithel to Sir Francis Willughby in which he endeavours to clear himself from being any means of sowing discord between himself and his good Lady dated An: D: 1572.

There are severall copies of letters writ by Sir Francis Willughby An: D: 1573 which express much pitty and compassion for his Wife, who was then in a very ill state of health, and I believe advised to goe to London for better help in her illness than she could find in the Country.

There is the copy of a letter writ by Sir Francis June 1573 to his Cousin Mr. Thomas Willoughby,[xiii] to let him know that earnest business would not permit him to goe to London, and his Uncle George Willughby was obliged to travell to the West, and thereby his Wife would not be so well provided for, as he wished in this time of her sickness, and therefore he prayed him that he would vouchsafe to accompany his Wife in Town, if his own affairs would suffer him. And that during his abode with her, he would take care that

---

John Dudley, 2nd earl of Warwick, in 1550. Dudley died in 1554 after being imprisoned, and Anne remarried. Another countess of Warwick was Anne Dudley (née Russell), countess of Warwick (1548/9–9 Feb. 1604), lady-in-waiting and close friend of Queen Elizabeth. She married Ambrose Dudley, 3rd earl of Warwick, the eldest brother of Robert Dudley, 1st earl of Leicester in 1565. Given the reference to her 'sister Willoughby' the reference is probably to Anne Seymour Dudley, although, since the two countesses were sisters-in-law themselves, it could also be Anne Russell Dudley.

[143] Richard Catesby (d.1553/4) had six sons with his two wives Dorothy Spencer and Elizabeth Astell. Possibilities might be: the daughter of William Powell who married George Catesby; Elizabeth who married Richard; Elizabeth Porter who married Edmund; Elizabeth Whorwood who married Edward; or Anne Throckmorton who married William.

[f. 73] she should want nothing which might either content her mind or be for the recovery of her health. And in his so doing Sir Francis Willughby writes, that he shall not only discharge all the charges which he shall sustain, but also requite him with such friendship as shall rest with him during life.

I don't find who this Mr. Thomas Willughby[xiv] was,[144] but believe he was the Father of Sir Percivall [Willoughby].

[f. 72v] There is a letter from Lady Willughby to Sir Francis Willughby dated the 16th year of Queen Elizabeth being An: D: 1574, in which letter she thanks Sir Francis for the venison that he sent her to London, which she thought the best she ever eat [sic]. She writes that her phisitians think it is very dangerous for her to travell. She would have got their leave to have gone to her Cousin Thomas Willoughbys in Kent, and would have made two days journey of it, but they would not consent to it. She writes that she thinks tis very unlikely that she should goe forth her time, if she be with Child, as she trusts in God she is, and yet some of her phisitians think the contrary. She desires they would give her something, either to help or else to dispatch her quickly, for she thinks death would be a thousand times more welcome to her than to live as she now does continually sick.

She writes that she has sent him a hat, (which she chose for him herself) which is of the newest fashion, and she thinks a very good fashion for him, because it is not high crowned, so that when he rides a hunting he may go under the bushes and never pull it off.

[f. 73 cont.] There is in the Library at Wollaton a letter writ by Sir Francis Willughby in March 1574 to a servant of his that was then in London with his Lady to enquir of him how his Lady does and what weekly charges do arise. He writes that he gave commandment that the horses should be sent down, but he perceives her mind is now changed, and thereby he is disappointed for the conveying of the

---

[144] Thomas Willoughby (*c.*1538–1596) held lands in Bore Place, Kent. He was admitted to Lincoln's Inn 30 Apr. 1558, was executor to the will of his mother, Briget Willoughby, 18 Aug. 1558, and served as sheriff of Kent 1573–1574 and 1590. Sir Percival was the eldest son of Thomas and his first wife, Katherine Hart, daughter of Sir Percival Hart of Lullingstone Court in Kent. Thomas and Katherine were married in 1557 and had 10 children. After Katherine's death Thomas married Mary Weston, by whom he had three daughters. Thomas Willoughby was first cousin to Sir Francis Willoughby, making Percival and his wife Bridget second cousins (they shared great-grandparents: see Table 1). See 'Pedigree of Willoughby', in Frederick Arthur Crisp (ed.), *Visitation of England and Wales*, 9: *Notes* (London, 1911), 1, https://archive.org/details/visitationofengl3ohowa. In *The Continuation of the History* (pp. 23–24), Cassandra concludes, based on reading many of his letters, that Thomas Willoughby was 'a very kind Father and a very just man […] a very prudent, and a very good man'. Mi, LM 27, fo.19. Thomas was buried at Chiddingstone, Kent on 2 June 1596. For his will, see Mi, 6/178/52 and 53; for his inventory see Mi, I 27 and 28.

ACCOUNT OF AN ELIZABETHAN FAMILY 107

children to Middleton. He knows not the meaning of this, unless it be to increase his charges, and if that should exceed the rate he was contented to allow, it would be hardly gotten at his hands, and London standing in the eye of the world, it would not stand greatly with her credit to be still riding in the streets. He would be advertised what time she means to continue in London. He also writes to know if Mr. Creme[145] can find him any treble lutes fit for his purpose.

[1574–1578: More Troubles and a Possible Visit from the Queen][146]

There is a letter from Sir Francis Willughby dated May 1575 to Dr. Smith[147] to thank him for the care he had taken of Lady Willughby during her illness, and since he thinks Buxton Waters[148] necessary for her, Sir Francis Willughby writes that if she would [f. 74] accomplish what he would wish her to doe, then he would come himself up to London, and if his leasure would permit him he would goe with her himself to Buxton. And where=as he advised her to live in a wholsome air and eschue disorder in her diet and perturbations of

---

[145] Unidentified.

[146] Although Cassandra generally follows a chronological progression in the Account and *The Continuation of the History*, in this section she reaches back to 1572 for some of her materials.

[147] Based on the assumption that Francis would have hired a physician of some note, there were two members of the Royal Society of Physicians named Smith who practised medicine in London in 1574, both named Richard. One was a notorious Catholic and opposer of the Reformation. The other, Richard Smith, MD (d. *c*.1599), is the most probable candidate. Dr Smith was born in Gloucestershire (*c*.1540s) and earned his MD from St John's College, Cambridge in 1567. William Munk (ed.), *The Roll of the Royal College of Physicians of London* (London, 1878), 68. There are numerous references to Dr Smith attending not only Elizabeth Willoughby but also other members of the household in Mi, A 57, a surviving account book for Nov. 1572 to Feb. 1575.

[148] Buxton, a spa town in the High Peak Hundred, Derbyshire. Phyllis May Hembry, *The English Spa 1560–1815: A Social History* (London, 1990); Mike Langham and Colin Wells, *The Baths at Buxton Spa* (Leek, 2005). I would like to thank Amanda Herbert, at the Folger Library, for these references. One of the earliest mentions of a visit to St Anne's Chapel (and presumably the waters) at Buxton is in *HMC Middleton*, 367, for Sept. 1524. Under the patronage of the earl of Shrewsbury in the 1570s, Buxton had a four-storey building with 'galleries, exercise equipment, airing rooms, "most decent" privies and lodging for all classes, including a dormitory for the poor'. See Norman Jones, *The Birth of the Elizabethan Age: England in the 1560s* (Oxford, 1993), 206–207, and 281 n. 58, for references to treatises printed in 1562 and 1572 describing the baths. The spa charged differential fees based on one's class, with gentlemen paying 3s 4d, plus 4d for administering the bath. It was frequently visited by Mary, Queen of Scots, in the 1570s and 1580s. Alexandra Walsham, *The Reformation of the Landscape* (Oxford, 2011), ch. 7 discusses Buxton spa in the context of the Reformation.

her mind. For[xv] the air he writes that he thinks she will not mislike the place where he is disposed to dwell, being unwilling himself to be in any air which they could find hurt by, but in this point he desires she will consider her duty rather than to suffer her self to be guided by self will. For his [her?] disorder in diet and the perturbations of her mind, she, only, must help that; for his part, he would not give her any just occasion of trouble, if reason might take place, and willfull will be laid aside.

By these and many more copy's of letters that are in the Library it appears that Sir Francis and his Lady lived very unhappily together. There is the copy of a letter from Sir Francis Willughby dated June 1575 to Sir John Lyttleton, in which letter he gives Sir John notice of his Wives intentions to goe to Buxton, where he writes she means to stay a fortnight, but to what place she will return he knows not, and to be in other mens houses, refusing his own is not convenient. Such journeys are very chargable and sometimes bring more discredit then relief to a sick person. Plain dealing he knows, has bread dislike between her and Sir John, but to let her follow her fancies would be meer phrensie.[149] Would Sir John and his Lady or any other friend of hers come to confer with him before her going, he would stay her journy some time, but if not before, he would expect to meet them at Buxton; or else at their return from thence at Middleton, where, (if she would goe thither) she should be used as became Sir John Lyttletons Daughter and his Wife, but if she [f. 75] refused, she should have but small maintenance or comfort from him. He expresses sorrow for writing so much, but says necessity forces him to shew his private pain, not that he would stain her good name, but he feared she would injure it, by her own inconsideration.

There is a letter from Sir John Lyttleton to Sir Francis Willughby dated from Prestwood[150] June 1575 in which Sir John expresses himself very affectionately, and friendly, to Sir Francis, and beholden to him for his plain dealing touching Lady Willughby who he hoped would suffer reason to take place, for she had now faithfully promised that she would be directed by her Husband as duty required, and that she would refer her self and cause to him, to order as he should think well off [of] and that at her return from Buxton she would come to Middleton to him, and remain there, or at any other place, where he should think good, not weighing her health, or life, so

---

[149] '[A] crazy notion or wild idea; also, a craze or mania', *OED*. It is also defined as a mental derangement. This reads more like foolishness, however.

[150] Prestwood manor farm in Staffordshire was purchased by John Lyttleton in 1554. See Text n. 187 below.

much as contenting him. This done Sir John writes, that he shall then become her friend notwithstanding what before had happened.

There is a letter which Sir Francis Willughby writ to his Lady at Buxton in which he wishes, that with the recovery of her health, she may also put on a tractable mind, and let her self will give place to reason, and that she would take the wholsome advice of her best friends. He writes that the horses shall be sent, and he desires she will repair the next way to Middleton, that he may have the horses against the time he must goe to Killingworth. He desires her to be as good a Wife as she would make shew of being to the world, and let her example cause him to do the like. Thus wishing you as my self etc.

[f. 76] There is a letter from Lady Willughby to Sir Francis in which she says she finds great benefit by the Bath at Buxton, and would gladly have staid longer, but she writes, that her Sister Hollys[151] must return home, and having taken her as she did, she thinks herself obliged to see her safe at home again.

This good accord, which now seemed to be begining between Sir Francis Willughby and his Lady, did not last long, as will hereafter appear, but I shall here stop to mention Queen Elizabeth's going a progres through that part of England, about this time. Upon this occasion Sir Francis Willughby sent to inform himself by George Willughby what would be fit for him to doe. In answer to which there is a letter from Georg Willughby dated June 1575, to let Sir Francis Willughby know that he had advised with severall of the Country Gentlemen, where, and in what manner they intended to meet the Queen, and by what he can learn, their servants need only to have plain livery coats, but he thinks Sir Francis's number of servants should in no wise be less then fifty, as well because heretofore he had not shewed himself to the Queen, as also that his estate was very well know[n] both to her Majesty and the whol Cownsel, to be nothing inferiour to the best. For himself, George Willughby writes, that he thinks he cannot make less than three sutes of apparell for he is well assured that his attendance will be expected a week.

I shall here copy a letter from Sir Francis Knolls[152] to Sir Francis Willughby to give him notice of the Queens coming to Wollaton.

---

[151] Most likely Eleanor Sheffield, daughter of Edmund Sheffield, 1st Baron Sheffield, who married Denzel Holles (1538–1590). Her father was killed in Aug. 1549 during Kett's Rebellion, as was Francis's father. Less likely would be the second wife of William Hollis (father of Denzil), Ida Grosvenor of Cheshire, whom he married in 1570.

[152] Sir Francis Knollys (1512–1596), councillor to Queen Elizabeth until his death and a member of Parliament from 1559 until 1593. At one point he held the wardship of Sir Francis Willoughby (see Introduction, p. 32). For more on Knollys, see Alexandra F. Johnston, 'Sir Francis Knollys and his progeny: Court and country in the Thames

Letter

Her Majesty is determined to tary two days at your house that is to say tomorrow night and Thursday all day, whereof I thought good to advertise you betimes. Wherefore I think it best for you not to defray her Majesty, but rather that you should give her some good present of beefs and muttons, and to keep [f. 77] a good table yourself in some place, if you have any convenient room for it, two messe[153] of meat. But do herein as you shall think best, but you had need to consider how your provision of drink etc may hold out. This Tuesday the 20th of July 1575.[154]

Your loving friend
F: Knolls

There is no account book or papers that I could find, which shewed in what manner the Queen was received and entertained at Wollaton.[155]

There is a book which gives a particular account of Sir Francis Willughby's expences from November 1572 to February 1574,[156] but no book (that I could find) of accounts for the next year.

In this book from November 1572 to 74, there is large sums set down for travelling charges, and often money is set down for servants board wages, which makes me believe Sir Francis Willughby and his Family removed very often, the discontent which was then between him and his Lady, I believe made every place uneasie to him, and she being sickly would often fancy the air she was in was unholsome, and therefore still be desiring to change it from one house, to another, for I find they were sometimes at Wollaton, sometimes at Middleton, sometimes at Kinsbury Hall, sometimes at Coventry, and sometimes at London, and besides these removes from one, to another, of their own houses, they were sometimes with Sir John

Valley', in Norman J. Jones and Daniel Woolf (eds), *Local Identities in Late Medieval and Early Modern England* (New York, 2007), 131–155.

[153] 'A quantity [...] of meat [...] sufficient to make a dish', *OED*, under 'mess'.
[154] See STB 2 (1), book 1, fo. 18–18v. In Cassandra's notes, this letter was dated 26 July 1575. Neither is correct, however. In that week of 1575, Tuesday fell on 22 July. Elizabeth visited Kenilworth from 9 to 27 July 1575. Cole, *The Portable Queen*, 188.
[155] W.G. Cooke, 'Queen Elizabeth never slept here: Cassandra, Duchess of Chandos as an authority for royal progresses', *REED [Records of Early English Drama] Newsletter*, 14:1 (1989), 18–20. Cooke counsels caution when using Cassandra to trace the movements of Elizabeth I. Cole lists a visit from Queen Elizabeth to Middleton but not Wollaton on 28–29 July 1575. Kinney and Lawson list Francis Willoughby as having being made knight at Middleton on 27 July 1575. Cole, *The Portable Queen*, 188; Kinney and Lawson (eds), *Titled Elizabethans*, 199. It would appear that Elizabeth never did travel to Wollaton.
[156] Mi, A 57 is a large account book of 92 folio pages that begins 8 Nov. 1572 and continues to Feb. 1574/5. See also *HMC Middleton*, 421–451, although Stevenson only copies down a small portion of the information.

ACCOUNT OF AN ELIZABETHAN FAMILY   III

Lyttleton and other of their friends, as appears by the Account Book for Riding Charges. By many books of accounts and papers of the orders in the family it appears that Sir Francis Willughby was very exact in keeping the account of his income, and his expencis, and that he was very reguler in his family. But many of these papers are so decayed by time, that they remain very imperfect. The only sheet I found intire of those orders to be observed by his houshold servants I shall copy on the other side.

[f. 78] A Copy of Some of the Orders Which were to be Observed by Sir Francis Willughbys Servants at Wollaton, I believe about the year 1572.[157]

Item that Foxe[158] supply the place of the usher, whose office is first of all to see that the Hall be kept clean, and that his groom sees no doggs come there at all. He is diligently to have good regard of every person that comes into the Hall, to th'end that if they be of the better sort notice may be given to the Master, or some head officer that they may be entertained accordingly. If of the meaner sort then to know the cause of their coming, and to give advertisement over, to the end they may be dispatched and answer'd of their business, provided always that no stranger be suffered to pass without offering him to drink, and that no rascall or unseemly person be suffer'd to tarry there. The covering of the boards doth appertain to the under butler.

Upon intelligence given from the clerk, or the cook, that the meat is ready to be served, he is with a loud voice to command all Gentlemen and Yeomen to repair to the dresser. At the neither end of the Hall he is to meet the service, saying with a loud voice, give place my Masters, albeit no man be in the way, and so to goe before the same service untill he come to the upper end of t'hall carrying a little fine rod in his hand which at all other times he is to carry in his bosom whereby he is to be known of all strangers to be the usher. He is also to appoint some one Yeoman, at his discretion in the winter time, to carry the torch before service in the night time.

---

[157] Pamela Marshall, *Wollaton Hall and the Willoughby Family* (Nottingham, 1999) spends two pages on the 1572 household order for the old hall at Wollaton (pp. 22–24). 'For another detailed set of rules and orders drawn up in 1595 by the second Viscount Montague setting out in wearisome detail how his domestic servants were supposed to cater to his every need, see S.D. Scott, ' "A booke of orders and rules" of Anthony Viscount Montague in 1595', *Sussex Archaeological Collections*, 7 (1854), 173–212, cited in Questier, *Catholicism and Community in Early Modern England*, 15.

[158] Unidentified, unless this Foxe is related to George Willoughby Fox. See Text n. 27 above.

The Dining Chamber being served, he is to place in the Hall in dinner and supper time, all noble=mens, men [f. 79] which be fellows together, and all Gentlemen according to every of their Masters degrees. But before their placing and sitting down, he is to give notice unto the clerk that so many mease [meals?][159] are to be provided for, but in this matter the diligence of the clerk is no less required than the usher, to the end that they may both to their Masters worship, see the same very well served according to the degrees, and number of the strangers there. If any great press of strangers shall be, then three or four of the meanest sort of servants,[xvi] as namely the slaughterman, the carter, and some of the best of the grooms of the stable, or such like are to be appointed by the usher to attend in t'Hall. If no strangers be, then the grooms of the stable, and the allowed pages and boys in the house, to attend upon the first dinner, and they to have the remainder thereof with some little help out of the kitchen, as the usher shall see cause. And likewise the pages at the latter dinner to attend upon the Gentlemen and Yeomen, and the remainder of the meat at, after both the dinners and suppers, presently by the usher to be put into the almes table, which is always by him to be kept safely locked, to be distributed among the poor, such days as shall be appointed. Imediately after supper if there be any strangers th'usher is with a loud voice to command all Yeomen waiters to attend upon the buttery hatch, for the serving of [blank.][xvii]

All disorders in the Hall are by the usher to be reformed, and if there shall be any stubborn persons he is to expell them out of the Hall, and to command all men at dinner and supper time (if any great noise shall be) to keep silence, saying with a loud voice Speak softly my Masters. His part is also to walk up and down the Hall, and especially in the time of the first dinner or supper, and only [f. 80] to call and to command the buttler the pantter[160] and such as be attendents to bring or fetch any thing that shall be wanting, but not in any wise to doe any service himself, otherwise then diligently to look to the tables. The benefit of the play in this as in many places doth belong to the buttler, but in most unto th'usher.

He is diligently too see that no meat filched forth of the Chamber be brought into the Hall, nor yet to suffer any waiter to abide in the Hall during the time their Master is at dinner or supper, nor is he to

---

[159] 'Mease', was (in the late 16th century) a measure of herrings, *OED*. The word 'meals' makes more sense in this context, however.

[160] From the 14th century on, a panter was 'the officer in a household who supplied the bread and had charge of the pantry (an office later merged with that of butler); the controller of the bread or food supplies in general in a large establishment, esp. a royal court', *OED*.

suffer any filchen[161] through the Hall from the buttery, kitchen, or such like places. For he is an officer of great trust and credit and next to the usher of the great Chamber (if any be) in degree above either cooke butler yeomen of the Chambers or porter.[162]

Penne being appointed to the buttery, his office is ever to keep clean and sweet his buttery, and likewise his plate and cups, making sure every day to have fresh and clean water, and for the most part twice a day to wash the same withall. His jacks[163] appointed for the Hall are to be kept from furring[164] and unsweet savour. His office with th' aid of an under butler is to keep the great Chamber clean to make fires there, and to provide for lights in due season, and to cover the boards, and cupboards there, having very good regard to the cleanness of his linnen. And likewise to provide for cards and dyce, whereof he is to have the profit.

The under butler is to cover the boards in the Hall. He is to suffer no houshold servant to remain tipling or to be at all in[xviii] the buttery[165] but whosoever is disposed to drink to be served at the hatch,[166] and so to depart.

[f. 81] Neither is he to suffer any stranger to come in the buttery, other than such as shall be of worship or good reputation, and they to be brought in either by some of their officers, by th'usher of t'Hall or else by some discrete Gentleman, or Yeoman, for their better entertainment acording to their degrees and credit. He is to foresee that no breakfast, afternoon meats nor hancks[167] after supper be had or made there. Or if any houshold servant by reason of his business come after dinner and is to have some meat, he is to be served in the Hall and not in the buttery. But if any stranger of credit in like case come he is by th'usher or some other discrete servant to be had into the buttery and not to be served in the Hall.

---

[161] 'To steal, esp. things of small value; to pilfer. Occasionally in weaker sense: to take away surreptitiously,' *OED*. The exact form 'Filchen' does not appear in the *OED*, but the 'en' ending was a participle form in middle English. Cassandra's use of 'filchen' suggests she copied the letters verbatim.

[162] In the 16th century, porter could have meant either (or both) of two duties, 'a gatekeeper' [n.1] or 'A person employed to carry luggage, goods, etc.' [n.2], *OED*.

[163] 'A device for turning a spit for roasting meat over an open fire ... roasting-jack', *OED*.

[164] 'The process of becoming furred or incrusted', *OED*.

[165] A buttery is a wine/cask room. Fr. Late Latin buttis or barrel. A butler served wine and tended to the buttery. See Mark Girouard, *Life in an English Country House* (New Haven, CT, 1978).

[166] A buttery-hatch is 'the half-door over which the buttery provisions are served', *OED*.

[167] According to the *OED*, 'hanck' is 16th-century English for 'hank,' which means to coil or loop, 'To fasten by a loop or noose; to entangle; to catch by any loop-like part.' In this context, the word might refer to coiled sausage.

The buttler is also to use good discretion in serving forth of the bread and beer to the houses of office, as to the kitchen the bakehouse the nursery and such like, that he understanding the allowed number there, may so serve them, as it neither be with want, nor yet with over great excess. He is to fore=see that his broken beer[168] be safe, and clean kept in sweet vessels for the poor. The buttery door ought not without speciall cause to be set open till eight of the clock in the morning, and then so to stand till it be nine, and from thence to be shut again till between ten and eleven and then to remain open till all dinners[xix] be done, and so after dinner and supper be done to be shut again, till between two and three and then after half an hour or therabouts to be made fast till five and so to remain open till nine, and after by no means to be opened that night without speciall cause. The discretion of this officer is to fore=see, that no filching of bread or beer, be suffer'd, nor yet any want where reason doth require may be greatly both for his Masters profit and worshipp for it is an office both of good credit and great trust.

[f. 82] There is a book of accounts of Sir Francis Willughbys expences from November 1572 to December 1573,[169] in which the sum totall of every months disbursment stands thus.

	li	sh	d
November 1572 disbursments this month was	100	4	2
December-ditto this month came to the sum of	115	12	2
January-ditto this month	102	0	1
Feburary-ditto this month	71	11	2
March 1573 disbursements this month came to	36	18	1
April-ditto this month	31	2	11½
May-ditto this month	87	19	11½
June-ditto this month	45	13	8½
July-ditto this month	27	11	5½
August-ditto this month	86	7	6
September-ditto this month	178	10	6^{xx}
October-ditto this month	152	13	5
November-ditto this month	223	2	5½
December-ditto this month	135	10	11½
By which book it appears that Sir Francis Willughbys household disbursments for these fourteen months came to the sum off [of]	1394	18	8½

[168] 'Broken' in the context refers to remnants of food or drink, so left-over beer, *OED*.

[169] There is a surviving Account Book (Mi, A 57) that provides detailed accounts of expenses paid for by Thomas Shawe between Nov. 1572 and Feb. 1575. The relationship between the accounts described here and Mi, A 57 is not clear.

There is also a list of servants wages paid for one quarter of a year which I shall copy upon the other side. This list begins with Mrs. Willughby, who I believe must be Sir Francis Willughbys Lady for 13^{li} 6^s 8^d, must have been too large an allowance for a quarter of a year, for a servant, or companion to Lady Willughby.

[f. 83] A list of servants which did belong to Sir Francis Willughby and his Lady An: D: 1572, and their wages for a quarter of a year.

	li	sh	d
Paid to Mrs. Willughby[170]	13	6	8
To Mrs. Elizabeth[171]	1	0	0
To Marjory	1	0	0
To John	0	10	0
To John	0	5	0
To the landress	0	10	0
To Marjory	0	6	8
To Elizabeth	0	5	0
To Mary[172]	0	5	0
	17	8	4[xxi]
Paid to Henry Willoughby[173]	1	13	4
To George Gum	1	10	4
To Thomas Shaw	1	0	0
To Rigley	1	0	0
To William Marmyon[174]	0	15	0
To the coachman	0	15	0
To William Blithe	0	13	4
To Rice	0	13	4
To Gregory	0	13	4
To Holland	0	13	4
To Tom	0	13	4
To Roger C.	0	13	4
To James Coke	0	13	4
To the warrener[175]	0	13	4

[170] It is not clear who this would be, although it might be Elizabeth Willoughby, as Cassandra suggests. Mi, A 57 includes allowances for Elizabeth, and additional monies as needed.

[171] Perhaps Elizabeth Meringe. See fos 90–91, pp. 123–124 below.

[172] This may be the same person as Mary, Francis's fool, mentioned below on fo. 85, p. 118.

[173] For Henry Willoughby, see Text n. 177 below.

[174] See above, Text n. 135 and below, Text n. 266.

[175] 'A servant who has the charge of a rabbit-warren', *OED*.

To Sheperd of Arnol	0	10	4
To Sheperd of Basford	0	10	4
To John Penne	0	10	0
To Hugh	0	10	0
To Tom	0	10	0
To William Stock	0	10	0
To John	0	10	0
To William Derby	0	10	0
To Fox	0	10	0
To John Gold	0	8	4
To William Carter	0	8	4
Carry forward	34	15	8
[f. 84] Brought forward	34	15	8
Paid to John Smith	0	8	4
To Bright	0	8	4
To Robert	0	8	4
To John B	0	6	8
To Richard B	0	6	8
To Thomas S	0	6	8
To John S.	0	6	8
To John	0	6	8
To John Dun	0	4	0
To John P.	0	3	4
To the boy in the kitchen	0	3	4
To the clerk of the church	0	5	0
The armorers wages one quarter	0	10	0
The musitioners[176] wages one quarter	5	0	0
	43	19	8

This account of servants makes no mention of any belonging to[xxii] the nursery, tho before this year 1572 I believe most of Sir Francis Willughbys Daughters were born.

The two John's set down amongst the women servants I believe might both belong to Lady Willughby in particular, and Henry Willoughby who is set down first in the list of the Gentlemen servants, was I believe Sir Francis's chief Gentleman, and by the spelling of his name with an O I believe he was of the Eresby family,[177] though

---

[176] Musicians.

[177] There are two Henry Willoughbys of the Eresby line of Willoughbys: 1) Henry Willoughby (1540–1606, born to Dorothy Willoughby), younger brother of Thomas Willoughby of Bore Place, Kent who was the father of Percival, and 2) a younger brother of Percival Willoughby, but Cassandra is probably wrong in her surmise, as Henry Willoughby, the uncle of Percival, married Frances Kerle in Aug. 1578 (Chandos, *The*

that distinction of the names of the two families I don't find always observed, but that Sir Francis Willughby himself did sometimes write his name, ou, and that Sir Percivall[178] sometimes with the u only. Therefore 'tis very likely that both families might originally be the same, and so spell their names alike, though through this book I have made that distinction because I most often find Sir Francis Willughbys name spelt without the o, and Sir Percivall Willoughby's name spelt with it.[179]

[f. 85] There are many letters which shew that towards the end of the summer An: D: 1575 Sir Francis Willughby and his Lady lived very unhappily together, and that notwithstanding her fair promises to her Father, that she would be directed by her Husband, she had not been long returned from Buxton, before she shewed the contrary.

Continuation of the History, 21 n. 5) and cannot be the same Henry Willoughby in the Wollaton household for whom several marriages were being considered between 1579 and 1581 (see below, p. 204). Henry Willoughby, Percival's younger brother could not have been this Henry Willoughby as he was probably not born until c.1570 (*ibid.* 23). The Henry Willoughby serving in Francis Willoughby's house in 1572 may have been the son of Hugh Willoughby of Risley, the navigator, and his wife Joanna (or Jane) Strelley. In Mi, A 57, fos 32v, 66, 81 Harry Willoughby is listed as part of the household in 1573 and 1574, and see *HMC Middleton*, 433, where he is described as Sir Francis's 'man for books'. See above (fos 83–84, pp. 115–116), where he is listed as one of the more important members of the household. There is a 1579 letter written by Sir John Byron, uncle to Henry Willoughby and husband of Alice Strelley, asking Francis Willoughby to provide an annuity of £20 per year to support his nephew Henry Willoughby in his suit to marry the daughter of Sir John Byron's uncle, a widow with four children. Mi, 5/168/73. By 1581 Henry Willoughby had been commended to the service of Henry Hastings, earl of Huntingdon, and the earl was writing Francis to ask for a marriage of Henry with Francis's second daughter, Dorothy (see below, fos 162–163, pp. 204–205). In 1595 there is an exchange of letters between Bridget Willoughby, Clement Fisher, and Clement's wife Mary in which Mary Fisher claims that at the time that Sir Francis was arranging a marriage for Bridget with her cousin Percival Willoughby (1579–1580), Henry Willoughby, still within the Wollaton household, had practised to steal her away and marry her and that he had written a letter to her to this effect. See below, fo. 148, pp. 188–189. At the time of this exchange of letters in 1595, this Henry Willoughby (the son of Hugh Willoughby) was dead. There is another Henry Willoughby, son of George Willoughby, who came of age sometime before June 1565. *CPR 1563–1566* Elizabeth I, iii, 212. See fo. 163, p. 205 below. Even Francis Willoughby, the naturalist, was confused. For Clement and Mary Fisher, see Text n. 191.

[178] In *The Continuation of the History*, Cassandra notes, 'There is an account of Sir Percivall Willoughby's Entertaining King James the first at Middleton Hall, & that he was there Knighted by the King An.D. 1603 by which it appears that I have given him the title of Knighthood many years before it was due to him, & that I should have only writ him Mr. Willoughby, & not called his Wife Lady, till yt year 1603.' Chandos, *The Continuation of the History*, 37; Mi, LM 27, fo. 33. In fact, Percival Willoughby was knighted at Worksop, not Middleton, in 1603.

[179] Cassandra gives an account of the Willoughbys of Eresby, going back to the early 14th century, in *The Continuation of the History*, 3–23; Mi, LM 27, fos 3–19.

Some alteration I believe Sir Francis had a mind to make in her marriage settlement, which might displease her.

There is a letter from George Willughby to Sir Francis dated in October 1575, which shews that he did ill offices between Sir Francis and his Lady, for in this letter he desires Sir Francis Willughby would banish his Wife from him, if after her many promises she would not at least yeild to pass the fines[180]

There is in the Library at Wollaton the copy of a letter writ by Sir Francis Willughby to Sir John Lyttleton, An: D: 1575 full of complaints of his Wife, amongst other things he writes that one day at Wollaton, as he was talking with Mary his fool[181] of going to Kinsbury, his Wife answer'd she would not goe thither, upon which he asked her if she would stay at Wollaton, or goe to Middleton. She answer'd that she would not stay there, and that if she had not been lately very sick; he would not have found her there, for she would have been gone before he had returned. He asked her whither, to which she answer'd, her friends would not see her destitute, and she would not bear so much as she had done, and that she would not with her good will tarry any longer with him, who she said kept her but as a fool, to jest, and flout at.

There is the copy of another letter from Sir Francis Willughby to Sir John Lyttleton in which he tells him that one night Sir Thomas Cocken[182] supped with him and his Wife at Nottingham, and used many friendly speeches to perswade her to be in a better temper, calling her Sister, and telling her he did so, because he had but one Sister, [f. 86] and her name was Lyttleton, but Lady Willughby grew very angry and wished him to fall to his meat, if he had no other speeches to impart to her. Sir Thomas Cockin comended some of the servants for being men of honesty, and wished she would not be so much offended with them, to which she replyed they were the veryest villins that ever Woman was troubled with.

There are several letters from Sir John Littleton[183] to Sir Francis Willughby in behalf of his Daughter, which letters shew that he

---

[180] 'Fine' used in a phrase meant (Obs.) 'In the end, at last.' To 'pass the fines' [fin] was to end the dispute, *OED.*

[181] See fo. 83, p. 115 above, where a Mary is listed among the servants. See John Southworth, *Fools and Jesters at the English Court* (Stroud, 1998). Most fools and jesters were men rather than women.

[182] Sir Thomas Cokayne of Ashburne, Derbys. (1520–1592) held many offices in that county, most notably from 1555 to his death as justice of the peace and in 1585 and 1592 as member of a special commission to investigate Jesuits and seminarians. C.J. Black, 'Sir Thomas Cokayne', *The History of Parliament Online:* http://www.historyofparliamentonline.org/volume/1509-1558/member/cokayne-sir-thomas-1520-92.

[183] The Lyttletons of Frankley spelled their name with a 'y' rather than an 'i', and Cassandra normally does so also.

endeavoured as much as he could to reconcile Sir Francis and his Lady. In one of these letters he assures Sir Francis that he would by no means plead for his Daughter, if he did not believe her very innocent, concerning those aspersions which had been cast upon her by malicious people, and such as had ill designs upon Sir Francis.

In answer to these letters there is the copy of a very long letter wrote by Sir Francis Willughby to Sir John Lyttleton, in which he gave a large account of his Wives behaviour. He wrote that he had long born her froward humour with secret sorrow (which now long of herself was become so publick) and to keep her in temper, he had forborn having his only Sister a night in his house for eight years, and then because she came to have stayed three or four nights, his Wife went down to the Vicarage, and sent for him, but he refused to goe to her. The next day she sent to him, to know if he would suffer her [to] come into the house to speak with him. He answered, that he never forbid her the house, but he desired she would carry herself as she ought. Nevertheless, upon her coming into the house she called his Sister abominable names, and swore she would neither eat, drink, or sleep, till she was revenged of her.

[f. 87] Sir Francis Willughby did not write how this dispute ended, but by many papers it appears that from this time they lived very unhappily together, and that Lady Willughby would often fall into passions which made her say very provoking vexatious things to Sir Francis, who seems to have been a man of great piety and learning. There are in the Library at Wollaton a great many very pious discourses writ by him, and severall sermons which he made for his own chaplains to preach, and a collection of the most learned books of his time. By copys of his own letters and other papers he appears to have been of a very mild sweet disposition, and a lover of hospitality, but a little too apt to be imposed on, by stories from his servants, who I believe made some advantages to themselves by agravating those unhappy differences between himself and his Lady,[184] who seems to have been a woman of wit, and virtue, but of a turbulent spirit, and ungovernable passions as one may judg

---

[184] Another assessment of Sir Francis Willoughby from a member of the family came from the pen of Montague Wood, husband of the youngest daughter Frances. He wrote, in 1626, that, 'Yett in that time of government he kepte as greate hospitalitye as any man in his shire. He bought as much lande as he sould, he spent as much in buildinge, yet in givinge to many confidence he was deceaved of more land than he soulde and more then would have payd his debts and his buildings.' Mi, 2/76/3–16, quoted in Alice T. Friedman, *House and Household in Elizabethan England, Wollaton Hall and the Willoughby Family* (Chicago, 1989), 37 and in Richard S. Smith, 'The Willoughbys of Wollaton 1500–1643 with special reference to early mining in Nottinghamshire, 1500–1643', PhD thesis, University of Nottingham, 1964, 69.

by copies of many of her letters and dialogues some of which I shall copy here.

It is before mention'd (Page 70) that the Lady Stanhop was one of those Ladys which Lady Willughby most often viseted, and from her doing so I believe some of her enemies would have raised a jealousie in Sir Francis, that Lady Willughbys friendship with the Lady Stanhop did proceed from her liking to be in Sir Thomas Stanhops company. This made an uneasyness between Sir Francis Willughby and the family of the Stanhops of Shelford.[185]

There is an account that upon Christmas Even Sir Francis left his Lady and went to Coventry, and that he took with him great part of the plate, but yet left enough with his [f. 88] Lady for necessary use. At his going away from her, he did requir of her a jewel in which was Sir Thomas Stanhops picture, but she bid him content himself, for he should never have that whilst he lived, and also many other disrespectfull things she said to Sir Francis Willughby at their parting.

This jewel, in which was Sir Thomas Stanhops picture, I find by letters to Lady Willughby was bought by Sir Thomas Stanhop for his own Lady, but Lady Willughby having desired Sir Thomas upon his going to London that he would buy her some such diamonds, and he not meeting with them, writ a letter to excuse his not buying the diamonds for her, and with that letter sent the jewel which he had bought for his own Wife in which was his own picture, which picture he desired might be returned to his Wife, and if Lady Willughby liked to keep the diamonds the price of them was sixty six pounds.

There is a letter from Sir Thomas Stanhop directed to the worshipfull Mrs. Marrows (who I believe was Lady Willughbys Sister).[186] He writes, that he had received the jewell, but knew not why Lady Willughby's having the jewel or wearing it should breed

---

[185] Sir Thomas Stanhope of Shelford (1540–1596) was the heir of Michael Stanhope (beheaded 1552). See Cobbing and Priestland, *Sir Thomas Stanhope of Shelford*. If the accusations of Thomas Stanhope's wife, Margaret Port, are to be believed, he used her cruelly; she calls him a tyrant and accuses him of 'blasphemy, misdemeanor, whore hunting, drunkiness, mischief and all naughtiness'. Married in 1557, they separated from 1581 to 1585. *Ibid.*, ch. 10, esp. p. 145. Based on reading some of Sir Thomas Stanhope's letters to Francis Willoughby, Cassandra also offers an unflattering description of Stanhope as a 'very haughty captious Gentleman' (fo.103, p. 134 below). See Wallace MacCaffrey, 'Talbot and Stanhope: An Episode in Elizabethan Politics', *The Bulletin of the Institute of Historical Research*, 33 (1960), 73–85.

[186] Margaret Lyttleton was the second daughter of Sir John Lyttleton. In 1561 she married Samuel Marrow, heir of Thomas Marrow of Berkswell, Warks. W.B. Stephens (ed.), *A History of the County of Warwick: VII*, VCH (London, 1964), 59; see TNA, C142/132/38, Inquisition *post mortem* of Thomas Marrow.

any harm, for he bought it reasonably cheap, and meant his Wife should have worn it, and therefore caused his own picture to be put therein, but my Lady her Sister having desired him when he went to Town to lay out such a sum upon a jewel for her, and he finding none for her price, at his return sent this picture and a letter with it for her to shew her Husband with the jewel and the picture, and if upon consideration thereof they both liked the jewel for the money it cost, then they might keep the jewel and return him the picture. This letter was dated from London March 1578. This and other letters shew Lady Willughbys inocency concerning this picture, but such was her anger when she and Sir Francis [f. 89] parted she had no mind he should have the comfort of believing her so.

Before Sir Francis went this Christmas Eve from his Lady (who I believe might be then at Kinsbury) to Coventry, I find by a letter from Sir John Lyttleton dated November 1578, that she had gone from Sir Francis to Frankeley. In this letter from Sir John to his Daughter he blames her for coming with others with her to Frankeley, without giving them warning, when she knew that her mother was at Prestwood.[187] He wrote that he referrs it to her own rash head what wisdom was in this, and because he hears she intends to come to Prestwood, he thinks fit to let her understand that he is not well, and the sight of her will not mend, but greatly disquiet him, and therefore he trusts never to see her more. She has forgot the duty of a Daughter to him, and he will forget her as his Daughter, in every thing, but that of praying for her, that God would bless her and her children and send her grace to shew herself both in life word and deed a dutifull Wife to her Husband.

In the long account which Sir Francis Willughby gave Sir John Lyttleton of his Wives behaviour to him, he writes that three weeks after he had left her, he sent to Henry Draycott[188] to goe to her,

---

[187] The Lyttleton manor farm of Prestwood had been purchased 12 Feb. 1554 from Sir Edward Hastings, master of the queen's horse; it had originally been part of the duke of Northumberland's (or Dudley) estates but was not included in the restoration of those estates to the 4th Lord Dudley. *CPR 1553–1554*, 1 Philip & Mary, vii, 194, licence to Hastings to alienate Prestwood to John Lyttleton of Frankley, with remainder to Gilbert Lyttleton, his son and heir. The Dudleys, however, felt that they still had a claim to the property, and when the 4th Lord Dudley died in 1586 and John Lyttleton died in 1590, Lord Dudley's son claimed that Sir John Lyttleton had received from him £200 as earnest for an eventual sale of the property to him for £2,600. Lord Dudley seized the property in 1590 with a force of 120 men and a lengthy lawsuit ensued that was decided, ultimately, in favour of the Lyttletons. TNA, STAC 5/L27/10, 5/L6/3; Tonks, 'Lyttletons', 54–59.

[188] Henry Draycot was, several times, placed in charge of the Willoughby household in 1578. See below, fos 89, 92, 119, 164: see pp. 125–126, 150, 189, 205. This may have been the same Mr Draycot who was fostered and supported with books and clothing in the Willoughby household in the 1520s (*HMC Middleton*, 358, 365, 383, 385, 396), or that

and let her know that he was going to her Husband (on purpose to try what message she would send).[xxiii] Her answer was, she would send no commendations to him, for she cared not for him.

He writes that soon after he went himself to Kinsbury taking with him Sir Fowlk Grevell,[189] Mr. Boughton[190] and Mr. Fisher.[191] Of what passed there, Sir Francis gives in this letter to Sir John Littleton a short account, and else where I find it writ down to this effect,[xxiv] viz: that after they had supped at Kinsbury Sir Francis Willughby sent to his Lady (who had before refused to come to supper) to requir her to speak with him. She sent word she would speak with him in the Gallery, where they all went. What Sir Francis said at first [f. 90] going into the Gallery was not heard by the company, but his Lady answer'd in great coller, I will blaze your armes and make you better known. Sir Francis pressed her to be reconciled to his Sister, which she refused [*she answered, she would not be reconciled to his Sister, nor come in her company but in other matters she would doe what he required of her, if reasonable, and what she should approve off. But being moved that these unkindnesses might pass, and old love be again renewed. She answered she could never love him, and that by his forward dealing, her heart was hardend against him. Upon telling her that he heard some of the servants which he had discharged, did loyter about the house, she Answered they were no charge to him, and would be there abouts in the Country in spite of him. Being again required to submit herself to him and take some better course, she answered she should never require his good will so long as she lived, wth divers*

Draycot may have been his father. In 1547 a 'Mastre Draycott' received an annuity of £3 10s for half a year. *HMC Middleton*, 317.

[189] This Fulke Greville is either Sir Fulke Greville (1536–1606) or his son, Fulke Greville (1554–1628), 1st Baron Brooke (Lord Brooke).

[190] Edward Boughton (*c*.1545–1589) of Causton was high sheriff of Warwickshire in 1579. According to the parish registers at Newbold-on-Avon, Edward Boughton, Esq. of 'Cawson' was buried on 13 Sept. 1589 (Dunchurch). A grandson, Edward Boughton, was baptized 31 Mar. 1572 (Newbold). A marriage between him and Elizabeth Catesbye was recorded at Newbold on 27 or 28 Oct. 1593. George Fanshaw Bridgeman (ed.), *Memorials of a Warwickshire Family* (London, 1906), 49–50, 56–57.

[191] Clement Fisher (*c*.1539–1619), of Great Packington, Warks. In the mid 1570s he worked for the earl of Leicester. He was a justice of the peace in Warwickshire from 1579–1590. Enis, 'The Dudleys, Sir Christopher Hatton and the Justices of Elizabethan Warwickshire', 18, 28. In 1585 he acted as treasurer for the earl of Leicester's expedition to the Netherlands; he received his knighthood from King James I. See Text n. 177 above and fos 146–149, pp. 186–187 below for the difficult relationship that developed between Bridget Willoughby and Clement and Mary Fisher. Clement Fisher had many financial dealings with Sir Francis Willoughby, at one time (in 1595) lending him a thousand pounds (fo. 149, p. 189). Later, Percival Willoughby owed him £330. Chandos, *The Continuation of the History*, 33; Mi, LM 27, fo. 30. Mary Fisher, according to Cassandra, was the daughter of George Willoughby (see below, fo. 141, p. 181), but she appears to be the step-granddaughter of George Willoughby and the daughter of Richard Repington.

other opprobrious, undecent, and spitefull speeches.][192] He then asked her if in all other things she would be ruled by him, to which she answer'd she would not be ruled by him. Upon which Sir Fowlk Grevell said why, Madam, will you refuse to be ruled by your husband. She answer'd she was the Queens sworn servant and knew not but Sir Francis might command her something against her Majesties proceedings, to which Sir Fowlk said that was an evil objection for a Wife to lay to her Husband.[193] Mr. Boughton would have perswaded her for her childrens sake and her own (for to discredit her Husband was to discredit herself and posterity) that there might be a good agreement and love between herself and Husband. She answer'd that her heart was hardned against Sir Francis, and she could not love him as she had done. Sir Francis answered her that since his first marrying her to this day her actions had shewed the little love which now her speech made manifest. He asked her how she could answer keeping those servants which he had discharged contrary to his liking. To which she gave him a very passionate answer and many more disrespectfull speeches are set down in this dialogue, from her to Sir Francis, who told her of somethings which he disliked, to which (says this writen account) she answer'd in mockage that she thanked him, and if she had had a cap she would have put it off to him. Many more spitefull disrespectfull speeches she made which are there copied, but this I think is sufficient to shew the nature of their uneasiness, and too much to be noted down by a Grandaughter in the fourth descent from this Lady.

This meeting which seems to have been design'd in order to have reconciled the unhappy difference between Sir Francis and his Lady, served only to increas that breach which was already made. Mrs. Mearing,[194] Lady Willughby's woman was with her Lady in the Gallery, and to Mr. Fisher expressed her sorrow for what had passed.

---

[192] STB 2 (1), book 1, fos 24–25.

[193] For a discussion of a married woman's allegiance to the Crown under Common Law, see Barbara J. Todd, 'Written in her heart: Married women's separate allegiance in English law', in Tim Stretton and Krista J. Kesselring (eds), *Married Women and the Law: Coverture in England and the Common Law World* (London, 2013), 163–191, noting that, throughout the early modern period, 'the principle of a wife's personal separate allegiance, though challenged, remained intact' (p. 182).

[194] She is named Elizabeth on the next folio. There were Meringes in Nottinghamshire going back to the 14th century. See the 1546/7 will of William Meringe of Saundby, Esq., *Testamenta Eboracensia*, 6, Surtees Society, CVI (Durham, 1902), 248–250, in which he names brothers, cousins, nephews and nieces; the Meringes intermarried with the Markhams; an earlier Elizabeth Meringe married John Strelley. William Meringe's widow and executrice was Elizabeth Meringe.

Sir Francis having left his Lady at Kinsbury Hall went into [f. 91] Nottinghamshire, after which Lady Willughby would have sent some of the men out of the house, but they sent her word that they would not goe, upon which she went down herself being led by Mrs. Elizabeth Mearing, and another of the maids, to have seen them turned out, but meeting Cludde[195] with his sword under his arm, Lady Willughby cry'd out in a fright, what will they murther me in my Husbands absence, and upon this sending down some of her maids to raise the Town, there came in Penn[196] and Green and divers others after them, who not being able to appease or sattisfie my Lady, she desired them all to guard her to the Vicarage, which they did.

Sir Francis being advertised of this disturbance at Kinsbury left his business which he had at Colearton,[197] and returned to his Lady, taking with him Mr. Beaumont.[198] The reception he met with from his Lady was not more kind then before, and much such another discourse passed between them, which remains writ down amongst the old papers in the Library at Wollaton.

There is a letter from Mr. Beaumont to Sir Francis Willughby dated from Kinsbury, in which he writes that he came thither the night before, where he found Lady Willughby very sadd (and in the house they told him she had not been well). He asked her what was the cause of the matter that was now fallen forth. She answer'd she should be glad to know that herself. She was sure no dishonesty could be laid to her charge, and therefore her care was the less. He told her he perceived Sir Francis meant not to lay any such matter to her charge, but only to reform the disorders that had been in his house amongst his servants, and others, who resorted thither. To which she answered, she was well content, and would not dislike what you [Sir Francis] did, save only that you should not force her to see Lady Arundell, who she thought had wronged her, and she could not endure her presence with out doing [f. 92] her some mischief and therefore she would avow it. He writ that he had used all

---

[195] Cludd is later described (fos 147–147v, pp. 186–188) as a cousin of Clement Fisher. On fos 92, 119, pp. 15, 150, he is referred to as J. Cludd.

[196] A John Penn is mentioned in the list of servants from 1572 (fo. 83, p. 116, above).

[197] Coleorton, Leics. Francis Willoughby was working coal pits at Coleorton in the 1570s that were owned by Nicholas Beaumont. Smith, 'The Willoughbys', 179–184, 196. Francis also tried to buy the Beaumont manor, and his loss of that opportunity gave rise to a suit at chancery in 1576, TNA, C. Eliz. W 14/19. He did, however, take on the debts of Nicholas Beaumont from the revenues of the coal pits to his financial detriment.

[198] Huntingdon Beaumont (c.1560–1624) was an innovator in coal mining, later a partner of Sir Percival Willoughby in the construction of perhaps Britain's first railed wagonway, known as the Wollaton Wagonway. R.S. Smith, 'Huntingdon: Beaumont Adventurer in Coal Mines', *Renaissance and Modern Studies*, 1 (1957), 115–153.

the perswasions his wit would serve him with, but Lady Willughby was so resolute, that nothing which he could say was able to stir her.

By some of the old papers it appears that Lady Willughby was[xxv] after this with Sir Francis at Coventry, but those papers don't shew when she went to him. By many circumstances in them, one may judge that they lived there, most unhappily together.

[1578–1588: Separation]

There is the copy of a letter from Sir Francis Willughby to Sir John Lyttleton, in which he writ, that being to goe to London he had set down directions for his men to observe in ordering of his family during his absence from Coventry, viz: that Joahn should look to the ordering of the children. To which his Wife said, who ever should take upon them to order her children, in her presence, she would mischief,[199] [*she said Joahn was his Whore*][200] and she would not be left amongst such villains, but would goe into the Town. To which he answered, that she should not, to make such an uproar as she had done before at Kingsbury. Then she desired to goe to an Inn, and send for some of her friends to her, and upon his denying her that, she fell into a most violent passion [*and sitting down called for a knife*] threatning to make away with herself, and being denyed a knife would have struck her scisors into her belly if she had not been prevented, [*and then she said she would never eat or drink more, but with the same knife she was next to eat with would kill herself.*][201]

There remains now in the Library at Wollaton those orders which Sir Francis Willughby left with his servants, Henry Dracot and J: Cludd, when he went from Coventry to London, February 1578, and left his Lady in that disturbance which his letter to Sir John Lyttleton gives the relation off.

> A Copy of the Orders left by Sir Francis Willughby to his
> Servants at Coventry to be observed during his Absence

That prayers be said at ten a clock in the morning, and at five a clock in the evening, that the children be there present, [f. 93] and that after service is done diner, and supper be presently brought up.

---

[199] In this context, could mean 'come to an end or harm', *OED*.

[200] There is a Johan Beardmore mentioned as taking care of the children in Jan. 1573. She is referred to again in the accounts in Oct. 1573. Mi, A 57, fos 16, 31. Another Johan listed in the household during these years is a Johan Poker.

[201] The additions to this letter come from Cassandra's earlier notes: STB 2 (1), book 1, fo. 22v.

That those persons which I have discharged from my house do not repair thereto, nor have any conference with my Wife, or any of her friends till my return.

That she shall have nothing to doe with the children, but that they shall be orderd by such as I shall appoint for that purpose.

That the household be ordered by the discretion of Dracot and Cludde, and such as I shall authorise, the weekly charges not exceeding 4li 13s 4d.

That my Wife shall not discharge or receive any servant, nor strike or evil entreat any servant.

That Arthur Buckly do not suffer any horses to be employed at my Wives command.

That there be no stuff bought in the Town without ready money paid for the same.

That who I shall appoint doe keep the chamber where the stuff is laid, and not suffer my Wife to buy or lay any other stuff there. That she have no authority to comand any thing in the house except necessary diet for herself.

That in my absence she shall not send any servant of any message to any place.

That Dracot and Cludde shall discharge all such as shall break these orders and place others in their rooms, if there be need to have any greater number.

That the children doe goe to bed strait after eight [f. 94] a clock at night and are made ready before eight a clock in the morning. And after it is nine a clock at night no body must be in the Great Chamber, but that the fire be raked up and the door locked.

That the servants be not gading into the Town, but give their attendance at dinner, and supper, and all other times.

Lady Willughby could not bear being thus left at Coventry with so little power in her family, and her servants so much, as appears by a letter from her directed to Sir Francis Willughby at London, and dated this February An: D: 1578.

Her letter was to this effect, that at Sir Francis's late going to London, his pleasure was that she should remain in his house at Coventry, if she could like the same, and further he did order that the Mayor[202] and Aldermen of the said Citty should provide her a house, not being an Inn, if she did not like to continue in his

---

[202] William Sewell the younger (1542–1624) of Warwickshire was mayor of Coventry in 1578. Sewell and his wife Ann (née Wagstaff) kept a public house named 'The Thistle' in Coventry. A brass plate in the name of Sewell providing this information is located in the ruins of the Cathedral Church of St Michael.

house. She writes that after he was gone the servants did deal with her so cruelly that she was not able to bear it, fearing that both herself and the child she went with must have been both lost, such was her grief. – For which reason she went out of the house to meet her Brother and some other friends and kinsfolks to confir with them what course she had best to take, minding to have returned home imediately after, but the servants refused her enterance, which forced her to goe to a house which the Mayor and Aldermen had provided for her, in which house she now was, in want of all necessarys, having no apparell but what was upon her back, nor any money to bear her charges.

She desires he will remit and forgive her offence to him in words, and hopes at his return to be received by him, that they may live with comfort together, and till then she desires [f. 95] his answer by the messenger what she shall doe.

I could not find (by any of the old papers) what answer Sir Francis Willughby sent to this letter from his Lady, but believe he gave her no invitation to come home to his house again, and it is very likely that in this time of his being in London Lady Arundell might help to perswade him that he might live more happily from his Wife than with her, who by her ungovernable passions made her self so very vexatious to him.

There is the copy of a letter from Sir Francis Willughby to Sir John Lyttleton, which I believe might be writ about this time. In which letter Sir Francis Willughby says that if he, or her mother, will receive his Wife into their house and endeavour to reduce her to a better temper, he shall be contented to make her a fit allowance. [*But in that I perceive Sr Franceis was very delaytory, for about the year 1582, I find he was obliged by the Queen to allow his Wife 200li a year for separate maintenance.*][203]

There is a letter from Lady Arundell (who 'tis probable might bear her Brother company when he return'd again into the Country, and that she might write him this letter soon after her returning home). In it she says, that she hears his Wife is very joyfull for her departure out of the country, and that her gosseps[204] give out that she will use all the

---

[203] STB 2 (1), book 1, fo. 26.
[204] Acquaintances or friends. See also Laura Gowing, review of Bernard Capp, *When Gossips Meet: Women, Family and Neighbourhood in Early Modern England* (Oxford, 2003), in *Reviews in History*, Institute of Historical Research (Nov. 2003), http://www.history.ac.uk/reviews/review/365 (accessed 11 Sept. 2017). According to Gowing, 'A contemporary term for companions in childbirth, "gossips" also swiftly became a derogatory term for women talking: the slippage begs important questions about the meaning of female friendship and conversation in contemporary culture.' It is probable that Elizabeth was pregnant at the time.

means she can to come to his presence and use speeches of great submission, altho, she means not to perform them. And that the Mayor and Cittyzens of Coventry have promised her so diligently to solicit the matter, that there is no heart so hard as not to be moved to pitty, much less his, whose natural disposition is to be courtious.

[*By this Lady Sr Francis Willughby had six Daughters when they parted; the Son w[hi]ch was born after at Sr John Littletons dyed young. In the time that Sr Francis and his Lady lived a sunder the three Daughters were married.*][205]

[f. 96] There are in the Library at Wollaton many letters which were writ by Sir John Lyttleton to Sir Francis Willughby in this year An: D: 1579 in behalf of his Daughter. There is one dated from Prestwood April 1579 in which he writes that Sir Francis only blames his Wife in the Generall without charging her with any particulars. He writes, that he hopes Sir Francis will offer her as wrong, and that natural affection forbids him to see her suffir it, and by order of law he may redress her, and if she have offended, he shall leave her reformation to the law, and in her cause he will deal and doe what he may by order of law.

There is another letter from Sir John Lyttleton to Sir Francis Willughby dated November 1579, in which he complains of his age and unfitness to travell, and for that reason he intreats Sir Francis to take the trouble of coming to Frankley, where he would be as wellcome as any friend, and when they were together he hop'd they might put an end to the difference between himself and his Lady, in which cause he thought no body was so fit to deal, as he her Husband, and himself her Father.

There is another letter ditto to ditto, dated the same month, to put Sir Francis in mind of his Lady, and little Son, who he seemed so careless, nay forgetfull, off [of].

There is the copy of Sir Francis Willughbys answer to this letter, in which he writes that he is contented to yeild more for his Wives relief than any seeking of hers, or, her demerit towards him, have deserved.

[f. 97] There is another letter from Sir John Lyttleton to Sir Francis Willughby dated December 1579. In which he writes that he has sent to his Daughter to know what she would desire Sir Francis Willughby should allow her for maintenance, to which she had answer'd, that she requested nothing but to be reconciled to his favour, and to live with him. Sir John in this letter heartily desires Sir Francis to accept the same. But if he will not; then he desires he will consider whose Wife she is, and of what family she is descended from, and accordingly proportion his allowance to her during the time of their separation. He

---

[205] STB 2 (1), book 1, fo. 26.

writes, that he thinks she can't have less than a gentlewoman to attend her, a nurse for her young Son, a maid to help the nurse and to be landress to them all, a boy needfull about the nurse, and to make his Lady's fires, and a serving man to wait upon his Lady. And for their tabling he trusts Sir Francis will allow for his Wife sixteen pence a day, and for each of the servants eight pence a day, and for wages he thinks he can't give less than fifty three shillings and four pence a year a piece to the woman nurse and man, and to the landress and boy twenty six shillings and eight pence a piece.

He leaves it to Sir Francis to name what he will allow for apparel, for his Wife and little Son (who he prays God to bless with many happy years) and with money he will allow her for other needfull expences. He thinks it will be also needfull for her to have a couple of geldings to use when she shall have occasion to ride.

There are severall letters which were writ by Lady Willughby to Sir Francis in this year An: D: 1579, in which she desires to know where he would have her goe, and if he still continues to like of her going to board with Mr. Beaumont. In these letters which are dated from Barkeswell[206] she desires he will give his blessing to his Son, and subscribes herself his obedient Wife.

[f. 97 v.] There is a letter from Sir Foulk Grevill to Catesby dated An: D: 1579 to propose his taking Lady Willughby to Board with him.

[f. 98] One of those letters from Lady Willughby to Sir Francis, dated from Barkeswell An: D: 1579, is to advertise him that a Pursevant [court summoner] had been with her to appear this terme in the Starre Chamber, but seeing her in a state not able to travell he had promised to give notice thereof to the Court, but said the next terme she would be forced to answer, not at the sute of Paramour[207] but of one that was under the Lord Leycester. She

---

[206] Elizabeth was staying with her sister Margaret and brother-in-law Samuel Marrow. The manor of Berkswell, Warks., 'was among the manors granted in 1553 to John Dudley, earl of Warwick and duke of Northumberland, but on his attainder reverted to the Crown. In Apr. 1557 the manor was granted to Thomas Marrow and Alice his wife, with remainder to their son Samuel and his heirs'. Salzman, *County of Warwick: IV*, VCH, 27–34. Samuel married Elizabeth's sister Margaret in 1561 (see Text n. 186 above).

[207] This refers to a lawsuit regarding the estate of Drayton Bassett mortgaged to the London tailor Richard Paramour in 1575 who dispossessed Thomas Robinson (a known recusant) in June 1578. Robinson's grandfather had been granted a 77-year lease on the land by Thomas Pope in 1538. Robinson maintained that foreclosure of a £1,200 debt for an estate worth £8,000 was usury. Paramour, frightened off Drayton Bassett in July 1578 by a 'large body of country gentry', perhaps including Francis Willoughby, appealed to Lord Leicester, who sent Henry Ferrers and George Digby to regain possession (fee simple was held by the crown). A struggle followed, leaving one man dead. The Privy Council became involved, and the case appeared before a rump Star Chamber in 1580. '*Paramour v. Robinson, Carie, and others*', TNA, STAC 5/P65/6. Simon Adams, *Leicester and the Court:*

desires to know Sir Francis's pleasure; what she should doe. In this letter she complains for want of money for necessary use, and writes that if he thinks there be cause why she should be so hardly dealt with, she was ready to answer it, which he would call her thereto. But she trusted that he would forget words past and accept of her as heretofore he had done, which would be to her great comfort. If not she desired he would fix the place where he would have her dwell, for she would not chuse for herself.

There is another letter from Lady Willughby to Sir Francis, in which she writes that she had kept no copy of her answer in the Starre Chamber.[208]

There are many letters from Lady Willughby to Sir Francis, in which she acknowledges herself to blame for her unhansome speeches, and disrespectfull carriage to him. In one she writes that she had been his Wife 16 years, and born him 12 children – that he cannot accuse her of any breach of her marriage covenant – all the faults he charges her with are disrespectfull speeches, which she is sorry for. And once more she offers her humble submission to him, it being the fourth time, which she protests was first sealed with her heart, before it was signed with her hand. But if he thinks this not sufficient, she desires he will set her down any other reasonable form, and he shall [f. 99] find her both ready to yeild to it, and willing to perform it. She desires he will consider how many false stories he has given credit to, told by those who mortally hate her, as that in truth she was not with child when she left him, but only feigned herself to be so. Afterwards that the child was dead, and even now, that it is suborned and none of her own.

There are also some letters from Lady Willughby, to Sir Francis, full of complaints, for want of an allowance, and for having her children taken from her etc.

There are severall letters which were writ by Sir Francis, and Lady Willughby's friends, about this time in order to reconcile those unhappy differences which were between them. Amongst which there is one from Thomas Duport[209] who expresses great good will

---

Essays on Elizabethan Politics (Manchester, 2002), 340–341, 372 n. 242, 387. For citations to Star Chamber records, see D.C. Peck, 'The Earl of Leicester and the riot at Drayton Park, 1578', *Notes and Queries* 27 (Apr. 1980), 131–135. Peck mentions that both Francis and Elizabeth were interrogated by the government but not charged.

[208] Since Elizabeth was interrogated separately regarding Paramour, and Cassandra chose to incorporate the communication with Star Chamber here, this reference is probably about Paramour and not the Willoughbys' separation.

[209] Thomas Duport (c.1513–1592) was an attorney employed by Henry Grey, marquis of Dorset. He was the executor, for example, of Mary Grey's will. S.T. Bindoff, *A History of Parliament, The House of Commons, 1509–1558*, XI (London, 1982), 69.

to Sir Francis Willughby and his family. He writes that he knew his Father Mr. Henry Willughby and Lady Ann, his Mother, and also his Grandfather, Sir Edward Willughby dwelling in Dorsetshire, and also his Great Uncle, Sir John Willughby dwelling at Collarton who all lived, worshipfull in their callings, and he hoped yet to see himself and his Lady live happily together for the good of them both, as well as their children who were now in a manner bereft of loving parents, and good educations. He begs pardon for his rude writing, wishing to see him live in such worship and estimation as his ancestors, in his knowledg had done, concluding – Yours to my little power.

There is a letter from Aldridge, who I believe was the Minister of Wollaton,[210] to Lady Willughby, to perswade her to submit herself [f. 100] to her Husband.

There is a letter from Bromley Cancell[211] to perswade Sir Francis Willughby to be reconciled to his Lady, who, he writes he is perswaded will use all diligence in her endeavours to content him, and gladly yeild him all due submission.

There is a letter from Sir John Lyttleton to Sir Francis Willughby dated June 1580, to desire they might have a meeting in order to reconcile himself and his Lady.

There are severall letters writ by Lady Arundell about this time to her Brother Sir Francis Willughby. In one she puts him in mind of taking a house against he comes to London, and tells him there is one to be had in White Freers, which stands near the Temple of

---

[210] Robert Aldridge (d.1616) was appointed rector of Wollaton by Francis Willughby on 15 Sept. 1576. In 1578 he was also appointed vicar of St Mary's, Nottingham by Queen Elizabeth. Apparently Wollaton went without a rector for some years in the 1590s. Aldridge was back performing marriages at Wollaton in 1613 after having been found derelict by the churchwardens in his attention to St Mary's. George Fellows, 'Wollaton Church', *TTS*, 6 (Nottingham, 1903), supplement, pp. 41–42. John T. Godfrey (ed.), *Notes on the Parish Registers of St. Mary's Nottingham, 1566 to 1812* (Nottingham, 1901), 15; W.P.W. Phillimore and T.M. Blagg (eds), *Nottinghamshire Parish Registers: Marriages*, 8 (London, 1905), 60. It was Aldridge who appointed John Darnell, puritan and, apparently, fraudulent exorcist, as curate of St Mary's in the 1590s. See Marion Gibson, *Possession, Puritanism and Print: Darrell, Harsnett, Shakespeare and the Elizabethan Exorcism Controversy* (New York, 2015), 84–92.

[211] Cancell is an abbreviation for Cancellarius. Sir Thomas Bromley (1530–1587), was appointed lord chancellor (Cancellarius) of England on 26 Apr. 1579 after the death of Nicholas Bacon. A possible date for this letter might be 1580; in that year his daughter Muriel married John Lyttleton, the nephew of Elizabeth Willoughby and the grandson and heir of John Lyttleton. Thus, he can be considered one of Elizabeth Willoughby's friends.

which the half years rent will be six pounds,[212] and another house is to be had in Chanon Row, which was the Controlers.[213]

In another letter she writes that she has sent her geldings, for his coach, being glad to hear of his bringing his children to London. She writes that if he will go forward with his determination it will make his Wives stout stomach to yeild, and he will find many friends, to take his part. She advises that if his Wife does not come to Town, he would order her to remove out of the house and Town of Kinsbury, lest she should cause some mischief to it, which he would be forced to recompence.

There is a very long letter from Lady Willughby to Sir Francis, in which she writes that it is now near two years since she had been banished his company and forbid his house, in which time she had suffer'd great travell of body and trouble of mind, wandring from place to place and depending wholy for relief, upon borrowing of friends.[f. 101] Upon how slender causes offence was taken and a quarrell pick'd, his own conscience can tell, and God knows, who she trusts will in time redress her wrongs and revenge her cause upon their heads who first blew this fire of discord between them, which flames she had many times essayed to quench by personall submission, friends mediation, and divers humble letters. Could he charge her with incontinency or breach of her marriage covenant, she desired her accusers might appear, and she be made a publick example. Would he but look into his own actions half so precisely as he examined hers; and see the duty of a Husband to a Wife, as well as hers to a Husband, she doubts not but he would find himself blameworthy.

She complains in this letter, that her children were taken from her, her servants allowed to use her disrespectfully etc. She writes that she had three times offer'd her humble submission to him, and does so now a fourth time, beseeching him now to accept of it, and not only to receive her into his fellowship, but freely to forget and to

---

[212] See Nick Holder, 'The medieval friaries of London: A topographic and archaeological history, before and after the dissolution', PhD thesis, University of London, 2011. The Carmelite monastery in Fleet Street, known as White Friars, was dissolved on 10 Nov. 1538. Houses were built on the property and many were rented as full houses or tenements.

[213] Chanon Row (Cannon or Canon Row) was a 'thoroughfare in Westminster which led from the New Palace to the Privy Garden'. It was named after the residence of the deans and canons of St Stephen's Chapel. Chanon Row was notable for attracting gentry, 'divers Noblemen and Gentlemen', following the dissolution. Fran C. Chalfant, *Ben Jonson's London: A Jacobean Placename Dictionary* (Atlanta, GA, 2008), 53. Today Canon Row is located off Bridge Street across from Parliament. This might be the house of the comptroller of the household. In the 1580s this would have been Sir James Croft. 'Controlers' could also refer to comptrollers of the ports, of Windsor Castle, or of her Majesty's Navy, *OED*.

forgive her all her former faults, as she willingly treads under her feet all the injuries that have been done her.

But if he will no longer look upon her as his Wife; then she desires he will make her such an allowance as becomes Sir John Lyttletons Daughter. She desires his speedy answer, that in case her friends should not think the offers he should make reasonable, they might then proceed to have her cause otherwise redressed.

There is a letter from Trussell (who seems to have been Lady Willughby's friend)[214] to his Uncle Marmion (one of Sir Francis's servants). In this letter he expresses to his Uncle a great value for Sir Francis Willughby's family, and hearty concern [f. 102] that some catterpillers about him do eat up the branches of his good name. He writes that Lady Willughbys cause will be heard by the Earl of Leicester, and Sir Francis Walsingham, and reported to the Queen.[215]

There is the copy of a very melancholy letter writ, I believe, about this time by Sir Francis Willughby to Sir John Lyttleton, in which he laments his misfortunes, and wishes for death, rather than, to continue so vexatious a life. He writes that he is now threatned by his Wife that she will complain of him to the Queen; which would be to discredit herself.

There are many letters from Lady Arundell, which seem to have been writ about this time, to her Brother, that shew a good deal of ill nature towards Lady Willughby. And one of those letters is upon a quarrell which had been between Sir Francis and the Stanhops. She dates it from the Court, and writes that she hop'd they should have met, and had conference together of such things as had hapned, since their last being together. She had made enquiry (she writ) for the Lord Talbots coming up, who she had heard was to have ended matters between himself [Francis]

---

[214] See fos 55, 105, 136, pp. 86 and n. 83, 136 and 176, where a Henry Trussell is mentioned. Henry's mother was Bridget Marmion Trussell, and his uncle, her brother, would have been a son of Henry Marmion who is mentioned as one of the executors of the will of Henry Willoughby, Francis's father and described as 'a trusty servant'. *HMC Middleton*, 49; see Text nn. 83 and 134 above.

[215] Most likely her cause would have been heard in the court of requests under the jurisdiction of the lord privy seal. Sir Francis Walsingham (*c*.1532–1590) was the lord privy seal from 1576 until his death. The court of requests originated under Henry VII and conserved the idea of a monarch, upon petition, as 'a dispenser of patriarchal justice'. B. Quaritch, *Introduction to Select Cases in the Court of Requests 1497–1569* (London, 1898), x–xii. The court could entertain petitions for justice between spouses 'in clear defiance of the common law prohibition against litigation between spouses'. Tim Stretton (ed.), *Marital Litigation in the Court of Requests 1542–1642* (Cambridge, 2008), 1. The court of requests documents are catalogued by bundles in the National Archives. There are over 300 bundles with numerous cases in each bundle. They are currently not searchable except through volumes of a handwritten catalogue that lists the cases neither alphabetically nor by date.

and the Stanhops,[216] but being to goe out of Town now herself she could not speak with him but she wishes it were urged in this sort, that they should openly acknowledg that they had abused him, and so to desire his good will, or else she would not have him end matters with them. And for that proud fool Edward Stanhope,[217] who made comparison, to be as good as Sir Francis Willughby she would have his servants revenge it of him, till he should be weary, and glad [f. 103] to give over, and seek his favour, She writes that their braging, and his suffering it, occasions parly [partly?] to his discredit. In this letter she says, that Lady Willughby was now at Sir Edward Suttons[218] who would give her certain knowledg of her behaviour.

There are some letters to Sir Francis Willughby, which makes Sir Thomas Stanhope appear to have been a very haughty captious Gentleman, and by the copy of a letter from Sir Francis, to Sir Thomas Stanhope, I believe tho they were neighbours, they were not very good friends. One of the paragraphs in this letter was, and wheras you desire me to be my own secretary, for that you love not embassages by servants penns, I have at this time sattisfied your request, but to be always so far tied, would be very much for

---

[216] This particular dispute in unclear. By the 1590s the Talbots and Stanhopes would scarcely have been speaking to one another, given a series of disputes over contested properties and Stanhope's building of locks and a weir on the River Trent; the Talbots could not have acted as honest brokers by the 1590s. By 1590 the disputes between the Talbots and Stanhopes were already 'old and increasingly bitter'. W.J. Tighe, 'A Nottinghamshire gentleman in court and country: The career of Thomas Markham of Ollerton (1530–1607)', *TTS*, 90 (1986), 37. The dispute mentioned here may have involved marriage proposals between the Stanhopes and the Willoughbys that did not come to fruition. Cobbing and Priestland, *Sir Thomas Stanhope of Shelford*, chs 16, 17. In a letter of 1591 from Thomas Stanhope to his brother Michael, Thomas recalled a time 'when he "fell out" with Sir Francis Willoughby' with regard to a plan to marry his son with one of the Willoughby daughters, a plan foiled by Thomas Markham (who was allied with the Talbots). *Ibid.* 222. The suggested date of these letters from Margaret Arundell (early 1580s) may refer to negotiations with regard to Margaret (b. 1571) or with regard to Dorothy (b. late 1560s?), both of whom married in 1587. In a letter of 24 July 1584 Sir Francis wrote to Thomas Willoughby that he had 'byn in some talke for the mariage of my daughters, and like enough to conclude for the one, if lyking shall grow betwixt the parties, withowt the which I wyll never presse them'. *HMC Middleton*, 157; Mi, C 17.

[217] Michael Stanhope and Anne Rawson had two sons named Edward. It seems likely that this refers to the first Edward, their second son (*c.*1543–1603). A lawyer who functioned as a surveyor of crown lands in Nottinghamshire, he married the daughter of Thomas Colshill of Chigwell, Essex, and was MP for Nottinghamshire, 1571–1572; from 1587 he was a member of the Council of the North and, in 1601 an MP for Yorkshire and knighted in 1601. Edward the younger (*c.*1547–1608) was a doctor of laws, master in chancery, and chancellor to the bishop of London. Cobbing and Priestland, *Sir Thomas Stanhope of Shelford*, *passim*.

[218] Edward Sutton, 5th Baron Dudley, perhaps at Castle Dudley, Sutton's seat and main home. Dudley Castle was sequestered in 1593 for unpaid debts.

me etc. It does not appear how this quarrell with the Stanhop's ended.

There is a letter from Lady Arundell in which she writes her Brother word that she heard his Wife was come to Town.

In another letter she writes to Sir Francis Willughby, that the Secretary [Sir Francis Walsingham] had told her that his Wife had caused wittnesses to be brought up to be examined of her behaviour.

In another letter dated from the Court Lady Arundell writes Sir Francis Willughby word that Sir Foulk Grevills coming would stand him in some sted, if he should need a wittness against his Wife. In this letter Lady Arundell writes, that she had provided a woman, which she thought very mete for the purpose, and that it was requisite for his Daughters, to have such a won [one], to take care of them.

There is another letter writ by Lady Arundell to Sir Francis Willughby to perswade him to draw a catalogue of his Wives faults, and send papers with it to the Secretary Walsingham, and the Earl [f. 104] of Leicester, to prevent their interceeding with the Queen in her behalf. Here Lady Arundell reckons up faults to be noted down viz: Lady Willughby's disorderly life, her watching late contrary to his liking, her keeping such company as he did mislike, her turning away Robinson[219] out of the house at a time great matters did depend, her maintaining servants in Warwickshire which he had turned away, her riviling him to his face, her runing out of the house and raising the Town at Kinsbury.

In another letter Lady Arundell writes Sir Francis Willughby that 'tis bruted his Wife is dead, but she believes that he finds it is her own quickness, and not deadness, that troubles so many; she writes that she often resorts to the Court, and there talks her pleasure of her, thinking thereby to hide many of her own faults, which if she could, she was to be borne with, for the number of them was not a few, and to lye of others, was no deminishing of them. Her friends (she writes) wish she would come up to answer her, but she means not to bestow her time so ill. She writes that the Lord Chancellor will be

---

[219] There are several candidates in the *ODNB* for this Robinson. One is John Robinson (d.1598), president of St John's Oxford until 1572 and archdeacon of Bedford; another is John Robinson, fellow of St John's Cambridge and rector of Little Gransden, Cambridgeshire, and of Somersham, Huntingdonshire. A third is John Robinson, rector of East Treswell, Notts., in 1556, who may be the same John Robinson who died in 1598. Another candidate is Thomas Robinson (fl. 1570–1609), a well-known lutenist and composer who would have been just starting his career in the 1570s. In 1603 Thomas published the first instructional book in English for the lute titled *The Schoole of Musick*. Given the reference to the discussion of 'great matters', it is likely that one of the John Robinsons is the person indicated here.

earnest with him for her, to get rid of her, for she is so importunate with him, that it is very troublesome.

It does not appear how these matters in dispute between Sir Francis Willughby and his Lady ended, but there is a writing which shews that An: D 1582, he was obliged by the Queen to allow her two hundred pounds a year for separate maintenance.

[f. 105] There is a letter from Henry Trussell, dated December 1580, to Sir Francis Willughby to give him an account of the death of his little Son, which occasion'd great grief to all about him, but especially to the comfortless Lady, his Mother, who he writes had been very sick ever since. He solicits Sir Francis Willughby to be reconciled to his Lady, concluding with a prayer that they might both forget what was past, and be inspired with perfect love for the future.

There is a letter from Lady Willughby to Sir Francis writ some time after this childs death, in which there is many tender expressions in relation to the family. She writes that she had lived from him till she was above forty years old,[220] and she fear'd if a reconciliation could not soon be made, she should be past child=bearing, and that now, though she could not expect it without hazarding her life, yet she would contentedly run that hazard, with the hopes to establish the house of the Willughby's.

There remains no answer from Sir Francis Willughby to this letter from his Lady, but upon the death of this little Son, I believe he imediately resolved to marry his eldest Daughter Brigit, to Percivall Willoughby, the eldest Son of Thomas Willoughby of Boreplace in Kent, whose great Grandfather was Christopher Lord Willoughby of Eresby in Lincolnshire, which family of the Willoughbys I shall hereafter give an account of.

This Percivall Willoughby was I believe a youth of tender constitution, and therefore advised while he was very young to travell. There are letters from his governour writ from France to Mr. Thomas Willoughby which give a long account of him chiefly[xxvi] in relation to his health. *There are a great many Letters in my Brother Willoughbys ^Study^ writ by this Tho: Willoughby, to, and off, his Son Percivall which shew, him to have been a very kind Father, & a very just Man, when Sr Percivall was a Child he sent him into ^France^ as appears by a long account of him, writ by his Governour to Tho: Willoughby. He was then too young to*

---

[220] Elizabeth Willoughby would be above forty years old after 1586. 'Above' may also mean 'about'; in the early 1580s she was in her late thirties. This letter would have been written some years after the death of their young son but before their reconciliation in 1588/9, perhaps in about 1585. Francis had earlier, on 24 July 1584, written to Thomas Willoughby mentioning reports 'of gyving over my howse, etc., and for receiving my wife being now reconsiled, for this last part ther is no such determinacion that I am pryve of as yett'. *HMC Middleton*, 157; Mi, C 17.

improve his judgement by his travels, and by a letter which Sr Percivall writ his Lady from France after he was married (with this expression, that he was with a people which he understood not) I find he did not then learn the language, and therefore I believe Tho: Willoughby sent him into France this first time, on account of his health.[221]

There is a letter from Lady Arundell to Sir Francis Willoughby writ[xxvii] about the time that the Duke of Alanson,[222] left England. In this letter she says that Monsieur is at the sea side to take his jour=[xxviii] [f. 106] journey to Flanders; where he is desired to take the government. The Lord Leicester and the Lord Hunsdon[223] are to accompany him thither; Her Majesty with most of the Court are gone to bring him to the sea side#,[224] and if his journey thither, be no more prosperous then it hath been here, Lady Arundell judges he will make fewer hereafter. In this letter she writes that her Cousin Percivall Willoughby was going into France, which she thought would doe him good. She dates her letter from the Lord Admiralls house Purford,[225] but the date of the year is not put to any of Lady Arundells letters; that of this, may be known by the Duke of Alanson who after three months stay in England took his leave of it in February An: D: 1583.[226]

[f. 105 v.] #Sir R. Baker says that in February An. D: 1581/2 the Queen brought the Duke of Anjou on his way as far as Canterbury, and then comanded the Earl of Leicester, the Lords, Charles Howard, Hunsdon, Sheffield, Willoughby, Windsor, Sir Philip

---

[221] STB 2 (1), book 2, fos 19–20. See fos 114–118 below for Percival Willoughby's trip to Europe.

[222] Francis, duke of Alençon, later duke of Anjou (Hercule François 1555–1584), the youngest son of Henry II of France and Catherine de Medici. Hercule changed his name to Francis to honour his brother Francis II, husband of Mary Stuart, Queen of Scots. Francis was courting Queen Elizabeth, but the Queen ended the putative engagement after he attempted to take Antwerp by force in 1583 and lost badly. Guy, *Elizabeth: The Forgotten Years*, pp. 33–34.

[223] Henry Carey, 1st Baron Hunsdon (c. 1524–1596), rumoured to be Henry VIII's bastard son by Mary Carey, née Boleyn, Anne's sister. Hunsdon became the Lord Chamberlain of Elizabeth's household and patron of William Shakespeare's theatre company, the Lord Chamberlain's Men,

[224] Cassandra uses the hash mark to add material that she originally left out. See the hash symbol at fo.105v, below, where she includes the additional information.

[225] The manor of Pyrford belonged to Westminster Abbey until the Dissolution. In 1558 Queen Mary granted it to the new priory of Sheen, refounded in 1556–1557. Elizabeth granted the manor to Edward Clinton, earl of Lincoln and lord high admiral of England in 1574. H.E. Malden (ed.), *County History of Surrey*, 3, *VCH* (London, 1911), 431–436.

[226] The duke of Anjou crossed the Channel to England in late October 1581 and departed England in early February 1582. Cassandra corrects her dating information on the verso of fo.105. Elizabeth may have accompanied Francis all the way to Dover. Cole, *The Portable Queen*, p. 193.

Sidney, Sir Francis Russell, Sir George Bourchier, and some other prime Knights to accompany him to Antwerp, where he was made Duke of Brabent, Limburgh, and Lorrain.[227]

[f. 106 cont.] There is a letter from Lady Arundell, dated from Hampton Court, to let Sir Francis Willughby know that Pen[228] had reported to her great likelyhood of her Sons good success in learning etc.

There is a letter from Lady Arundell to her Neece Briget Willughby to enquire if the Traveller which she looked for, was yet come, and in this letter she desires to know when her Son Arundell[229] meant to return (by which I believe her Son went to France with Mr. Percival Willoughby). She writes, that when her Husband last saw Sir Francis Willughby, he told him that he had once thought of sending for her, and her Sisters home, for the summer, but he had alter'd his mind thinking it unfit for them to be in his house without some woman of discretion to advise them. This made her think that when her Cousin Percival did come home, they would not be sent for, and therefore she look'd that they should both come, and rest with her all the summer and at Michaelmas she would bring them up to Town and be at their wedding. She writes that she was likewise desirous to have her Sister [f. 107] Dorothy and to keep her, with her, till she was bestowed in marriage, for she thought her house a meetter place for her then where she was. And therefore she desired her neece that when she next sent to her Father she would let him know how willing she was to have them.

There are severall letters from William Arundell to his Uncle Sir Francis Willughby complaining of hard usage from his Father, which he writes must proceed from want of affection for him, because he never was undutyfull to him. His Brothers marriage[230] he writes goes on very happily, with which his Father is contented; And he alone remains rejected. He writes about trees (which I

---

[227] Sir Richard Baker, *Chronicle of the Kings of England* (London, 1670), 381.

[228] A John Penn is listed among Francis Willoughby's servants in 1572. He is further mentioned many times in the Account Book Mi, A 57 between 1572 and 1575.

[229] This reference to Margaret's son may have been to Thomas, the oldest (*c*.1560–1639) or William, the youngest (d. *c*.1591); it is most likely Thomas. Thomas was briefly imprisoned in 1580 for being a Roman Catholic and a suspected spy. Andrew J. Hopper, 'Arundell, Thomas, first Baron Arundell of Wardour (*c*.1560–1639)', *ODNB*. From these letters it appears that William was involved in mercantile and monetary matters.

[230] Thomas Arundell married Mary Wriothesley, daughter of Henry, 2nd earl of Southampton, in 1585. His father-in-law Henry was in open religious conflict with the Queen. George Cockayne, *The Complete Peerage*, ed. Geoffrey H. White, XII, Part I: (London, 1953). Arundell's brother-in-law, Henry, 3rd earl of Southampton was the subject of some of Shakespeare's sonnets. See G.P.V. Akrigg, *Shakespeare and the Earl of Southampton* (London, 1968), but see also *ODNB* entry for the 3rd earl of Southampton.

suppose Sir Francis Willughby had employ'd him to get for him) and says in his letter, that those which my Lord had were given him by merchants, and that unless he were Lord Treasurer he should not have them at that price, and that the times were now so dangerous, that no merchants durst venture over.[231] But if Sir Francis Willughby would let him know, he would do what he would have him, about getting the trees.

There is a letter from this William Arundell to Mr. Jefery[232] for a servant of Sir Francis Willughbys to offer him twenty Angells[233] to perswade his Uncle to sell him Bloxford.[234] In this letter, he complains of his Uncles unkindness to him, and mentions services which he had done his Uncle, by procuring him money etc.

There is an account of Sir Francis Willughby's settling an annuity of twenty pounds a year upon this William Arundell.

[f. 107v] There is in the Library at Wollaton a book which gives an account of money raised by Sir Francis Willughby above the produce of his land An: D: 1579 in which the sums totall are.

	li	sh	d
For wood sold at Wicken, Kinsbury etc	281	0	8
For fines lett	20	13	0
For iron made at Middleton which had cost Sir Francis in geting received	604^{li}	0^{sh}	5^{d}
	752	12	6
And for cole sold from An: D: 1576 to An: D: 1580[235]	1652	17	10

[f. 108] There is in the Library at Wollaton, a book of Sir Francis Willughbys accounts for An. D. 1580, which book shews that Sir Francis with ten servants set out from Wollaton upon the 2^{d} of November, begining a journey then towards London. This book is very particular in the account of his expences upon this journey viz: that at Packington he spent 13^{sh} 4^{d}. That the next day at

---

[231] Perhaps referring to the growing threats of a Spanish invasion after 1585.

[232] Perhaps James Jeffreys or Jeffrey, gentleman of Wellow, Hants, whose will is probated 11 Feb. 1601. TNA, PROB 11/97/104.

[233] A gold coin minted in England between 1465 and 1642. Its value varied; after 1550 it was worth 10 shillings.

[234] Possibly Bloxworth, Dorset, for which there are many court rolls, deeds and grants in the Willoughby archives. See Mi, 5/164–67, 170, 174, 179.

[235] R.S. Smith notes that this amount refers only to the profits from the coal mines at Bedworth, which were mortgaged to pay down the debts of Nicholas Beaumont. Smith, 'Willoughbys', 185.

Daintry he paid for supper, break-fast, and for horse meat 3^{li} 7^{sh} 0^{d}. By this account he lay the second night at Brickkill,[236] there is set down the particulars of his expences there, which for supper, breakfast, and horse meat, in all comes to 3^{li} 8^{sh} 4^{d}. There is also set down the particular account of what he spent at St. Albans, for supper, breakfast, and for horse meat, the sum of which was 3^{li} 11^{sh} 2^{d}.

This book does not tell where he rested by the way upon this journey, but shews that he did not get to London till Friday November the 8th and that he with only one man supped at Mr. Thomas Willoughbys house.[237] There is set down in this book, for the supper that night, for eleven of Sir Francis Willughby's men, and three carters, and for Mr. Fisher and three men paid at the White Hart in Holbourn[238] the sum of 11^{sh} 8^{d}.

This book shews that November the 9th being the next day; Sir Francis Willughby began to keep house in Lincolns=Inn Grange.[239] The particulars of that days dinner is set down, and that thirty four persons dined

---

[236] Cassandra has written Brickkill but certainly means Great Brickhill, Bucks. The journey would have been from Packington, Leics., to Daventry (rather than Daintry, as Cassandra has written it) to Great Brickhill, along the same route as the M1 motorway today.

[237] Both men kept London lodgings, presumably for business. Thomas Willoughby's London town house, was a short walking distance from Francis Willoughby's Grange. Thomas Willoughby's estate, however, was Bore Place. Bore Place in Chidingstone, Kent, entered the Willoughby family through Percivall's great-grandmother Bridget née Read (1485–1558), who inherited it from her mother Margaret Alphew (or Alphegh). Bridget married Thomas Willoughby (1486–1555), who then moved with her to Bore Place. Thomas and Bridget's second son Christopher inherited the barony of Eresby. Percivall's grandfather Robert (1511–c.1555) inherited Bore Place from his mother. He married Dorothy Willoughby (1512–1550s?), daughter of Sir Edward Willoughby of Wollaton and niece of the Navigator; this marriage ended in divorce on 13 Feb. 1553/54 owing to acknowledged adultery on the part of Dorothy Willoughby with James Rogers, Esq. Mi, 1/7/1 and Mi, 6/179/46; *HMC Middleton*, 150. Thomas, Percivall's father inherited Bore Place from Robert, although his grandfather, Thomas Willoughby, had disinherited any issue of Robert and Dorothy for 'many consideracions and causes [...] whiche I am right sorry for'. TNA, Prob. 11/30/589, fo. 307v. Edward Eldridge Salisbury and Evelyn McCurdy Salisbury, *Family Histories and Genealogies*, I, Pt. 2 (New Haven, CT, 1892), 590–591.

[238] Holborn (Holbourn) in the mid 16th century was a small village adjacent to London, bounded on the east by Chancery Lane and Gray's Inn Lane, on the west by fields, and on the south by Lincoln's Inn Fields. See 'Plan of London (circa 1560 to 1570)', in *Agas Map of London 1561* (n.p., 1633), British History Online http://www.british-history.ac.uk/no-series/london-map-agas/1561/map (accessed 23 Aug. 2016).

[239] In 2016, Lincoln's Inn Fields was the largest square in London. In the late 16th century, it consisted of three fields: Cups Field, Purse Field, and Fickett's Field. It is unclear exactly where the Willoughby grange was located. See Elijah Williams, *Early Holborn and the Legal Quarter of London*, 1 (London, 1927), 1083–1084. A grange was a country house of a gentleman not enclosed within a city wall or where farming was practised, *OED*.

with Sir Francis. The sum of that days expences was 1^{li} 8^{sh} 11^{d}. And that the next day 48 persons dined with Sir Francis Willoughby, and 42 persons supped with him. Every dish of meat is there set down [f. 109] and what it cost. The whol sum for diner and supper was 2^{li}—16^{sh}—11^{d}. Thus particular each days expence in London is set down in that book from November the 8th til the 30th that day Sir Francis went into Kent to the wedding of his Daughter Brigit.

There is set down in this book of accounts paid for Mrs. Brigit Willoughby's wedding apparel as by the bills at large may appear, 156^{li}—18^{sh}—9^{d}. And paid to Mr. Thomas Willoughby in part of wedding goods 500^{li}. Paid to Mr. Repington for drawing books between Sir Francis Willughby and Mr. Thomas Willouby 2^{li}—6^{sh}—8^{d} And paid his man for ingrossing them 1^{li}. Given to Mrs. Brigit Willughby two pounds, and to her taylor for going three times into Kent, and mending the gound [gown] ten shillings. Given to the trumpeter going into Kent six shillings and eight pence. Given to the buttler at Boreplace 6^{sh} to the yeoman of the celler six shillings, to the cook ten shillings, to the chamberlain four shillings, to the pantlor[240] three shillings, to the usher of the Hall three shillings. To the servant that help'd to dress the horses one shilling. And given to a pursevant 6^{sh}—8^{d}.

This book shews that Sir Francis stayed at Boreplace till the 6th of December, and that he came that night to London and stayed there till the 17th. The particulars of every dinner and supper and the number of people that dined with him every day is set down in this book, during the time which he stayed in London. This book also shews that December the 17th he lay at St. Albans, and that his supper, breakfast and horse meat came to 4^{li}—6^{sh}—10^{d}.

His expences upon this journey at Northampton, Harborough, and Leicester is also set down in this book.

There is another book of accounts for An: D: 1584 which shews the particulars of Sir Francis Willughby's weekly expences that whole year, which in all amounted to the sum of — 1847^{li}—1^{sh}—3½^{d} There is set down this year, for two butts of sack 22^{li}—10^{sh}—0^{d}.

[f. 109 v.] There is also a book which gives an account of money raised by Sir Francis Willughby this year An: D: 1583 for his wood etc. as follows

	li	sh	d
Rec'd of Blyth for cole	351	13	4
For wood	138	0	0

---

[240] Variation of panter. 'An officer in a large household who was in charge of the bread or pantry', *OED*.

Money borrowed   2181   0   0
                                              2670   13   4

Money raised by Sir Francis Willughby An: D: 1584
Rec'd of Blythe for cole   1026   12   3
For fines   306   13   4
For wood sold   88   0   0
Money borrowed   1468   4   4
                                              2889   9   11

Money raised by Sir Francis Willughby An: D: 1585
Rec'd of Blythe for cole   772   2   10
For wood sold   186   1   6
Of Sir Christopher Haddon[241] for the manor of   0   0
   Laughton Wallieste, in part of a greater sume   1300
Of Mr. Heyman for the mannors of Heringe
   and Sellinge,[242] in part of a greater sume   1000   0   0
Money borrowed this year   2007   0   0
                                                        5265   4   4

Sum total of money raised by Sir Francis Willughby these 3 years
above the produce of his land was   10825   7   7[243]

---

[241] Sir Christopher Hatton (1540–1591), a favourite of the Queen, was made lord chancellor of England in 1587. See Alice Gilmore Vines, *Neither Fire Nor Steel: Sir Christopher Hatton* (Chicago, 1978). Hatton appears to have been a moderating force in terms of religion in Warwickshire, balancing the growing influence of the Dudleys and reforming Protestants within the county over against a still significant number of Catholics and Catholic sympathizers. See Enis, 'The Dudleys, Sir Christopher Hatton and the Justices of Elizabethan Warwickshire'. Francis Willoughby may have been part of the Hatton network. See a letter from Christopher Hatton to Francis Willoughby, dated 7 Feb. 1582/3, thanking him for his courteous dealing with regard to the sale of Willoughby lands in Langton Wallis to Hatton. Mi, 5/167/184. In this letter Hatton expresses his gratitude and readiness to requite the favour.

[242] Ralph Heyman, son of Peter Heyman, a gentleman of the bedchamber of Edward VI, purchased Heringe and Sellinge from Francis in 1585. Edward Hasted, *The History and Topographical Survey of the County of Kent*, 8 (Canterbury, 1799), 313–314: http://www.brit-ish-history.ac.uk/survey-kent/vol8/pp303-314 (accessed 10 May 2016). Langton Herring Manor or Langeton Herynge is a fortified manor house in the county of Dorset.

[243] This income is important for assessing Francis Willoughby's ability to finance the rebuilding of Wollaton Hall.

[Bridget and Percival]

[f. 110] There are many letters from Mr. Percivall Willoughby to his Lady both before and after their marriage,[244] severall of which are so torn as to be hardly legible. In one he writes, that his pen is insufficient to express his joy to receive a letter writ with her own hand, the pattern whereof he tenderly harbour'd in his heart. But he is amazed to see her term him a master, to her, whom in heart he honors, in duty reverences, in love and loyalty, faithfull serves, and obeys, in all intire affection, is most carefully tender; and of whom he always desired, and to his power deserved, if not to be entertained as a faithfull friend and servant, at least to be retained as well wisher, remaining in her power and pleasure to be commanded, etc.

He writes, that we, unadvisedly sowing the seeds of our joys, are altogether ignorant when to make our harvest. Delays my only dear breeds danger, and doubtfull minds suspect the worst, yet doubt you not of this, that I love, and live to be only yours.

Some think it an ease to have a partner in their grief, but sorry should I be to have thee partaker of my sorrows.[245] I wish thee part of all my joys, but in grief I would suffer alone.

[f. 111] My letters should be longer, good heart, if business did not force me to make them short. But though my hands faint, my heart shall never fail. Though pen and paper wast, my love and liking shall increase, and albeit my ink freeze for cold, my good will in fervency shall try, so long as life shall last or you with like affection vouchsafe to blow the coles of my hot desire, I crave only that thou believe try and trust me.

I heartily thank you for the mirth in your letter, and am sorry my melancholy mood will not suffer me to be as merry with you. Wherefore till I am better disposed my dear adeu.

---

[244] In addition to the letters copied here which come from early in the marriage, Cassandra includes descriptions of other letters from later in their marriage in *The Continuation of the History*, 27–28, 39, 41, 45–47; Mi, LM 27, fos 23–24, 34, 36, 41–43. There are two original letters from Percival to Bridget dated 1610 in the Middleton collection: Mi, 6/170/136/4–5. For other correspondence, see Mi, 6/170/138/1–8. Cassandra concludes 'By many letters and old Papers this Lady seems to have had a very good understanding, and to have been very carefull of her Family, and to have acted with great discretion in those unhappy ^differences^ between her Father and Mother, and Sir Percivall and her Father, She appears to have been a Lady fit for business, and very well able to graple with those difficulties which their perplexed affairs often brought her under'. Chandos, *The Continuation of the History*, 27; Mi, LM 27, fo. 23.

[245] Percival is probably referring to the recent death of his mother, which must have occurred about this time, as his father was to remarry and father three more children prior to his death in 1596.

>His own never, if not yours ever
>Percivall Willoughby

Another letter he begins thus

My best beloved Black
I have used all means possible for your coming to Town but can't preveil. Your Father doubts if you were here you would either see your Mother or your Mother see you, which he in no case would, while he is in Town, otherwise our marriage had been here etc. I pray send up the measure of your finger for your wedding ring etc.

>Yours only
>Percivall Willoughby

[f. 112] There is no account of Lady Willughby's being at all consulted in the affair of her Daughter's wedding, and by this letter, which says Sir Francis would not let his Daughter be married in Town for fear she would see her Mother, I am apt to believe that Lady Willughby did not approve of the match.[246]

I believe Mr. Percivall Willoughby and his Lady were both very young when they married,[247] and that it might be intended by both their Fathers that Mr. Percivall Willoughby should travell the spring after they were married.[248]

There is a letter from Mrs. Willoughby, dated from Boreplace in Kent, to her Father Sir Francis, full of expressions of great duty, and respect to him, and of distrust of her own being able to indite a letter to him as she ought. Her small skill, and little use of writing, she hopes will make him excuse this her first letter.

She writes that she is very well used by her Father and Mother=in=law, and her Cousins, for which she desires when he sees her Father=in=law he will return thanks.

She writes that Mr. Percivall is now upon beginning his travells, which she prays God to prosper, and grant him well to return, and

---

[246] In Cassandra's notes, she states, 'otherwise their marriage had been in London. These letters bear no date but I believe they married the end of the year 1580. By letters I find soon after they were married they went to live with Mr. Thomas Willoughby at Boreplace in Kent'. STB 2 (1), book 2, fo. 22. For their marriage settlement, see a 1581 draft of terms of agreement (Mi, 5/168/74) and copies of the marriage settlement in 1583 (Mi, 5/168/75–76).

[247] He was 20 or 21.

[248] He travelled to France and Switzerland. *HMC Middleton*, 553, 557–558.

begs Sir Francis will not forget him in his absence. Her Aunt Arundell is now at the Lord Lincolns.[249]

This letter bears no date, but Sir Francis Willughby's answer to it, is dated March An: D: 1581. He writes, that he is glad to hear she is so well used by Sir Percivalls relations; but of that he was always well assured, and, to continue it, must be her own care; for 'tis not beauty nor fortune [f. 113] but good qualities and a virtuous disposition which makes a Gentlewoman esteemed. Therefore 'tis her good behaviour that must gain her own credit. He desires she will learn by others in time (she may ghess who he means) to be wise and not repent too late. That now at first entrance she should frame herself a dutyfull Wife, and that she should take care to be indeed, such a woman as she desired to be esteemed, and thus she might encrease and long enjoy her friends, in order to which two things were needfull, serving God and knowing herself. He bids her know herself, what is, and what is not fit to be done, that she may follow the good and refuse the evell, he bids her therefore serve God first in the morning, and last at night, with earnest affection, even from the heart, and not for custome sake. Next he bids her be carefull to keep good company, because ill company soon infects those that are well enclyned. etc.

There is the copy of a very affectionate and respectfull answer from Mrs. Willoughby to this letter from Sir Francis her Father; in it she returns him many thanks for his fatherly counsel to her which (she writes) she will endeavour to follow; she thanks God that she is placed amongst good company, honest and well disposed people, who shew themselves very friendly to her. Her duty to her Husband she will unfeignedly be carefull to perform, having the example of others seldom out of her mind, and cause to learn to be wise by others harms. She writes that the week before, she had a letter from her Husband, who was going to Geneva, at his departure (she [f. 114] writes) that he told her he would gladly hear by letter from Sir Francis what he would have him chiefly labour to learn in his travells, and he had writ to him to that purpose.

By this and severall other letters one would believe[250] there had been a perfect good agreement between Mr. Percivall Willoughby

---

[249] Edward Clinton (1512–1584/5), 9th Baron Clinton, 1st earl of Lincoln, lord high admiral under Edward VI. Lady Arundell did not accompany Queen Elizabeth on this visit, since Elizabeth was hosted by the earl of Lincoln in July 1580 and not again until Sept. 1582. Cole, *The Portable Queen*, 217.

[250] In Cassandra's notes, this line reads from 'believe': 'Sr. Percivall Willoughby had been designed to travell by both his Fathers after he was married and that it was not from any resh [rash?] resolution of his own, after his marrying upon some discontent between him and his Lady, (as his own letters which follow) make one believe that put him upon travelling.' STB 2 (1), book 2, fo. 23v.

and his Lady, and that[xxix] his travelling was design'd before they married, and not the effect of any discontent between themselves after. But there are other letters from him to her which shew the contrary, though they do not shew from what cause the uneasiness which was between them did proceed; their discontents I believe they kept to themselves, and concealed from their nearest relations. His letters shew he had a very tender affection for her, and 'tis likely he thought she did not make him those returns which his kindness for her deserved. And perhaps she might value herself as being heiress to Sir Francis Willughbys great estate, and upon that account carry herself more haughtily to him than he liked.[251] They both seem to have had good spirits, and I believe both desired to govern, and from that cause 'tis likely there might at first happen some disputes between them, which when they grew older, and wiser, were all laid aside, for by all the accounts which remain of them, they seem to have been a very affectionate couple, and had their affairs been easie, as their humours appear to have been, afterwards, to each other, I should believes [sic] the whole course of their lives had been more happy than usuall; but I must hereafter shew the difficaulties they had to strugle with; and shall here copy some of his letters which make it appear that they were not in good humour with one an other when he went to travell.

[f. 115] The Copy of a letter from Mr. Percivall Willoughby to his Lady before he went to Travell.

Hard's the hap that some men have, and who is born under an unlucky planet[252] must seldom or never look for good fortune—etc. To you I have linked my liking and liberty, plighted my faith and troth, and yielded my self to your courtesy and subjection, all which how inwardly you esteem'd I know not, but outwardly it rather seems to be rejected than accepted, the greater is my grief and the more in silence do I sorrow etc. Might I be privie to your fancyes, I would frame my self to your fashions etc. Little I know I do deserve and less I desire. My sute and service I confess not to be much, and yet such, as if any of them might please you, there should be no want in me! But alass how may I please, when I must not know what breeds

---

[251] Cassandra finished this thought following 'liked': 'but 'tis only to be guessed at, for none of the letters shew the cause of that uneasiness which Sir Percival Willoughbys letters make appear there was between them, his letters shew that he passionatley loved her, and that discontent from her carriage to him had made his resolve to travell. But before he went, he writ to his Lady a sad complaint of his hard fortune, he accuses his own little desert, and goes on thus'. STB 2 (1), book 1, fos 23v–24.

[252] See Patrick Curry, *Prophecy and Power: Astrology in Early Modern England* (Princeton, NJ, 1989).

your displeasure; you utterly estrange your self and your discontents from me, and rather shew me your tears, than impart the cause. Words may slip unawares from me or be taken wrong, but would you friendly and freely impart your mind to me, I would as willingly mend what were a miss, as I am sorry I should offend there where I love most, for whom, and to whom I only live and care, and in whose joys I repose my greatest felicity. But if you shall secretly sorrow before me, and feed me only with lowring looks, as one not able for sorrow to endure the sight of it, I shall be constrained to forsake both my friends and country, till such time, as I shall certainly both hear and believe you to be more affectionade [*sic*] to him who loves you best. Thus not knowing when again to see you, and finding you unwilling to speak to me I have used this for want of conference as my last and best farewell, desiring you (what misery so ever I endure) to think of me [f. 116] as I am, that is yours, and only yours.

> O sorrow must my senses tast
> Which once did swim in bliss
> Sithe fortune hath me tied so fast
> And bids me leave to wish
> The silly ship wherein I sailed
> And past from place to place
> At anchor tied must still abide
> Thus alter'd is my case
> The wandring wings of my free will
> Are clipped to my pain
> And in this plight to take my flight
> I labour all in vain
> The pleasant winds are all now ceas'd
> Which _____ xxx
> But seas of sorrow are increas'd
> Which beat against my boat
> Such heavie hap is him bequeath'd
> Which sought a place of joy
> But now of solace quite bereaved
> Is harbor'd in annoye.

More faithfull then fancied
Percivall Willughby

The Copy of a letter from Mr. Percivall Willoughby
To his Lady when he was abroad.

My dear, the only solace of my solitary mind, if the thoughts thereof had not continuall recourse to thee, my pensive passions, would set my heart a float to all kind of sorrows, [f. 117] and so still languishing I should both see and suffer a daily pain, and in a short time my all and finall confusion. The only comfort which now I receive since parting, causes me to judg of my past happyness, when I did enjoy thee being present, and now in absence worthily to esteem the greatness of so great a pleasure by wanting it.

Pardon me I pray thee, in that so rashly I went from thee, and condemn me not of discourtisie. The penance which I suffer, may seem sufficient for such a fault, and the little ease which as yet I receive in my journey (whenever I return) will learn me so much wit as to think my self well, when I am well. The case good heart, is so much altered with me, to come from my friends and all thats dear, to those I know not, a people which I understand not, and who when they speak most friendly, mean least good. Their meat and kind of dressing I rather loath than like, their drink being wine, I can't away with. Thus lead I a life full of discontent both in body and mind. So that perswade thy self though I can't make any greater place for thee in my heart, than I have done, I shall both love and like my country far better. In the mean time however I doe, make thou thy self happy as thou mayst, and so sweet soul my love and life is only thine.

Percivall Willoughby

[Cassandra drew a heart with crossed darts which was perhaps in the original letter.]

[f. 118] There are severall other very kind letters from Mr. Percivall Willoughby to his Lady while he was travelling, and letters wherein he desires Sir Francis Willughbys commands and directions in his travells, what would be most proper for him to see or doe. In his last letter to his Lady he tells her, that he wants money to pay what he owes in France, and to bring him home, which he desires her to get of his Father for him. In this letter he laments the sadness of his case, in being absent from her, and near no friend, and without a penny of money.

Most of these letters are very much torne, and the dates of them not legible, so that it does not appear how long time Mr. Percivall Willoughby spent in his travells. But by one of those letters I find he was at Lyons in July 1583 and by a letter dated from Boreplace August 1583, which he carried from his Lady to her Father it appears that he was then returned home.²⁵³ Her letter was to this effect. That though she could write nothing which she would not commit to this bearer by word of mouth, yet she thought it her duty by letter humbly to beg his daily blessing etc. What she could certifie him off [of] from thence, she would leave to Mr. Willoughby's report, and only let him know that her Aunt Arundell had writ to her from Shafbury [Shaftesbury] to desire her to let him know that she desired her neece Dorothy Willughby might come to her, and remain with her, till she should be bestowed in marriage.

At this time that Mr. Percivall Willoughby went to viset Sir Francis at Wollaton, I believe, Sir Francis might invite him and his Lady to come thither to live with him, because I find by the old papers that soon after Sir Percivall came home from his travells, he and his Lady went to live at Wollaton.

[f. 118v] #²⁵⁴ Since the writing of this book I have found that Sir Percivall Willoughby was knighted by King James the first in Middleton Hall An: D: 1603, and that I have here given him the title of Knighthood twenty years too soon.

[f. 119] #It does not appear in what year Mr. Percivall Willoughby was knighted, and therefore from this time I shall call him Sir.²⁵⁵ While he was at Lyons he took a French Gentleman to teach him Italian who was I believe a very proud haughty person. His name was Francis Conrados.²⁵⁶ This servant Sir Percivall seems to have been very kind to, and there is an account that at his first comming to Wollaton he desired Sir Francis would give him leave to eat at his own table, and that he would have had Marmion's Chamber for him, but that Sir Francis would not grant but I think he had Cludds Chamber. Marmion and Cludd were two of Sir Francis Willughbys favouret[xxxi] servants.²⁵⁷

---

²⁵³ Following this sentence in Cassandra's notes, she wrote: 'There is no letters or paper which shew how Sir Francis or Mr. Thomas Willoughby, approved of Sir Percivalls travelling, nor is there any letter writ by Sir Percival Willoughbys Lady while he travelled to be found.' STB 2 (1), book 2, fo. 28.

²⁵⁴ The hash mark indicates additional information that Cassandra discovered after this Account was completed; it corrects her misunderstanding regarding Percival's knighthood on fo. 119.

²⁵⁵ On the place and date of Sir Percival Willoughby's knighthood, see Text n. 178 above.

²⁵⁶ For a history of the Marmions that includes the tale of Conrados and William Marmion, see Alfred Thomas [Scrope] Goodrick, 'The Original Marmion', *Blackwood's Magazine* 193 (Mar. 1913), 390–399. There is a Francis Conrado of Bristol and his wife Elizabeth, widow of John Cleyton of Bristol, draper mentioned in the Chancery Records, TNA, C 781591, in 1591 and in Francis Collins (ed.), *Feet of Fines of the Tudor Period*, Pt. 3, 1583–1594, Yorkshire Archaeological Society Record Series, VII (London, 1889), 196, for 1593.

²⁵⁷ 'Marmion and Cludd were two of Sir Francis's favouret Servants, men of ill principles and wicked designes, as is before mentioned in the account of Sir Francis; now th[e]se two Men were both highly provoked at Sir Percivalls asking their Chambers, for his French

Marmion was an ill man as[xxxii] appears from his endeavours to asperse his Lady, and cause the separation which was between Sir Francis and his Lady. 'Tis likely Cludd too might have been in that cabal, because when Sir Francis left his Lady at Coventry, in February 1578 Henry Dracot, and J = Cludd were the two servants which he trusted with the care of his family, and who must have been chief, which Lady Willughby writ, to complain off [of], to Sir Francis; in which letter she says, that after he was gone to London the servants dealt so cruelly with her that she was not able to bear it.

These, and I believe many more of Sir Francis's servants had very little regard to the interest of their Master or his family, but made it their chief care to enrich themselves which I believe they found more easie for them to doe when Sir Francis lived by himself, than when his Lady or any of his Children lived with him. And therefore 'tis very likely that they might resolve when Sir [f. 120] Percivall came to live at Wollaton, that they would make Sir Francis uneasie with him as soon as they could, and so make them part again. This unlucky request which Sir Percivall made in behalf of Conrados his man, gave them but too good an opportunity to put in practice what I believe they might resolve by any means to bring to pass; there are letters which shew that Marmion and Cludd were both extreamly angry at Sir Percivalls asking for their Chambers for his French man, and Conrados trusting to his Masters kindness for him, did I believe carry himself very insolently in the family, for it appears that prety soon after Sir Percivall came to Wollaton there grew very great discontent and uneasiness amongst Sir Francis's servants.

There is a letter from Mr. Thomas Willoughby to his Son Sir Percivall dated April the 14th 1584.

In this letter he advises his Son to be careful how he meddled in the differences amongst Sir Francis's servants, because if he took part with the one, that would make the other his enemy.

This advice I believe Sir Percivall followed. I also believe that he soon grew uneasie at the haughty carriage of his man Conrados,[258] and repented that he had not at his first bringing him to Wollaton kept him to a more humble and respectfull behaviour towards Sir

man, and from his first coming to Wollaton I believe they studyed how to be revenged of Sir Percivall, Conrados trusting to his Masters kindness for him, did I believe carry himself very insolently in the family, so that there soon began to be great uneasieness amongst Sir Francis's Servants.' STB 2 (1), book 2, fos 28–29.

[258] The language in Cassandra's notes differs: 'After some time Sir Percivall (seeing the disputes dayly increased) resolved to part w[i]th his French Man, in hopes by that, to make himself and the family more easie.' STB 2 (1), book 2, fo. 29.

Francis's servants, whose quarrells amongst themselves, and their dislike to Conrados gave him so much trouble, that he soon found it would be necessary for him to part with [f. 121] Conrados in order to make himself more easie. Conrados had great expectations from his Masters kindness to him, and finding that he was to be turned out of his service,[259] and that Sir Percivall would take no farther care for him, he turned so base a villain to his Master (as appears by letters and old papers in the Library) that he joyned in confederacy with Marmion and Cludd, before they parted, to render Sir Percivall as odious as was possible to Sir Francis, by reporting scandalous stories, of their own making, to Sir Francis, of Sir Percivall.

Marmion and Cludd I believe had long been striving to make Sir Francis believe that Sir Percivall only courted and respected him, till he could get his estate made secure to him, and that when ever he did settle that upon him he would find that Sir Percivall had very little regard for him, and that self interest was the only cause of his good behaviour to him now.

These wicked servants found Conrados a proper tool for them to work by, and as soon as he was gone away from his Master they had contrived a letter for Conrados to write to upbraid Sir Percivall for his breach of promise in turning him away as he had done. In this letter Conrados enlarged upon his own faithfull services, and blamed his Master's ingratitude to him, and then accused his Master for being guilty of many[260] ill actions, and in this letter told him of many disrespectfull words which he [f. 122] had spoke of Sir Francis, and that he had threatened that if he could but get Sir Francis Willughby's estate made secure to himself, Sir Francis should not live long after. Much more to this effect there is in this letter concerning Sir Francis, and in it he also accuses his Master of saying many reflecting[261] things of Sir Francis's Lady [*(who was then parted from her husband)*].[262]

This letter (of which a copy now remains in the Library at Wollaton) was contrived by Sir Francis's servants to be given to Sir Francis instead of Sir Percivall. Sir Francis receiving the letter read it, and never suspecting the designs which those villains had upon him, believed all that which Conrados had writ was true of Sir Percivall. 'Tis easie to believe that Sir Francis was highly provoked by such treatment from his Son Percivall who till then he had used

---

[259] 'This Francis Conrados had great expectations from his masters kindness for him; and when Sir Percivall had turned him away, without doing any thing for him, this villain was so base, as to resolve he would be revenged of his Master'. STB 2 (1), book 2, fo. 30.

[260] STB 2 (1), book 2, fo. 30. Cassandra's notes say 'guilty of many abominable very ill actions'. 'Abominable' is crossed out.

[261] Casting or bringing reproach or discredit on a person, *OED*.

[262] STB 2 (1), book 2, fo. 30.

with a fatherly kindness. And there are many letters which shew that Sir Percivall suffer'd under excessive grief for being thus slandered, and not able to make his innocence appear. [*These rogues had so well contrived their stories, that at first Sir Percivall's own father had doubtfull thoughts of him.*][263]

There is a letter from Mr. Thomas Willoughby to his Son Sir Percivall dated March the 24th 1585, writ, I believe upon his first hearing of Conrado's accusation against his Master, by a letter from Sir Francis to him.

In this letter Mr. Thomas Willoughby blames his Son's behaviour[264] and want of wisdom, if he had ever had, any such discourse with his man Conrados, as his enemies make appear. He desires him to take heed; and not seek to revenge himself, which might disquiet Sir Francis, but to endeavour to purge himself from this pretended infamy by all honest means. He writes that the letter which he received from Sir Francis was opened before it came to him, and that he hears there is [f. 123] a copy of that infamous letter come to Lady Willughbys hands, who for the good=will she bears him will suffer no body to have a copy of it, but reads the letter herself to all that come to her. Mr. Willoughby writes that he heard Mr. Thomas Markham[265] gave Lady Willughby the copy of the letter, and that he had caused Francis Conrados to justifie the letter before the Lord Talbot.[266]

Old Markham hated Sir Percivall because he [Percival] had opposed the match between his Son and Margaret Willughby, the treaty whereof I shall hereafter give an account off [of].

---

[263] STB 2 (1), book 2, fo. 31.

[264] 'For appears by + + a letter ## from Mr. Thomas Willoughby ≠≠ March the 24th 1585 to Sir Percivall, to tell him he thought his behavior and desert very ill, and his wisdom very small, if he had, had such discourse with his man Francis Conrados, as his enemies make it appear.' STB 2 (1), book 2, fo. 31. Cassandra used the symbols to re-order different parts of the text.

[265] Thomas Markham of Ollerton, Notts., and Kerby Bellars, Leics. (c.1523–1607) was the eldest son of Sir John Markham of Cotham by his third wife Anne, daughter of John Strelley and widow of Richard Stanhope. Thomas Markham's wife was Mary, daughter and heiress of Ryce Griffin. Markham was high steward of Mansfield, standard bearer to the Queen's band of gentlemen pensioners, ranger of Sherwood Forest and, in 1578, high sheriff of Nottinghamshire. Two of his sons, Griffin (about more later) and Robert Markham, were famous recusants. David Frederick Markham, *A History of the Markham Family* (London, 1954), ch. 4.

[266] George Talbot, 6th earl of Shrewsbury (1528–1590). In 1568 Elizabeth I gave Talbot the responsibility for guarding Mary, Queen of Scots. He was made earl marshall in 1572. See Text n. 216 above for more on the Talbots and their differences with the Stanhopes; see also Text n. 135 on William Marmion, the servant mentioned at length here, who had been a servant in the Talbot (Shrewsbury) household and had, apparently, been part of the reason for the difficult relations between Lord and Lady Shrewsbury.

[insert from f. 122v] #²⁶⁷ There is a letter from Mr. John Adams²⁶⁸ to his Brother Sir Percivall, dated from Boreplace August the 24. In this letter he begs Sir Percivall will not hazard himself with Markham, but rather bear the tempestious rage of so foolish a storm. (He writ) that Markhams first plot was upon his reputation, which in the end would turn to his own discredit, but now that he seeks his life, he begs he will trust to himself and other friends to revenge the quarrell. He desires Sir Percivall to consider that he is a married man and that the propigation of two honourable houses, rests on him etc.

There is another letter from Mr. John Adams to his Brother Sir Percivall dated An: D: 1587, to let him know that he had heard that his drawing²⁶⁹ upon Markham by the Lord Chancellors house was taken very hainously, and therefore he thought it would be well for his Cousin Robert Willoughby²⁷⁰ and his Father to viset the Lord Chancellor, and open the whol cause thereof to him.

By some of the old letters it appears that Markham had concern'd himself very much in the affair between Sir Percivall and his servant Conrados, which Sir Francis took so ill from him that he gave that for one reason why he was against marrying his Daughter to him, saying the dislike which he had to Sir Percivall upon a light French report (the author infamous, and of no credit) might cause a division amongst his children.²⁷¹

---

²⁶⁷ According to Cassandra's hash mark, all of fo. 122v should be inserted here in the middle of fo. 123.

²⁶⁸ John Adams (b.1560) was the brother-in-law of Percival Willoughby, married to his sister Frediswith, 'Phridelwide' or Frideswide (b. c.1575). Letters to Percival from Adams, whom Cassandra calls 'the Councelor', show, according to Cassandra, 'that he was a very kind friend to Sir Percivall', Cassandra also mentions that there were several kind letters from Phridelwide to Bridget, her sister-in-law. 'In one of her letters she writ that – There is no woman in the world that she more esteems, but her Husband does not care she should goe journeys from him [...] so she has no hopes of seeing her, but must sit mopeing at home by her fire side turning Apples – and may goe to Church to pray for her friends.' Chandos, *The Continuation of the History*, 26; Mi, LM 27, fos 21–22. See also Chandos, *The Continuation of the History*, 43; Mi, LM 27, fo. 38.

²⁶⁹ Presumably drawing a sword upon Markham.

²⁷⁰ This cousin is mentioned later in relation to Robert Spencer, Margaret Willoughby, and the Markhams. On fo. 181v, p. 232 there is a letter from him to Francis Willoughby. He may possibly be Robert Greville (born c.1540), a younger son of Fulke Greville (d.1559) and Elizabeth Willoughby de Broke, 3rd Baroness Willoughby de Broke.

²⁷¹ One of these letters is copied in full by Cassandra below (fos. 179v–180, pp. 229–230) and includes the date: in her notes, she wrote 'but there is a letter from Sir Francis to his cousin Markham dated 1 Nov. 1586, in which Sir Francis gives several reasons why he is against matching his daughter to his Cousin Markham's Son, whereof one was the dislike which he had to Sir Percivall Willoughby upon a light French report (the author infamous and of no credit) which would he says cause a division amongst his children. This shews

[*This shews that Sr Francis was then convinced of the falseness of F: Conrados letter and villanous reports of his Master.*][272]

There is a very kind letter from Sr Francis to Sr Percivall dated Dec: the 19[th] 1587, In which Sr Francis writes that he doth not understand what his Cousin Markham doe report of him, but he knows nothing w[hi]ch can either touch Sr Percivall or himself; concerning the match (he says) Markham broke of w[i]th him and not he with Markham, which Markham has s[ai]d many times an in many places, he has likewise said that he never claimed any promise or contract, nor would by any means seek Sr Percivalls good will w[i]thout his own better liking. In this case Sr Francis tells Sr Percivall he must depend upon the uprightness of his own conscience.][273]

[f. 123 cont.] There are severall letters from Mr. Willoughby to his Son Sir Percivall, which shew that he took great pains to discover and lay open Conrado's knavery, and also to justifie his Son and make his innocency apparant, and also letters to comfort his Son, who (by the account of this affair) appears to have suffer'd under extream affliction for being thus aspersed, and not able to clear himself.

In one of his letters he tells Sir Percivall, that he did before admonish him, that no means would be wanting to discredit him to Sir Francis, and to lessen his character in the world; but now he desired he would ease his mind by considering that this sort of dealing had been usuall in all ages, and that at length shame would be the reward of such infamy, for time would hear truth. [f. 124] He advised him and his good Wife with all reverence to serve God, and to neglect no duty to Sir Francis whose honest nature would, he doubted not, in time be cleared from false suggestions and abuses. Wherefore not respecting worldly advancement his prayer for him was, that God would give him a contented mind amidst such broiles as this world was pestered with.

There is a droling [in jest] letter from John Pickerell[274] to Sir Percivall, in which he writes, that he had daily expected to hear of his death and distruction, and to have seen his finall end upon

---

that Sir Francis was then convinced of the falseness of Francis Conrados letter and villainous reports of his Master'. STB 2 (1), book 2, fos 35–36.

[272] STB 2 (1), book 2, fo. 36.

[273] STB 2 (1), book 2, fo. 36.

[274] 'Drolling' means to act facetiously, in jest, or as a buffoon, *OED*, derivative of 'droll'. Apparently Conrados, who was unpopular in Francis Willughby's house, attempted to smooth tensions with Francis's other servants, who then put him up to fabricating a letter accusing Percivall Willoughby of some malfeasance and blackmailing him with it. Francis trusted his servants overwell, and the letter caused a rift between Sir Francis and Percivall. Even Thomas Willoughby, Percivall's father, expressed doubt in his son's character. Francis and Percivall were eventually reconciled. See fo. 125, p. 155. A John Pickerell of Shipbourne, Kent registered the baptisms of four children. Frederick Arthur Crisp, *Registers of Shipbourne, County Kent* (London?, 1921).

Nottingham gallows, for the fancyed murther of Sir Francis Willughby, which he believed had rather been intended by his accusers than ever thought of by himself. He desires Sir Percivall not to grieve, but remember whence he is, and despise such false hearted foes. He advised him to shake off his melancholy, and to spend his patrimony in the defence of his reputation and God would be his buckler.[275]

There is a letter from Mr. Willoughby to his Son Sir Percivall to let him know that he had been three times with the villain Francis Conrados, and that he had sent to tell him, that if he would give him forty pounds he would justifie his Master to Sir Francis Willughby, and confess the whole truth; which was that Blyth, Marmion, and Clud, had set him on, so to defame his Master. Clud he said was the greatest knave, and had given him money and promised him more. In answer to [f. 125] this, Mr. Willoughby told him he should have such a reward as his villainy deserved. In this letter Mr. Willoughby tells his Son, that he has writ this account of Conrados at large to Sir Francis.

There is a letter from Mr. Willoughby to his Son Sir Percivall dated June the 9th 1585[xxxiii] in which he writes, that Sir Francis Willughbys Lady, and he, are grown so great friends, that she opens all her griefs to him, of Marmion, Clud etc.

There is another letter from Mr. Willoughby to his Son Sir Percivall Willoughby dated An: D: 1585. In which he advises his Son to live more thriftily. He desires him to consider the expence which he has been at for him already, and writes that he must raise fortunes for his Brothers and Sisters. But lets Sir Percivall know that he has sent him such linnin as he can spare, and a silver salt. In this letter he writes that Sir Francis is so followed by Markham, Fisher, Cludd, and Marmion, that he hardly does any thing without them.

I could find no account, how, or when, Sir Francis was reconciled to Sir Percivall, but by many letters from Thomas Markham and copys of Sir Francis Willughbys answers An: D: 1586 to 1587, it appears that Sir Francis and Sir Percivall were then good friends.

There are no papers which shew what part Sir Francis [f. 126] Willughby's Lady took in this troublesome affair, but by what Mr. Thomas Willoughby writ his Son Percivall of her, viz: that she had a copy of Conrados's letter, which she read to all that came to her, one may believe she took no pains to doe him justice.

---

[275] A buckler is a small round shield (origin Old French, *c*.1300); both Marlowe (1593) and Shakespeare (1595) used the term buckler to mean 'to act like a buckler; to shield, defend, protect' or 'to ward or catch (blows)', *OED*.

There are letters which shew that this Lady Willughby spent part of the time she lived from her Husband, at Hogsden,[276] and that while she was there her Daughter Brigit Willoughby[277] was in London, and never went, or sent, to see her Mother.

There is a letter from Sir Percivall to Lady Willughby to exuse his Wife on that account, to which letter there is Lady Willughby's answer dated May the 18th 1584, in which she writes, that she does not think him answerable for his Wives faults, and that if in forgeting her duty, to her, she had contented, any other (#I believe meaning Sir Francis Willughby)[xxxiv] it was well done, and she was content to make a virtue of necessity, trusting hereafter to have to have more comfort of her. In this letter she assures Sir Percivall that her only hopes [sic] was in him, that he would doe his best to reconcile her Husband and herself, which was the only thing she wished for in this world.

[Elizabeth and Francis, 1585–1588, and the Building of Wollaton Hall]

[BL, Lansdowne MS 46 no. 30, fos 60r–60v][278]

60v: *Lady Eliz. Willoughby to Sr John Littleton her Father 1585*

60r: *My very good father: Many and those very grevous, have bene the discomfortes of my lyfe, synce the tyme of my seperation from Sr Frauncis, my husband. But emongste them all, there is none that hath trobled me more, or toucht me nearer, than the alienation of yor good opynion & fatherly affection towardes me. And albeit it had not pleasd yow to take yor pore daughters part so farr as to releyve her wants, and to redress her wronges, yet me thought in reason I might iustly hope for both a good opynion of me in yor self, and of yor good report of me to others. Especially synce I am caste of[f] of by Sr Fraunces wthout profe, and yll thought of by yow wthout cause. For if all reportes shalbe beleived as true and all accusations receyved as iuste, it comes all to a reckininge to be faultie or free, giltie or innocent. But synce there never hath been hitherto, nor never shalbe*

---

[276] Hogsden is most likely Hoxton in London's East End in Shoreditch, just north of the City of London.

[277] Bridget's last name, now that she was married, changed from Willughby to Willoughby in Cassandra's Account.

[278] This letter, along with the three other Lansdowne letters included here are to be found among the papers of Lord Burghley in the British Library. Three of these letters (nos 30, 32 and 33) are not included in Cassandra's Account, and she may never have seen them. See Alice Friedman, 'Portrait of a marriage: The Willoughby letters of 1585–1586', *Signs* 11 (1986), 549–555.

any matter of dishonesty proved againste me, why am I thus cruelly delt wthall of my husband. Why am I thus hardly thought of by yow. Why is yor tender love turned into hatred and yor dayly blessinges into bitter and deadly cursinges. Why spare yow not to speake yll of me to suche persons, as reioyce in my myshapps, and are ready messengers of suche newes [illeg.][279] *to my husband. Alas my good father, if yow from whom I should looke for, comfort in my greifes, assistance in my trobles, and succor in my necessities ioyne hands and take part wth my adversaryes, what hope can I conceyve ever to be reconcyled to my husband, or what ioye can I take in suche a wretched & miserable life. Therfore I beseche yow for the love of god, take pitie of me as of yor naturall childe have compassion of me as of a distressed woman. Encrease not the reioycing of my yll willers, wth the encrease of my sorrowes. And wth teares upon my knees, I moost humbly crave at yor handes, to suspend yor iugment (or at the leaste yor reporte in suspicions without profe and receyve me agayne into yor accustomed favor, and good opynion, wch I more desyre and hold dearer then any thing in this world. And so beseching almighty god to blesse yow wth good and longe health, and to dyrect yow wth his holy spirite in all yor endevors, I humbly take my leave*

By yor distressed, yet moste

dutifull daughter.

Eliz Willoughby

There is a letter in the Library at Wollaton which was writ by this Lady Willughby to her Husband in December An: D: 1585.[280] The letter was to this effect. That notwithstanding the manifold wrongs and wants which she had sustained for the space of seven years past, and the just cause she had to hate those who by their leud and false reports had been the contrivers thereof, yet she [f. 127] solemnly protested that she heartily forgave them. She returned him her humble thanks for vouchsafing her his company and conference; a happy entrance she hoped to a full and perfect reconciliation betwixt them, to which as on her part she should in all good and convenient sort be directed by him, so she trusted he would hold her excusable if by the advice of her good and wise friends she should refuse to enter into hard conditions; which she does not believe could come from his own disposition, but from the malice of those who have labour'd all they can to keep them a sunder, of which she could name many, but

---

[279] A word is crossed out here.
[280] This letter was copied by Cassandra into this Account, in part, from BL, Lansdowne MS 46 no. 31, fos 61r–62v. For the original from the British Library, see the appendix to the Introduction and Figures 4 and 5 on pp. 59–63.

would only mention one who fearing a likelyhood of their comming together, and finding false reports to him of her took not the effect he expected, like a cuning [cunning] woodman, changes his course, and under collour of friendship to her would insinuate that Sir Francis went about to sue a divorce between them, for which purpose certain fellows had undertaken to find out a supposed child,[281] which suspicion had been bruted, greatly to her discredit, wheras if it had pleased him at first, when this slanderous report was brought to him, to have called her to answer for herself, his mind might have been better sattisfied and her reputation not so much impaired, in defence whereof she still stands, and will to her dying day, in defyance of any villain or verlett that shall impeach it.

In this letter, she offers to come from London, if he will send for her and receive her again into his house, with his first favour, as his honest and lawfull Wife.[282] She prays for his health and long life, and desires he will give to her poor children, the fruitless blessing of their unfortunate Mother.

BL, Lansdowne MS 46 no. 32, fos 63r–64v

64v: *Sr. Fra. Willowby to my Lady Willowby*
Decbr 29, 1585
To my loving wife the
Lady Wyllughby give this

63r:
I have not such convenient leysure as to answere yor letter particularly as I would. This only I think, that as there is some parte wch may be reasonably

---

[281] The irony of this rumour is that, among Cassandra Willoughby's papers, written by Cassandra and now archived at STB 2 (2) with a date of 1584/5, is the following uncatalogued copy of a baptismal certificate: 'William Deverell alias Willoughby Son of Katharine Deverell, & as she hath confess'd him, ye Son of Sr Francis Willoughby Knt of Nottinghamshire Baptized ye 4th day of March 1584. This is a true Copy taken out of ye Register of Laughton in le morthing [Laughton-en-le-Morthen] in ye County of York, & Attested by Robt Barnard Vicar.' See also Rosemary O'Day, *Women's Agency in Early Modern Britain and the American Colonies* (Harlow, 2007), 143–144, for a reference to this. This may be William Willoughby whose birth is listed in *Boyd's Marriage Indexes* for 1584. See Percival Boyd, https://www.findmypast.co.uk/articles/world-records/full-list-of-united-kingdom-records/life-events-bmds/boyds-marriage-index-1538-1840. See the Yorkshire bishop's transcriptions of burials for a William Willoughby who died in 1634 and was buried at New Malton. There is a further irony in that one of the examples Francis wrote down with regard to the responsibilities of a justice of the peace was to seek out adulterers. He provides an example of the ancient (legendary) law-giver Zaleucus, who took out his son's eye for adultery. Mi, O 16/9.

[282] It is perhaps relevant that, in a 1585 inventory of the old hall at Wollaton, one of the rooms is allocated to Lady Arundell. Mi, I 5; J.H. Hodson, 'The first Wollaton Hall', *TTS*, 72 (1968), 62.

excused content me, so there is muche more that may minister occasion of offence as I suppose any indifferent reader will iudge) onles I should acknowledg my self faultie in yt wherin I knowe my self moost giltles.

I do not fynd as yet by yor letter, ether that yow confesse yor fault or require pardon therof in suche humilitie as is mete and convenient for the recovering of my goodwill or as yow would seme to make showe to the world.

Yow would covenant & condition wth me, yt if I would recyve yow into myne owne howse, wth my former favor, and send for yow, that then yow would moost willingly come, otherwise yow would contynew at London till yow had satisfied yor debt. Further yow alleage that ther is no cause why yow should make any greate hast, if either [it] is or were true, or that yow did beleve the report wch yor freind in secrete & in like good will did declare to yow of my hard deling pretended & vowed against yow.

For my part I will not go about to persuad yow the contrary. Only thus farr yow may iudge of me, that yor owne doinges & desertes shalbe the ballance. that yow shalbe wayed by, wch as they be good or badd, even so make yor full account to recyve. Yow say yow will endeavor to frame all yor woords & behaviors as they may best content & please me. Yow have not knowne that against any other I have bene suche a tyrant to doe so hardly wth them wch in this sort do sett me muche lesse. Against yor self whom I sought by persuasion & in all myldnes to wynne to dutie & obedyence, if by any meanes xii or xiii yeares sufferance could have wrought yt effect wherin yor father & yor owne conscience may be sufficient iudges. Nay, I may iustly saye the contrary. In usinge some severitie I sought reformacion & not revenge. To punishe was a punishment to my self. I never did it but wth greif & endevored rather by persuasion then correction, both by my self & others to recleyme yow, wth wch kind of deling because yor stubborne & froward mynd would not be bowed, my softnes hath rather deserved reprehension then comendacion. The husbandes lenitie ought to be such as to encrease the wyves folly.

In excuse of yor faltes wch I obiected yow told me that yor younger yeares and foolish counsell were the causers. Be better advised in latter yeares. Elder yeares require riper iudgment. Take good hede what counsell you followe.

63v: This I write in yt respect: that yow say yor frend in secrete & wth like good will did thus advertise yow of my entent towardes yow. Evel counsell geven & followed hath bene many tymes the destruction of the counsellor & of them that recyved the counsell. Frame yor self to a better course, even for yor owne reputacion, & althoughe peraventure yow fynde not that yow desired, yett better than hitherto yow have deserved.

Send me the particular note of yor debtes. Wullaton the xxixth of December 1585. Yors as yow knowe, Fra. Wyllughby

BL, Lansdowne MS 46 no. 33, fos 65r–66v

65r: *To Sr Fr Willoughbye from his Lady.*

About ye beginning of 1586

66r:

Sr. F: I am very hartely sory that either my hole letter, or any part therof should mynester any the least occasion of offence towardes yow. For I protest unto yow before god, it was no part of my meaninge so to do.

And to the end, that nothing should either ignorantly or negligently slype from eschape me, that might brede either quarel or question about it truly Sr F I reade it both very often, & very considerately before I would send it, And synce the retorne of yr answere I have also more precisly perused every sentence and as I may say sillable therof. Wherin as my conscience is cleare from any yll meaninge towardes yow so the matter it self in my poore understanding doth mynester neither iuste cause nor so muche as any reasonable coulor of offence Wherin I refer my self with yow to any equall & indifferent reader.

And for yor self if it would please yow but to examyn more exactly the contentes of my letter, and compare them wth the particular of yor answere, yow shall easly fynd and confesse, that yow have mystaken both the my meaning & the matter also.

For the wch cause I will not troble yow wth any new repet[ic]ion of myne owne letter or any particular answere to yors.

Only wheras yow write that yow do not fynd as yett by my letter either that I confess my fault or require pardon for it in suche humilitie as is mete & convenient for the recovering of yor good will, & as I would faine to make show to the world, To this I must answere that I knowe not what to answer except I knowe by yor general charge, what particular fault yow meane.

For if yor meaning be that I have made yow any fault by any dysolute & incontenent kynd of life (as I have bene most lewdly & falsly both suspected & reported, then I say agayne as I sayd before and will say whilst I lyve that I defye any villeyn or varlett parson [person] that shall go about to impreache me. And towardes yow if I be found faultie in yr behalf, I require no one iote of favor at yor handes. So I pray God to dele wth me further as wth a moost faithless & periured parson both towardes him and yow.

66v: So againe if yor meaning be to have me acknowleg of my former forgettfulness of my dutie many wayes towardes yow for & concernige howshold matters only, then my answere is, that that hath bene donne many tymes & long synce, both by my letters, and by my self upon my knees. And for yor further & full satisfaction herin, I do here once agayne confesse to yow under my hand & seale that I have behaved my self towardes yow both unadvisedly & undutifully both in worde & dede many wayes & many tymes, for the wch I have bene & am very hartily sory, humbly requireth yow both to forgive me & forgett it.

And as towching the tyme to come, if it shall so please god that we may come together agayne, I crave no other usage at yor handes than my good or yll behavior shall deserve, being wayed in the ballance of truthe & reason together, as yow yor self have sett downe.

So for the better increasing & continuing of a firme & unfeynidd love & lykng betwixt us I humbly beseche yow as my hope is, to waye of me as of yor lawefull wife and to say all in a word, that it will please yow truly to love her that will both faithfully & humbly love & obey yow.

I have sent yow herin enclosed according to yor commandment the particular note of my debtes here in London. ~~I be also endebted to diverse others of my freindes in the country as namely to Mr Thomas Markham x^h wch I have very necessary occasion to use he very freindly lent me I thank him for I thought not good to remember them unto yow because god willing I meane to discharge them myself of the money wch I hope to recover against the warden of ye marshallsea as sone as I can make tryall by [halve?]~~

And so geving yow most harty thanks that it hath pleased yow to vouchsafe to write to me (though somewhat bitterly & sharply), my humble dutie towardes yow remebred, I take my leave of yow comytting yow & my pore children to his_____ own who is best able to kepe yow.

[another hand]
Madame as I have altred this letter
Yow may wth good warrant send it to
Sr F, but in any wise, remember the condicions how they
Stand wth yow that yow be not overtaken wth them][283]

[f. 127v] There is a book of Sir Francis Willughbys houshold accounts beginning March the 4th An: D: 1586.[284] For things bought, besides what the stock produced. This book gives an account

	li	sh	d
That he came from London and spent that week at Wollaton	3	18	4
And that from March the 4th to the 11th he spent there	4	17	9
And from the 11th to the 18th was spent	5	8	11
And from the 18th to the 25th part of which week Sir Francis was at Middleton			

---

[283] Sometime between 1585 and 1586, Gabriel Marmion, one of Sir Francis's servants distrusted by Lady Willoughby, wrote a letter to Sir Francis in which he reports that Lady Willoughby was displeased with him, charging him with speaking evil of her. Marmion acknowledged that, responding to 'speech of yr hard deling with her', he said that she had always been a most willful gentlewoman, and that if she loved Sir Francis, as she would make the world believe, she would come to live with him with greater haste and gain back some part of the credit she had lost by her absence. Marmion did not think, however, that she was going to change. Mi, 6/170/124/5.

[284] Mi, A 69/1–2, fos 1–13v for these accounts, beginning 4 Mar. 1586/7; there are a few minor discrepancies between the account book and Cassandra's transcription.

Spent that week at Wollaton	3	18	5

An: D: 1587

From March the 25th to April the 1st Sir Francis being himself at Middleton, his family at Wollaton spent that week	2	13	1
And from April the 1st to the 8th the family at Wollaton spent	2	9	9
And from April the 8th to 15th, Sir Francis returning on Wednesday to Wollaton, spent that week	4	3	4
Before the end of that week Sir Francis went again to Middleton spent at Wollaton from April the 15th to the 22th	2	9	9
From April the 22th to the 29th spent in his absence at Wollaton	2	13	0
And from April the 29th to May the 6th spent at Wollaton	2	8	0
Upon Monday Sir Francis Willughby returned to Wollaton from the 6th to the 13th	5	3	3
From May the 13th to the 20th Sir Francis went to Belvoir Castle[285] and stayed there 5 days spent that week at Wollaton	4	11	1
Upon Friday Sir Percivall came to Wollaton, from the 20th to the 27th spent	6	10	9
From the 27th to June the 3d upon Wednesday Sir Thomas Stanhope and more company dined at Wollaton New Hall spent that week	7	15	9
From the 3d to the 10th Sir George Hastings and more company came to Wollaton and stayed 2 days, spent that week	7	10	4
From the 10th to the 17th Sir Thomas Mannors and more company dined one day at the New Hall,[286] spent that week	6	14	10
From the 17th to the 24th Sir Francis Willughby was absent 3 days, spent	5	11	8

---

[285] Belvoir Castle was the seat of the earls of Rutland, the Manners family.

[286] This seems to suggest that the New Hall at Wollaton was largely completed by 1586, although most accounts (including Cassandra's on fo. 129, p. 164), give 1588 as the date of completion. For the building accounts between 1582 and Nov. 1588, see Friedman *House and Household*, 103, 187 (app. B) and 205 n. 39. Francis did, however, begin to entertain at his New Hall before 1588. Account books for 1587–1588 show that two or three large gatherings of local gentry took place at the New Hall, including a lavish dinner for 120 people on 11 Nov. 1587. Work was still being done on the interior of the New Hall, however, in the early 1590s. Friedman, *House and Household*, app. B and p. 205 n. 39, citing Mi, A 70.

From the 24th, to July the 1st, Sir Percivall
stayed all the week, and more company 2 days,
spent that week   6   14   11
From July the 1st to the 8th Sir Francis
spent at Wollaton   7   4   1
From the 8th to the 15th spent that week   5   11   5
From the 15th to the 22 the Earl of Rutland[287]
and others sup'd upon Tuesday and dined upon
Wednesday at Wollaton, spent that week   7   14   2
From July the 22th to August the 5th spent
those two weeks   11   5   7

This week Sir Francis removed from Wollaton to his house at Nottingham. This book gives an account of the names of the men servants which Sir Francis Willughby then had but makes no mention of the women servants. The number of men servants was between 30 and 40. Some weeks there was 6 or 7 men more than other weeks.[288]

[f. 128] There is a letter from Lady Arundell to Sir Francis Willughby which seemes to have been writ about this time and is to this effect.

Methinks the time long now, since I either saw you or heard from you, and therefore I could not pass so good an occasion of sending as I now have, that thereby I might learn in how good state of health, both you, and yours, now are, which in my self I feel so to decay, as it maketh me more mindfull to enquir of the state of my friends etc. I pray let me know how well your purchase, and your building goe forward, which you have in hand. They both together seem to me great matters, to go forward at one time. From the Court February the 14th Your Sister

Margaret Arundell[289]

The building which Lady Arundell means, was I believe Wollaton New House. The Old Hall was built near the Church. What now remains of that old building is turned into 3 or 4 farme houses, of which one is about a quarter of a mile from the rest, which was

---

[287] John Manners, 4th earl of Rutland (c.1551/9–1588). John inherited the earldom from his brother Edward (b.1549) a few months before dining at Wollaton. Edward died on 14 Apr. 1587. Sibyl M. Jack, 'Manners, Edward, third earl of Rutland (1549–1587)', *ODNB*.

[288] Mi, A 69/1–2, fos 10v–12v, dating from 15 July to 29 July 1587.

[289] This is the last letter from Margaret Arundell in this Account. Given what she says of her decaying health, she may have died soon after this letter, which Cassandra tentatively dates in 1587. Various online genealogies give her death date as 1591, but given the circumstances, it is likely that she died prior to Elizabeth Willoughby's return to her husband in 1588.

the Dairy house to the Old Hall.²⁹⁰ The New House is placed upon a hill about half a mile from the Old Hall, from whence there is a very noble prospect of the country round it. One side of the house looks upon the Castle and Town of Nottingham, from another, there is a fine view of Clifton House and gardens the seat of Sir Gervas Clifton.²⁹¹ From^xxxv the other sides of the house there is the prospect of severall houses and little villages, and each corner and middle of the house pretty near point to churches that are about 2 or three miles off. The house it self is a very [f. 129] noble pile of building, but it being less easie to discribe it by writing, then by drawing, I design to place at the end of this book a draught and a plan of it,²⁹² and shall therefore only mention here that Sir Francis Willughby began this building [*while he lived from his Lady*]²⁹³ An: D: 1580 and finished it An: D: 1588.²⁹⁴ The master workmen which built the house he sent for out of Italy as also most of the stone figures which adorn the house. All the stone which it is built with, was brought from Ancaster in Lincolnshire, by the people who dwelt there, and who exchanged their stone with Sir Francis for his cole, which they carried back from Wollaton. But not withstanding the stone, and its carriage, cost nothing but the return of cole which Sir Francis made for it, and that at that time labourers wages was [*sic*] at that time^xxxvi very small, yet it appears by a very particular account of the building which still remains in the Library, that the building of that house cost Sir Francis Willughby four=score thousand pounds.²⁹⁵

---

²⁹⁰ For a detailed description of the Old Hall, see Hodson, 'The first Wollaton Hall', 59–67, although he mistakenly thinks that Queen Elizabeth stayed at the Old Hall in 1575. Most of his information comes from two inventories, one taken *c.*1550 and the other in 1585. *HMC Middleton*, 474–485 and Mi, I 1/2 and Mi, I 5. See also accounts for 1565 and later, Mi, A 47, 53, 56, 57 for repairs and renovations to the Old Hall.

²⁹¹ Sir Gervase Clifton (1587/8–1666) was born the year his father died of consumption. His seat was at Clifton-on-Trent, Notts., south of the River Trent. John P. Ferris, 'Clifton, Sir Gervase, 1st Bt', Andrew Thrush and John P. Ferris (eds), *The History of Parliament: The House of Commons 1604–1629* (Cambridge, 2010).

²⁹² This plan is not now included in the MS.

²⁹³ STB 2 (1), book 1, fo. 28.

²⁹⁴ Robert Smythson (*c.*1533/7–1614), architect and surveyor, moved to Wollaton in 1580 to design and build Sir Francis Willoughby's house. He spent much of the rest of his life there and was buried in St Leonard's Church in Wollaton. Mark Girouard, *Robert Smythson and the Architecture of the Elizabethan Era* (London, 1966); Friedman, *House and Household*, ch. 4.

²⁹⁵ For an analysis of Cassandra's description of Wollaton New Hall, see Friedman, *House and Household*, 164–65, where she writes that the cost of building was more likely 1/10 of the £80,000 Cassandra reported. A note of debts owed by Sir Francis and due between Aug. 1587 and Feb. 1589/90 alone adds up to £11,956. Presumably many of these were loans for the building, making the total figure of £80,000 in loans and income seem not impossible. Mi, 6/170/32.

One of the account books for An: D: 1587[296] makes mention of Sir Francis Willughby's dinning at the new house November the 11th it being Lenton Fair time, and that the Earl of Rutland and his Lady,[297] Sir Thomas Mannors,[298] and his Lady[299], and Sir Gervas Clifton and his Lady,[300] Sir Anthony Strelley[301] and his Lady, and divers other Gentlemen, with their retinue to the number of a hundred and twenty persons, all dinned with Sir Francis at Wollaton New House. The account of things bought for that diner I shall copy on the other side of this leaf. [f. 129v]

The account of things bought for a dinner at Wollaton New House November the 11th 1587. The provision of beef mutton etc being killed at home.

Paid for	sh	d
Butter	9	4
Eggs	6	10
Milk for custards	1	[blank in MS][302]
2 Piggs	2	8
5 Capons	6	2
8 Chickens	2	2
4 Woodcocks	1	4[303]

[296] *HMC Middleton* includes extracts from this household account book. The specific reference to this 11 Nov. dinner is on p. 456. Mi, A 69/1–2, fo. 19.

[297] John Manners, 4th earl of Rutland, died the February following this dinner. His wife was Elizabeth Charlton, daughter of Francis Charlton of Apley. He was earl for only one year and was also lord lieutenant of Nottinghamshire and custos rotulorum of Nottinghamshire from 1587 to 1588.

[298] Sir Thomas Manners (1537–1591), John Manners' uncle and fourth son of Thomas Manners, 1st earl of Rutland, by his second wife Eleanor, née Paston. Thomas was known as 'Lusty' Manners to his family, Sir Thomas was a soldier who accumulated military fame; between campaigns, he was the constable of Nottingham Castle but then was outlawed for debt and died in disgrace. 'Manners, Sir Thomas (1537–91)', in P.W. Hasler (ed.), *The History of Parliament: The House of Commons 1558–1603* (1981): http://www.historyofparliamentonline.org/volume/1558-1603/member/manners-sir-thomas-1537-91 (accessed 14 Sept. 2016).

[299] Theodosia née Newton, daughter of Thomas Newton. Married in 1571.

[300] Probably Sir Gervase Clifton (1516–1588). See above, Text n. 291 for his son Gervase. His second wife, Winifred, (m. Sept. 1565) was a recusant. C.J. Black, *History of Parliament*, http://www.histparl.ac.uk/volume/1509-1558/member/clifton-gervase-1516-88 (accessed 31 Mar. 2018).

[301] Sir Anthony Strelley (1528–1591) married Joan, daughter of George Baynham. For the Strelley family, see Charles Kerry, 'Notes to the pedigree of the Strelleys of Hazlebach' in *Journal of the Derbyshire Archaeological and Natural History Society*, 14 (London, 1892), 95–97. Strelley was notoriously litigious. His will is dated 1591 (Borthwick Institute, York, Prob. Reg. 26, fo. 287).

[302] Stevenson has 'mylke for custerdes, 12d', *HMC Middleton*, 456; Mi, A 69/1–2, fo. 19.

[303] 16d in the MS.

5 Snipes[304]	0	10
4 Plover	0	10
Bread for the kitchen	0	8
Ale to seeth[305] fish in	0	2
6 li of Sugar	10	0
3 li of Raisins	0	9
3 li of Corans [currants]	1	3
3 li of Pruins	1	0
½ li of pepper	1	0
℥ ii[306] of Cynamon	1	4
℥ ii of Ginger	0	4
℥ ii of Mace	1	6
℥ ii of Cloves	1	0
1 li of Bisquet	1	8
Paid for Musk Comfects[307]	2	6
[total]	2	14	4

[f. 129 cont.] It appears by this and other account books that Sir Francis Willughby then dwelt at [f. 130] Thurland House in Nottingham, but it does not appear whither that house was then his own, or not, but of late years it has belonged to the Earl of Clare,[308] and tis probable his ancestor bought it of ours.

In this year An: D: 1587 Sir Francis Willughby married his second Daughter Dorothy to Henry Hastings,[309] the Son of

---

[304] A common straight-billed marsh bird, *OED*.

[305] To poach. *The good Huswifes Handmaide for the Kitchin* (London, 1595): www.staff.uni-giessen.de/gloning/ghhk (accessed 31 Mar. 2018).

[306] ℥ is the alchemical symbol for ounce, so this would be two ounces of cinnamon.

[307] Entry for 'musk', *OED*: 'They lefte a very sweete sauour behynde them sweeter then muske.' *HMC Middleton*, 456; Mi, A 69/1–2, fo. 19.

[308] Thurland Hall was built about the year 1458 by Thomas Thurland, nine times mayor of Nottingham. It was sold to Thomas Markham in the late 1540s. The hall passed by purchase to Sir John Hollis. See 'Nottinghamshire History', http://www.nottshistory.org.uk/articles/briscoe1905/thurlandhall1.htm (accessed 31 Mar. 2018), taken from J. Potter Briscoe, *Bypaths of Nottinghamshire History* (1905). The website features a drawing of the hall prior to 1840. See James Orange, *History and Antiquities of Nottingham*, II (Nottingham, 1840), 734–736 and J. Holland Walker, 'An itinerary of Nottingham', *TTS* 39 (1935), 1–4. Thomas Markham may have rented Thurland Hall to Francis Willoughby. He seems to have sold it to John Holles in the 1590s. John Holles was made earl of Clare in 1616, after which the Hall was, for a time, called Clare Hall.

[309] Henry Hastings (c.1561–1650) was the second son of George Hastings (see below, Text n. 310) According to the *ODNB* (T.Y. Cocks, 'Hastings, Henry (bap. 1562, d.1652') Henry was an eccentric sportsman with a hospitable table provided from his farms and fishponds. The pulpit of a disused neighbouring chapel formed his larder. Anthony Cooper, Lord Shaftesbury, who was a near neighbour, described him in a plaque with

George,[310] the younger Brother, of Henry Earl of Huntyngdon.[311] There are a great many letters from this Earl (who spells his name Huntyngdon) to Sir Francis concerning this match, part of which I shall copy in the account which I shall hereafter give of this Dorothy Willughby and her four younger Sisters.

There is the copy of a letter writ by Sir Francis to this Earl Huntyngdon to excuse himself for not keeping their wedding at his house, nor desiring that the young couple should stay with him till Michealmas, because by reason of his wives absence, and the furniture of his house being much decayed, he had not designed to keep house this year, and therefore had not made such provision of corn, and cattle, and other necessaries as would be needfull for him to discharge himself with credit to such an assembly, and therefore he hoped Lord Huntyngdon would hold him excused for their continuance with him after the wedding. This copy of a letter is not dated, but another which is writ upon the same sheet of paper, and I believe at the same time is dated June: 1587: which makes me believe they were married about that time.[312]

---

gold letters that was fixed under an original portrait of Henry. Among other information, he described Henry Hastings as 'well-natured, but soon angry, calling his servants bastards, and cuckoldry knaves'. 'He was low, very strong, and very active … his clothes always green, and never worth, when new, more than £5 [...] He had all manner of sport hounds that ran buck, fox, hare, otter and badger, and hawkes long and short winged [...] His house and hall were crammed with litters of cats, hounds and spaniels, hawks and fox skins, with dice, cards, tobacco pipes and every manner of hunting equipment.' See Henry Nugent Bell, *The Huntingdon Peerage*, 2nd edn (London, 1821), 91–98. Shortly after the death of Dorothy Willoughby in 1638, he settled part of his estate on one Jane or Anne Langton of Woodlands who seems to have been his mistress and whom he may have afterwards married.

[310] George Hastings (1540–1604) succeeded his brother Henry as the 4th earl of Huntingdon in 1595 and was in turn succeeded by his grandson by his first son Francis, Henry Hastings (1586–1643) in 1604. James William Edmund Doyle, *The Official Baronage of England* (London, 1886).

[311] Henry Hastings (*c*.1536–1595), 3rd earl of Huntingdon was a fervent Protestant and a potential successor to Elizabeth I, descending, as he did, from George, duke of Clarence, brother to Richard III. Henry supported Edward's selection of Lady Jane Grey as his heir, for which he spent time in the Tower under Mary. He was a dominant force in Leicestershire and in 1572 Elizabeth appointed him lord president of the Council of the North. In part because of the demands of this position, and also because of the care he took for his siblings, nieces and nephews, his support of Protestant scholars, ministers and preachers, the costs of law suits, and the demands placed on his estate by his father's will, the 3rd earl was plagued by debts and died leaving a reduced estate burdened by as much as £20,000 in debts. On at least three occasions (1570, 1571, and 1572) he borrowed £800, then £1,500, and then £3,000 from Francis Willoughby. Cross, *The Puritan Earl: The Life of Henry Hastings*. For the monies owed Francis Willoughby, see the appendix, pp. 329–330.

[312] For other letters from the earl of Huntingdon, his brother George Hastings, and his nephew Henry Hastings to Francis Willoughby regarding the prolonged negotiations

Wollaton New House was not finished till the year after this, and 'tis likely Sir Francis Willughby did not care to buy any new furniture till he went into that house.

[f. 130v] The book of houshold accounts mentioned before page 127 shews Sir Francis Willughbys weekly expences, where he went, and what company came to him at Thurland House in Nottingham, after the same maner as is set down page 127 concerning his expences weekly at Wollaton. This weekly account is continued from August the 12th 1587 to the end of October. This book gives an account that upon the 21th of October the Earl of Rutland with ten servants; Mr. Spencer, and Mr. Robert Willoughby with two servants each, came to Thurland House that the two latter stayed with Sir Francis two days, and that the Earl of Rutland and his retinue stayed with him till Tuesday night and then his Countess came, and as I understand by that book they borrowed Thurland House of Sir Francis Willughby for it is there set down that then the Earls officers entered upon 32 hogsheads of beer, and what other provision remained in the house, and that Sir Francis had his diet with the Earl, except that now and then he walked to Wollaton.[313]

November the 18th Sir Percivall Willoughby came to Wollaton, as that account book shews, with two men, but Sir Francis continued to stay at Nottingham with the Earl of Rutland. The expences at that time at Wollaton upon Sir Percivalls account is set down in that book, and also an account of many dinners which Sir Francis had at Wollaton to entertain company there, and that in his absence his servants were left at Wollaton at board wages.[314] There is also set down an account of many dinners which Sir Francis had to entertain company at the Chauntry,[315] that the Earl of Rutland dinned with him there in Christmas week, and the week after Sir Percivall, and severall others which are there named came and stayed with Sir Francis from Monday till Thursday, that in January the Earl dinned with him again. And the 9th of February Sir Francis went to Mr. Spencer at Allthorp, and stayed till the 18th and that then he returned and supped at the Chauntry. There is an exact account of his expences weekly, and of the dinners he had there all this time,

---

leading to this wedding, see Mi, 6/170/124/1–7. For various papers relating to the marriage settlement, see Mi, 6/170/125–130. These documents are all dated 1585.

[313] *HMC Middleton*, 455–456. Cassandra's excerpts from this household account book for 1587, copied down by Stevenson, are again quite accurate.

[314] *HMC Middleton*, 456.

[315] Francis had a house at the Chantry at Wollaton, which was purchased by Henry Medley from 'Rawfe Pynder, grocer of London', in 1562 for £34 15s: Mi, A 42, fo. 12 and *HMC Middleton*, 417.

till April the 6th 1588, and then the servants at board wages were taken into the house which he then kept at the Chauntry.³¹⁶

[f. 131] There are ~~other~~^{xxxvii} letters in the Library at Wollaton which shew that this summer An: D: 1587 Sir Francis Willughby married his third Daughter Margaret to Robert Spencer of Wormleighton in Warwickshire, descended from the ancient Barons of that name, which Robert being a person of a great estate, was, by letters patent (bearing date July the 21 the first of King James) advanced to the dignity of a Baron of this realm, by the title of Lord Spencer of Wormleighton.³¹⁷ The ceremony of his creation was performed at Hampton Court, and soon after he was sent to the Duke of Wirtenburgh,³¹⁸ with the ensigns of the most noble Order of the Garter. From this Robert Spencer and Margaret his Lady the present Earl of Sunderland is descended.

Before Sir Francis Willughby began to build I believe he had a great estate in money [*but Building Wollaton obliged him to borrow money, because many sumes w[hi]ch Sr. Francis had lent out before, he could not then get paid.*]³¹⁹ There is a letter from him to George Willughby dated An: D: 1574 to treat about buying,^{xxxviii} an estate of the Earl of Huntyngdon. But before he had near finished building his house it appears by the old letters that he wanted money, and that Mr. Thomas Willoughby the Father of Sir Percivall had supplyed him with it. There is a letter from him dated June the 5th 1584 in which he tells Sir Francis that he has offered an estate of his in Kent to sail [sell], but is profered but 5000^{li} for it, much less (he writes) than he thinks the estate worth; and therefore he must defer

---

³¹⁶ *HMC Middleton*, 456–457.

³¹⁷ Robert Spencer (1570–1627) of Northamptonshire was the son of Sir John Spencer and Mary, daughter of Sir Robert Catlin. He was created 1st Baron Spencer of Wormleighton in 1603. Margaret, his wife and third daughter of Francis Willoughby, bore him seven children and died 17 Aug. 1597 at the age of 26 following the birth of their last child. This child, Margaret, was born 14 Aug. 1597. Robert Spencer never remarried. He fought for twelve years to gain a large part of Francis Willoughby's estate but in the end only recovered ⅛ of the manor of Lambley, which he then sold for £900. At the accession of King James I, he was reputed to be the most moneyed man in England. He was buried at Brington beside Margaret, writing in his will that he wanted to be buried 'by the monument which I have made for Margaret my beloved wife'. See below, fo. 184v, p. 237. See *HMC Middleton*, 455, 456, 457, 458, 566, 568, 571, 608; *CSP Dom.* 1595–1597, p. 557, no. 81 for his struggle to gain some of the Willoughby estate from Percival and from Dorothy Willoughby as well as from Arabella Stuart. Spencer carried on various diplomatic missions for James I.

³¹⁸ Württemberg (or Wirtemberg) in the 16th century was a duchy near Stuttgart in Swabia, Germany. Ludwig III was the duke of Wirtemberg in 1587.

³¹⁹ Uncatalogued paper in Cassandra's hand titled on fo. 1, 'Amongst Sr Fr. W:ˢ Ladys Letters'. STB 2 (2), fo. 3 of this document.

to sell it which he is sorry for, and writes that he knows the land to be worth 300^{li} per Annum.[320]

There is a letter from Sir Francis, to Sir Percivall Willoughby to borrow money for him. He desires he will goe to Sir Henry Goodrick[321] to know what he had done concerning the money [f. 132] which he had promised to provide for him. And in a postscript writes, if Sir Henry be not home himself you need not make his Lady privie to it, or any else, for they can make no answer. This letter is dated July 1587 and directed to Newhall as many letters to Sir Percivall about that time were. In this letter he also desires to know if Mr. Willoughby of Nuneaton[322] would help him to 300^{li}.

There are in the Library at Wollaton severall letters and papers which were writ An: D: 1588 that shew that there was a very villainous design carried on by one Payne a servant of Sir Francis Willughbys to render him suspected by the Queen and Councel of joyning[xxxix] with the Spaniard at the time of their invasion, and a copy of articles exhibited in her majesties behalf, by this Robert Payne against Sir Francis Willughby to the Lords of her Privie Councel, whereby he would maliciously have made it appear that Sir Francis Willughby was in the Spanish interest, that he had plotted with severall priests to aid and assist the Spaniards in their[xl] intended invasion, that he had hindred the firing of the beacons, to give the people notice of their danger. That he had made a deed of gift of his estate which Payne said he believed was done in order to defraud her Majesty, if any concealment of treason should be found against him. That for fear of Paynes discovering all this Sir Francis had endeavoured to get him murdered, and that he had[xli] corrupted Payne's counsel so that he could not prosecute him in the Star Chamber, and therefore he petition'd the Privie Counsel in behalf

---

[320] In July 1585, in another letter from Francis to Thomas Willoughby, Francis reports that a Mr Huitt, draper in Candelwick Street, had offered him £5,500 for his land in Kent. Francis would not sell for one penny under £6,000. In the letter, he thinks Huitt will come to his price, although he also notes that a Mr Wilford in Rie is interested. In this letter Francis describes his efforts to sell Langton Welles for £3,000 and warns that if these sales do not go through he may have to go abroad to negotiate them. He asks to borrow £300 with interest at the same time he plans to send £500 to Thomas Willoughby to settle a debt with a goldsmith and with Thomas Willoughby. He says, 'I have byn in some talke for the marriage of my daughters, and like enough to conclude for the one [probably Dorothy Willoughby].' His charges have grown so large that he may have to discharge some of his unnecessary servants. Mi, C 17; *HMC Middleton*, 157.

[321] Probably Sir Henry Goodere (1534–1595), who built Polesworth Hall, Warks., on the site of a nunnery. See Text n. 385.

[322] William Willoughby of Normanton and Nuneaton, who, however, wrote his will only a few months later on 3 Oct. 1587 and died that year.

of the Queen, against Sir Francis Willughby, laying before them these articles of accusation against him.[323]

[f. 132v] There is a letter from Mr. John Adams to his Brother-in-law Sir Percivall Willoughby dated June the 15th 1588, in which he writes that he heard Sir Francis was sent for up by a Pursivant to appear before the Lord Chancellor.

[f. 133] There is no account how this matter ended, nor what became of Payne, but I am apt to believe Sir Francis would not let him go unpunished. And it appears that one of our family viz: Sir Ambrose Willoughby was[324] one of those Gentlemen, who at their own charges hired ships to joyn the English Admiral in order to encounter the Spanish Armada. This Sir R: Bacon [*sic*] gives an account of.[325]

It appears by many of the old papers that there was about this time a great scarcity of money in England,[326] and that Sir Francis

---

[323] Robert Payne of High Wycombe, Bucks., had proposed growing woad at Wollaton in 1585. There is a 1586 petition from Robert Payne to Lord Burghley to continue sowing woad on certain conditions, notwithstanding the Queen's 1585 proclamation restricting the cultivation of woad. BL, Lansdowne MS 49/38. In 1586 the Privy Council granted permission to Payne to continue his operation. See a six-page MS by Payne published in R.S. Smith, 'A Woad Growing Project at Wollaton in the 1580s', *TTS* 65 (1961), appendix II; BL, Lansdowne MS 49/33, fo. 33; Lansdowne MS 121/21; Smith, 'Willoughbys', ch. 16. For a 1585 letter from Robert Payne to Sir Francis, see Mi, 5/165/96 and Mi, 5/165/95. For a description of the fraught relationship between Payne and Sir Francis, see Hayden, 'Sir Francis Willoughby,' 140–149. See Mi, 5/165/117-118, 123-126, 128, including a handwritten testimony by Draycott, one of Francis's servants, against Payne. See also Mi, 5/167/189. In 1591, Sir Francis appeared before the Privy Council regarding a private dispute with Payne over monies owed. Payne was released from his Majesty's Bench until the dispute could be heard. *Acts of the Privy Council of England*, New Series, Vol. 22 (1591-1592), 170–171, 240–241. If Paine failed to show up, 'their Lordships doe promise to graunt to Sir Frauncis Willughbie their warrant for the apprehencion of the said Paine, where soever he maie be remaininge within any parte of her Majesty's dominions'. Payne responded with accusations that Sir Francis had plotted to assist the Spanish invasion in 1588. In Feb. 1591/2 a settlement was reached, although Payne returned to prison and died there as a result of an action for debt by Sir Francis. For many Middleton documents regarding woad cultivation and Robert Payne, see Mi, 5/165/95-128.

[324] Sir Ambrose Willoughby (whose seat was at Malton, Gloucs.), was the second son of Charles Willoughby, 2nd Baron Willoughby of Parnham. He was one of the Queen's esquires of the body. Based on John Foxe's *Book of Martyrs*, and repeated many times since, Ambrose Willoughby was one of those who provided a ship at his own expense and joined the English fleet in 1588 at the time of the Spanish Armada.

[325] Baker, *Chronicle of the Kings of England*, 396 ff.

[326] Lawrence Stone's contested *The Crisis of the Aristocracy 1558–1641* (Oxford, 1967) argues that there was a crisis of indebtedness in the aristocracy after 1585 and for the last 20 years of Elizabeth's reign. See esp. pp. 247–48. See N.J. Mayhew, 'Population, money supply and the velocity of circulation in England, 1300–1700', *Economic History Review*, NS 48 (1995), 252–253, where he concludes that: 'though V [velocity] peaks for the 1561 estimates (a calculation perhaps still affected by the debasement), it seems to have fallen markedly through Elizabeth's reign before stabilizing in the second half of the 17th century at a velocity level below that of 1300. If some allowance is also made for the increasingly widespread use of negotiable paper contributing to M [money], the impression of falling V becomes

Willughby, by his building; and in the midst of that; marrying two of his Daughters, had run himself in debt, and that he often employed Sir Percivall, and Mr. Thomas Willoughby his Father to borrow money for him and to be bound with him for it.

There is a letter from Edward Willoughby to his Brother Sir Percivall dated November 1588, in which he writes that money grows every day scantier than other, and that those that have money stick not to ask twenty in the hundred for it, and that such are mens wants that rather than they will goe without it, they daily give it. In this letter, he tells this story of Alderman Catcher and Alderman Skinner, that they were both by order of the Privie Counsel committed to the fleet, for whiping two Gentlewomen in Bridewell as common whores, and it was supposed it would cost them 2000^{li} before they got out, the Queen taking the matter hardly against them, their fine was like to [f. 133v] be the greater.[327]

One of these Gentlewomen was Wife to him that sue'd to be Lord Latimer, the other was Captain Nunames Wife.[328]

There is the copy of a very angry letter from Lady Willughby to this Alderman Catcher, who I believe had writ to her in behalf of Sir Percivall, at a time when she had a quarrell with him, which I believe hapned very soon after she was reconciled to Sir Francis her Husband.

---

still more marked.' Apparently, the money supply continued to rise, but the rate of circulation of money decreased. Also, an increased population resulted in a decline in real national income and per capita income, which plummeted. All of these calculations are affected by the rise in other forms of money (e.g. paper credit) and growing proportion of silver coin to gold. The evidence for growing poverty and unemployment in the 1590s is unmistakeable.'

[327] A similar but much lengthier version, described in the introduction, is told by John Adams in a letter to his brother-in-law Percivall Willoughby in Aug. 1588. Mi, C 18; *HMC Middleton*, 158–159. After a term as sheriff of London in 1587–1588 John Catcher (d.1638) became a City alderman and in 1590 attracted the high subsidy assessment of £56. He surrendered his aldermanic position in 1596. Thomas Skinner (d.1596) was sheriff in 1588 conjointly with John Catcher and succeeded Catcher in the Aldermanry of Cripplegate when Catcher was discharged due to financial difficulties. In Dec. 1588 Alderman Skinner was detained in custody for disobedience to an order of the Queen-in-Council. Whether this was related to the incident described here and elsewhere is unclear, as it may also have been in relation to London's inability to contribute toward expenses required of the Crown. Skinner was made Lord Mayor of London in 1596 upon recommendation of Queen Elizabeth but died shortly thereafter. http://www.historyofparliamentonline.org/volume/1604-1629/member/catcher-sir-john-1568-1638; John James Baddeley, *The Aldermen of Cripplegate Ward from A.D. 1276 to A.D. 1900, together with some account of the office of Alderman, Alderman's Deputy, and Common Councilman of the City of London* (London, 1900).

[328] P.H. Reaney and R.M. Wilson, *A Dictionary of English Surnames* (London, 1991), 2259, Newnam.

The copy of part of that letter from Lady Willughby to Alderman Catcher.

You causlessly condemn me of unkindness to Percivall Willoughby. I will forbear to repeat his unfriendly behaviours, because I will not disclose his faults to a babling fool. Expecting no better than the worst you can practice, I stay my own trouble, and stay you your tongue for al=be=it, I am Fatherless,[329] I am not Husbandless nor friendless, but

                A Dispiser of vain Fools
                Elizabeth Willughby

[1588–1595: End of Separation and Death of Elizabeth Willughby]

[f. 134] It was I believe about Christmas 1588, that Lady Willughby came to live with Sir Francis.[330]

There is a letter from Edward Willoughby to his Brother Sir Percivall dated from Boreplace December 1588, in which letter he desires Sir Percivall will have care of old Spencer, and his Cousin Robert,[331] who he believes have some ill design against him; and writes that they now labour to bring Lady Willughby to live with Sir Francis.

There is another letter writ the same month from Edward Willoughby to his Brother Sir Percivall to let him know that Lady Willughby now speaks marvilous well of him, and that she had told him, her Son in law Spencer had been with her, and told her that Sir Francis Willughby was a most wise man for not disposing of his land in his own life time, and for his part if Sir Francis should dye, he would keep possession of one of the turrets of the new house.

---

[329] Sir John Lyttleton died in Feb. 1590. 'His dissolute heir, Gilbert Lyttleton, gave him a pauper's funeral, "neyther mourning gowne, clothe nor cloke was given for him"'. (Tonks, 'Lyttletons', 59–60, citing L38/12, deposition of John Lynold). No tomb was erected over his grave, and the provisions of his will were not respected. For his will, see TNA, PROB 11/75/268. Cassandra has placed this letter here, in 1588, because of the mention of Alderman Catcher and the events of 1588, but it must properly be dated after Feb. 1590.

[330] Her return to Wollaton may have been precipitated by increasingly poor health. On 11 Aug. 1588 John Adams reported to Percivall Willoughby that 'My Lady Willughby was dead and in a mortale sound [swoon] by the space of j. hower full, and could not be revived. There weare none in here chamber but here mayde, and a jentelman's man wiche lay over here, hereing the mayde to cry out, came downe and helped to rubb and recover the good lady, and soe in the end thereof recovered here.' Mi, C 18; *HMC Middleton*, 159.

[331] Robert Willoughby?

Spencer also told her that Sir Percivall kept his Wife from viseting her, to which she answer'd that she could not believe that, because Percivall Willoughby had told her that his Wife should come to her whenever she pleased; to which she said Spencer answer'd, that Sir Percivall could afford her little if he could not afford her fair words.

It is very probable that the reconciliation between Sir Francis and his Lady was made in London,[332] and that Sir Percivall might come up to them in Town, on purpose to wish them joy of it, and perhaps find some opportunity to press Sir Francis to make a settlement of the estate upon him, and it is also very probable that Lady Willughby might take this very ill from Sir Percivall and perhaps this might be the reason why Alderman Catcher writ to her in behalf of Sir Percivall, and occasion'd her writing that angry letter to the Alderman. [f. 135] I believe at this time while Sir Percivall might be in London with Sir Francis Willughby and his Lady my Grandfather was born.[333] For there is an affectionate letter writ by Sir Percivall to his Lady dated from London An: D: 1588, to congratulate her upon the birth of her Son. He stiles her his best beloved, and writes, that upon the news her Mother was sadly out of humour, and vented her anger upon her maids. But Sir Francis seemed to be very glad, though as yet he would doe nothing for the child, and was every day in a thousand minds what to doe with his estate. [*and has been lately so ill yt he doubts ye worst.*][334] He expresses great concern for his leaving her, and promises not to be long absent from her again, writing that if Sir Francis had not promised him as he was a Christian to see him sattisfied he should not have stayed from her, with such grief and vexation of mind as he had now done. He desired she would cherish and content herself, and prayed God to send their Son happyer days than his parents. [*By this and many other letters, tis plain that Lady Willughby had no true kindness for Sr Percivall, I believe she hop'd to have a Son of her own to inherit Sr Francis's estate, and therefore could not w[i]th patience look upon Sr Percivall & her*

---

[332] 'It was about this time [Dec. 1588] that Sir Francis Willughby and his Lady were reconciled.' STB 2 (1), book 2, fo. 39.

[333] Francis Willoughby (1588–1665). 'The eldest child of Percivall and Bridget, Francis was brought up initially at Middleton, Warks., but from 1599 principally at Wollaton Hall. He was educated at Magdalen College, Oxford, from 1607, and entered Lincoln's Inn in 1609. He returned to live at Middleton with his family from 1615. He succeeded his father in 1643, but never lived at Wollaton Hall, which had been badly damaged by fire in 1642.' Francis was Cassandra's grandfather. University of Nottingham: https://www.nottingham.ac.uk/manuscriptsandspecialcollections/collectionsindepth/family/middleton/biographies/biographyoffranciswilloughby(1588-1665).aspx (accessed 18 Sept. 2016).

[334] STB 2 (1), book 2, fo. 39.

daughter Brigetts ^children^ as their Heirs; and now upon the birth of my Grandfather, I believe she fear'd Sr Francis might be preveild w[i]th to settle the estate upon them and their Heris, and therefore she was so angry at the news of her Grandsons birth I believe she continued this unkind carriage.][335]

There is a very angry letter from Lady Willughby to her Son percivall, which is not dated, but I believe might be writ about this time. In this letter she tells him, that she marvels much he dares be so saucy, to medle where he had so little thanks. And that he came for no other end but to cozen Sir Francis of his money, and to tell him lyes, and tales, but it were good for him to get home in time for fear of afterclaps, and say he had fair warning.

I will not vouchsafe my name at this time, because if thou can'st not guess right, thou mayst goe shoot at rovers[336] this fair weather with thy silence keeper.

[f. 135v] The before mentioned account book shews that in April 1588 Sir Francis Willughby began again to keep house, and I believe the Earl of Rutland and his family might then return to his own house, for it appears by this book that Sir Francis's family were sometimes at the Chauntry and sometimes at Thurland House in Nottingham;[337] his weekly expences, as before, is there set down, and also what company came to Sir Francis and where he went himself. That from April the 6th to the 13th Sir George Hastings stayed with him two days, and that the expences that week came to 5^{li}—14^{sh}—4^{d}, from the 13th to the 20th Sir Percivall and his Brother Edward Willoughby staid 5 days with Sir Francis whose expences that week was 5^{li}—11^{sh}—10^{d}. From the 20th to the 27th spent 5^{li}—5^{sh}—0^{d}. That May the 4th Sir Percivall came and stayed 2 days, and other commers and goers were there that week, and that the weeks expence was 4^{li}—11^{sh}—4^{d}. From May the 4th to June the 15th the same particular weekly account is set down in that book which added together in that time the sum totall was 29^{li}—18^{sh}—7^{d}. June the 16th the Bishop of York,[338] Sir Thomas Mannors, Sir Thomas Stanhop, and divers other Gentlemen dined with Sir Francis at Thurland House,[339] spent that week 8^{li}—5^{sh}—11^{d}. From the 22th to the 29th spent 4^{li}—16^{sh}—4^{d}. in which time Mr. Sacheverell was at

---

[335] STB 2 (1), book 2, fo. 40.

[336] See *OED*: 'An arbitrarily selected mark at an unknown distance from the archer, esp. as used to provide practice in range-finding and long-distance shooting.' 'Silence keeper' remains a mystery.

[337] Home of Thomas Markham. See Text n. 308.

[338] Edwin Sandys (1516–10 July 1588) was archbishop of York from 1577 to 1588; John Piers (1522/3–1594) succeeded him.

[339] *HMC Middleton*, 457. Cassandra includes more detail in the following excerpts than Stevenson.

Wollaton 5 nights.[340] From June the 29th to July the 20th Sir Francis was most of the time[xlii] in Warwickshire spent in that time at Wollaton 14^{li}—2^{sh}—7^{d}. August the 3^{d} Sir Percivall and his Brother and much company dined at Wollaton, spent that week 4^{li}—18^{sh}—0^{d}. The same company stayed at Wollaton the week following spent from August the 3^{d} to the 10th 8^{li}—5^{sh}—1^{d}. Sir Percivall and his Brother continued at Wollaton part of the next week and Mr. Spencer also came, spent from the 10th to the 17th 5^{li}—18^{sh}—10^{d} from the 17th to the 23th much company dined at Wollaton spent that week 6^{li}—3^{sh}—7^{d}. From the 23^{d} to the 31 spent 5^{li}—5^{sh}—0^{d}. The first week in September Sir George Hastings, and the next week much other company were at Wollaton, after which Sir Francis went to Warwickshire and stayed there till the end of that month, spent at Wollaton in September 19^{li}—6^{sh}—4^{d}. From October the 5th to the 12 Sir George Hastings and his Son, and Mr. Palmer[341] stayed 3 days at Wollaton with Sir Francis, spent that week 5^{li}—13^{sh}—2^{d}. From the 12th to the 26th spent 11—16—10. In which time J: Bartowes[xliii] weding[342] dinner was kept, and much company dined with Sir Frances [*sic*] after at the Chauntry, from the 26th to November the 2^{d} spent 5^{li}—16^{sh}—0^{d}. Sir Percivall stayed with Sir Francis from Monday till Satturday, the week after Sir Francis lay 3 nights at Nottingham, spent from November the 2^{d} to the 23th 16—5—0. The 23th Sir George Hastings came with 5 men, and Sir Percivall Willoughby and others who all stayed from Monday till Thursday spent that week 8^{li}—2—3. Spent the next week 8^{li}—2—3. Spent the 1st week of December 8—1—7, spent the 2^{d} week in December 9—14—11.[343]

[f. 136] There is a letter from Henry Trussell to Sir Francis Willughbys Lady dated February the 23th 1588/9, to congratulate her upon her coming again to live with Sir Francis. In this letter

---

[340] *HMC Middleton*, 257. Henry Sacheverell, Esq. of Nottingham, *c*.1548–1620, Ratcliff-upon-Soar (Notts.) and Morley (Derbys.). His father John fled England in 1559; his lands were taken in hand by the Queen but were recovered by Henry in 1575/6 for a leased rent of £200. *CPR* 1575–1578, 18 Elizabeth, 100. His wife was Jane Bradburne (1559–1621), from whom he separated after at least four children who survived him. In 1593 he was in the Fleet for not repaying her dowry. Subsequently he took up a mistress, Elizabeth Keyes, by whom he had three sons, two reputed (Ferdinand Valence and Francis Sacheverell) and one acknowledged named Valence.

[341] Probably Robert Palmer of Wingham, Kent (*c*.1541–1626), son of Sir Henry Palmer of Angmering, Sussex. Robert Palmer was high sheriff of Kent in 1595 and was knighted in 1603. He served in Parliament for Arundel in 1586 and 1601 and was a gentleman of the privy chamber to James I. *History of Parliament*: http://www.historyofparliamentonline.org/volume/1558-1603/member/palmer-thomas-ii-1541-1625 (accessed 19 Sept. 2016).

[342] Unidentified.

[343] *HMC Middleton*, 457–459; the text, from J. Bartowes on is written along the margin in tiny script.

he writes, that he hopes soon to see such a reformation in Wollaton House as shall make Sir Francis sufficiently sensible of the loss he had sustained in her absence, and that he shall be heartily glad to see Wollaton reassume its former credit.

There is a letter from Lady Willughby, to her Husband, Sir Francis, dated from the Grange[344] July 1589, full of complaints against his servants. Those who he most trusted she writes were not faithfull to him. One of them was a near kinsman to the Lord Huntyngdon and prevented his selling his western land, out of regard to his young Mistress their Daughter [Dorothy Willoughby Hastings].[345] She writes that she desires he will conceal this till he comes down (which she hopes will be quickly) and then she will let him understand such a plot of knavery amongst his own men as she believed was never used towards so good a Master as he had been to them. She desires in this letter that he will keep his Son Hastyngs out of the mess till she has spoke with him.

In this year An: D: 1589 there is an account of Lady Willughbys going to London for the recovery of her health.[346] There are in the Library severall very kind and submissive letters writ by her to Sir Francis while she stayed in Town.

In one dated November 1589 she tels him that their Daughter was deliver'd of a girle. And writes that she had been to try her Brother Willoughbys house in London which she did not think fit for them to be in, the furniture was so mean that she was fain to have all her own found, and besides the house was so cold [f. 137] that in winter she could not be able to endure it. She beseeched him to have a care of her health, for though she must bear the [word missing][347] he would the charge of her sickness.[348] But what was his will, she would willingly obey. She writ that she marveled his charges should

---

[344] Wolvey Grange, Warks., where Nuneaton House was located.

[345] 'In other letters she tells him she is ill-used by his servants, which she will make appear at her return; she writes that it is they which hinder his selling or letting his western lands, [Woodland, Dorset] and that they are set on by Lord Huntington'. STB 2 (1), book 1, fo. 31. See below, 166–169, pp. 208–212, especially.

[346] In Apr. 1589 Elizabeth and Francis had been to the spa at Buxton. On 26 Apr. 1589 Sir Francis Willoughby wrote to Elizabeth Hardwick Talbot, countess of Shrewsbury, to ask her to lend her horse litter and furniture to Elizabeth Willoughby to come home. Elizabeth, he says, 'hath beene longe sicke' and 'having receaved noe healpe is growne to suche weakenesse' that she cannot manage to travel home by horseback or by coach. Folger Shakespeare Library, X.d.428 (126).

[347] There is a word missing here. Perhaps 'pain' based on her earlier notes.

[348] 'and beseeches him to have a Care of her health for he must bear the Charges tho she does the Pain, but what is his Will she will Willingly obey.' Uncatalogued paper in Cassandra's hand titled on fo. 1, 'Amongst Sr Fr. W:ˢ Ladys Letters'. STB 2 (2), fo. 2v of this document.

arise to ten pounds a week since her comming away. Before, when things were dearer, at the most their weekly expences was but eight pounds. She writs that she leaves him to judg if his charges has not been lessen'd since her comming home. She desires in this letter that her coach horses may be sent to fetch her home again.

In another letter Lady Willughby tells Sir Francis that she has found but little benefit by her medicines, though her phisitians spare neither his purse, nor their own pains, tho she writes they take but twenty shillings a day, and come twice for it.

[*Despairing of a Son of her own, grew more kind to them; for there are severall very affectionate letters from her, to her Daughter Brigett, writ in the years 1592 and 93, and about that time I believe it was [by her intersession] that Sr Francis made the settlement beforementioned of Wollaton Cossall and Trowell, Middleton and Kinsbury, upon Sr Percivall and Bridgett, and their Heires. From this time until Lady Willughby's death I believe they lived very easie and happyly.*][349]

There is a very kind letter from Lady Willughby to her Daughter Bridget dated An: D: 1592, in which she offers them the Chauntry to dwell in, which if she and Sir Percivall approves off [of], she will have the house repaired, and they shall have the keeping of twenty cows and Sir Percivall Willoughby's geldings, which (by her manner of writing) she thought would be better for them than to continue at Middleton.

There are also very kind letters from Lady Willughby to her Daughter Bridget An: D: 1593, who was then big with child. In one she mentions sending her wine etc, and desires Bridget Willoughby will not make strange of any thing which she can pleasure her withall, but believe the more bold she is, the more she shall think she loves her.

[f. 138] There are severall letters from Lady Willughby to her Son Percival some very kind, and others the reverse of them. In one letter to him she complains, that when she was absent from her Husband and in want, her other Sons-in-law often remembered her with many good things, but he never sent her any thing, nor lent her a groat.

In a letter An: D: 1593 Lady Willughby desires her Son Percivall will get for her a tunn [tun=a large cask or barrel] of the best claret wine and a barrell of sack.[350]

There is another letter from Lady Willughby to her Son Percivall, in which she promises to use her utmost endeavour to get Sir

---

[349] STB 2 (1), book 2, fo. 41.

[350] White fortified wine from mainland Spain or the Canary Islands. Most sack was probably sweet and matured in wooden barrels for a limited time. It was very popular with the Elizabethans. Typical sack may have resembled cheaper versions of medium Oloroso sherry.

Francis's estate made secure to him, provided he would help discharge his debts. She tells him he is too apt to take offence, and confesses she is herself to blame for sharpness of nature, but if he will trust her, she will be kind to him, and evermore friend and assist him, in which should she fail, she bids him then lay her own hand writing to her charge. She prays for his good success in his business at London, and that Kinsbury may be redeemed. And hopes that he and Henry Willughby may soon come down to Wollaton to let leases and provide sumes of money to untie the many mortgages.

[*Sir Francis Willoughby had been reconciled to his son Percivall some years before his Lady dyed,*]³⁵¹ There are in the Library at Wollaton many very kind letters from Sir Francis Willughby to Sir Percivall writ from An: D: 1587 to An: D: 1593. Many of those letters were writ to desire Sir Percivall would help him to money, and to desire he would be bound with him for severall sumes of money.

In one of these letters Sir Francis desires Sir Percivall will find him [f. 139] a chapman [a trader or dealer] for Steeple Hall, for his debts grow so great that without the sail [sale] of that and some other things, the interest money will eat up the profit of his revenue.

There is a letter from Sir Francis to Sir Percivall, dated An: D: 1591 to desire he would be bound with him for the sume of 1600ˡⁱ to Thomas Peyn,³⁵² for payment of 800ˡⁱ which he was to lend to Sir Francis Willughby.

There is a letter of Attorney dated An: D: 1593 from Sir Francis Willughby to Sir Percivall, to inable him to sue for, and levie debts due to Sir Francis.

Sir Francis seems then to have employed Sir Percivall in all his affairs, and to approve of what he did, and gave him a writing (which was drawn by Mr. George Lyttleton his Ladys Brother) to secure to him the inherritance of Wollaton, Cossall and Trowell, and of Middleton and Kinsbury.

The hopes of this settlement I believe made Sir Percivall Willoughby and his Father, so ready to assist Sir Francis with what money he wanted; and by so doing to engage themselves in those debts which he contracted, and which after Sir Francis's death fell

---

[351] Uncatalogued paper in Cassandra's hand titled on fo. 1, 'Amongst Sr Fr. W:ˢ Ladys Letters'. STB 2 (2), fo. 2 of this document.
[352] Possibly the son of William Payne (d.1615) who bought half of Medbourne Manor House, Leics., in 1551. Thomas (d. aft. 1591) bought the other half in 1563. Nick Hill, 'The Manor House, Medbourne: The development of Leicestershire's earliest manor house', *Transactions of the Leicestershire Archaeological and Historical Society*, 75 (2001), 39; J.M. Lee and R.A. McKinley (eds), *A History of the County of Leicester: V*, VCH (London, 1964), 229–248. http://www.british-history.ac.uk/vch/leics/vol5/pp229-248 (accessed 13 Sept. 2016).

very heavie upon Sir Percivall, as will hereafter appear in the account I shall give of Sir Percivall [in the second volume of her Account].

This settlement of Wollaton etc, and of Middleton and Kinsbury upon Sir Percivall Willoughby and Brigitt his Wife and their heirs, was I believe made by perswasion of Sir Francis Willughbys Lady about a year before her death, her state of health being then grown so bad that she could not expect to live long, and at that time I believe Sir Percivall and his Lady were much in her favour, and often with her.

There is a letter writ by Sir Percivall Willoughby to his Lady [f. 140] to give her notice that her Mother was then very sick, and to desire she would send her some of her preserved barberrys, and some cherries, and to send his dogg because they wanted a dog to kill partridges for Lady Willughby, and with this letter, there is a copy of a very affectionate letter, which he desired she would write to her Mother.

There is a letter writ I believe about the same time to Lady Willughby by Robert Spencer her Son-in-law, dated An: D: 1594, in which letter he expressed great concern for her sickness, which continued so long upon her, and which he had heard was so extream, that he doubted of her life, and that put him now upon writing plainly to her, which he hoped she would pardon, because he did it for the good of her children that were unmarried. Upon which account the world blamed her, saying that if Sir Francis and she had not come together again, they would have been as well, or better, bestowed than the rest of their Sisters, which was very unnaturall in her and she must expect God would lay the burthen of their offences on her if they should do otherwise than well. He himself (he writ) had made divers motions for their marrying such men of worth, both for living and behaviour, as had he had Sisters of his own he should have been glad they might have had them. But those offers she had received so contemptably, that had not her extream sickness now hapned, he should have used no more speeches about them, but that made him write his opinion that she should now take care for them and shew the world that she did not hate her own flesh. For should God call her, she might be sure Sir Francis would marry again, [f. 141] and then she might judg what regard would be had of her children.

There is no account of the time when, Lady Willughby dyed but I believe this was her last sickness, and that she dyed An: D: 1594.[353]

---

[353] The date of Lady Willoughby's death has been variously reported. Friedman follows Cassandra in writing 1594, while Hayden writes 1595. Concern with Lady Willoughby's bequests and inventory in June and Aug. 1595 (fos 191–191v, pp. 245–246) suggest that she died in 1595, at which time she was 49 years of age. There is a reference in the Feet of Fines to a dispute, dated Easter [26 Mar.] 1595, between Ralph Whalley, Esq., plaintiff,

[After Elizabeth Willoughby's Death: Francis Willoughby Remarries]

There is a letter without date from Abigail Willughby to her Sister Brigitt in which she writes, that she hoped they should now have happyer days, and that her Father would send for her again to Wollaton, to supply her Mothers place, which she found herself unfit for.

Lady Willughbys uneasie temper, and the severity she shewed to all her Daughters made them bear her death (I believe) with very little concern. If Sir Francis had any thoughts of having Sir Percivall and his Lady come to live with him at Wollaton, (as their Sister Abigail hoped) tis very probable that his servants, Marmion and Cludd etc. might joyn with Fisher another of Sir Francis Willughbys servants (who had married George Willughbys Daughter)[354] and prevent Sir Percivalls coming to live with Sir Francis; in order to effect this 'tis probable[xliv] they strove again to renew the old quarrell that has been between them.[355]

There is a letter in the Library which was writ by Sir Francis Willughby to Mr. Thomas Willoughby An: D: 1595 I believe soon after his Ladys death to borrow his house in Lincolns Inn Fields. To which letter there is Mr. Willoughbys answer that he was very sorry that he could not furnish him with that house, having let a lease of some of the rooms half a year before. This house I find was often borrowed by Mr. Willoughby when he was in the Country himself. In March 1595 Robert Sackville[356] writ a letter, which yet remains in the Library, to borrow it for his Wife and the

---

and Francis, Elizabeth, and Percival Willoughby, defendants, cited in S.H. Skillington, 'Medieval Cossington', III, ch. 5, *Transactions of the Leicestershire Archaeological and Historical Society*, 19 (1936–1937), 275–292, esp. 289. See also TNA, *Calendar of Proceedings in Chancery in the reign of Queen Elizabeth*, 3, 1597 (London, 1832), 299. In May, 1595 Frances Willoughby, the youngest daughter, left her mother and father because of the cruelty of her mother. Mi, 2/75/2/8/1. R.S. Smith states that Elizabeth Willoughby died on 4 June 1595. Smith, 'Willoughbys', 56. See Mi, F 12/98 for a 19th-century annotation that she was buried 4 June 1595. Francis Willoughby remarried in Aug. 1595.

[354] George Willoughby, the illegitimate uncle of Sir Francis Willoughby, who figures prominently earlier in this letter collection. See Text n. 27 above. His step-granddaughter was Mary Repington, wife of Clement Fisher and daughter of Richard Repington. For Clement Fisher and Mary Repington also, see Text n. 191 above.

[355] Cassandra's earlier notes say, 'soon after her death Fisher and the rest of Sr Francis's designing servants ^by letters wch remain appear to [hav?]^ renewed the quarrell between him and Sr Percivall, as is before mentioned in the account of Sr Fra: Willughby where is put down what particulars I could find relating to that quarrell.' STB 2 (1), book 2, fo. 41.

[356] Robert Sackville, 2nd earl of Dorset (1561–1609).

Countess etc. [f. 141v] There is a letter from Sir Percivall Willoughby to Sir Francis dated June the 1st 1595, in which he writ, that Mr. Fisher had always sought his overthrow and disgrace, and to make himself by Sir Francis's spoyles.

[f. 142] By the old papers in the Library at Wollaton there is reason to believe that Sir Francis Willughby's servants did intend to get from their master some of their Lady's jewells, after she was dead. It was a fashion at that time in very rich embroadrys upon cloaths to mix pearl upon spangles with the gold and silver. Such a sute of cloaths I believe this Lady had when she dyed, part of which I believe still remains in the wardrobe at Wollaton. This garment was made of crimson velvet, the body of which seemed to have been richly embroadred but the embroadry was picked off. In the skert of the gowne there was ten breadths of the velvet about a yard and a half long, the bottom of which by the marks upon the velvet appear'd to have been embroadred about 4 inches deep and also an embroadry of the same breadth had been on each side of the fore part of the skert of the[xlv] gowne, the velvet was also marked quite round the skert about 14 inches from the top which shew'd that it had been gethered there, which made the farthingall round the hips, which old pictures shew was the dress of that time. With this gowne I found in the wardrobe a muff which was a square piece of rich embroadry upon which there was some pearl, the other side was sabl and this muff was made to tye together with ribbons. There was also a cap richly embroadred, and two long feathers, one black, and the other white which I believe was to be worn with it. Such a cap this Lady Willughby's picture is drawn with upon her head, and she is[xlvi] also painted in[xlvii] such a gowne as I believe this might have been. There was also with these cloaths a frame of wire for the hair, which was to fix jewels in, to ware upon the head. There was also some scolloped lace which I believe had been a ruff and severall holland head bands, and quoives [coifs] for the head made of fine holland embroadred with silk gold and spangles, design'd for such a dress for the head as many of Queen Anne Bullen's [Boleyn] pictures are drawn with. There was also in the wardrobe another gowne with a farthingall skert made of black farrendon and laced with black and gold lace. There was also two white wrought waistcoats to be worn with petticoats which I believe was the[xlviii] un=dress [under-dress] then in fashion.

After this long digression which these old cloaths have led me into I must return to the first sute upon which I believe the pearl might have been, and also that part of that pearl Lady Willughby might have borrowed of her Daughter Brigitt, because I found a letter from her [f. 143] writ to Fox (which was one of Sir Francis's servants)[357] after his Lady's death to desire she might have such jewells returned as she had lent to the Lady her Mother viz

pearl[358] to the value of	30^{li}
buttons of gold valued at	18
and in old gold	14
and also some other small jewells.	

In this letter she writ that Russell[359] had worn some of the pearl since her Mothers death, and she had seen some of the buttons worn, and for the old gold, her Mother had most of that about her when she dyed.

It is very probable that Sir Francis's servants might represent this letter in such a manner to him as might make him take it very ill from his daughter, and that also they found ways of giving him again ill impressions of Sir Percivall.

[*I don't find any account of Sr Percivall or his Ladys being at Wollaton for any time after Lady Willughbys death, and do believe that Fisher (who married George Willughbys Daughter, and had insinuated himself very much in Sr Francis's favour) joined wth Cludd and Marmion two of Sr Francis's servants, who before had been chief instruments in making those unhappy differences between Sr Francis and his Lady, and after between Sr Francis and Sr Percivall, now after Lady Willughby's death thought to enrich themselves by keeping Sr Percivall at a distance from Sr Francis and by their instigation I believe it was that Sr Francis began to have hard thoughts of Sr Percivall and his Daughter Brigett.*][360]

There is a letter from Sir Francis to Sir Percivall dated April the 24 1595, to let him know that he would have him meet him at London, and [*bids him*] that he should [*fail not*] bring with him the rents of Middleton Kinsbury and Wyken, and the accounts of the iron mills, and also he must bring with him that writing [*the Assurance*][361] which did secure to him the inheritance of Wollaton, Cossall and Trowell; Middleton and Kinsbury.

I could find no account of Sir Percivall's going to London at that time, and believe he might excuse it; fearing to trust Sir Francis with that writing which he had order'd him to bring.

The old papers shew that Sir Francis made but a short stay in London and that at his return to Wollaton, he sent to Sir Percivall

---

[357] Unidentified, although he may be related to George Willoughby aka Fox, illegitimate half brother of Henry Willoughby, father of Francis, who is mentioned throughout.

[358] There is more discussion of pearl necklaces (a great pearl and of little pearls laced with rubies) in the correspondence of Abigail Willoughby, fo. 191v, p. 246 below.

[359] Wife of William Russell, steward of Sir Francis. In July 1595 it was Russell whom Sir Francis sent to London to seek a new wife. See fo. 144, p. 246 below.

[360] STB 2 (1), book 2, fos 4–5.

[361] Insertions are from STB 2 (1), book 2, fo. 9v.

to come from Middleton to him there, and that at this meeting at Wollaton there passed so much unkindness between the Father and Son, that Sir Percivall went away from Wollaton upon the 23th of July 1595, without taking any leave of Sir Francis.

There is the coppy of a letter which Sir Percivall writ soon after his return from Wollaton to Middleton, to Green,[362] who had been his friend, by pleading in his behalf to Sir Francis. In this letter he tells Green that he had been sent for in hast to Wollaton, but his entertainment was such that he stay'd not long. And that hereafter he would frame himself to endure loss and disgrace [f. 144] with less disturbance. He desired Green because he had been an old servant, a loving friend, and a faithfull peace=maker, to meet Sir Francis at Fox's, but writ, that he believed his Father=in=law was so resolute in his own overthrow and the utter undoing of him and his, that no good would be done.

[*I find no ^other^ account of what passed between Sr Francis and Sr Percivall at this meeting ^at Wollaton^ but believe by the help of Fisher, Marmion, and Cludd, there was some hot disputes between them, and to avoid more at their parting, was (I believe) ^perhaps might be^ the reason* …][363] It is very likely that the reason why Sir Percivall went a way from Wollaton without taking leave of Sir Francis, might be to avoid unkind word at their parting; but what ever the cause was, this action, together with what had before passed between them made Sir Francis so very angry with his Son Percivall that he imediately sent Russell his steward to London to seek him a Wife. This Isley Cranewell,[364] gives Sir Percivall an account off [of], in a letter dated from Wollaton July the 23th 1595, being the same day which Sir Percivall went from thence. He also writ word that the person that Russell would recommend was Mrs. Tamworth, who had been called in question for her honesty, and was separated from her Husband. Russell was very quick in performing his Masters orders, for there is a letter from Russell to Sir Francis dated August 1595 in which he writes that he had carried wedding gloves to Mr. Sutton. By which it appears that they were then married. This Ladys name was Dorothy.[365] She was the Daughter of Thomas Coleby, of Greyes Inn, and the widow of John Tamworth.

---

[362] Possibly relating to the Green family who were long-term tenants in the region of Halesowen, especially on the Manor Abbey Farm purchased by Sir John Lyttelton, 'Halesowen Abbey', Romsley and Hunnington History Society, http://www.rhhs.org.uk/local-history/halesowen-abbey.html?start=9 (accessed 5 Oct. 2016).

[363] STB 2 (1), book 2, fos 6–7.

[364] Isley Cranewell appears with Sir Percival in chancery court *c*.1599 regarding leases on mines in Derbyshire during the life of Sir Francis Willughby. TNA, C 2/Eliz/Z1/12.

[365] For Dorothy Colby, see the introduction, p. 49. According to the *ODNB* entry by R.S. Smith on Francis Willoughby, the steward chose Dorothy, 'an astute widow', and

There is a letter from one Lewes[366] writ (I believe soon after Sir Francis was married) to Sir Percivall, to advise him to comply as much as he could with Sir Francis, because his Lady had many great friends, and was a woman of a greatdeal of wit (as her actions shew'd). Her Mother also was a very [f. 145] wise woman, and was to live with them in London, in a house with 15 beds which Sir Francis had taken for them, and he now threatned that the Star=Chamber should decide the difference which was between them.

There is a letter writ by Sir Francis Willughby and dated from Sherfield [Shenfield, Essex?] August 29th 1595, which orders sending a buck to Dr. Smith, and if the Lord Huntyngdon can't send him a stag from Windsor (which he believes will be hard for him to doe, if the Queen comes thither) then he would have a brace of bucks sent for himself. He also ordered a pretty nagg to be found for him to give to Dr. Smith, which should have its runing at grass at Sherfield within thirty miles of London, from whence he might use him at his pleasure. Besides that at Wollaton (he writes) that his Wife needs a phisitian, and will use him, if he will be contented to come to her, which he thinks he will not refuse, to pleasure her; and Sir Michael Mollyns[367] will bid him heartily wellcome.

It appears by the old papers that Sir Francis was very fond of this Lady, who I believe took great care to please and oblige him, and thereby soon gained an absolute power over him. They were in so

---

Willoughby married her immediately. They remained in London, and he lavished jewels and plate on her, but a mere fifteen months later, after a short illness, Willoughby died. His death was so sudden and his burial so rapid in St Giles Cripplegate, that his family suspected he'd been poisoned. Dorothy was left pregnant. Had Dorothy given birth to a son, this son would have inherited the Willoughby estate. The child, however, was a daughter, Frances, born on 3 May 1597 and dying in infancy. Years of litigation with the Willoughby heirs followed. In Oct. 1597, Dorothy married for the third time, taking as her husband Philip, 3rd Baron Wharton (23 June 1555–26 Mar. 1625). He settled £1,000 a year on her, £310 of which she immediately gave to the lord chancellor, Bacon, to decide in her favour in a suit respecting the Willoughby estate. This third marriage proved unhappy. In 1602, she was writing letters complaining of Lord Wharton's ill-treatment.

[366] Lewes may be the father or grandfather of Thomas Lewes (b. c.1619) a very wealthy vintner and alderman of London. whose progeny eventually owned Stanford Hall, Notts.

[367] Stepfather of Dorothy Colby Tamworth Willughby by his second wife Elizabeth née Gilbert who was the widow of Thomas Colby. According to the entry for Michael Molyns (d.14 May 1615) in the *History of Parliament*, Moleyns, who was left in charge of Willoughby's estates, may have been the second husband of Dorothy's mother. Sir Michael Molyns was the 3rd son of William Molyns of Sandall or Sandhills, Hants, and Mackney by his 3rd wife, Ann née Culpepper. Molyns served in Parliament, representing Wallingford in 1589; he was also a warden of the Fleet prison. Molyns undertook the management of Dorothy's claims. Alan Harding, 'Molyns, Michael (d.1615)', *History of Parliament Online*, http://www.historyofparliamentonline.org/volume/1558-1603/member/molyns-michael-1615#footnote5_1m2opp6 (accessed 31 Mar. 2018).

much hast to marry, that writings could not be drawn, but Sir Francis articled to tye severall Lordships upon this Lady as a security for her joynture which was to be 2000 mark a year. But this Lady liking the land tyed for her security[xlix] better than the[l] joynture which was to have been settled upon her, took care to prevent that settlement [f. 146] from being made. [*she finding that that the difference between Sr Francis and Sr Percivall, was like to be for her advantage did her endeavor I believe to continue it.*][368]

It is very likely that the servants who had made this match were intirely in this Ladys interest, and it appears by the old papers that she, together with them, had worked up Sir Francis to such a degree of anger against Sir Percivall and his Lady that he did not care what became of them. There are in the Library severall very unkind letters from Sir Francis to his Daughter Brigit writ this year; one very long one in justification of Fisher, and to express his anger for her carriage to him, and that in passing by Fisher he would have saluted her, but she bid him spare that curtisie for others that had a better opinion of him. Fisher (he writ) had deserved better usage from her, and Percivall Willoughby had ill requited him for the good he had done him, for if it had not been for Fisher an estate which he settled upon him, would not have been settled so. In this letter he also writ that her Husband was grown so froward that nothing would content him but what agreed with his own humour, and he was become so imperious, that he would not allow him to chuse his own friends, or to place his children, where he thought best. If Percivall Willoughby thought he would bear this from him he was deceived. He would therefore have her make him understand, that he should presently use Middleton House himself and therefore they must leave it, for he would no longer permit such contrary and rebellious humours to be in his house. This letter is dated September 1595.

In answer to this letter Lady Willoughby writ that her Husband was not at home, and she could wish it might please him, that somebody else might tell him of his dislike, rather than herself. That as [f. 147] to her Sisters, she had never heard her Husband speak of their being place'd, nor had she known him ever meddle with any friend of his, if they would but let him alone, and for Mr. Fisher his own friends and kindred did not spare to report how ill he had dealt with them. Even his Son Dilkes[369] had reported, that if she would have been perswaded by him and his Cousin Cludd, she should have been so basely bestowed. This she had concealed, and should still, but that he was offended with her for him whom she

---

[368] STB 2 (1), book 2, fo. 8.
[369] Thomas Dilke of Maxstock married Clement Fisher's daughter Anne.

had just cause to dislike. She desired he would not take hasty courses with her Husband by the perswasions of others, but first hear what he could say for himself. And that he would not condemn her upon Mr. Fisher's reports, without hearing her speak.

[*By what I can learn of Sr Percivalls Lady, she acted wth great discretion in all these quarrels which hapned in the family, there are a great many letters of hers, writ, w[i]th a great deal of spirit, she seems to have been a woman fit for business, and very carefull of her affairs, and family, which by what I could learn ^from those old letters^ she governed w[i]th great wisdom and prudence# (f. 41v) I believe she was a lover of musick because in one of her letters to her Aunt Arundel she expresses concern that she hears nothing of her virginals, and writes that she believes if they are sent it must be by her procuring#*

I believe she patiently suffered many injuries from Sr. Francis's servants, in hopes to keep peace between him and Sr Percivall, but ^in^ this last quarrel between them Fishers provocations drew from her an angry letter][370]

Lady Willoughby was so much provoked by Mr. Fishers ill treatment of her, that at the same time that she answer'd her Fathers letter, she writ a very angry letter to Fisher, which he was so enraged at, that he threatned to trouble her for it. Upon hearing that, she writ a letter to Sir Percivall who was then in London to this effect.

I have sent you, so near as I can remember a copy of what I writ to Mr. Fisher, because he threatnes to call me before the Counsel, but I hope there is nothing but what may be well answered if he were far better than he is, seeing it is all too true. He dealt so ill with me to my Father, that I could not forbear him in any thing that I knew. Come what may of it, I hope for your part (being a common enemy to us both) you will think no otherwise than well of
    Yours
    Brigitt Willoughby

[f. 147v] A copy of Lady Willoughby's letter to Mr. Fisher.[371]

I had received at this instant letters from my Father, wherein I have his displeasure for not pleasing of your worship; I am sorry he knows you no better, but I hold your tongue for no slander, that is so busie in all matters, and spareth not Lady's and Gentlewomen of greater account than my self. Thou hast used thy pleasure in bad speeches of the Countess of Shrewsbery, of Mr. Thomas Spencers Wife, and

---

[370] STB 2 (1), book 2, fos 42–43 and 41v.
[371] There is an analysis of this letter within the context of vituperative letter writing in Michelle O'Callaghan, '"An Uncivill Scurrilous Letter", "Womanish Brabb[l]es" and the Letter of Affront', in Daybell and Gordon (eds), *Cultures of Correspondence in Early Modern Britain* (Philadelphia, PA, 2016), 174–177.

others. Thou hast practiced dissentions betwixt my Husband and me from the begining. Thou hast set my Father and him at jares, because thou mightest the better fish and inrich thy self as thou hast done with their spoyles. Thou wouldest (being in thy house) have married me to thy Cousin Clud, a poor cozening knave of my Fathers, that came lowsy to him, and therefore in thy heart couldest never since abide me, tho hitherto I have concealed it.

I was once before for thy pleasure and perswasions, little better then hurled out of this house, being great bellied, when thou didst hope both by that means might have perished. And now again I, and mine, for not worshiping of thee, must upon small warning goe wander, as thou thinkest, a great conquest of such a worshipfull justice as thy self, that employest all thy wits and means to doe mischief. It is well known to all the Country, that my Father of himself, never offer'd such measures to the worst servant, or tenant that he had, [*having no farther benefit then house room.*][372]

At thy being at Middleton, thou toldest me that thou camest to cross my Fathers marriage, and to take that stumbling block [f. 148] out of my way. And yet now no man so ready to cog and desemble with them as thy self. And not withstanding all this and much worse then this thy ordinary protestation is, by the faith of an honest man. Malicious knave, thou art, that canst not spare poor Gentlewomen, and infants, with thy tongue and practices. Gentleman thou know'st thy self to be none. And tho at this instant I have no better means of revenge, than a little ink and paper, let thy soul and carkes [carcass] be assured, to hear and tast of these injuries in other sort, and tearms, then from and by the hands of a woman.

And seeing by thy practices and theirs, to whom by oath thou art confederate with, I am like to lose my Fathers favour (which was all the world to me) while I am able to speak thy treacherous knaverys shall not rest altogether concealed, and complain to my Father if thou dare again.

The answer to this letter still remains in the Library. Tis dated from Packington, and writ by Mary Fisher, to Lady Willoughby, and is to this purpose viz:

That her Husband had shewed her, her letter, so full of outrage and incivility as hardly beseem'd a Gentlewoman, and in which she had charged him with many things not true, as that he would have married her to Cludd, when she was in his house. If Cludd had, had any such dealing with her, she was sure it was unknown to Mr. Fisher. But it was well known that while she was in their house, Mr. Henry Willoughby (then living) did practice both with

[372] STB 2 (1), book 2, fo. 45.

Cludd and Dracot to have stole her away and married her; and that she had received a letter from Henry Willoughby to that effect, herself, and divers others could witness;[373] and also that Mr. Fisher fell out with them for offering such practices in his house. Sir Francis Willughby being then in treaty with Sir Percivall Willoughby's friends, this her Husband had made Sir Francis acquainted with, but had he concealed it, she had [f. 149] not then been Sir Percivall's Wife.

In this letter she used many angry expressions not behind hand with Lady Willoughby's, and asserted her Husbands inocency of doing any ill offices between herself, Sir Percivall and Sir Francis, but the contrary which she had ill requited him for.

And whereas she threatned his carcas, and bid him complain to her Father if he durst. Should any peril fall on Mr. Fisher, her untemperate letter would be a good testimony from whose malice his evil came.

It appears that Fisher did complain to Sir Francis, by the copy of a letter from Sir Francis to Fisher dated September the 13th 1595. This letter is about other business, but in it Sir Francis tells Fisher that he is sorry Brigitt Willoughby has carried herself so ill to him, through her Husbands folly, and that for her ill expressions, as revenging herself upon his carcas etc, she shall repent it, when it will be too late. And if he had known so much before his last going to Middleton, her Sisters should rather have lodged in an ale house than there. It appears by some of the old papers that Mr. Fisher had lent to Sir Francis a thousand pounds, and that perhaps may be one reason why Sir Francis shew'd him so much friendship. [*June ye 1st 1595 Sr Percivall writ Sr Francis that Fisher had always sought his overthrow and disgrace and to [enrich] ^make^ himself by Sr Francis's spoyles and doubtless that was Fishers designe, he had lent Sr Francis a thousand pounds, (which perhaps was his own before) and Fisher I believe expected that would bring him an estate. [T]o be sure his ill designs upon Sr Francis was the reason he strove to keep up the difference between him and Sr Percivall.*][374]

There are severall very unkind letters from Sir Francis to Sir Percivall dated from Sherfield and from Wollaton in September and October 1595, some full of threatnings to force him from Middleton, others angry ones, that he does not vouchsafe to answer his letters, and in one of his letters to Lady Willoughby he writes thus.

Belike you learn these ill tempers of your Husband, whose base account of me is such as he disdaineth to answer any letter of mine. Tell him from me, that if a man write to his better, [f. 150]

---

[373] With regard to Henry Willoughby, see Text n. 177 above.
[374] STB 2 (1), book 2, fos 9–10.

if he answer it, it is curtesie if to his equall, duty; but if to his inferiour, the not answering it is ill manners.#[375]

[f. 149v][li] #There is a letter from Edward Willoughby to his Brother Sir Percivall dated August 1595 to let him know that his Brother Hastings had been with Sir Francis Willughby and his Lady, and that he had taken the Woodland of Sir Francis for three lives, and that he was contented to joyn with Sir Francis in the settlement of his Ladys joynture, and the confirmation of other leases, and that he had yeilded to Sir Francis all that he had desired of him, in the doing wherof he had gain'd the good will of Sir Francis. Edward Willoughby in this letter to his Brother desires and advises him also to comply with Sir Francis in things that are reasonable, and entreats him to confirm and farther his Ladys joynture. And writes that he had heard a good report of the Lady

There is the copy of a letter from Sir Percivall writ [*Jan. 8*][376] An: D: 1595[377] to W: Agard,[378] in which he writes that he is sent for to meet Sir Francis, and that there is such shews of a pretended peace as should please all parties, but he doubts, such is the minute necessity of declyning estates in these days, that nothing will stay their downfall, and that his hopes are small in so shaken a house, where the principall piller hath, and ever will ly open to all manner of pestilent blasts.

[f. 150 (cont.)] Sir Francis Willughby's Lady; and his deceitfull servants, I believe made great advantage from this quarrell which they had made between him and his Son Percivall.

There is a very flattering letter which was writ by Russell to his Master Sir Francis, dated from Wollaton October 1595, in which he heartily wishes him heirs by his new Lady, for which he writes that he had the hearty prayers of all the Country, and if he did but hear the daily good wishes that himself and Lady had from all sorts of people, it would yeild him cause of joy, and invite him to live at Wollaton. He writ that Mr. Henry Willughby[379] had said, that he did hear, and like very well of his Lady, but said he had done her great injury in regard her joynture could never be secured by reason of

---

[375] Cassandra indicates, with the hash mark, that fo. 149v should be inserted here.

[376] STB (2) 1, book 2, fo. 42.

[377] The date of his letter would be Jan. 1595/6.

[378] William Agard, Esq. In 1585, William Agard acted as receiver of the Queen's possessions belonging to her honour of Tutbury. The Agard family held the manor of Bromley Regis, Staffs.

[379] Which Henry Willughby is this? Is this the younger brother of Percivall? Or Percivall's uncle Henry Willoughby (1540–1606)? The fact that Cassandra spells his name 'Willughby' would suggest that he is not related to the Willoughbys of Eresby. See Text n. 177 above for a description of many Henry Willughbys/Willoughbys.

all the land being so intangled, and tyed upon Sir Percivall. With many other circumstances which Henry Willughby intended to write upon to his worship himself, Russell in this letter enlarged upon his own fidelity, and concluded, with humble duty service and faith to himself and good Lady, comitting them both to the terrestrial, and celestiall paradice.

There is no letter or account book which I could find that mention this Lady's bringing any fortune to Sir Francis, but by severall one may guess that he was very fond of her person, and that she and her relations [f. 151] by their care to flatter and please him, soon gain'd great power in the management of his affairs.

Therre is a letter from Sir Francis (which bears no date) directed to his loving Wife the Lady Dorothy Willughby who 'tis very likely he might leave at Sherfeild while he went upon business to London, before she could goe. In this letter Sir Francis, writ that he had inclosed 4 letters which he desired she would send, one to Sir Micheal [Moleyns], one to Mr. Talbott, one to Sir John Conuay,[380] and the 4th to Mr. Beamont. He writ that his cause against Parramore in Chancery, had not been hear'd because of my Lords sickness.[381] He wishes her to care of herself in comming up to London, and concludes, comitting her, and the Lady her Mother, and his Sister Brigit [Sister-in-law?][382] to the tuition of heaven.

In the postscript he writes. I did think this process would partly amaze Percivall Willoughby and his hangers on, and Mr. Robert Willughby[383] doth utterly condemn him, touching his detaining of the houses from me, Middleton, and the Hote.[384] I would gladly hear an answer of the letters sent to Sir Foulk Grevill, and Sir Henry Godiers[385] executers. If Savage[386] advertized you how the

---

[380] John Conway or Conuay (1535–1603), from Arrow, near Alcester, Warks., married Elene Greville (1545–1580), the daughter of Fulke Greville and Elizabeth Willoughby Greville.

[381] See Text n. 207 for an account of a 1578 case with Paramour. For Chancery, see *Wylloughby v. Paramoure* TNA, C21/W19/8. See also a 1602 covenant between Percival Willoughby and Richard Paramour, Mi, 6/178/26.

[382] Perhaps a daughter from her mother's marriage with Michael Moleyn.

[383] Possibly Percivall's brother Robert Willoughby (b.1565) or Robert Willoughby, son of Fulke Greville (see Text n. 270 above). There are no known Robert Willughbys (as Cassandra spells the last name of the Willoughbys of Wollaton) near that generation.

[384] Unclear.

[385] This is probably Sir Henry Goodere (1534–1595). According to Sir Samuel Rush Meyrick (ed.), *The Heraldic Visitations of Wales and Part of the Marches Between the Years 1586 and 1613, Under the Authority of Clarencieux and Norry* 1. (London, 1846), 149 n. 5, n. 317, 'The Godiers or Goodorea, were a Herefordshire family.' The family name has a wide array of spellings/pronunciations: Goodere, Goodyer, Goodrich, Goodrich, Goodrea, and Goodricke. One of the major players against Paramour was a Henry Goodere, otherwise loyal to Leicester. Adams, *Leicester and the Court*, 340–341.

[386] Most likely John Savage (1554–1615) of Clifton, Cheshire.

Lord Huntington [Huntingdon] did take the matter touching his Son [nephew] Henry, I would gladly understand thereof.

Sir Francis had no Sister but Lady Arundel and therefore I conclude, that Brigit, named in the letter, was his Lady's Sister.

[f. 152] There is a letter from Sir Francis Willughby to his Daughter Brigit dated from Wolaton February 1595.[387] This letter is to tell her that he finds missing of her late Mother's apparel a velvet gown, and much other apparel containing many pearl's, and also a great quantity of bothe fine and coarser linnin, all which he charges her to send him by the bearer, for he will not suffer her to rob and spoile him.

There is the copy of Lady Willoughbys answer to her Fathers letter still remaining with his letter, tis dated February the 11th 1595 [1595/6], and is to this effect.

I did never rob, nor spoile you, nor commit any graceless action, and am sorry my better deserts, can have no better consideration with you, if at your being at Middelton, your steward Russell would have suffer'd me to have come to you, I would have sattisfied you of as many of my Mothers things as either my Sisters left here, or otherwise I did hear off [of], not meaning to desire any of them, but only such things as she had of mine, which might have been fitter for me, (as I thought) again, than for Russell and strangers, to have worn. I have deliver'd to Fox a note of such things as they left here, and he may fetch them at his pleasure, and if he had listed [listened; been attentive] he might have let you understand, being at his house, that I would have spoke with you about some causes of my Mothers. If this may not sattisfie you, I will repose my self in the inocency of my cause, and bear as I may these and other your hard course[s].

[f. 153] There is another letter from Sir Francis to his Daughter Brigit dated from Wollaton February the 13th 1595, to this effect.

I have sent you a note under Abigail's hand what things she sent to you, which I would have to be safe delivered to the bearer hereof, and likewise since the writing of the note, she has said and others do well know, and have seen a whole set of these pescoddes [a fashionable doublet], whereof I have sent you a pattern, which were deliver'd by her to you, and divers other things, with a carkenett [necklace or collar] of aggetts, and one other trymming of a gown with pearl, which I would have to be sent to me likewise.[388]

There is also Abigail Willughby's letter to her Sister Brigit. In it she expressed much concern for her Fathers anger, and writ that she had sent a note of the cloaths and linnin mention'd in her

---

[387] 1595/6 This sequence of letters is dated Feb. 1595.
[388] See below [fo. 191v, p. 246] for letters between Sir Francis and Abigail Willoughby regarding jewellery left by Elizabeth Willoughby.

Fathers letter, which he had made her set down in a note, and she fear'd if she should not send them it would be the worse for her.

It is very probable that Sir Francis Willughby might want all those things mentioned in the letter, to present to his Lady, who was then with him at Wollaton, as appears from a letter writ by John Atkinson to the Lady Dorothy Willughby at Wollaton, this letter is dated from Nottingham February 1595. In it he writes, that by the symptoms he believes her Lady to be with child.[389] He also gives in this letter an account of his care of others in the house.

[f. 153v][390]

[f. 154] (which makes me believe he might be the family phisitian) and adds his duty to Lady Mollyns, which shews that that Lady was at Wollaton with Lady Willughby.

It does not appear who that Lady Mollyns was, but finding mention of her in most of the letter's writ about that time; and that by other letter when Sir Francis married his second Lady, that her Mother was to live with them, I conjecture that this Lady Mollyns might be her Mother, and that after the death of Thomas Coleby, who was that Lady Willughby's Father, she married Sir Micheal Mollyns.[391]

---

[389] Lady Dorothy Willoughby gave birth to her daughter Frances in May 1597, six to seven months after Francis died. If she was pregnant in Feb. 1596/7, she must have lost this child.

[390] Attached to fo. 153v is the following partial text: 'purpose to give my information of an # # unfortunate Family which has been formerly of Great Authority tho now in a Low Ebb of Life. – But I stand at too great a distance from your Grace, to presume to Enter upon the # # particulars of it in this, the whole being tedious, and only thus far, I beg Leave to inform your Grace that one Christopher Willoughby [1453–1488/89, 10th Baron de Eresby] was the first that setled at Knoyle (the present seat of our family in Wiltshire) who was a Branch of the Nottingham family, in the reign of Henry the 6th. This my Father was often used to tell me, who had the honour of being particularly intimate with my late Lord Weymouth [Thomas Thynne, bap. 1640–1714, buried in Wiltshire near Knoyle] & of leaving behind him a character which was an honour to his Country. If it be your Grace's goodness & pleasure That I should pay my Duty of Attendance at Cannons, your Grace will please to order your servant to acquaint me of it, which will ever be most greatefully acknowledged as the greatest Honour conferred upon me.

May it please your Grace
I am Mad^m [Madame]   Your Graces most Dutifull and Obedient
                                           Lewis
Willoughby

Southampton Buildings in Chancery Lane 12 July 1726'

[The author of this text was most likely a descendant of Sir Christopher Willoughby (1508–1570), second son of the 10th Baron de Eresby, who is recorded as Willoughby of West Knoyle. Cannons (Middlesex) was the home of James Brydges, duke of Chandos, and Cassandra Willoughby Bridges. This letter was presumably addressed to Cassandra.]

[391] See information on Dorothy Colby Tamworth Willoughby above, Introduction, p. 49; fos 144–146, pp. 184–186 and Text n. 367.

There are some very friendly letters writ by John Atkinson to Sir Francis Willughby. There is one dated from Nottingham in June 1596, about selling of wood, and to let Sir Francis know that the reseits for what had been sold at Wollaton would be upwards of 200^{li}.

There is another letter writ by him the same month to tell Sir Francis that he is very ill used by his servants at Wollaton who abuse him sadly in selling his wood; at such a rate (he writes) they sell it, as if they have one half to have the other fetched away. He also writes that by the use of his money they make their own gain, and that he is betrayed by those he most trusted. This letter is directed to Sir Francis Willughby at his lodgings in Smithfield.

There is a letter from Sir Francis Willughby to Fox; about selling Lamley for 4000^{li} and Carlton, Carrolton, and Sutton for 2500^{li}.[392]

[f. 154v] [*These troubles obliged Sr Percivall to be often in London, his Lady I believe chose to stay at Middleton, that she might keep at a distance from her Father who was then so very unkind to her and her children. Sr Francis would have had Middleton from Sr Percivall, he I believe insisted upon his own right to it and so would keep possession.*][393] There is a letter from Sir Percivall to his own Father, Mr. Thomas Willoughby, which gives a long account of his troubles. How, that when he was from home, and had left his Wife big with child, Sir Francis had sent a troop to take possession of Middleton, that his servants resisting, they went off to the Town, after having broke down a wall and two doors.

He writes that the new Lady and her friends endeavour as much as they can to disgrace Sir Francis's children, and old followers, and perswade to fit him better with new feathers and plomes of their imping[394], than any which either himself hath bred, or his own experience could approve. And when they have plomed him bare, he may sit like a bird, to be a scorn to all the world. This letter is dated April the 12th 1596.

[*Amidst these great afflictions, Sr Percivall's own Father, Mr. Thomas Willoughby dyed in London. Sr Percivall was then in town and June 21th 1596 writ to his Lady at Middleton an account of his Father's illness which letter was to this effect that it was not her Father's troublesome courses, not the overthrow of his house, nor any worldly concern that ever touched him so nearly as the*

---

[392] Sir Francis did not sell Lamly. It stayed in the hands of his wife Dorothy after Sir Francis's death. On the eventual descent of Lamly after Dorothy Willoughby's death in 1621 to Sir Francis's six daughters, its division into sixths, and its disposition, see below, fo 194v, p. 253.

[393] STB 2 (1), book 2, fo. 47. '[…] of this made Sr Francis send a troop to take possession of the house when Sr Percivall was from home and h[a]d left his Lady big with=Child'.

[394] Grafting; adding feathers to repair a hawk's wing, *OED*. Percival is accusing Dorothy of trying to replace Sir Francis's family and friends with her circle in an attempt to take all of his property.

pittyfull spectacle of his own Father, who with a few days sickness, was much weakned in mind and memory, his great care was for his Father's health, and omitting to move him on account of worldly affairs, left her (who of all other did worse deserve it) the full scope to effect, which she [Mary Weston, Thomas Willoughby's second wife] *had effected; for she and her followers omitted no opportunity to contrive matters which might tend to the benefit of her, and hers, from which I fear much trouble will arise; they have procured a will from which yet I can't get a sight off. Such and so unfortunate is our case, to have such Step=Mothers, step into our houses, from whom God deliver us and ours.*[395] *Mr Tho Willoughby dyed that day June 21th 1596. Sir Percivall sent his brother Thomas Willoughby to take possession of Boreplace, after his Father's death.*][396]

Tho: Willoughby [*Percivall's younger brother*] *writes Sr Percivall, that his Brother-in-Law Rogers would keep him out; he desires Sr Percivall will come himself, for he fears, he will suffer wrong, the oxen he writes are driven away, and some packs of linnen are sent away.*

July 1596 Tho: Willoughby writes Sr Percivall that many of the neighbouring Gentlemen have been at Boreplace to see him, and express their joy that he keeps possession of it; but are more glad to hear he intends to live there.

In August 1596 Mr Tho: Willoughby writes his Brother Sr Percivall, that their Mother-in-Law[397] *sells all the goods etc and makes horred and unjust complaints of them for wronging her, and her Children* [...]

There is a letter from Tho: Valency to Sr Percivall dated Dec: 24th 1596. He writes to desire Sr Percivall will come to Town to look after his business, which requires his attendance, he writes whoever encounters with one Mother-in-Law, has enough to do; but he that has to deal with two, has the divell and all; from whom he prays God send him a good deliverance#[398] [insert at #] *There are severall friendly letters from Tho: Valency, and also several from John Pickaral to Sr P:W: and also many from his Bror-in-law John Adams*[399]

See a letter from Ned Will: Book 1st Page 26[v]

---

[395] Another copy of this letter, with slightly different wording, is in Chandos, *The Continuation of the History*, 24; Mi, LM 27, fo. 19, STB 2 (1), book 2, fo. 49.

[396] STB 2 (1), book 2, fo. 50. STB 2 (2), Uncatalogued paper in Cassandra's writing dated Novem^r 1596, fo. 1, under subtitle 'In another letter to his Lady', fo. 1 of this document.

[397] In this case, mother-in-law means stepmother.

[398] All of the above letters are also described in Chandos, *The Continuation of the History*, 20; Mi, LM 27, fo. 20. The 'mother-in-law' mentioned is Percival's stepmother, Mary Weston, by whom his father had three daughters. Thomas Valence is probably Thomas Valence of Lincoln's Inn who leased the top floor chambers and a gallery in Willoughby House, Lincoln's Inn's Fields, from Thomas Willoughby in 1595. *Ibid.* 25 n. 2; *HMC Middleton*, 322.

[399] This sentence is inserted at the hash mark.

So hard was Sr Percivalls case, that before he had ended his disputes, wth his own Mother-in-Law [step-mother], he found himself involved in far greater troubles by his Lady's][400]

[f. 155] [*Sir Francis cut down all his timber.*][401] There are other letters and papers which shew that Sir Francis leased out the greatest part of his estate for three lives.[402] The money raised by these leases as also that, by the sail of the land and wood, 'tis very likely Sir Francis Willughby's Lady got secured for herself.

There is an account of Sir Percivall's prefering a bill in Chancery[403] against Sir Francis, which 'tis probable might be upon this occasion that so he might secure to himself, that part of the estate which the law would allow him, in right of the settlement which Sir Francis had made of Wollaton Cossall and Trowell, and Middleton and Kinsbury, upon him, and his Lady, and their heirs.

There is a letter from Sir Percivall to his Lady dated May the 13th 1596, which said that her Father had preferred a bill against him, but that would be easie enough answer'd. In this letter he writ that her Father said none of his name must [c]ome near him, for fear of troubling his Wife, and that he would care for no body[404] that loved Sir Percivall.[405]

There is another letter from Sir Percivall to his Lady dated June the 20th 1596 in which he writes that her Father would have all for his Wife Dorothy; but since she had made choice of him for her Husband, he would never yeild to that while he lived. At last, he writes that Sir Francis was content to chuse Mr. Micheal Murrin [Moleyns], and he his Cousin Henry Willughby,[406] to end all matters – but their demands were so unreasonable that he expected no good would be done.

---

[400] STB 2 (1), book 2, fos 50–51. Cassandra describes a letter from Edward (Ned) Willoughby to be found in STB 2 (1), book 1, but it is on fo. 26v, not fo. 26.

[401] STB 2 (1), book 2, fo. 12.

[402] An estate of three lives allowed the lessee to hold the estate for the length of three lives which might be understood to encompass the lives of the lessee and the next two generations or it could mean the lessee, his surviving wife, and a son or some combination thereof.

[403] Not located.

[404] In Cassandra's earlier notes: 'would hate all those that loved Sir Percivall, his only care was to enrich his new Lady'. STB 2 (1), book 2, fo. 47.

[405] R.S. Smith cites a Jan. 1598 letter from Rhys of Cossall, who oversaw the Codnor ironworks for the Willoughbys, to Bridget Willoughby, suggesting that Francis may have had, too late, some misgivings about his treatment of Bridget and Percival. See R.S. Smith, *Sir Francis Willoughby of Wollaton Hall* (Nottingham, 1988), 36, for the relevant text of the letter which includes the following: 'Your father did use many times to deliver to me many speeches touching you [...] and told me that if Percival and I do not agree before that I died [...] he is like to be hardly handled, which I would prevent, and I know not well how to do it.'.

[406] It is unclear if he is the Henry Willughby who was the son of Hugh Willughby. See Text n. 177 above.

I could find no account how this refference ended, but believe it produced no good to Sir Percivall, and from the [f. 156] old papers one may believe that Sir Francis neglected all his children, and made it his chief care to raise a great sum of money for his Lady. And thus having charged his estate with as much money as it could bear, he fell very sick. There is a tradition in the family that his friends suspected his Lady had given him poyson, but whither that was so, or not, is uncertain. All the account which I could find of his sickness, was from a letter writ by Sir Percivall to his Lady, which letter was to this effect.[407]

That again the black messenger salutes her, and God with his many blessings hath, and doth, intermingle many troubles, that we may the better know, and acknowledg from whence both proceed. He writ that her Fathers case was lamentable, that he had been ill a fortnight, and shut up from all his friends, that the whore and her minnion had stript him both of goods and land, and left him nothing where he lay but what hung upon his back, and that he now sits haling for life, and breath, and that in this case he was solicited to see him. Dated November 1596.[408]

There is no particular account either of his death or buriall, more than that he dyed in November An: D: 1596.[409]

---

[407] Cassandra noted a 'Letter from Percivall Willoughby to Bridget November 1596 describing Sir Francis's last illness'. STB 2 (2), Uncatalogued paper in Cassandra's writing dated Novem^r 1596.

[408] Percival had heard from an informant within Sir Francis's household that 'Sir Francis is past all recovery, and therefore in all your pretences leave no time. It should seem something was feared here to be done, for that one cottage this morning was filled full of writing boxes, jewels and the like and so sent to the Fleet [Michael Mollyns was a warden of Fleet prison]. Here is some weeping but not much, yet I think passports [permission to remove goods?] be plenty. This intelligence I had from the wife of the house who watched with him all night and had a great desire you should know this much.' Smith, *Sir Francis Willoughby*, 34. The source is not provided. Smith also provides information, again with no citation, from a deposition by William Atkinson, who said that Sir Francis had been invited to dinner at the Fleet. Lady Willoughby then entreated Atkinson to go see the Lord Mayor and the sights there, 'although Atkinson had not asked to go'. The next day Sir Francis began 'to purge and scour violently, and this lasted three whole days. A few days before his death, a broth was brought to him, whereupon he was alleged to have said 'away with poison'. Ibid. 33–34. William Atkinson, an apostate priest and a spy for Robert Cecil, had offered to poison the earl of Tyrone in 1595. *CSP Dom.* 1595–1597, p. 14, no. 49.

[409] Francis Willoughby died intestate. There exist four different draft wills by Francis Willoughby. See Mi, 1/13/4a, Mi, 1/13/11, Mi, 1/13/5 and Mi, 7/180/5. For his Inquisition *post mortem*, see Mi, 1/2/2/1. Bridget Willoughby attested 'That the said Lady Willoughby conceived so little grief for the said Sir Francis his death and took so small care for his funeral that she caused him to be buried the same day that he died as she believeth, and did never acquaint this respondent's husband or any other the said Sir Francis his dearest friends with her intent or purpose touching his funeral'. Smith, *Sir Francis Willoughby*, 34. Francis was buried at St Giles Cripplegate 16 Nov. 1596. In a

After Sir Francis Willughby's death, his Wife being with child, Sir Percivall was under great apprehensions that she might impose an heir upon him, and in order to prevent any such imposition, he obtain'd of the Queen a troop of guards [f. 157] to watch and search every body that came to the house, where she then was.[410]

There is a letter from Sir Percivall to his Lady in which he says that her Mother=in=law [step-mother], had a strange woman next door to her who in the night was brought to bed of a Son. He writes that God knows whither she was not brought thither by design.

This Lady in right of the child she went with, kept possession of all the estate which Sir Francis Willughby left. This engaged Sir Percivall in very expensive law sutes.[411]

Upon May the 3^d 1597 she was deliver'd of a Daughter. There is the copy of[lii] a letter from Sir Percivall Willoughby dated October 1597 to the Lord Burghley, then Lord high Treasurer of England, who had given the wardship of that child to his Son the Secretary. In this letter Sir Percivall desired the Lord Burghley that for the avoiding of the malice of his adversaries, and the better establishing of his perplexed estate he would vouchsafe so far to recomend his humble sute to his Son, that he might have the wardship of the child, for the land only, for such

---

1597 appeal that Sir Percival sent to Lord Burghley, he wrote, 'For she, which was so unkynde a wyfe to so over loving a husbande, as having absolutely contryved and gotten to herself and her heires the greatest parte of his landes, coulde not afford his dead corps the leaste part of those rightes and obsequies which weare due to suche a man.' Mi, F 10/32; *HMC Middleton*, 620. See the parish register for St Giles Cripplegate, London Metropolitan Archives P69/GIS/A/002/MSO6419/001, under 16 Nov. 1596: 'Sir Francys Wylloughby knight'. Those buried at St Giles in the same month include children of or family members from a dycemaker, shoemaker, yeoman, labourers, clothier, baker, vintner, glover, householders, and one other knight, Sir John Buck. The individuals buried at St Giles seem to come, for the most part, from the trades, crafts, and labouring classes

[410] 2 June 1597 letter from Percival Willoughby to William Cecil, Lord Burghley. Mi, C 25; *HMC Middleton*, 618–619: 'for that Sir Mychaell Molyns, (as by sufficient proofe I made it knowen to the judges of the common pleas) had practised with a gentlewoman in Nottinghamshier to exchaunge a sonne of hers (if neede weare) for a daughter of the said Lady Wyllughbyes; which practise of his, howe daungerous it mighte have proved to me (as my case stood), I leave it to your honorable censure and consideracion'.

[411] Percival began a Common Law suit in the wake of Sir Francis's death, suing for recovery of Wollaton, Cossall, Trowell, Kingsbury and Middleton. Dorothy Willoughby countered with a suit in chancery, obtaining an injunction against Percival, 'the Prequator [*sic*] of the Common Pleas to staye the entering of a recovery which was knowledged to barre an Infant in Venter sa Mere'. Cambridge University Library, Gg2.31. fo. 411, cited in Maria Cioni, *Women and Law in Elizabethan England with Particular Reference to the Court of Chancery* (New York, 1985), 65. In the course of these law suits, Bridget Willoughby wrote to Percival 'that the Lady Wharton had sent to serve her with a proces as she was going into Church, which they would have had the Priest to have read in the Church, but he refused it'. Chandos, *The Continuation of the History*, 28; Mi, LM 27, fo. 24.

considerations as should seem good to his Honour. And that he might the better judg of the value of it, Sir Percivall writ that he had inclosed the particular of those lands, and by that particular, he would also see what lands this Lady the widow of Sir Francis Willughby, by the help of Sir Micheal Molyns, and the rest of their accomplices, had got for herself and her heirs, though her usages of Sir Francis had been such, that she had ill deserved it.[412]

[f. 157v] By the journal of the House of Lords April the 4th 1621 it appears from the 2^{d} article of the charge against the Lord Chancelor Bacon, that he took as a bribe from the Lady Wharton 310^{li} in a cause depending between her and Sir Percivall Willoughby.[413]

[f. 158] With this letter Sir Percivall sent to the Lord Burghley a present of a gelding.

Amongst the old papers in the Library at Wollaton I could not find any copy of that inclosed particular of the estate which Sir Francis Willughbys widow got from the family, but many circumstances shew that it was a very considerable estate in land, of which I believe the Dorsetshire estate was a part.[414] The money which Sir Francis raised by leases, and selling wood etc and gave to this Lady, must have been a great sum; and by tradition the goods in Sir Francis's houses (all which he gave this Lady) must have been of great value, I have been told by some of the family that there was an inventory of the plate in which there was an account of a hundred large silver dishes, and very larg quantities of all other usefull plate, all which this Lady very soon carried to the Lord Whartons family, by marrying that Lord some months after Sir Francis Willughbys death.

This Ladys Daughter dyed soon after Sir Percivall had beged the wardship of her lands.

There remains in the Library at Wollaton the following account of the estate in land and goods which Sir Percivall Willoughby and Brigit his Wife had from Sir Francis Willughby her Father. And also of the debts which the estate was charged with.[415]

---

[412] Mi, F 10/32; *HMC Middleton*, 620–621. (See the Introduction, pp. 15–16.). There are several other letters from Sir Percivall to Lord Burghley in 1597. See Mi, 2/75/3/9 and Mi, C 25, dated 2 June 1597; *HMC Middleton*, 618–620. Lord Burghley wrote, in response, 'I shalbe content to heare any mocion in the Court of Wardes to morrow, towching this request. And upon profe of Sir Michaell Molyns practice I will change my opinion.'

[413] See Mi, 2/75/3/1–28 for the Cause papers in *Percival Willoughby vs. Molins and Wharton*. See also Mi, 2/75/3/9 (undated) and Mi, C 25, dated 2 June 1597.

[414] '[B]ecause from that time I could find no appearance of any profit to our Family from that Estate, and ~~by tradition I [illeg.]~~ the Money taken for Leases ^#^ (which Sir Francis Willoughby gave his Lady)^#^ upon that Estate which came to Sr P:W.' STB 2 (1), book 2, fo. 13v.

[415] In Cassandra's earlier notes she writes: 'Jan the 2d 1602 Henry Willughby writes to advise Sr Percivall to sell land & clear all he owed, he tells him Sr F Willughbys first debt

[f. 158v] An Account of the Land which was Settled upon Sir Percivall and his Lady by Sir Francis Willughby.

These 5 mannors were conveied to them by their heirs male viz

    Wollaton and Sutton
    Cossall   in Nottinghamshire
    Trowell

    Middleton
    Kinsbury   in Warwickshire

The goods which Sir Percivall had from Sir Francis Willughby, were I believe, only the locks hinges and other iron, etc, which were fixed to the houses, for which Sir Francis obliged Sir Percivall to pay 1000^{li} as set down on the other side.

All these 5 Lordships, with some other quit rents in each County, upon a late improved rent, the tenants being leased by Sir Francis Willughby, for three lives, after his second marriage, were by the yearly value then but – 807—16—0 per Annum

Annuities charged by Sir Francis Willughby upon these 5 mannors some for years and some for lives were – 257—0—0

Which deducted out of the yearly income of those 5 Lordships, reduces the sum which Sir Percivall was to receive per Annum to be but – 550—16—0

[f. 159]

An Account of the Money which Sir Percivall Willoughby
was to Pay out of the Estate which he had from
Sir Francis Willughby.

	li	sh	d
For goods, iron works etc at Middleton and Wollaton Sir Percivall was to pay	1000	0	0

---

was but 500 Markes, wch he continued upon usery till it grew to be very near 20000^{li}.

To this Sr Percivall answers, he that hath ever been blown by contrary winds may sooner wish than attain an end of his travails. He says tho he has used all means and attendance, yet God knows when he shall see an end. In the meantime he offers any Land to free himself, nor would he be unwilling to undergoe any course in some sort to ease his mind and heavie burthened estate, which he doubts will cost too dear before it be secured.'
STB 2 (2), Uncatalogued paper in Cassandra's writing dated Novem^r 1596, fo. 1v of that document. See below, fo. 184, pp. 235–236.

To three of Sir Francis Willughbys Daughters in part of their portions Sir Percivall was to pay[416]	4000 0 0	
Debts which Sir Francis left for Sir Percivall to pay	1786 0 0	
and for interest money due which Sir Francis left for Sir Percivall to pay	1370 0 0	
For iron works which Sir Percivall had undertaken for Sir Francis upon his promis that Sir Percivall should be no looser by it, Sir Percivall was to pay	3000 0 0	
Sir Percivall was bound with Sir Francis for the debt of 21000^{li} without any other consideration then that of Sir Francis's promise to leave to him and his Wife the whole remainder of his estate, this debt Sir Francis left for Sir Percivall to pay of[f]	21000 0 0	
The trouble which the Lady Wharton (the late wife of Sir Francis Willughby) gave Sir Percivall before he could get the possession of the estate which Sir Francis left cost Sir Percivall in law sutes the sum of	3000 0 0	

35156 0 0

There is an account of other mortgaged lands which Sir Percivall had[liii] a power of redemption, upon paying 3050^{li}, which with other things imposed upon them by Sir Francis, was as much as they were worth. It is probable that Willoughby and those other Lordships which Sir Percivall sold of his Lady's estate, might be included in these mortgaged lands.

To raise that 3050^{li} at that time was I believe pretty hard for [f. 160] Sir Percivall to doe; and the lands themselves were so encombered that no body would buy any of them. And therefore I believe Sir Percivall was forced very soon to sell his own Kentish estate to raise this money; and also the 4000^{li} which he paid his Ladys Sisters, and also money to enable him to carry on his law sutes with the Lady Wharton.

Thus when Sir Percivall first enjoy'd Sir Francis Willughbys estate he found himself engaged in excessive troubles, for from those 5 Lordships which were settled upon him he could receive but

---

[416] In 1597 Edward and Winifred Willoughby, in addition to Abigail and Frances Willoughby took Percival Willoughby to chancery court with regard to these manors [and these payments?]. TNA, C 3/294/13.

550^{li}—16^{sh}—0^{d} per annum, and those Lordships were charged with the debt of 35156^{li}.[417]

Having given this account of the shattered condition which Sir Francis Willughby left his estate in, to Sir Percivall, and of the neglect which he seemed to shew of all his children before his death. I think I ought to be so just to his memory as to note down, that from the papers which still remain in the Library at Wollaton it plainly appears that this Sir Francis was a man of great piety and learning. There is still remaining a collection which he made of the most valuable books of his time, and many notes and remarks upon them writ with his own hand. There is also in the Library severall other little manuscripts writ by himself upon divine subjects some of which seem to have been heads of sermons for his chaplains to preach upon.

By the papers which direct the orders which Sir Francis Willughby would have to be observed in his family, and the remaining books of his accounts, one may believe that he was a very good oeconomist.

It was the fashion of those times for families of distinction to maintain as their retinue, in their own familys, and to be always ready to

---

[417] For an additional description of his encumbered estate, see the 2 June 1597 letter to Lord Burghley in which Percivall refers to his overwhelming financial burdens, including annuities, promised portions for the younger Willoughby daughters and at least £8,000 in debits, with an annual income of only £400. Mi, C 25; *HMC Middleton*, 618–620. For more on the ongoing financial difficulties that Percival Willoughby experienced, see Chandos, *The Continuation of the History*, 29–30, 37–39; Mi, LM 27, fos 26, 33–35. In 1597 the money received from the whole estate from Sir Francis as well as the money raised in the sale of coal was £585. His expenses for the Christmas season alone were £103. In 1604 Sir Percival was forced to pawn and sell plate. In 1605 he leased Bore Place Park, and by 1606 he was confined in the Fleet prison for debt for nearly the entire year. Cassandra wrote, 'There are some very melancholy letters writ by Sir Percivall to his Lady while he was confined to the Fleet, in which letters he complains most grieviously of his misfortunes, and how heavily his troubles opress him.' Chandos, *The Continuation of the History*, 39; Mi, LM 27, fo. 34. Later in volume 2, Cassandra summarizes Percival Willoughby's problems: 'He was himself cumbered with a great deal of business occasion'd by the very great debt which Sir Francis Willoughby left the Estate charged with, and the troublesome law sutes which he was engaged in by Sir Francises Widow […] By the account books which remain in the Family one may believe that Sir Percivall and his Lady were both very good managers, and that the losses which they sustaind were more owing to their being oppressed, with too much business then to their want of care.' Chandos, *The Continuation of the History*, 65–66; Mi, LM 27, fo. 69. In addition, Percival Willoughby had responsibility for the debts of his own father, demands from his wife's sisters and also from his many brothers and sisters and the children of Thomas Willoughby's second wife. For chancery suits initiated by Frances Wood and her husband and by Abigail Willoughby Pargiter in 1598 against Percival, see TNA, C2/Eliz/W23/57, C2/Eliz/W3/59 (1598), C78/129/16 (1598), and C21/jas1/415/22. In Jan. 1596/7 both Henry Hastings and Dorothy Willoughby Hastings withdrew from suit against Percival Willoughby. Mi, 6/170/134v.

attend them upon any occasion, many Gentlemen, who were really born, so, and who looked upon it to be no disgrace, to be so, retained by the great families then in England, but rather the contrary, for it was then usuall for Gentlemen to get their Son's placed in a man of qualities house, as a means to gain them a better education, [f. 161] than by continuing in their own little families they could have had. Of this sort of Gentleman Sir Francis Willughby always retained a great number, as appears by many of the old papers, as well as George Willughbys letter page 76,[liv] who is there mention'd to have writ, that he had advised with severall of the Country Gentlemen, where [and] in what manner they intended to meet the Queen, and by what he could learn, their servants need only to have plain livery coats, but he thought Sir Francis Willughbys number of servants should in no wise be less than fifty.

Some of these Gentlemen servants which Sir Francis retained, had I believe gain'd his friendship so much as to have thereby a power to perswade and influence him in the affairs of his family, and this power (I believe by the old papers) they used only for their own advantage, and finding those unhappy divisions between Sir Francis and his Lady, and afterwards between him and his son Percivall, and Daughter Brigitt Willoughby, might prove profitable to them, they helped to make, and continue that breach as wide as they could between these near relations; till after that Lady's death, and Sir Francis Willughbys second marriage; which second Lady defeated their projects, and soon shew'd she had subtlety enough to out wit them, so much as to make all their plotting turn to her own advantage, and thereby to gain to herself such immense wealth, as has been already shewed that she raised, by making use of the declyning age and last part of Sir Francis Willughbys life.

Before I proceed in my account of Sir Percivall Willoughby and his perplexed affairs,[418] I shall here set down what particulars I could find in those old papers relating to Sir Francis Willughby's five younger Daughters, which with their Sister Sir Percivalls Lady[lv] were all the Children which Sir Francis left for I think I need make no farther

---

[418] Cassandra expanded on Percival Willoughby's 'perplexed affairs' in *The Continuation of the History*, 25–39; Mi, LM 27, fos 19–35. Many of the details relating to the problems attending Francis Willoughby's second marriage and the contested inheritance that ensued are not included in Cassandra's Account. The gist of Sir Percival's complaint can be followed in his bill in Star Chamber. Mi, 2/75/3/10. Additional materials relating to this suit are in Mi, 2/75/3/4–9. Bridget and Percival eventually came into possession of the major part of Sir Francis Willoughby's estates but not without years of litigation. Their troubles included time spent by Percival in debtors' prison in London in 1605.

mention of that girl which his Widow was with child off [of], because she lived but a few months.

[Dorothy Willoughby Hastings]

[f. 162] Concerning Dorothy Willughby the Second Daughter of Sir Francis.

I shall here copy part of a letter from Henry Earl of Huntyngdon, which I believe was writ to Sir Francis Willughby upon this Daughters account – for I think it could not mean Brigett the eldest Daughter because this letter is dated August 1581, and by the account book it appears that Brigitt was married to Sir Percivall Willoughby An: D: 1580 being the year before.

The letter was to this effect.

It was my hap yesterday to pass in my journey towards York nigh your house, where you were not, or else I hope I should have spoken with you so as this letter might have been spared. There is a matter that I think fit to be moved to you without delay, which in divers respects 'tis meet you should give a favourable ear to. Henry Willoughby your kinsman, and by you commended to my service, hath been, and is a suitor to one of your daughters for marriage.[419] The liking between them is great, but without your liking to proceed to a match would be thought hard, for your favour this [Henry?][lvi] is a suitor. And by me he hath chosen to make the means, because you first commended him to my service, and by his being with me, I find him such a one, as for good parts, honesty, and good nature, I may be bold to commend him, worthy of much more than I am able to doe for him, and yet what I can doe for him, he shall not want. I am bold to pray the continuance of your [f. 163] favour to him, and that in this his suit, you would vouchsafe to shew it to him.

If God send you no Son, what Willoughby is there that can be more meet to taste of your liberall favour than this gentleman. I could say more than leasure will now serve me to write. Truely I wish with all my heart it may please God to send you a Son of your own; but if that fail, till I hear more I can't change my opinion which I have uttered, and so heartily praying your favour for this my Willoughby, with my most hearty comendations I doe commit you to

---

[419] It is difficult to identify the Henry Willoughby being referred to here. Cassandra's spelling of his name would seem to suggest that he was of the Willoughbys of Eresby. If this is the same Henry Willughby who was trying to marry Bridget at one time (fo. 147), he could be the son of Hugh Willoughby, as surmised by Francis Willoughby, the naturalist and father of Cassandra.

the tuition of the Lord, hastily from Mansfield the 17th of August 1581.

Your Loving Friend
Henry Huntyngdon

Upon the Back of this letter from Lord Huntyngdon there is a Query, whether this Willoughby was a son of Sir Hugh's, writ by my Father.

Amongst the old papers I could no where find any copy of Sir Francis's answer to this letter, nor any other mention made of this Henry Willoughby, except in Mrs. Fisher's letter page 148; which person, 'tis likely, might be the same Henry Willoughby, who she there writ, had practiced with Cludd and Dracot, to have stole away, and married Brigitt Willughby while she was in Mr. Fisher's house. And at the same time that Sir Francis Willughby was in treaty with Sir Percivall's friends.[420]

There are in the Library severall letters which were writ some years after that which is copy'd above, from this Henry Earl of Huntyngdon to Sir Francis Willughby, concerning the match between his Nephew, Henry Hastings, and Dorothey Willughby. Some of those letters were dated An.D. 1584, tho by what I can judg from those old papers they did not marry till 1587 as is already [f. 164] noted page 130. It is reasonable to think that the estate which the Earl of Huntyngdon offer'd to settle upon his Nephew might be less than Sir Francis thought his Daughter deserved, and that therefore this match was so long in debate.[421]

There is with the letters from Lord Huntyngdon concerning this match, a paper which seems to be writ by a very good friend of Sir Francis Willughbys, in which is drawn up ten considerations, and reasons against the match between Henry Hastings and Dorothey Willughby, of which the most materiall were these, viz

---

[420] On this Henry Willoughby, see Text n. 177 above.

[421] The writing up of and the terms of the negotiations are discussed in several surviving letters from Henry Huntingdon to Sir Francis between June 1585 and Jan. 1585/6. On 21 Sept. 1585 Henry Huntingdon committed certain rents and hereditaments to Henry Hastings and Dorothy Willoughby and their heirs to the clear yearly value of £200, the manor of Puddletown [Dorset] or some other lands to the clear yearly value of £400, as well as a commitment not to make any leases of the jointure land that was to be available to Dorothy if she survive Henry, and fourthly £2,000 to be paid over the course of five years. In both this note and a subsequent letter of 7 Jan. 1585/6, Henry Huntingdon requested a meeting with Sir Francis particularly urgently as he reminds Sir Francis that he (Francis) had promised Henry Hastings that the marriage would take place before Shrovetide 1585/6. Mi, 6/170/124/1–3. The extended negotiations that took place can be traced in the letters and numerous drafts of agreements relating to the marriage settlement beginning, apparently, in May 1585. See Mi, 6/170/124–136.

That a great part of the land was design'd to descend to the heirs of Francis Hastings, in whom, and to whose issue the Earldome was to be restrained.

That the Lady Hastings hath a great part in jointure by Act of Parliament which intervein other demises.

That the Earl is above 20,000^{li} in debt which may greatly charge his land, and that much of this money must have come by the credit and bonds of others.

That in respect of procuring such sumes of money there may be hidden mortgages upon the land, except the Earl upon his honour do confess them. The sale of Ware, and Ware Park made by the Earl to Mr. Fanshaw,[422] may teach you to beware.[423]

When you have paid two thousand pounds with your Daughter, that is not their sattisfaction. They shoott at another mark, for though you pay your money, yet at the marriage there shall be a key to your land, and their desire they think to bring to pass with the countenance of their honour. God send you your hearts ease. I doubt this match will not breed it. The young gentleman is half Stanhop. A word to the wise is enough.[424]

I don't understand why the author of this paper calls the young gentleman half a Stanhop. His Mother was the Daughter and co-heir of Sir John Port of Etwall in Derby Shire.

In the papers relating to this marriage I find no mention made of George Hastings who was the Father of this Henry,[425] who married

---

[422] For information on the sale of the manor of Ware, Herts., to Thomas Fanshaw (1533–1601), Remembrancer of the Exchequer, in 1580 for £410, see TNA, C 2 Eliz./ F4/49. In 1574 Thomas Fanshaw had leased Ware Park for 50 years for £191 12s 2¼d to the Exchequer for the first 30 years until [Christopher Hatton's] debt was paid, after which 100 marks p.a. were to be paid to Katherine, the dowager countess and to Huntingdon. The same year [1574] the dowager countess of Huntingdon released her dower in Ware Park in exchange for an annuity. Hastings Manuscripts, Herts. Deeds, cited in Cross, *The Puritan Earl*, 319, 334, 337.

[423] This assessment is very similar to the assessment of the state of the earl of Huntingdon's estate described by Cross, *The Puritan Earl*, ch. 3. There is an undated letter to Sir Francis Willoughby from Gabriell Marmion, written about this time, that relays a discussion that took place recently in Fleet Street in London concerning the marriage. The reported opinion of Mr Markham was that the earl of Huntingdon meant to hold Francis to the bargain already agreed upon. The conversation concluded that the match should move forward, despite those who were opposed to it, and it was now too late to back out, as the two young people were so 'assured' that she would be taken away and any rescue would be difficult Mi, 6/170/124/5.

[424] Thomas Stanhope married Margaret Port. Henry Hasting's mother was Dorothy Port. Both were daughters and co-heirs of Sir John Port of Derbyshire, as Cassandra notes in the next paragraph. For the difficult marriage of Thomas Stanhope and Margaret Port, see Text n. 185 above.

[425] There is a letter from George Hastings to Sir Francis, dated 3 Mar. 1585/6 concerning the protracted negotiations between Sir Francis and Henry, earl of Huntingdon in

Dorothy Willughby, but the whole affair seems to have been [f. 165] transacted by his elder Brother, Henry Earl of Huntyngdon, who had no children himself, and Francis, the elder Brother of our Henry, and the eldest Son of George Hastings, married, and dyed, in his Father's life time, but left a Son Henry who after became the Heir of his Grandfather George, and Georges elder Brother, Henry Earl of Huntyngdon, the person who managed the affair of this match with Sir Francis Willughby, and who 'tis likely might give Sir Francis reason to believe that he had more kindness for his Nephew Henry than the rest of his family and consequently that after his death he might give him hopes of such a part of the estate as was not entailed upon the child who was the heir to his title.

There is a letter from Francis Hastings [the older brother of Henry Hastings] (who was I believe the Father of that child) to Sir Francis Willughby, in which he earnestly desires Sir Francis Willughby to lend him a hundred pounds. This letter is dated An.D. 1577.

In this treaty of marriage there seems to have been many rubs before it could be brought to a conclusion, tho the particular reasons do not appear. There are severall letters writ by Henry Hastings to Sir Francis Willughby both before and after his marriage. In one of those letters to Sir Francis, he expresses great fears that by the perswasions of some, Sir Francis's thoughts may be drawn from him, which he is very sorry for, knowing himself to be clear from offending him, and writes that my Lord is easie to be drawn to any thing that in reason shall seem fit and convenient. He hopes Sir Francis Willughby will weigh and consider a young mans case, having settled his affection so deep that nothing but death shall alter it, he begs Sir Francis Willughby will remember his own youth, and then he will the better consider of him, who is determined as long as he lives to persecute him to death, that shall goe about to marry her, for he thinks 'tis better to dye and end his grief, than to live without her. He assures Sir Francis Willughby that it is not the heat of youth which causes him to write thus, but an honest affection, so surely settled, that he is sure never to have a quiet mind without her.

This letter is dated from London, April but not the date of the year.[426]

---

which George testifies to the good faith of his brother, confirms his own friendship with Francis, notwithstanding, however, that he will not forbid his son to have recourse to Dorothy Willoughby. He refers to the 'lewd parsones' attempting to 'delewd' Francis to be wary of his friends, of whom George counts himself. Mi, 6/170/124/4. This undoubtedly alludes to the anonymous author (and others) citing reasons listed above against the marriage of Henry Hastings and Dorothy Willoughby as well as the conversation reported by Gabriel Marmion (Text n. 423 above).

[426] This letter may follow upon that of Hastings's father on 3 Mar. 1585/6, thereby tentatively dated Apr. 1586. There is a further letter from Henry Hastings to Sir Francis dated

[In Nottingham University Library is the following, undated, declaration:]

Memorandum that Dorothe Willughbie hathe declared before Robt Markham & Mary his wyfe & Mr. Martin Hill that true it is that Between Mr. Henry Hastinges & her self in pryvate hathe ben promysed faythe & troth other to other But not in precence of any other. Ro: Markham][427]

[f. 165v] There is a letter from Henry Hastings to Sir Francis Willughby dated from Loughborough October 1587.

To desire a lute with 14 strings which he once gave to Sir Francis, and seeing it is not now occupied (he writes that) he is the bolder to crave it again, that his Wife may sometimes use it.

By this letter it appears that they were married before October 1587.[428]
[f. 166] In relation to this wedding I could find amongst the old papers nothing[lvii] to add but what is already set down page 130 in this book.

There is a letter from the Earl of Huntyngdon to Sir Francis Willughby dated from York April the 9th 1588 to let Sir Francis know that there is reason to believe that his Daughter Hastings is with child, and therefore he thinks it will be inconvenient to her, to have his Nephew continue to sojourn with her so, as they doe at

---

10 Apr., written from Loughborough prior to his trip to London and therefore, most likely, just prior to this letter: 'The greafe which I sustained at my last beyng at Woleston [*sic*], beyng dreven to depart from her compannya, whom I love the dearest in the worlde did so troble me att that time, that I forgot many things that I pourposed to speake unto you, and seyng that I maye not retorne [return] without your displeasure, I ame determined to defere them untill my commyng ^from London^ hoping that you will not deale so hardly with me, as to forbide ^me^ your howse, protestyng before ^God^, that never since my commynge thether, I have don any thyng ether by worde, or deade that mighte, ether dishonnor you, or discredit my selfe, if it weare knowne to the hole worlde, wherfore good Sir Francis, and I trust father, I doe most humbly desire you to continnewe that care which you semed once to have of me, but until suche time, as you maye evidently perceave me nothing worthy of it: I tought it good to lett you understand that upon Wensdaye next God willyng I meane to goe towards London, and if it woulde please you but to take so muche paines as to write to my Lorde your minde, I shall thinke then indeade that you doe not utterly reiecte me, but att that my Lord performynge what he hathe promised, you are ready to doe the like. Thus praying to the almighty, to preserve and blesse you I end: from Loughborrowe the 10 of April. Yours to commande for ever Henry Hastings.' Mi, 6/170/124/7. This letter is printed by kind permission of Lord Middleton.
[427] Mi, 6/170/124/6.
[428] The wedding should have taken place between Apr. 1586 (the date of these letters from Henry Hastings) and June 1587 (see fo. 130, pp. 167 and 205 n. 421 above) but not before Shrovetide 1586 as Francis had promised. The date for the wedding was 9 July 1587.

present, and he has not any house in his own hands to offer his Nephew, for which reason he is a suitor to Sir Francis Willughby, to let them have the Woodland, they paying him so much rent for the house and grounds about it, as he now takes, which Lord Huntyngdon undertakes that his Nephew shall truely pay. He desires Sir Francis will answer his request by a few lines to Harry.[429]

With this letter there is a copy of Sir Francis Willughby's answer, in which he writes Lord Huntyngdon word that he had sent for his Nephew to come to him that they might confer together touching his request concerning Woodland. He writes that the burthen of his debts makes him not willing to grant a lease for the yearly rent of Woodland, but by fine to set the same for 3 lives, or else by sale of some of the land there to ease himself of the debt. This he motion'd to his Lordship the last time he spoke with him, but had no direct answer, which is the cause that at this time he can't come to a resolution. Certain persons are now very desirous of the demeasnes of Woodland, which he must part with before he can pay his Lordship the hundred pounds which he is now to pay. He has offered other lands [for] sale, which these troublesome [f. 167] times considered his chapmen being of good ability would not stand too. He has been and is willing to borrow that sume upon interest, but sees no hopes of obtaining it. And therefore it rests with his Lordship what to determin herein. He hopes his Lordship will not think that he would enforce a hard bargain to his Nephew, either by setting[430] or selling this estate, for of his credit he shall know the parties and their offers, and the money that it is

---

[429] There are additional papers in the Middleton collection relating to the negotiations between Francis Willoughby and his son-in-law Henry Hastings over settling the estate of Woodland on them. As is clear from what Lord Huntingdon says, after the marriage Henry and Dorothy lived at York with the earl of Huntingdon until after the birth of their first child. See Cross, *The Puritan Earl*, 54. Although the following correspondence takes place in 1588, there is further correspondence and agreements in the Middleton Collection that show this was not resolved until 1589. There is a letter from Henry Hastings on 7 June 1589 that asks for Sir Francis's help, describing the loving care which Sir Francis would seem to have toward him but also the problematic state that he and Dorothy will find themselves in without his help. (Mi, 6/170/124/8.) Francis Willoughby was clearly reluctant to turn over the promised Woodland to them, however. The 1589 agreements between Francis Willoughby and Henry Hastings include £20 annual income from parcels of the demaines of Woodland as well as a payment of £2,000 upon the death of Francis Willoughby without a male heir, Mi, 6/170/132–136. Mi, 6/170/137 is a letter from Dorothy Willoughby Hastings to her sister Bridget, most probably written after the death of Sir Francis, asking for evidences for Woodland and Knolton, which suggests that they were still insecure in their holdings. Bridget seems to have re-used the letter to write down a shopping list as well as tasks that needed doing, including feeding the capons and ducks. See Figures 6 and 7 below, pp. 216–217.

[430] Leasing, e.g. leasing land to a mining company.

sold for shall come to him or his. He writ that he had offer'd to his Lordship Whmbrok[lviii] for 2000^{li} which estate he had since sold for 400^{li} more.[431] And if his Lordship would forebear the 500^{li} which he was to pay his Lordship, for one year (for which he was willing to allow his Nephew, or where else his Lordship should other wise appoint it) or by other convenient means find a way for him without forefeiture of his bonds, to detain the demeasnes of Woodland in his hands. The farme of Cane[432] standeth five lives from Henry Hastings, viz: his own Wives and three lives granted to Myller and his children, the yearly rent is but 20 li tho the quantity of tyled (drained) ground is above 400 acors. This estate he hoped he could sell to Myller for 2000^{li}. If his Lordship would like of it Myller should be bound with him for the payment of his Lordships money. And that Henry Hastings should be no looser himself and Percivall Willoughby would enter into bonds that the sum which it is sold for, shall come to his hands. This (Sir Francis Willughby writes) is what he can offer, and he leaves it to his Lordship and Henry Hastings to chuse what they like best, so that he may be freed from any forefeiture and pleasure them.

[f. 167v]

The Lord Huntyngdon's answer to this letter from Sir Francis Willughby still remains in the Library at Wollaton. It is dated May 1588 and is to this effect.

The bearer hereof your Son-in-law being a Father, he now the more earnestly intreats you to be good to him and his, and therefore renews his former request touching Woodland. He is sorry that Sir Francis should have cause to sell any land, but more, now, that his Daughter has a Son by his Nephew, he is sorry that he should sell any of his western lands. He believes his turns may be served as well by the sale of land in other places, without touching any of his land there or in Nottinghamshire, or Warwickshire. He had been told Sir Francis Willughby did once intend to sell some land in Essex, which he wished he would rather be contented to doe, than to sell in the west (if he must sell any land at all). But if there is no remedy and he will sell Cane, then he had advised his Nephew to make certain requests to him,[433] one of which he

---

[431] Perhaps Winbrook or Wynbrook. Unknown.

[432] Most likely Caine's Farm which was also in Dorset and would fit the requirement of western land that Sir Francis might be willing to sell.

[433] In an undated draft memo (most likely dated 1587 or 1588), it was agreed, with Henry Hastings, that Sir Francis shall have freedom to sell Cane manor, after which he would pay Henry £100 and his heirs would pay Henry £1,500 more in the years after the death of Sir Francis in the case of a lack of male heirs of his body, lawfully begotten. It was also agreed that Henry Hastings should have from certain parcels of the demaines of Woodland £20 a

hoped, he would be contented to grant to him, and the more favour he shew'd him, the more bound he should be to him; and himself, and all his friends, would think themselves the more beholden to him, to whose good favour he leaves his Nephew and his cause. And whereas his Nephew had desired them both to be Godfathers to his child, Lord Huntyngdon desir'd Sir Francis Willughby would grant the name because his Daughter was the Mother.

[f. 168] There is another very pressing letter upon the same subject from the Earl of Huntyngdon to Sir Francis Willughby. It is dated from Wadley[434] August 22th 1588. And in it he desires Sir Francis, that if ever he would doe any thing for his Daughter and Henry Hastings, he would now, by letting them have the mannor of Woodland, at so reasonable a rent as might enable them to welcome both him, and their other friends. He begs Sir Francis will not alienate that love and affection which he once seemed to bear his Nephew, and which he acknowledges to have been greater than he could deserve, unless his perfect love and duty to him, might deserve it. But he doubts his Nephews continuall absence, and the ill offices from some about Sir Francis (whose vilainy he hopes time will discover) has alter'd his mind towards him.[435]

There are a great many letters which shew that Henry Hastings used his Wife very ill, and 'tis likely some stories of that sort might have been brought to Sir Francis, and that Lord Huntyngdon might strive as much as he could to make his Nephew appear inocent.

There is a letter from Henry Hastings to Sir Francis Willughby dated from Hinton[436] May the 23th 1593, to importune him again to let them have the Woodland. He writes that his Wife does not like to dwell so near the sea side, and that the place does not agree with her. And in this letter he says, that he has heard Sir Francis has been told that he does not use his Wife well. He desires he will send to her (which he may easily doe and he not be privie to it) and hear her answer, and if he finds him blame worthy to condemn him, otherwise to suspend his judgment and let him have his

---

year or else £200 in money at his election. Mi, 6/170/132. This memorandum also gives Sir Francis the option to lease Cane for three lives or any number of years.

[434] Wadley House or Manor, Littleworth, Berks.; owned by Oriel College, Oxford but, at this time, leased to the Unton family.

[435] There is a letter in the Middleton collection, dated 7 June 1589, in which Henry Hastings writes that Sir Francis can see 'howe your dauters case and mine standethe therefore if you helpe not, it will not be so well w[i]th us, as otherwise it woulde [...] If it please god yt you may see us settled, I hope it will be to your comfort'. Mi, 6/170/124/8.

[436] Hinton, Hants.

good will. He hopes for such an answer as shall sattisffie his expectation. And ends his letter with commendations to himself and Lady.

[f. 168v] There is another letter from Henry Hastings to Sir Francis Willughby dated from Duning-Park[437] the 11th of April 1593, in which he writes that if he had known Sir Francis Willughby would have spoken with him, he would have been with him that night. But now his journey is fix'd so that he must lye at Middleton tomorrow and set forward towards the west upon Monday. He desires Sir Francis Willughby will command him, if he may stand him in any stead, and assures him that he shall always find him an honest man; and that he never served him or his Lady for the hope he had to gain by them, nor whilst he lived would he flatter them, but his regard and respect to them both was honest, and so it should be forever.

There are no letters which shew what notice Lady Willughby took of her Daughter Hastings. But by that letter of hers to Sir Francis enter'd in this book page 136 it appears that she blam'd Lord Huntyngdon on account of his preventing the sale of the western land.

After Lady Willughby's death, and Sir Francis's second marriage, Henry Hastings endeavour'd to make that second Lady and her Mother his friends in this affair of the Woodland, as appears by a letter from him dated from Middleton October the 2^d 1595. This letter is directed to the Honorable Ladys, the Lady Willughby and the Lady Mollyns. In it he writes thus.

My acquaintance with you both is yet so small, that I am in doubt whither I should be so bold as to^{lix} trouble you with my small affairs, but your kind entertaining of me imboldneth me, at this time to be an earnest suitor to you both, to obtain at Sir Francis's [f. 169] hands that I might have a lease of Woodland granted to me, my Wife and child in fee farme.[438] But if Sir Francis will not grant to you this small request for me, then let him know that if I may have of Mr. Woodall 200^{li} more, I will except of it, and he shall have the lease. Sir Francis thinks he hath given me 200^{li} on the bargain, but I am sure no man will give more than I have done, as you shall easily find.

I believe Sir Percivall Willoughby and Henry Hastings were very friendly to one another for some years. I shall here copy two of their letters.

---

[437] Presumably between Wollaton and Middleton.

[438] In fee farme is a sub-feudal land estate. In this case, Hastings would hold Woodland and be entitled to its rents but would pay a rent to Sir Francis. Title (fee simple) would be retained by Sir Francis and his heirs. As fee farme was a kind of fee tail or restricted ownership, the possessor had no right to alienate the title to the land.

The Copy of a letter from Henry Hastings to Sir Percivall Willoughby.

My good Brother
   I was so bold in your absence to send to your bayliff of Middleton, for some fish against my Lord and my Fathers families came [come?], but hearing since that you are in the Country, I have sent this messenger to you, to desire you would send my Lord some. I am sure it will be very wellcome, and for my own part you shall command me in the like. And so with my hearty comendations to yourself, I end, and will ever rest

Your assur'd loving Brother for ever
Henry Hastings

I left my Wife well when I came
out of the west, and am sure she
will be very glad to hear of her
Sister's and your health.

Sir Percivall Willoughby's Answer.

Sir
   I shall be ever glad you would command me in any [word missing] and am very sory it was not my happ to be at Middleton; where, and here, you shall ever command both men and master, and whatever the places may afford. Though my troubles for Sir Francis's occasions, and the Lord Chancellors heavie undiserved displeasure, have made me a stranger to my own houses, and to have little pleasure in the world. [f. 169v] And were it not that I am a recommended prisoner to the Fleet, after so many heavie payments and chargable suits, for not satisfying Sir William Breretan[439] 1500^{li}, I would both see you and tender my love and duty to my Lord. My Lord and his house I have and ever will honour. And thus being very glad to hear of your health and my Sisters, I leave you both to the tuition of the Almighty.

Yours ever to his power
Percivall Willoughby

---

[439] William Brereton (1550–1631), 1st Baron Brereton, built Brereton Hall in Cheshire. For a case in chancery that William Brereton brought against Percival Willoughby over the manor of Smallwood, see TNA, C2/jasI/B1526. Francis Willoughby had had a suit in chancery in 1576 against William Brereton over a breach of contract regarding Brereton's failure at that time to complete the purchase of Smallwood Manor. TNA, C2/Eliz./W14/19.

[f. 170] There are in the Library a great many letters from Dorothy Hastings to Sir Percivall Willoughby, and his Lady, some of which I shall here write an abstract off [of]. [Figures 6 and 7]

There is a letter from Dorothey Hastings to Sir Percivall Willoughby to tell him my Lord — is minded to set his iron works, and hearing that he is desirous to deal in them, he desires he will come over to him that they may talk about them. She writes, that he is offered 1100^{li} per annum for them, but had rather Sir Percivall should have them, than any body, and therefore offers him the refusall of them. This letter is dated from Ashby.

There is a letter from Dorothey Hastings, to her Sister the Lady Willoughby. In which she writes that she wondred her Sister Frances should continue so obstinate, that she refused to come to live with her Brother and herself, and offers to try if she can perswade her to come to them, if Lady Willoughby thought that would stand her in any stead, for she should be sory to hear she would not be ruled by her best friends.[440]

There is a letter from Dorothey Hastings to her Sister the Lady Willoughby (dated from the Woodland). In behalf of her Sister Winifrid Willoughby, who she writes is under so much sorrow, that it is uncomfortable to them all to see her. She desires to hear how herself Sir Percivall, and all their little ones doe, and whither Winifrid was like to have her house or no, for she should be glad to hear that she had a home again.[441]

There is another letter from Dorothey Hastings to Lady Willoughby, dated from Woodland May the 9th 1615. In which she writes that she is willing to pay her Brother Wood [Montague Wood, the husband of Frances Willoughby], as soon as she can, all his [f. 170v] charges in law, but she hoped her Brother Willoughby would not see her a looser by Cranway[442] because she had done what she did at his request.

There is another letter from her to her Sister, dated from Woodland June the 24th 1619. To desire her Sister to ask Sir Percivall if he knew of any lease for a hundred years made by her Father before she married, of all the Dorsetshire lands to four of his younger Daughters. Her Brother Wood has writ her a letter to that effect.

There is another letter from Mrs. Hastings to her Sister the Lady Willoughby dated December the 10th 1619. To desire she would give

---

[440] See fos 193v–195, pp. 249–254 below with regard to Frances and her troubles.

[441] See fos 185–190, pp. 237–244 below with regard to Winifrid and her marriage with Edward Willoughby.

[442] Unidentified.

her tenants warning to pay no more rent to her Brother Wood, who she fear'd would get Lady days rent before hand, for he had play'd her a vile part in disappointing her of her own before, which she desires her Sister to get from him if she can. She writes that she has found him very false in his dealing, but it is Gods will to plague her with vile men. The letter which she sent by her Son Henry she doubts was opened, because it was not her own seal. Therefore when she writes to her she desires she will take care who she sends her letters by, for she knows some have been opened and read and sealed again before she had them, therefore she dares not write her mind to her at large, but desires that she and Lady Peckham[443] will seal up her secrets, and pray for her. [f. 171]

She writes that Mr. Hastings gives her continually threatning words and she has her health very ill. She hears that her Son Ralph will be with Lord Huntyngdon that Christmas, and she doubts he may do her wrong, by geting her rent from the tenants, if Lady Willoughby will not prevent it by warning the tenants not to pay to any body but herself, for she knows all her children dessemble with her for their own advantage. She concludes pray God to send all her friends long life, and herself speedily to heaven.

There is another very melancholy letter from her, to her Sister, dated from Woodland July the 3^{d} 1620.

She writes Mr. Hastings opened, and read, her last letter before he gave it her. She heartily wishes herself with some of her friends. She is daily vexed with false witnesses which say she set her hand to that which she never did. She thinks they will poyson her eare long, but hopes God will take her to his mercy, and desires her Sister to pray for her.

There are many such petious letters from Mrs. Hastings to her Sister Willoughby. In one dated April the 11th 1621, she writes that she has been most vilely used by Mr. Hasting's in words and deeds too long to write. He has threatned to lock her up and use her like a dog. She greatly fears that he means to poyson her. He wishes she could [f. 172] not write, and then he could doe well enough with her.[444]

---

[443] Possibly Katherin Peckham, née Trussell. Katherin was the daughter of John Trussell of Billesley (c.1515–1582), son of Avery Trussell of Billesley and nephew of the John Trussell who was the bailiff at Wollaton (see above, Text n. 83) and Mary, daughter of Grimston. She married Reynold Peckham of Kent, n.d., William Camden, *The Visitation of the County of Warwick in the Year 1619: Taken by William Camden, Clarencieux King of Arms*, ed. John Fetherston (London, 1877), 93 and 447 (index). More likely the sister of Hugh Willoughby who married George Peckham. See Text n. 449.

[444] This is an interesting comment that suggests that some women of the upper middle class may not have been taught to write. See James Daybell, *Women Letter-Writers in Tudor*

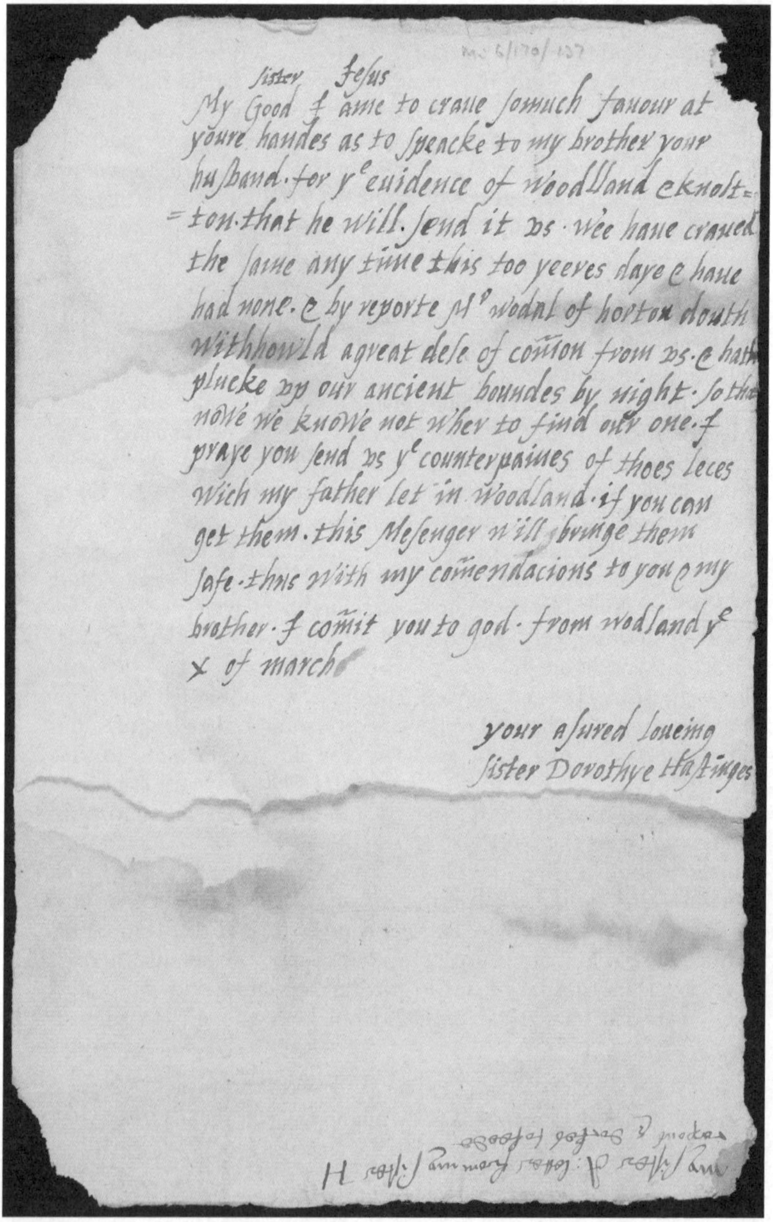

Mi 6/170/137

sister Jesus
My Good I ame to craue somuch fauour at
youre handes as to speacke to my brother your
husband. for ye euidence of woodland & knolt=
=ton. that he will send it vs. wee haue craued
the same any time this too yeeres daye & haue
had none. & by reporte Mr wodal of horton douth
withhowld agreat dele of comon from vs. & hath
plucke vp our ancient boundes by night. so that
nowe we knowe not wher to find our one. I
praye you send vs ye counterpaines of thoes leces
wich my father let in woodland. if you can
get them. this Mesenger will bringe them
safe. thus with my comendacions to you & my
brother. I comit you to god. from wodland ye
x of march

your asured loueing
sister Dorothye Hastinges

Figure 6. Letter from Dorothy Willoughby to her sister Bridget Willoughby (*c.*1600), asking for evidences and leases for two properties, in colour online. Reproduced by permission of Lord Middleton and the University of Nottingham Library Manuscripts Collection, Mi, 6/170/137.

Figure 7. Reverse of the same letter from Dorothy Willoughby to her sister Bridget Willoughby (*c.*1597), with a list of cloth, lace, lining, buttons, and other items for Bridget Willoughby and the children, in colour online. The list, written by Bridget on the back of the letter, also includes feed for the capons and ducks. Reproduced by permission of Lord Middleton and the University of Nottingham Library Manuscripts Collection.

He, and Sir John Rives[445] told her, she had set her hand to writings which she never saw. She writes that they care not what they say or swear, to serve the turn they would have it.

In this letter she tells of a great escape they had of the house being burnt by a barne which was set on fire by one shooting through a hole in it. The wind blew the pouder into the thatch of the barn and so set it on fire, and had not the wind changed of a sudden so as to blow the fire from the house it must have burnt it. (She writ) that she had never been well since that fright, and desired her Sister if she could tell what was good for the trembling of the heart she would let her know it.

At the bottom of this letter it is writ by Sir Percivall Willoughby's hand. To garter your hoose below the knee, for the gartering above is not good for them which have the panting of the heart.

In a letter dated from Woodland the 30th of April 1622 she writes her Sister, that she would fain to speak to her not daring to write her mind, for fear the letter should be open'd. In this letter she tells her Sister that Mr. Hastings uses her worse than his servants, for they have wages and meat and drink, but she has nothing but meat and drink, neither cloaths nor money. She desired Lady Willoughby would write to him, to afford her some maintenance out of that estate which her Father left her, she being now in want of needfull things. And writes that he has put her out of her chamber, and threatens to lock her up, for what cause she knows not. She thinks she had best leave him. He threaten[d?] to cut down the woods at Lamly and let States [estates].[446] She desires to know if Kilborne,[447] and the rest of the tenants have sent up Lady days rent to London.

She desired Lady Willoughby would lend her 60^{li} to help her in her extremity, for she can't long endure Mr. Hastings vile using of her. She desired the bearer might bring her the money in gold sealed up [f. 172v] in a box.

England (Oxford, 2002). There is a suggestion here that illiteracy made it easier to abuse a wife.

[445] Sir John Ryves of Damay Court, Dorset, was Dorothy Willoughy Hastings's son-in-law and the husband of her daughter Dorothy; they married in 1617. John Ryves died Jan. 1624/5 without heirs of his body. See E.A. Fry and G.S. Fry (eds), *Abstracts of Dorset Inquisitions Post Mortem at the Time of Charles I* (London, 1894), 8–11. Dorothy Hastings Ryves next married Thomas Tregonwell.

[446] The woods at Lambley were mentioned in the Domesday Book. He threatened to cut down a forest at least 500 year sold and rent out the land in parcels.

[447] Unidentified. See Payne Kenyon Kilbourne, *The History and Antiquities of the Name and Family of Kilbourn (in its Varied Orthography)* (New Haven, CT, 1846) for various Kilbornes.

There is another letter to the same purpose from Mrs. Hastings to Lady Willoughby, dated from Woodland March 1624. In this letter she earnestly desires to see her Sister having more to say, than she can write to her. She desires she will receive the use money due to her, and send it by a sure hand, for her extremities are great. She writ that Mountiegue Wood keeps both the use and principle money from her, and that it is now near eight years since he had it, and he uses her vilely. She tells Lady Willoughby that she trusts to her more than to any of her Sisters, and has received more comfort from her.

There is another very melancholy letter from her to her Sister in which she writes, that she is alive though in great misery, being lame of one legg, and her sight fails her because of vexations which she has daily from Mr. Hastings.

In another letter from Mrs. Hastings to her Sister dated from Woodland May the 10th 1626 she writes that her Daughter Rives[448] is big with child and intends to ly inn at Woodland, and she wishes Lady Willoughby would be at her groning and help to comfort her. She writes that she is sorry to hear that Sir George Peckham[449] and his Lady are likely to lose Streley. Her Brother Wood she fears will defraud her of her money which he has owed her (and she has forebore him) these ten years. She desires Lady Willoughby will perswade him to pay her before strangers, for she hears his land is extended for debt.

[f. 173] There is a letter from Mrs. Hastings to Lady Willoughby, dated from Abes=Court[450] May the 5th 1628, in which she writes that she is now with her Daughter Rives, expecting her happy hour. She writes that she should be very glad to see her this summer, if the journey would not be too painfull, and too chargable.

There is another letter from Mrs. Hastings to her Sister dated from Woodland October the 31th 1628 in which she writ that she should be very glad to see her at Woodland, and desires she will bring the mare which she gave her, with her, because she wants one to take air upon, for Mr. Hastings uses the coach continually, so that she never have it except upon Sundays to goe to Church. She writes that she is grown so very sickly that she doubts she shall not live long,[451] and her

---

[448] By 1626 Dorothy Hastings Ryves had remarried, although her mother still refers to her as her daughter Rives.

[449] George Peckham, listed as a recusant in 1630, married the sister of Hugh Willoughby, whose first husband was Francis Strelley. Sir John Mitchell petitioned for a writ against Sir George Peckham for refusing to fulfil an award made by arbitrators appointed by the court of chancery as to payment for the manors of Shipley and the sale of Bilborough and Strelley.

[450] Perhaps Winterbourne Abbas, Dorset.

[451] Dorothy Willoughby Hastings died 4 Dec. 1638.

Daughter Rives is also grown very sickly with breeding her children, insomuch that she doubts neither of them will ever see Wollaton again.

Upon the top of all these letters from Dorothey Hastings, and many more of the old letters, there is writ either Jesus or else Emanuell. Which I believe was an ancient custome in writing letters.[452]

With these letters there is a copy of one from Sir Percivall Willoughbys Lady to Mrs. Hastings dated from Wollaton July the 9th 1620, to this effect.

The Kings coming into the west this summer will I believe prevent my seeing yourself my Brother, and my Neece Rives at Wollaton. And should I venture to come to you I doubt [f. 173v] my Brother would prevent it if he could, as he had thoughts to have done the last time. I will never come to doe either of you harme, for my heart desires to doe all the good offices that a loving well wishing friend may doe between you, and happy should I think my self if I could by any means work your likings and contents, which I pray God quickly to begin, and ever to continue; and that all jarrs and discords may be ended between you,[ix] and that they that are the causes may be banished from you. Thus comitting you to the protection of the Almighty, whom ever, I will intreat in my prayers to bless and keep you in all your indeavours in this world, and in the world to come, to give you everlasting happyness.

Your loving Sister

By some of the old letters one may believe that the first cause of the unhappyness of Mr. Hastings and his Lady might proceed from his desiring to have her estate in land sold, and her unwillingness to part with it.

[Margaret Willoughby Spencer]

[f. 174] Concerning Margaret Willughby the third Daughter of Sir Francis Willughby

It has been already shew'd page 131 that this Lady married Robert Spencer of Wormleighton in Warwickshire, but before this marriage there had been a long treaty of marriage for her, between Sir Francis Willughby and his kinsman Thomas Markham for Griffin Markham[453]

---

[452] See Figures 6 and 7, pp. 216–217. The letter from Dorothy Hastings to her sister Bridget includes the reference to Jesus.

[453] Sir Griffin Markham (c.1565–c.1644) was the oldest son of Thomas Markham (1530–1607) and Mary Griffin (1540–c.1633) of Ollerton, Notts. He was influenced by his mother's

his Son. This affair seems to have been first began by the young people unknown to either of their Fathers, who for some time, after they were made acquainted with it, appear to approve of the match but from the old papers it may be gather'd that neither of their Mothers were pleased with it, and also that Mr. Thomas Markham was unreasonable[lxi] in his demands of having more settled upon the Lady than Sir Francis Willughby was willing to part with from his estate.[454]

The relation between the two families had made a great intimacy amongst them insomuch that Mrs. Margaret Willughby used to be often at Mr. Markhams house for a great while together, when she was very young; it appears by letters that she was there when her Cousin Griffin Markham went first to Cambridg. There are agreat many letters in the Library at Wollaton which he writ to her from thence, part of which letters I shall here copy.

An Abstract of Letters From Mr. Griffin Markham
to his Cousin Margaret Willughby dated from Caius
Colledge in Cambridg.[455]

In the first letter which begins with Dear Cousin, he tells her that he has never been quiet in his mind since he parted from her so suddenly and with so few words, good will and opportunity not being wanting, but such was his shamefacedness that instead of speaking

Catholicism and became a committed Catholic. Markham accompanied the earl of Essex at the siege of Rouen in 1591, where he was made a knight, and then followed Essex to Ireland in 1599. He married Anne Roos, daughter of Peter Roos, Esq., of Laxton, in 1592. When James VI came to England, Markham was soon involved in the Bye Plot [Watson's Conspiracy] to raise Arabella Stuart to the throne. Or he planned to kidnap James and force him to assign the reversions of several estates belonging to his father. He confessed and was condemned to death, receiving an expected reprieve only on the scaffold. He spent the rest of his life in exile in Europe, with only occasional forays into England, probably acting as a spy for Robert Cecil and joining the English regiment in the Low Countries. His wife, Anne, corresponded with Cecil, offering to deliver the Jesuit, John Gerard, to him, if her husband was restored and pardoned. 'The quatercentenary of Sir Walter Raleigh's trial, Part IV: The Main and Bye Plots', *Queensland Supreme Court Library Historical Lecture Series* (2003): http://www.lexscripta.com/pdf/raleigh.pdf.

See the *ODNB* article by Mark Nicholls. See also Markham, *A History of the Markham Family*, 99–104. There are several post-1615 letters from Griffin Markham in the BL, Lansdowne and Harleian Collections. See also *CSP Dom.*, 1644, pp. 35–36, 45–46, 54–55, and 86.

[454] There is a copy of a marriage settlement between Sir Francis and Thomas Markham from 1585–1586. Mi, 5/168/80. See Mi, 5/168/81 for the revocation of the marriage settlement.

[455] Griffin and his brother Robert Markham were both admitted to Gonville & Caius College at ages 14 and 15 as commoners. Both became Roman Catholics. John Venn, *The Biographical History of Gonville and Caius College 1349–1897*, I (Cambridge, 1897), 21. 'Admitted at Gray's Inn, Ap[ril] 27, 1586'.

he used blushing, nor would he have spoke more to her before he went to Cambridg, but that from thence he might salute her with his rude lines which would not blush to let her perceive his stedfast unfeigned and faithfull mind towards her etc. If you will continue as I left you I don't dispare but my Father will procure the good will of yours, and then I shall hope that his perswasions, and my Mothers instruct=[lxii] [f. 174v] instructions your good will, will rather increase than deminish etc.

Yours to trust untill he be dust
G: M:

In his second letter he tells her, that her answer gave him great content, because by it he perceived her affection to him, and good will to his friends (as yet undiserved) which shewed her great clemency, good disposition and singuler virtue. He could neither attribute to his friends sufficient thanks for providing him such a match, nor make such returns as was due her, but would rest at her command, being ready to perform any thing which might be acceptable to her. Her letter had so abandon'd fear from him that he hop'd at their next meeting he should without blushing declare to her the sume of his faithfull and unfeigned mind etc. He desires to know as soon as she can certifie him what end their parents have made, and shall daily pray that it may answer their expectations, and that God would grant to her health prosperity and virtue, and so entirely to knitt the knott of amity betwixt them, that by no means it might be dissolved. I cease any further to trouble you from Cayus Colledg December the 24th.

Yours whilst life doth rule his vital breath
G: M:

In his third letter he writes that their meeting did not so much rejoyce him as their [?] departure does grieve him, for what greater grief can happen to faithfull friends than in the begining of their familiarity to be separated. But 'tis fond to strive against a stream, and best for them both to comfort themselves with hopes to meet again shortly, and although shortly, yet he should [f. 175] think it too long, but in the mean time he hoped they should often hear from one another by letters, which should carry the true meaning of his mind, who would forsake all others for hir sake, and vowed himself hers, to be true to her so long as they both should live. If [word missing] accept this I shall be sattisfied, and will labour by what means I can to deserve it hereafter, in the mean time account me yours and at your commandment, Caius Colledg 28th April.

Yours to command while life doth last.
G: M:

His fourth letter is dated from Westminster, May the 15th.[lxiii] In it he writes that he has been almost a week in London, and that he had dined that day with her Mother who was in good health, and tho not merry, yet she was merrier than she had been, hoping all would be well again, which he heartily prayed for, both for her own, and Fathers sake. He expresses himself very affectionately to her, desiring her pardon, for his rude and hasty letter, and that she would not condemn the invention, but marke the mind from whence it proceeded.

There is another letter dated from Caius Colledg June the 7th in which he writes, that he is very glad to be assured by her letter that she was grieved at their parting as well as himself, but his sorrow was now greater than it was then, because then he hoped to have seen her again this summer but was now almost out of hope of it, for his tutor labour'd all he could to prevent his comming, but it is his continuall desire that he may not prevail, because then he might perform by word and deed, what now he can only write, tho he finds the old proverb verified in him, that where he loves most he can express least, which was the reason why he gave her the first onset by [f. 175v] writing. But he does now in heart rejoyce that it is come to this point that he need not doubt, since they have both faithfully promised and by oath vowed to be true to one another. He hop'd they should be loyal as Ulices and Penelopy, for Ulices being twenty years engaged in the siege of Troy could never be moved to be false to the chast Penelopy, though there were many traps laid for him, and he fain to escape divers of them with danger of his life, all which time the chast and wise Penelopy remain'd at Greece, being solicited by many, but obtained by none, till at length it was blazed abroad that her Husband was dead, after which they were so importunate, that at last she promised, that if they would let her weave up a web which she had in hand, she would after consent to marry one of them, which granted, she always unwove at[lxiv] night, what she had wove in the day till her Husband came from Troy. Such loyalty I hope will be betwixt us, if we should be so long absent, which I pray God may not be a quarter of that time, and truely for my part I would rather sustain the labour of Ciciphus, or the thirst of Tantalus, than I would swarve,[456] and I hope you think so. I would be loath to be tedious to you, but hope you are of my mind, that can never be weary of reading your letters etc.

---

[456] Swerve, stray.

Yours or not his own
G: M:

[f. 176] In another letter from Cambridg, he complains of his not hearing from her on whom he has wholy fixed his fancy, and in whom is his whol delight, to her he yeilds himself as he is bound, for hers he is, and hers he will be so long as they live, he wishes himself with her that his words might express what now he writes. She has his heart, though he is so distant in person. He concludes praying for her health and prosperity.

Yours as his own
G: M:

In another letter he complains, that he could not procure leave to come to her, which would have been the greatest joy that he could possibly have had, but necessity having no law he must be content. He hop'd the time would come that they should be oftner together. What he had said to her was so printed on his heart that he vowed nothing but death should disolve it. He pray'd for the same good fortune to her that he wish'd himself, and concluded from Cambridg August 14th.

Yours at all assayes ready prest[457]
G: M:

In another letter he writes, that both present and absent he always wants either time or words. But he thinks tis now more than time to cast off that childish shamefacedness which has hitherto haunted him, and express his thanks to her for her curtisie to him. He assures her that during his whol life he will be at her comand. He desires God to grant her, her hearts desire, and to send them a merry and quick meeting, and concludes from Cambridg May the 16th.

Wholly yours both heart and mind during life
G: M:

[f. 176v] In another letter he complains that all his hopes of seeing her are frustrate, and his wishes invain, and that now by writing he must explain, what by words he would have made plain, if fortune would have granted him that favour which he expected, but the vulger proverb (things most desired and wished for seldom fall out) he daily

---

[457] 'ready prest'=willingly disposed

sees verified against his will, and knows no remedy, but to think of the joy their meeting will bring, when they may stay together as long as they please. These thoughts will drive away the tediousness of the time betwixt this and then, he prays for her health and concludes

Yours as he hath always said

In another letter he laments his long absence from her, which if he could have foreseen he would have used other means than now he can, but time past can't be recalled, which he is sorry for, but sorrow will not mend it, therefore he must arm himself with patience, and not look for what he so greatly desires, again, till he has enter'd the Park Pale, so many dterminations, so suddenly broke he never met with before, and thinks he never shall hereafter unless about the same matter, and from what cause he knows not, but hopes the best. He concludes his letter with most hearty commendations to her, and prayers for her health, and prosperity, from Deene the 17th December.

Yours assured as you know
G: M:

[f. 177] In another letter he writes that he has been in such grief since he last parted from her that it is great pain to him to conceal it from the company he keeps, yet he blames himself for being so sorrowfull at a time that he finds his desires granted beyond what he can think himself worthy of, or shall so long as he lives be able to deserve, but he finds nothing can content him but being continually with her. He desires she will let him understand wherein he may pleasure her or any friend of hers, and to his small ability she shall find his willing mind to perform it. What he has said she knows, and from the same, he will never start whilst life doth reign in his body. He concludes from Caius Colledg 23th of February.

Yours as you know willing in all things to pleasure you
G: M:

In another letter he writes with concern that through too much childish shamefacedness, he had lost the opportunity of shewing himself thankfull for her curtisie to him. And as for them which are against it, he weighs them not a rush, so long as she continues the self same mind, but hopes to be revenged of them either at London or when he comes into the Country. Some there be amongst the most, can doe least, but others he will not say can doe something (because he trusts in God their friends are wise enough) but if they leave not off quickly, they may paradventure crack their credit for their thankless office, and get what they don't look for. He commends her wisdom for not desiring to know them, which might breed inconveniencys if she could not have shewed them good countenance, as he thinks no body would, and has found by experience that he himself could not, for the greatest anger of his Fathers, because he would not vouchsafe good looks, and patiently bear with some of them. In truth he could not dissemble nor would he so long as he lived. And writ, I must here call my self back, lest I wander too far, and come to your letter for which I doe most heartily [f. 177v] thank you, as well for your good counsel, as your good affection towards me which if I live I will requite with the like if I am able. In the mean time desiring God to grant us both our hearts desire I cease any longer to trouble you from Cajus Colledg April the 12th.

> Yours whilst life doth endure as you have bound him
> G: M:

In another letter he says he has so much to write to answer both her letters, and to give her thanks for her great curtisie, that he knows not where to begin on [sic] when to end, and to give useless thanks is but a simple requitall, yet he hopes they will be accepted, and since she says it is not meet for him to express himself at her command, he will fullfill her request and answer with silence, but think what he list, being so bound to her, that he will say no more, because she requested him. He writ that he suspected some of his letters had been intercepted by the way, or plain knavery played with them, but he does not care, being fully resolute. He hoped to see her shortly, and concluded desiring God to grant her health with all prosperous felicity from Caius Coll: 15th of May

> Desirous of naught longer than he is yours
> G: M:

> The Copy of one of Mr. Griffin Markhams Letters
> To his Cousin Margaret Willughby

My good Cousin.

It cannot chuse but grieve me greatly that I should be such a sottish fool, that as the proverb saith I have not a word to cast at a dog, and especially when I have strayned to speak best, for which I am greatly ashamed but I can't mend it, and therefore I must fly to my old excuse, till time will serve. But where you say that I have been thankfull sufficient, and that you are indebted to me, I will never [f. 178] grant, for if it were but only for this one letter, which is nothing in comparison of your greater curtesie, I should be never able to requite it whilst life indured, but only by shewing my self thankfull for it, as I will during life, as you shall understand at our meeting if I can doe as I wish, in the mean time vowing my self during life at all assayes to be at your command. I cease any longer to trouble you desiring God to grant you health and prosperity, and to send a soon and merry meeting, from Caius Colledge this 9th of June.

Yours whilst his own
G: M:

In another of his letters he expresses great sorrow that he shall not see her, but yet he writes, that since his Mother hopes to, come, it is not reasonable that he should distrust it, but if he does not come she shall know his faithfull and unfained mind by his true messengers who will not blush. He now begins to be something rustical and bold but hopes she will pardon him. His heart she has, though in person he is absent from her, full sore against his will etc. He concludes biding her farewell, and praying God to grant her health and send them soon to meet – from Cambridg June the 27th.

Yours as his own
G: M:

All these letters begin either with my Sweet Cousin, my Good Cousin, or my Dear Cousin, but the date of the year is not set to any of them. Most of them are directed to my very Good Cousin Mrs. Margaret Willughby at Kirkbie Bellers and some to my loving Cousin Mrs. Margaret Willughby at Bestwood Park.[458] All these letters I found rolled up together, and remarks writ upon them with Sir Francis Willughbys hand, which makes me believe she had given them to her Father, but with these [f. 178v] letters there are no copys of Mrs. Margaret Willughbys answers to any of letters, but there are other letters of hers which express resolutions never to engage herself farther than her Father should approve off[of].

---

[458] Both Kirby Bellars and Bestwood Park were estates held by Thomas Markham. Kirby Bellars had been a priory dissolved in 1536, and Bestwood Park was a friary in Sherwood Forest, surrendered in 1539.

There is the Copy of a Letter from Mrs. Margaret Willughby
to a Cousin of hers whose name is not writ, nor the date.
The letter is to this Effect.

Cousin I understand by your letter to my Brother Willoughby [Percival Willoughby] that Mr. Thomas Markham useth liberall speeches, that either my Father, or my self, have made some promises of marriage to him, or his Son. Why he presumes this I cannot imagin, but can assure you this is very far from truth and honest dealing. You are not ignorant how he broke with my Father, and if he thinks to withdraw me contrary to his liking he is, and shall be very much deceived. It may be thought, that being some time in his house might occasion a liking between us, but to be plain with you, both his Father and friends do know, and my self did find the contrary. But had it been otherwise, I was not so hasty, as without my Fathers further allowance, nor ever will I without his presence yeild any consent or promise to any one in that behalf, hoping that as all my endeavours shall tend to please and obey him, so he will not urge me farther than shall be with my own free will and liking.

[f.179]

There is a letter from Mrs. Mary Markham who was the
Mother of Griffin Markham directed to her good
Cousin Margaret Willughby.

In which she writes that she had dealt with her Father (Sir Francis Willughby) who she found not only far from the matter, but he shew'd her no curtisie, which she took unkindly. But she would still follow it as earnestly as she was able, if Margaret Willughby would assure her of her friendship. But her word she could never get, but when Mr. Markham commanded it, and good will by constraint was little worth. Her kind letter to her had been worthy thanks – if she would yet answer it, she should be sattisfied, and proceed in the cause as time will serve to win her Father, and they both must be content to stay her Fathers time, which God grant to all their comforts, she concludes Your loving friend and kinswoman
M: M:

There is a letter from Mr. Thomas Markham to Margaret Willughby, in which he writes that at his return home he found his Wife weeping, and his Son sorrowful, but himself was pleased to see that she was so well beloved, whereupon he had writ a letter to Sir Francis Willughby, which he sent open for her to see, desiring to set the matter on foot again, and to conclude with Sir Francis's own offer rather than break, if she would let the bearer his Cousin Marmione (a person she might trust for to his knowledg, she had not a truer friend in England) know she desired it should be, and that hereafter she would frame herself to please his Wife, whom she would find a loving Mother-in-law. He concludes with blessing to her his best beloved Goddaughter. From Kirby Billars October the 31th 1586.

>Your loving Cousin and most assured friend
>Thomas Markham

[f. 179v] In a postscript to this letter he writes. These two letters I have sent unsealed, and my seal, to seal Sir Francis's letter, and pray you to further his coming both with your perswasions, and attendance hither,

>So Farewell gentle Hyne.[459]

In Mr. Thomas Markhams letter to Sir Francis Willughby, he writes of the sorrow which he had found his family in, and that he perceived this breach would be offencive to, and discontent, their best friends, and very well please, all their enemies, and therefore he had thought good to revive it again (if it pleased him) with the acceptance of his own offer, viz: Middleton and Wiken, he heartily prays that he would vouchsafe to come to Kirby, and bring Megge with him, where his Wife would lodg him warmly, and feed him wholsomly.

Sir Francis Willughbys Answer to this Letter was Copied to this effect.

In respect of you, which I would not have done to another, I was contented so much to leave my own determination as to yeild to that which I perceive might in the end greatly disquiet me, and therefore resolve never to grant the like again, esteeming my quietness the greatest benefit I shall enjoy upon earth. There are some speciall causes why at this time I will not enter into further talk of marriage for my third Daughter, first because it is a preposterous course, not having taken order; for the second, another cause is that paradventure it may occasion dislike from others towards [f. 180] you if all things fall not out to their content, which for old good will, I would be loath should happen to my friend, when both the cause and the suspition thereof may be avoided. A third cause is the dislike

---

[459] Hind: a young deer

settled against some upon a light French report[460] (the author not only being of no credit but infamous also) from which would follow such such[lxv] divisions and dissentions amongst my Children as I would be loath to run into. Other causes I will not commit to writing, but this match will not content all parties, and I would not advisedly minister occasion of offence to any. I find my self not fit for travell, else I would have seen you and your Wife at Kirby, to whom I desire you to make my hearty commendations. Wollaton this 1st of November 1586.

Your Cousin and friend to use
F: W:

It appears by this letter that Sir Francis Willughby was then[lxvi] satisfied of Sir Percivalls inocency, in relation to Conrado's wicked letter and report of him, for by what he writes (was the 3rd cause against the match, the dislike settled against some upon a light French report) he must mean the quarrell between Sir Percivall and Griffin Markham, which by Mr. John Adam's letters to Sir Percivall appears to have grown to such a hight that it was hard to prevent their fighting. By this letter from Sir Francis Willughby one may believe that he thought this match would not content his Lady, and that he was unwilling thereby to give her offence. That Lady Willughby was much against the match appears by a letter which she writ to her Daughter Margaret Willughby to this effect.

My Daughter, the motherly love I bear you (than which no love can be greater) constrains me to write hoping that you bear [f. 180v] a dutyfull care of my blessing and counsel. I desire the Almighty to bless you, and continue you in that faith which your Father and I carefully desired you should learn from your cradle, and as a Mother I charge and exhort you not to enter into any union which may draw you from the same. Marriage is honourable, but if religion fail on the one party, it is in my opinion a wicked joyning of the faithfull with the ungodly. I write this because I hear of a marriage motion'd to you, which for the religion suspected, or professed, is not to be received. I also hear that to procure your good will tokens have been given you which are markes and signs of popery, I mean crucifixes and such like. Either you must in time go back or God hath lost a servant, and my self a Daughter. Remember your calling, and your Fathers mind, and portion, to prefer you, and you shall find (I flatter not) that you may be sought in marriage of those

---

[460] See fos 119–123, pp. 149–155 and Text n. 256 for Conrados.

who are able to treble any thing you shall receive by this match. But were it to gain the whol world and lose God, your bargain were worse than I, or any one, can write, or think. Be not bewitched with foolish love, or blind superstition etc. I am by Gods pleasure, and at his sufferance severed from my Husband and Children, and find some of them not so dutyfull as God and nature commands. She writ with some resentment, that her Daughter Willoughby had been very near her, but never came to see her, and what her Son Willoughby had reported of her, (she writ) she knew not. She blamed Margaret for shewing her letters, and delivering them to others to keep, and then telling her Father, they were burnt, but she cares not who sees what she writes. She concludes from Holbourn February the 26th 1586.

> Your loving Mother if you be an obedient child
> Elizabeth Willughby

[f. 181] There is a long letter from Margaret Willughby to Sir Francis, her Father, dated from Eikle,[461] March the 28

She begins this letter with praying for his health, and desiring his blessing, and then repeats his last commands to her, that she should make him privie to any letter message or speech, which she should have from her Cousin Griffin Markham, and therefore she now writ to let him know that she saw her Cousin G: M: upon Wednesday, who then told her that his Father had met Sir Francis Willughby at London, and that a day was appointed for them to meet in the Country, and he hoped that end would be made which his Father and he most desired, but she remembring his last and grievous words to her, told him it was in vain for him or his Father to labour any more in it. At which he seemed greatly grieved, and asked to know her mind, and if she would goe back from what she had writ if Sir Francis Willughbys good will were obtained, to which she answered, No, If your good will were obtained, I would never goe back from what I had written. He then took his leave, and went to Northampton to bed, and the next morning writ the inclosed letter, and after came himself, desiring to be resolved what I meant to doe, to which I said I could give no other answer than what I had already given. He then took his leave, saying he

---

[461] Perhaps the parish of Eccles in Shropham, Norfolk where names of the Grey family and of William Willoughby occur. Francis Blomefield, 'Hundred of Shropham: Old-Bukenham', in *An Essay Towards A Topographical History of the County of Norfolk: I* (London, 1805), 369–394. British History Online http://www.british-history.ac.uk/topographical-hist-norfolk/vol1/pp369-394 (accessed 17 June 2018).

hoped his Father and you would agree. Thus dear Father craving this one request that if you put an end to this match, began with both your consents, you will leave me to rest as I am, because I can never marry any other without offending my conscience. She concludes praying for his health and long life etc.

Your obedient and loving Daughter till death
Margaret Willughby

[f. 181v] There is a letter from Robert Willoughby to Sir Francis dated from Eikle March the 27th 1587. In this letter he tells Sir Francis, that while he was with him, young Mr. Markham came to Eikle, and that his Wife would have prevented his having any private speeches with Margaret Willughby, but she could not, for after dinner before his Wife, and her Sisters he had some secret speeches with her, which he had desired her to give him an account of, and also to send him the letter which Mr. Markham had sent her from Northampton. This letter also mentions Mr. Markhams comming again the next day as her letter to her Father shews, with farther circumstance, that he came from Northampton with his four men up to the house, and two other men posted at the same time by the gate one having a broad buckler, the other was a double gelding with a pillion ready furnished.[462] He could not say these two men were of Mr. Markhams company, but he thought the presumption was great that they were.

It does not appear who this Robert Willoughby was. Sir Percivall's Grandfather who married the Daughter of Sir Edward Willughby of Wollaton perhaps might than be living as well as his Wife. His name was Robert, and 'tis possible he might dwell at Eikle, and that because of the double relation to them, Sir Francis Willughby might desire his Daughters should live with them some part of the time that he lived from his Lady.[463]

[f. 182] There is a letter from Sir Francis Willughby to his Daughter Margaret, dated from Wollaton August the 12th 1587, to

---

[462] According to the *OED*, a buckler was a small, round shield intended to catch a blow. According to James Howell, Esq., *A French and English Dictionary Composed by Mr Randle Cotgrave and another in French and English* (London, 1673), a double-gelding was a horse meant to carry two. A pillion is a term for a second pad to carry a passenger on a horse. Markham seems to have attempted to orchestrate an elopement.

[463] Percival's grandfather, Robert Willoughby, died *c*.1555. Mi, 6/179/46; *HMC Middleton*, 150. See also TNA, PROB Reg. 11/40/402, fos 289-291, the 1558 will of his mother Bridget Willoughby, in which there is no mention of her son Robert. See Mi, 6/179/41 for a draft of her will. See also Text n. 270 for a Robert Willoughby, son of Fulke Greville.

tell her he hears his Cousin Griffin Markham claimed some promise from her, which he thinks strange because she had said she would never proceed without his full consent. He comands her (in this letter) to advertize him presently what promise he could chalenge from her. And tells her there are many causes of dislike, and that fear of God is the only rule to continue liking between Man and Wife. She had been warned by Mrs. Luce Bricknell[464] what exact offices must be observed of pleasing the Mother and Grandmother, with offence inexcusable against the Divine Majesty.

There still remains in the Library at Wollaton a very hansome writ letter from Margaret Willughby to her Father in answer to this from him, which letter is to this effect.

She was sorry that he had been given to understand, that her Cousin Griffin Markham should claim any promise from her, and she had hop'd he had vouchsafed a better opinion of her, then that she could be so forgetfull of her duty as to yeild consent to any without his farther liking, which was not true. By Sir Francis's appointment she was some time at their house, and then her Cousin Griffin Markham made no shew of good will or affection towards her, but what he was urged to by his Father, and the rest of his friends, and besides his indifferency in the matter, his Mothers carriage was very unkind towards her even when she had used what means she could to metigate her displeasure, that she had told her, that if her Husband would be so overseen as to match her Son, with her (which she hop'd would never be) all the rest of her Children should have their portions well assured, and after that I must not look to live in the same house with her, by my presence to disturb her devotions, but be placed in some cottage at their pleasure. And Mr. Markham had told her that, if she could not frame, and fashion, her conditions to his Wives, and her Mothers liking, [f. 182v] she would have but a weary life of it in matching with his Son. From these causes (she writ her Father that) he might believe that it was unlikely that they should presume of any promise from her, (which was untrue). By this letter she seemed to desire her Father would put an end to the affair, and she assured him that she should rest intirely at his disposition. She wished her Cousin Griffin Markham such a Wife as he need not be forced to have, and that might content his friends without so many exceptions, and so she had told him at Eikle, where she had presumed to speak to him contrary to Sir Francis's pleasure. This letter is dated from Newhall August the 15th.

---

[464] Unidentified.

There is another letter from Margaret Willughby to her Father to let him know that since her comming from Mrs. Markham's she had received but only three letters from her, the two first about Christmas last at Wollaton, which she had deliver'd to him, to which Mrs. Markham not receiving any answer to her liking had sent her that letter which she now inclosed, by one of her own men desiring a present answer, which answer she had given to this effect. She was sorry if she had any way offended her, and if she came again to her house, she would (as she had already done employ herself every way to the utmost of her power to give her content.[lxvii]

[f. 183] There is a very obliging letter from Sir Clement Fisher to Mistress Margaret Willughby, in which he writes; that he as much wishes her well=doing, as that of the dearest Child he has; this letter is directed to Kirby, and in it he tells her that he[lxviii] is very glad she is so well placed.

Amongst these old letters at Wollaton, there is one from Mr. Thomas Markham, directed to the right worshipfull Mrs. Spencer at Sandy.[465] The letter is to this effect.

Because after so desparate an attempt as this has been, and now clearly broken, I don't think fit to trouble you nor my self with often repairing to your house, I send this letter, to pray you to make my true excuse to that good Lady your Mother, for not keeping my promise with my Wife and Daughter Margaret that we would wait upon you some time this summer.

His Daughter Margaret lay ill of the small pox, and now might she be glad, and in this respect himself not sorry, that he had not concluded with Mr. Robert Spencer, as he desired for had Mr. Robert Spencer affected his Daughter Margaret, then her company might have bread his danger.

By this you may see God doth all for the best, he hath shewed his love to you by preserving your Son, and his chastisment to me by punishing my Daughter; which I doe (by his promise) also take for a note of his love, and even so in love I end from the Court at Tybballs this 25th of July 1587.

Yours wherein I may
T: M:

Postscript
As for Mr. Spencer tho I have cause not to like of his hard dealing in matter of mattrimony (whereof now I heartily free him) yet his

---

[465] Mother of Robert Spencer? Tybballs may be Burghley's residence, Theobalds.

good company and mutuall friendship I will like [f. 183v] very well, as he shall perceive when he may have cause to use me.

This letter shews that there had been a treaty of marriage between Robert Spencer and Margaret, the Sister of Griffin Markham, as it is very probable that Mr. Spencer's acquaintance with Margaret Willughby might begin at Mr. Thomas Markhams house, where he came to make his addresses to Mrs. Markham, but finding reason to think Margaret[lxix] Willughby would be a better match for him, and coming to visit Margaret Markham, just at a time when Margaret Willughby had been ill used by that family who had claimed promises from her which she had never made, it is likely that Mr. Spencer found it no hard matter to perswade Mrs. Margaret Willughby to change those kind thoughts she once seemed to have had for her Cousin Griffin Markham to himself.

There are no papers which shew the particulars of this treaty of marriage between Robert Spencer and Margaret Willughby, but by the quick conclusion of the match one may believe, that Sir Francis Willughby was, from the first proposall, pleased with it; his last letter to his Daughter concerning Markham is dated August the 12, and by this letter from Thomas Markham dated July the 25th one may believe they were married before that time. It is already set down in this book page 131 that this Robert Spencer of Wormleighton in Warwickshire was descended from the ancient barons of that name etc.[466]

[f. 184] There are in the Library at Wollaton several very kind and friendly letters from Sir John Spencer (who was the Father of this Robert that married Margaret Willughby). These letters are to desire Sir Francis Willughby to look into his affairs, and sell land to clear his debts. One of these letters is dated April An: D: 1595. In which letter he writes that he understood by his servant Mr. Russell that his debt is now 19000[li] (which debt was greatly increased since their last

---

[466] See above Text n. 317. Robert Spencer, 1st Baron Spencer of Wormleighton married Margaret, daughter of Sir Francis Willoughby of Wollaton, Notts., in 1587. See Mi, 6/178/87 for the particulars of a final agreement between Robert Spencer and Margaret Willoughby, dated 1587. Margaret died on 17 Aug. 1597, See the Inquisition *post mortem* for Francis Willoughby, dated 14 Sept. 1597, which says that she died prior to the inquisition. Mi, 1/2/2/1; C 142/248/23. Spencer remained for life a widower, a fact to which Ben Jonson alludes in the lines:
Who, since Thamyra did die
Hath not brook'd a lady's eye,
Nor allow'd about his place
Any of the female race.
A.F. Pollard in *DNB*, LIII, 367–368. See also Richard Cust, 'Spencer, Robert, first baron Spencer (1570–1627), *ODNB*.

meeting) and that he was about selling land, and raising money by fines to pay off 14000^{li} of it. (He writes) that since he is now awake he hopes he will not again fall a sleep, and let the remaining 5000^{li} rest a growing debt. He desires to see him in Town the next term and assures Sir Francis, that himself with his best friends will be ready to help to restore him to a perfect good estate, whereby he might live with the reputation of his Fathers. He concludes wishing him contentment, and the speedy effecting his good purpose, with hearty comendation to himself and his Sister (I believe Lady Arundell might be with Sir Francis after his Lady dyed).[467] There is another letter from Sir John Spencer to Sir Francis Willughby dated from Althropp [Althorp] October the 15th to let him know that they are to muster their horsemen on Thursday at Northampton, and upon Satturday, Monday Tuesday and Wednesday they shall deliver their foot to the captains to be taken to London the week following.

In this letter also he puts Sir Francis in mind of his debts, and writes that knowing him to be forgetfull, he has also writ to his Sister to call upon him, for that he thinks at All Saints Day, he will answer the interest of very near 20000^{li}, and such returns are heavie.

[f. 184v] These, with other letters mention'd before from Robert Spencer the Son, are sufficient to make one believe they were both very good friends to the Willughbys, and that they had no designs upon Sir Francis to the prejudice of his family (as Mr. Hastings appears to have had) but that they acted with great honour and honesty endeavouring to doe what good offices they could[lxx] in those unhappy differences that (has been already shewed) were in the family.

By the old papers one may also find reason to believe that Mr. Robert Spencer and his Lady lived very happily together. They had four Sons, and two Daughters, Mary the eldest Daughter married Sir Richard Anderson Knight, and Elizabeth the other Daughter married Sir George Vane Knight. John their eldest Son was one of the Knights of the Bath at the creation of Prince Charles An: D: 1616. He died without issue. William their second Son married Penelope the Daughter of Henry Earl of Southampton.[468] He dyed An: D: 1636, and was succeeded by

---

[467] It is unlikely that Lady Arundell was still alive in 1595. See Text n. 289 above. John Spencer was probably referring to Dorothy Tamworth Willoughby, as he would now have considered Francis Willoughby his brother.

[468] The other two sons, and the third daughter of Robert and Margaret were: Richard, who married Mary Sandys, Edward, who married Margaret Goldsmith, and Margaret,

Henry his Son who in the 19th of King Charles the 1st was created Earl of Sunderland. His Son Robert was the Father of Charles, the present Earl of Sunderland.

Robert Spencer who married Margaret Willughby dyed at Wormleighton the 25th of October An: D: 1627, and was buried at Brinton, in Northamptonshire, where he had caused a noble monument to be erected in his lifetime, for himself and his Lady.

[Winifrid Willoughby]

[f. 185] Concerning Winifrid Willughby the fourth Daughter of Sir Francis Willughby

There are many letters which shew that Lady Willughby used her Daughter Winifrid with very great severity; she seemed by her letters, to have had a very tender affection for her Sister Brigitt, and it is very likely that in the time that Sir Francis and his Lady were both very angry with their Son Percivall, she might strive as much as she could to pacify them, and upon the same account I believe Mr. Thomas Willoughby might often send his second Son Edward with messages in behalf of Sir Percivall to Wollaton, or Nottingham, or where else Sir Francis might be. Winifrids affection for her Sister I believe made her always desirous to hear what news he either brought from, or was to carry to, Sir Percivall, and by thus conversing together they soon engaged each others affections.[469] It appears

---

who died in 1613 at age 16 but left behind a valuable account book with records from 1610–1613. For Margaret and her account book, see Edith Snook, *Women, Beauty and Power in Early Modern England: A Feminist Literary History* (London, 2011), 11. 86–87, 76–84, 195–196 nn.8 and 9. Diana, Princess of Wales, formerly Lady Diana Spencer, was a direct descendant, 12 generations removed, of William and Penelope Spencer.

[469] There is a slightly condensed version of this in Cassandra's earlier notes: 'There are a great many letters which shew, that this Lady must have been an extream severe Mother to all her Children, but especially to her fourth Daughter Winifrid, who I believe used to justifie her Sister Brigitt and Sr Percivall as much as she could, all the time Sr Francis and his Lady was so very angry w[i]th them, and this I believe might provoke Lady ^Willoughby^ to use her the worse in the time of this quarrel between Sr Francis and Sr Percivall (which you will find a relation of, in the account of Sr Percivall). Edward Willoughby, Brother to Sr Percivall used to come ^as I find reason from the letters to^ believe often to Wollaton as a mediator between Sr Francis and his Brother; ^there seems to have been a great^ friendship ^between^ Winifrid had for ^and^ her Sister Brigitt, soon ^and that I believe at first^ made her have wth a more common esteem for her Brother Edward[. T]o him she used to lay open her griefs ^as appears by his letters^ ^to PW^ and ease her mind by telling him how much she suffered from her Mothers cruelty severity to her, and those un=happy divisions in the family. [T]hese troubles used to oppress poor Winifrid so heavily, that she often expresses herself ^in her letters to Brig Will^ weary of Life; she seems ^by her way of writing^ to have been a woman of a tender sweet disposition and more then common piety, but

by the old papers that Edward Willoughby made his Brother Sir Percivall acquainted with this affair, and obtain'd his friendship towards the promoting it, in order to which one may believe by the old letters that Sir Percivall was very willing his Father should settle a good younger Brothers estate upon him; and it is reasonable to believe, that Mr. Thomas Willoughby [f. 185v] would not be displeased with this affair, provided they could gain Sir Francis's consent, in order to which Mr. Thomas Willoughby gave Sir Francis an account of the whole matter. Sir Francis had a very good opinion of Edward Willoughby (as one may judg by the old papers) and his Father offering to make such a settlement upon them, as they might live comfortably upon, and not requiring any fortune fro=m Sir Francis with his Daughter, being willing his Son should marry her without any money paid down to him, and to leave it to Sir Francis to give his Daughter what he pleased, and when he pleased. The asking no ready money from Sir Francis, was a gratefull proposall; to him, who by that time Wollaton was built, had found it difficult to raise any. Weighing this affair he at last resolved to yeild to what Edward Willoughby and his Daughter Winifrid, with great earnestness desired, only bid him apply himself to his Wife to get her good will (as appears by one of Edward Willoughbys letters).

There is a letter from Edward Willoughby to his Brother Sir Percivall dated December 1588,[470] in which he writes that what his Father has offer'd him, he will perform at any time, and therefore he desires his Brother to advise him whither he shall come down to Sir Francis now in the time of his being Sheriff or not.[471] His Father, he writes, would send two men and a boy to wait upon him, but being a younger Brother, he thinks one man and a boy would be sufficient, but in this he desires Sir Percivalls ad= [f. 186] advice, as also concerning his liveries, whither they shall be green clokes or coats.

---

being thus oppressed w[i]th grief, and ^often seeing^ Edward Willoughby ^who I believe might^ expressing his concern for her, in very [illeg.] ^a tender manner^, she soon added that of loving him to the rest of her troubles (ɸ) After this love intriegue had been kept private some time, Ned Willoughby ^as appears by their letters^ gets his Father Tho Willoughby of Boreplace, to make Sir Francis acquainted with it, Sr Percivall ^by his letters^ seems to have been very kind to his Brother in this affair and willing to have his father settle a good estate, for a younger Brother, upon him. And besides Mr [repeats and besides Mr] Thomas Willoughby offer'd to ask no fortune from Sir F:W to his daughter AB: being willing his Son should marry her without any money paid down to him and leave it to Sr F: W: to give his Daughter what he pleased.' STB 2 (1), book 1, fos 33–34v.

[470] Dated 1589 in Cassandra's earlier notes. STB 2 (1), book 1, fo. 35. 1588 appears to be correct.

[471] Sir Francis served as the high sheriff of Nottinghamshire in 1579, 1588, and 1593.

Thus Edward Willoughby seemed to have great hopes of gaining his beloved mistris when yet the greatest difficulty still remained, and that was to gain Lady Willughby's consent. In one of his letters he writes that when it was first proposed to my Lady she flew into violent passions both with Sir Francis and her Daughter Winifrid, and would by no means be prevailed upon to hear of such a match. And for fear least Winifrid should steal away and marry him privately, she kept her locked up, by such hands as he could not convey a letter to her, or get one from her.

In a letter from Edward Willoughby to Sir Percivall dated March the 18th 1589 he writes that Lady Willughby uses poor Winifrid with such severity that he fears she will be lamed.

There are severall very pittyous letters from Winifrid to Sir Percivall and his Lady. In one of her letters to Sir Percivall she writes that her Mothers illness grows worse and worse, and the doctors advise her to goe to the Bath, which she believes she intends as soon as she can. In this letter she desires Sir Percivall will find some way to get her from her Mother, who she writes leads her such a life as she is not able to endure, and now she does all she can to make her Father angry with her; she has turned away her maids now, and says Winifrid shall serve her in their room. In short Winifrid writes that she has not one quiet hour.

In another letter from Winifrid Willughby to Sir Percivall, she [f. 186v] writes; that her Mothers unkindness still continues, insomuch that at present she will not vouchsafe to call her Daughter, but Mrs.Winifrid.

Amongst Winifrid Willughbys letters, there is a love letter to her from Richard Pudsey,[472] in which he owns that he does not diserve her, and writes that words can not express the grief which he suffers for her sake. It is such, as almost drives him to dispare when he thinks of his luckless love. He beseeches her to accept of a simple token as a testimony of his good will, which undiserved curtisie will bind him to be for ever thankfull.

There is no copy of any answer from Winifrid Willughby to this letter.

There are severall letters from Edward Willoughby which express great concern for the[lxxi] ill usage which Winifrid suffer'd from her

---

[472] Richard was the oldest son of George Pudsey and his first wife, Maud Cotton, living in Langley, Warks. *HMC Middleton*, 454: 'Mr George Pudsie and his sonne came on Monday at nighte; Mr. George Pudsie and his sonne went away on Thursday morning.' 1 July 1588.

Mother. Which at last he found a way to free her from,[473] by geting her a way, and privately marrying her, of which there is this account in a letter which he writ to his Sister Brigit, dated from London, May An: D: 1590. That her Mothers cruelty and unnaturall usage of her Sister Winifrid, had made him take an extraordinary course for her quiet, for which he writes Lady Willughby threatens imprisonment and death shall be his portion with her; but he trusts as God has joyned them together, so he will help them and raise them up [f. 187] friends. And he hopes she will continue a Sisters love to them both.

There is also a letter from Edward Willoughby to Sir Francis dated May An: D: 1590, in which letter he expresses great concern for his heavie displeasure, assuring him that if he had not been pleased to give his consent, to his friends, as well as himself, he would never have been troublesome to him while he had lived; but having by his allowance settled his affections upon Mrs. Winifrid; pitty had moved him now to take her from such cruel hard usage as her Mother had made her indure, being he supposed rather incensed by others, than of her Ladyships own disposition, so unnaturall to her Daughter. He now heard my Lady had vowed she would have him slayn, but he hoped her Ladyship would not commit that office to any of her friends for fear he get little by the match. In this letter he writ that he had diserved better of my Lady (as others could witness) during her absence from Sir Francis. And he had now in most humble sort by all possible means which he could devise saught her good will, but this she had only returned with bitter words, and vehement protestations, that she would never give her consent. He hoped Sir Francis would not condemn him when he had considered his case. He always had, and would be ready in all dutyfull sort to doe him the best service that he may; he only craves his favour and good will towards himself, and his blessing with his Daughter, hoping that his course of life and usage of her, will hereafter gain his favour and affection.

[f. 187v] There are in the Library at Wollaton many very melancholy letters from Winifrid Willoughby to her Father acknowledging her great offence and beging he would forgive her.

In one dated January 1595 writ in very moving termes both to Sir Francis and his Lady,[474] beging if ever Child was heard of Father and

---

[473] Cassandra's earlier notes state that Winifrid was the one who freed herself: 'From such severe usage at last Winifrid finds a way to free herself, by privately marrying Mr Edward Willoughby.' STB 2 (1), book 1, fo. 36.

[474] Dorothy Willoughby, Sir Francis's second wife, if this date is 1595/6. Otherwise, this is addressed to Francis and Elizabeth in Jan. 1594/5.

Mother, they would not now stop their ears to her, who came to them with a wounded heart, for years and experience had shewed her, that the hand of God was streached out against her, which once again she begs them by their blessing to help to appease.

In another letter to Sir Francis, she begs if he will not look upon her as his Child, yet he would not let her be less than his servants.

By another letter I find Winifrid and her Husband took a journey to Wollaton, in hopes to have seen her Father (which he refused) and also to remove some goods, which I believe she had there, which had remained from the time of her going away.

Upon Sir Francis's refusing to see them, she writ to tell him that seeing their being there was offensive to him, they would seek some abiding place which should be far from him, but then she hoped he would allow her that 40^{li} yearly which he had vouchsafed to promise her, [f. 188] towards her maintenance.

Marrying as they did, unknown to either of their Fathers, it is very likely that, that settlement which Mr. Thomas Willoughby offer'd Sir Francis to make upon his Son, if he would consent to the match, might never be made, and perhaps Mr. Thomas Willoughbys second wife[475] to raise as much as she could for her own Children, might prevent his being very kind to his Son Edward. However this was, it is very apparent from both their letters which still remain, that they were often reduced to very low circumstances [*and to beg relief from them*][476]. He was engaged in a law sute, and by being bound for others was forced to pay more than he was worth, and run himself so much in debt that he was comitted to Warwick Goal.[477] Under these misfortune[s] Winifrid Willoughby writ her Sister Brigitt many very melancholy letters. In one of her letters to her Sister she desires she will send her a dish of fish against the assises, they being to have a great company of witnesses. [*but under these misfortunes I believe Sr Percivall and his Lady were very kind to them,* # [and by all their Letters they seem to have been happy in each other, their Tempers being perfectly agreeable][478]

---

[475] Mary Weston. See S.T. Bindoff, 'Willoughby, Thomas', *History of Parliament Online*: http://www.historyofparliamentonline.org/volume/1558-1603/member/willoughby-thomas-1596; http://www.tudorplace.com.ar/willoughby1.htm.

[476] STB 2 (1), book 1, fo. 37.

[477] The terms goal and gaol (jail) seem to have been used interchangeably in the late 16th century. Although the date of Edward Willoughby's incarceration is unclear from Cassandra's account, it must have been after 1590 and seems to have lasted until 1605. Warwick Gaol was located in Warwick Castle, which was owned by the Crown until 1604 when Fulke Greville was granted the Castle by James I.

[478] STB 2 (1), book 1, fo. 37. The hash symbol indicates that fo. 36v should be inserted. Most of that folio, however, repeats information already copied into the Account.

In another of her letters to Lady Willoughby her Sister, she writ that she had been procuring money against the tryall, but she doubts it will fall short. She prays for patience, and complains of grievous pains in her head.

There is another letter from Winifrid to her Sister Willoughby which she dates from her Aunt Moorows. In it she writ that she had been sent for to her Sister Abigal's against her lying inn, but fell so sick by the way that she was forced to stay at her Aunts, and shall now return home as soon as she was able. In that letter she writ that her Husband had sent a petition to the King in hopes of being released from his long imprisonment.

In another very pittious letter to her Sister, she writ that the sickness was within four doors of her Husband, and therefore she begged Lady Willoughby would solicit to get him released.

[f. 188v] There is in the Library the copy of a letter writ in a very moving manner to Mr. Burrell,[479] and signed by Thomas Cartwright, Wasllia Hynton, Richard Eaton, and Ed: Pod: dated April the 9th 1602, to solicit him to release Mr. Edward Willoughby from his imprisonment, desiring him to consider his weak state of health, and that in a short time if he be kept there, he must be utterly ruined, both himself and family, and then Mr. Burrell could have nothing but his bones. Whereas now the poor and wofull Gentlewoman his Wife, to gain her Husbands liberty (as they heard) would be contented to mortgage or sell all that she had even to the bed which she lay upon. They desire he will consider that the debt was not his own, but for suretyship for another, therefore they beseech him for Christs sake to shew some compassion to his miserable case, and if not to him, to his Wife and Children who had no share in the suretyship.

There is the copy of a letter to the same effect from Edward Willoughby to Mr. Burrell dated July 1605. In this letter he desires Burrell would let him have the use of his books.

By Winifrid Willoughbys letters to her Sister Willoughby it appears that under these bitter afflictions which she suffer'd Lady Willoughby was very kind in assisting her, for the most of these melancholy letters are full of acknowledgments to her Sister for her great bounty and kindness to her.

Many of these letters give accounts of her being very sick and weak as well as in want through her Husbands misfortunes.

In a letter dated October An: D: 1606, to her Sister Willoughby she wishes her Neece Brigitt a comfortable enjoyment of her marriage, and that her other Neeces may have as good matches, and

---

[479] See Burrell family papers in the Lincolnshire archives, ANC–9ANC.

wished her Neece, would think her Bess hansome enough to wait upon her.

[f. 189] There is an account writ by Sir Percivall Willoughby's own hand from An: D: 1596 to 1599. In it I found set down

Paid to Ned Willoughby in November 1597 in part of his Wife's portion 333^{li}—6^s—8^d and in November 1598 paid him 333^{li}—6^s—8^d being the whole sume then due. This book mentions severall times 40^{li} and 44^{li} paid to Ned Willoughby, which I believe might be his half years annuity. There is also set down severall little sumes paid by Sir Percivall Willoughby for, and too [sic], Ned Willoughby. And that An: D: 1599 Sir Percivall was bound with Ned Willoughby for 60^{li}. And again the same year for 50^{li}, and again the same year for 40^{li} and that the same year he paid debts for him which came to 81^{li}—5^s—0^d. And that Hurley men[480] demanded of Sir Percivall the sum of 368^{li}—15^{sh}—0^d, due from his Brother.

By this as well as severall other papers it appears that Sir Percivall and his Lady were both very kind to Ned Willoughby and his Wife.

There is a very moving letter writ by Winifrid Willoughby to her Father in behalf of her Husband and Children, beging that he would let them have one of his houses to live in, that they might have some resting place, for her present state was so deplorable that she would rather chuse her grave.

By this it appears that poor Winifrid began to want before her Father dyed. But I could by no papers find whither he, or his Lady, were reconciled to her so far as to see her before they dyed. Nor could I find any account what fortune he left her, or whither he made her any allowance during his life. Nor is there any account how long Edward Willoughby lay in Goal, nor by what means he got himself released.

[f. 189v] There is a letter from Winifrid to her Sister Willoughby to let her know that her God=daughter (who I believe was Winifrid's eldest Daughter) and her Cousin Hannam, had such an affection for each other, that her Husband and self had resolved to consent to their marrying. She had, had some scruples from their being so near of kinn, but upon discoursing with many pious good men she was sattisfied it was allowed by God, and good men, who had made her see that was no cause to break their loves, especially beholding the many graces God had endued him with, and true grace, and happyness, she thought could not be separated. Besides

---

[480] Possibly bailiffs, or hurling men, ball players, *OED*.

he had a compitent estate sufficient for them to live with content upon, and both of them being so near to her, doe now humbly beg her favour and consent to their marrying.

By this letter one may believe that Winifrid Willoughby and her Husband were then in easie circumstances, but her letters some time after show the contrary.

There is a letter from Winifrid to her Sister Willoughby dated May An: D: 1625, in which letter she writes that she is[lxxii] under very great affliction to part with her dear Son, who had been a great help to her, but was now going beyond sea. And writes that her griefs and wants were more than she could express. Her Son and Daughter Hanname with their Children now lying upon her for maintenance till her Husband could pay them her fortune. And her Son Swift had sued her [f. 190] Husband for that part of his Wife's portion which was not paid. With these afflictions (she writes) that her grieved heart was much cast down.

There remains no account of more Children left by this Edward and Winifrid Willoughby than this Son and two Daughters mentioned in her letter. Of the Daughters, I believe it was the eldest that married Hanname, who I think was a Major in the Kings service. They had many Children, but from them I think there now remains no descendants. The other Daughter married Swift of Worcestershire, from whom was descended that Swift who for many years was chose Member of Parliament for Worcester. He dyed without heirs, and so I think did the rest of her Children.

Thomas Willoughby, the Son of Edward and Winifrid, was bread a Hamborough [Hamburg, Germany] merchant. There is a letter still remaining in his Grand=daughters hands, which he had writ to his Wife, August the 25th, 1635, to desire her to receive 200^{li} then due to him, and with it to pay severall small debts which he had left owing which in all amounted to the sum of 206^{li}—2^{s}—6^{d}. This letter mentions his being then going to Italy, and gives an account of yarn, and of wine, in both which I believe he traded; there is an account of his being unfortunate in his business, and that after sustaining some great losses he went to the East Indies, and dyed there. He married, Elizabeth the Daughter of Robert Payne of Basingstoke in the County of Southampton, who brought to him the inheritance of the mannor of Barton Stacy in that County, being in value of 600^{li} per annum. They had two Sons and three Daughters. The eldest Daughter married Carpenter.

Ann, the second Daughter married – Lascoe a Drugster on Cornhill. She had a Daughter who dyed young, and a Son William who married Jane Stokes, by whom he had a Son Francis, and four [f. 190v] Daughters, which five children he left at his death to the care of Mr. Edwards of Soho Square.

Elizabeth the 3d Daughter of Thomas Willoughby, married Mr. Dards an oyle man, but left no Child.

Edward Willoughby the eldest Son of Thomas dyed unmarried, by this accident. He was riding out to take the air, with another Gentleman whose hat fell off. Mr. Willoughby by endeavouring to take it up fell off his horse and broke his neck, and dyed upon the spot.

Hugh Willoughby of Barton Stacy near Winchester in Hampshire heir to his Brother Edward, was a Docter of Phisick. He married Rebecca the Daughter of Theophilus Pointer[481] of Oxford, who was the Son of [blank] Pointer who was Dean of Christ Church. This Doctour Willoughby had a Son that dyed unmarried at 25 years of age and three Daughters, of which Rebecca, the eldest [blank].

Elizabeth the second Daughter of Dr. Willoughby dyed young. Elizabeth the third Daughter married Martin Wright a Counceller the eldest Son of William Wright a Welsh Judg.

[Abigail Willoughby Pargiter]

[f. 191] Concerning Abigail the fifth Daughter of Sir Francis Willughby

It appears by many of the old letters in the Library that Abigail Willughby had the care of the house during her Mothers sickness and after her death. There is a letter from her, to her Sister Willoughby, dated from Packington June the 12th but not the date of the year [probably 1595, right after Elizabeth Willoughby's death]. In this letter Abigail writ that she hoped since it had pleased God to take her Mother that she would come to Wollaton in her turn. This she hoped that herself and Brother [i.e. Bridget and Percival] would be willing to doe, because there were many things which her wits would not serve her to name, that would be spoyled for want of her help. She assured her from the bottom of her heart that it was not want of good will in her that they were not there at present. She desired her Sister would joyn with her to thank God for their happy deliverance from all their troubles, and prays God to send them a happy meeting at Wollaton.

---

[481] Probably Theophilus Poynter 'chirurgeon', son of John Poynter of Oxford (not a dean). Licensed as a surgeon Oct. 11, 1666. Joseph Foster, *Alumni Oxonienses: The Members of the University of Oxford 1500–1714* (Oxford, 1891): L–R, p. 1197.

In the postscript she writ that her Mother had given her clock to Russell had it been in her power she should have had it as willingly as she could desire it.

There is a letter from Abigail Willughby to her Father, to give him an account of keys, where they were, and also of those inventorys which she had in keeping, and to let him know that the new napkins were at the weavers when he went up to London, and that there was a great bucke [washing tub] of diaper and damask[482] which had been ill washed, laid in a diaper chest, because they could not be washed again before he went to London. She concludes thus. I leave Packington the 15th of June. Your loving and obedient Daughter

Abigail Willughby

[f. 191v] There is a letter from Sir Francis Willughby to his Daughter Abigail in which he writes.

My pleasure is that you deliver to Nuport the buttons set in billiment,[483] and also the great pearl which your Mother did wear in a necklace about her neck, if they be not there in your custody, I would have you ride to Wollaton, with one of Mr. Fishers men and Nuport and George Draicott who shall accompany you back to Mr. Fishers house. Thus in hast I commit you and your Sister to the tuition of the Almighty, who bless and keep you according to his dyngne [digne] pleasure, Sherfield the 13th of August 1595.

Your loving Father

This letter is directed to his loving Daughter Abigail Willughby at Packington

There is Abigail Willughbys answer to this letter, in which she writes that she had sent the buttons that was upon the billiment, but the necklace which her Mother[lxxiii] used to wear was of two sorts of little pearl, laced with rubys, or garnetts, and a diamond hanging down through the boots, which was in a chest in his Chamber etc. Thus craving your daily blessing I humbly take my leave the 19th of August 1595.

Your humble and obeydyent Daughter Abigaill Willughby

---

[482] Diaper was a patterned linen or cotton fabric; damask was a twilled linen fabric used mainly for table linen, *OED*.

[483] Biliment or a biliment is an ornamental article worn by women, most likely a hood or head-dress, *OED*.

Writ in a postscript
The necklace I cannot certifie
you off [of], but the ring that hung
at it Newport shewed me, as
I had writ the letter.

[f. 192] Amongst the old papers, I could not find any particular account of the time when Abigail Willughby married, but believe it was about two years after her Fathers death.

There is a book of Sir Percivall Willoughby's accounts of money paid and received by him in which there is set down 500^{li} paid in part of Abigail Willughbys portion February the 7th An: D: 1598, and that in April 1599 he gave his Sister Abigail a bond for a hundred pounds, and also that June the 15th 1600, he gave her another bond for a hundred pounds.

By this account book one may believe that she was married An: D: 1598. Her Husband was William Pargiter a Northamptonshire Gentleman.

There are in the Library severall letters from her, to her Sister Willoughby after she was married. In one she writ that her Sister Wood looked to ly inn every day, after which time, she would make what hast she could, to see her, who she pray'd God to bless and requite for all her Sisterly love to her, which she could only requite in love to her again.

There is a letter from Mr. William Pargiter her Husband to Lady Willoughby to desire she would speak in his behalf to Sir Percivall to give him land security for the debt which he owed him. He writ that he had been with his Cousin Henry Willoughby, to see what directions his Father had given him for a conveyance to be made of some parcell of land in Cossall or Trowell, but found that Sir Percivall had only writ in the generall, and nothing in particular to him, whereupon he had desired his Cousin Henry to make a draught of a tenement in Cossall, which he desired her Ladyship would approve off [of], and get it ingrossed for him at Wollaton, and sealed and delivered by Sir Percivall and herself, and possession given to his Brother Wood in his behalf etc.

Another sute he made Lady Willoughby in behalf of her Son Henry who was not only in want of maintenance, but also in want of liberty in respect of his engagements for his Father, and though she had not a power to get him relieved from the latter,[lxxiv]
[f. 193][484] There is a letter from Mr. Pargiter to Sir Percivall Willoughby[lxxv] from Greetworth September the 23th 1631 in which

---

[484] There are two folios 193. The first one, inserted into the text, clearly belongs after the second one. The editor has made that change.

letter he desired that himself his Wife and two Daughters and a Gentlewoman, and servants, might come to board at Wollaton with Sir Percivall Willoughby.

Greetworth was the name of Mr. Pargiter's house in Northamptonshire. They had five Sons, and four Daughters; Dorothy the eldest Daughter married [blank] Kirby of Huntingtonshire, and after his death her second Husband was Sir John Washington of Northamptonshire. She had severall Children but they all dyed without leaving any children. Grace the second Daughter of Abigail Pargiter, married [blank] Stratford of Merywell near Aderston [Merevale near Atherstone] in Warwickshire, by him she had six Sons and three Daughters, of which, Grace the eldest married Mr. Rushton of Flower in Northamptonshire. Abigail the 2d Daughter married Mr. Trotman of Warwickshire. Dorothy the youngest Daughter married Mr. Hood a descendant from the famous Robin Hood in Leicestershire. John the eldest Son of Grace Stratford married the Sister of Sir John Coomes of Davantry in Northamptonshire by whom he had one Son and two Daughters; Grace the eldest Daughter still lives unmarried, Abigail his second Daughter married Pilkington the Consull of Aleppoe by whom she has four Daughters.

John the only Son of Sir John Stratford married Mrs. Free the Daughter of the Governour of the Company in Hamborrough by whom he has one son. Edward the second son of Grace Stratford married Mrs. Taylor of Ansty in Warwickshire, by whom he has one Son and severall Daughters. He is still living and very near 90 years of age.

Robert the third Son of Grace Stratford was settled in Ireland where he married Mrs.Welsh and by her had two Sons and seven Daughters, of which Grace the eldest Daughter married Burton, Mary the second married Mr. Pearss, Elizabeth married Mr. Hickman, Jane the 4th married Mr. Carlton, Abigail the 5th Daughter married Mr. Canning, Catherine the 6th married Mr. Spencer, and Ann the seventh Daughter married Mr. Eyre, and is since dead.

[f. 193] Edward the eldest Son of Robert, and Grandson of Grace Stratford, married Mrs. Beasly of Northamptonshire, by whom he had three Sons and one Daughter. His second Wife is the Daughter of Sir Morrice Eustace of Ireland, by this Lady he has no Child.

Francis the second Son of Robert Stratford married Mrs. Free the eldest Daughter of the Governour of the company in Hamborough.[485]

---

[485] It appears that two of the male descendants married daughters of Free, the governor of the company in Hamborough [Hamburg, Germany].

William, Theodore, and Francis, the three youngest Sons of Grace Stratford who was the Daughter of Abigail Willughby, all dyed unmarried.

Elizabeth the third Daughter of Abigail Willughby (who married William Pargiter Esquire) married Francis Smith of Worcestershire, by whom she had severall children, who dyed without leaving any Children. And Ann her Daughter now living. This Elizabeth Smith who was the Daughter of Abigail Willughby lived to be 98 years of age, and not long before her death she was visited by her Sister Abigail Hickman, who was then 88 years of age, and came to let her know that her Sister Pargiter [sister-in-law?] who was then 94 years of age was very well recovered from a fit of sickness.

Ann the Daughter of this Mrs. Smith married William Friend of Northamptonshire, by whom she had three Sons and two Daughters. Ann her eldest Daughter married Mr. Delangley by whom she had one Daughter who now survives her. Elizabeth her second Daughter married Mr. Dobson, a Drugster in Ireland. She is also dead, and has left two Daughters.

Robert Friend her eldest Son, now Docter of Divinity and Master of Westminster School, married Mrs. Jane Delangley by whom he has three Sons.[486] William Friend, her second Son, a clergy=man had the good fortune to gain the 20000^{li} prize in the lottery An: D: [blank] He married Brigit Glover a ministers Daughter by whom he has two Daughters. John Friend, her third Son who is a Doctour of Phisick married Mrs. Ann Morrice, by whom he has one [blank].

[Frances Willoughby Wood]

[f. 193v] Concerning Frances, the Sixth Daughter of Sir Francis Willughby

There remains in the Library at Wollaton but little account of this Frances Willughby, the youngest of Sir Francis's six Daughters, but by her own letters, and some other letters which make mention of her, one may believe[lxxvi] that she strove to be her Mother's favoret, and as a means to make herself so, did help to aggravate those unhappy disputes which were in the family. But this course did not long keep her Mother from using her with as much severity as the rest of her Daughters, as appears by some of her letters, which are full of sad complaints of the hardships which her Mother made

---

[486] Robert Freind (1666/7–1751). The Freind sons can be traced in the *ODNB*.

her suffer, [*and this ill usage makes her leave her Mother*]⁴⁸⁷ her Sisters having, I believe, been before disobliged by her were not very friendly to her under these misfortunes, and this prompted her to make friendships out of her own family, and to goe away from Sir Francis and his Lady unknown to either of them, with Mr. John Drake. There remains in the Library a letter which she writ to Sir Francis upon this occasion. [f. 194] Her letter is to this effect.

That her Mother's cruelty to her had forced her to take this course, and though she was sensible she ought not to accuse her Mother, yet now such was her offence, that only her Mothers wrongs could render her excusable, and his knowing that she never used to displease him. She writ that Mr. Drake used her with great respect, and took care to preserve her reputation, and that her intention was to live for some time in his Uncle Richard Drakes house, whose Wife had an extraordinary good character, and there she hoped to carry herself so well as to merit his pleasure.

There is no copy of any answer from Sir Francis to this letter, nor does it appear how long she stayed at Mr. Drakes house, nor when she married.⁴⁸⁸ But by a letter from her to Sir Percivall Willoughby concerning some trouble she had about her fortune, one may believe she did not marry till some time after her Fathers death, and tis probable that she might live at Mr. Drakes house till then, and that after Sir Francis Willughby's death, Sir Percivall and his Lady might invite

---

⁴⁸⁷ STB 2 (1), book 1, fo. 38. On 7 June 1595 Frances Willoughby and John Drake, gentleman, answered to the High Commissioner for Ecclesiastical Causes with regard to her leaving Wollaton. They have objected that she left her mother and father without just cause and against her duty to God and to her parents. They object that she has fallen into the company of Mr John Drake with whom she has contracted marriage and that he has used her body and 'passed such familiarities as man and wife doe'. Mi, 2/75/2/8/3–4. In her answer Frances cites the severity, without cause, with which her mother treated her. She first fled to Arundel House, where she met John Drake, son of Sir Bernard Drake, a sea captain involved in early ventures off the coast of the New World. She stayed with Drake a few days and then travelled with him to Esher, in Surrey, the home of Richard Drake [his uncle]. She admitted that it was against her parents' good will and against the duty of an obedient daughter, but cites how cruelly misused she was. Drake admitted that he met up with her with some hope of a contract between them. Mi, 2/75/2/8/1–4.

⁴⁸⁸ Frances had not married at the time of the 1597 suit at chancery filed by her, Abigail, Winifred, and Edward Willoughby against Percival Willoughby. See above, Text n. 416. She had married Montague Wood, however, prior to Nov. 1598 when Montague Wood and his wife Frances joined a lawsuit at chancery together with Abigail Willughby against Percival and Bridget Willoughby, TNA, C78/129/16. There is an interesting book of poems by Robert Parry, gentleman, published in London in 1597. They are passionate poems upon his fortunes, 'offered for an incense at the shrine of the Ladies who guided these distempered thoughts', one of whom is 'Fransis Willoughby'. See Carleton Brown, *Poems by Sir John Salusbury and Robert Chester* (Bryn Mawr, 1913), xl–xliii. For the wardship of Frances Willoughby after her father's death, see Mi, F 10/32.

her to come from Mr. Drakes house to live with them, and that her refusing to doe so, was the reason why Dorothy Hastings in a letter to her Sister Willoughby page 170 writ that she wondred her Sister Francis [sic] should continue so obstinate, that she refused to come live with her Brother and herself. There are[lxxvii] severall letters from Mrs. Hastings to her Sister, writ after her Sister Francis [sic] was married full of complaints of her Husband [Montague Wood] that he had received the rents of her estate and she fear'd she [f. 194v] should not get it out of his hands, and that he had played her a vile part. But it was Gods will to plague her with vile men. By many others letters one may believe that this Mountague Wood[489] of Lamley was a very ill man, as well as a very ill Husband to this Frances Willughby, who I believe married him while she was at Mr. Drakes house, and tis very likely this match might be made for her by Mr. Drake, or else that she made it for herself without consulting with any of her friends. I believe very soon after they married, he began to use his Wife very ill and continued to doe so as long as she lived. There are many letters from her to her Sisters which give an account of his barbarity to her viz: that he turned her out of doors, beat her, and made her suffer the want of the necessarys for life, and other of her letters complain of the unkindness of his relations to her. So that upon the whole, one may judg that she had a very miserable life.[490]

Mi, C 29: Two Letters from Montague Wood to his 'Good Sister', c.1600, on Paper, front and back

LETTER 1

Good Sister I had thought not to have written unto you, untill I had sent you sum good news, but sutche occasions have happned of late, that I am forced to send you as ill news, as ever you herde and worst to me then to all the worlde besides. Soo it is that foure my last goinge to London, your sister Fraunces, by the evill perswationes of sum dishonest people hathe acquainted herselfe, withe a coople of gentlemen bothe strangers to her before nowe and to me, bothe unmaried men and of notorious fame, and hathe yelded soo mutche to her pleasures as she hathe not refused to goe to tavernes, to foll [fool] withe them, I knowe not howe often, and to staye at the taverne, whole nights withe them, she hathe ridden, to one of there howses, and hathe sent awaye her servaunte for the space of three dayes not sufferinge soo mutche as her mayde to staye withe her since siche tyme, she hathe geven [?] them entertaynement at her owne howse, and hathe lodged them with suche shamefull usage of her selfe [...] them, that all my servaunts, had I not cum home

---

[489] With regard to Montague Wood, see Introduction, pp. 18–19, 57.
[490] The two original letters that follow, however, show another side of the story, told by Montague Wood. They are printed with the kind permission of Lord Middelton.

as I did, woulde have lefte her, to her selfe, and of them hathe placed a mayde withe her to fitt her evill disposition, at this tyme wiche when I perceaved I turned awaye, and your sister desperatelye tooke her cloths and went awaye from me, yet I have used sutche meanes as she is cum againe, but she determinethe to goe as I thinke after those lewde felows. I tendringe [?] her creditt and the reputation of her freinds from whome she is descended, offered her that if she woulde forsake sutche companye, and live a modest and continent life, I woulde remitt those her faults passed, and suppresse the common reporte as mulche as I coulde, and defende her reputation by all possible meanes, I mighte, but she awneswared that she woulde not, but where she had binn once she woulde be tenn tymes withe them and if God Allmightye shoulde saye to her, that her soule shoulde have damnation she woulde not allter the course nor make anye reconciliation hereof, I thought good to advertise her nearest freinds, to see if they maye perswade her to more modesty omittinge to speake of manye particulars, withe care off her creditt if it maye be helpte, dothe cause me to conceale and thus leavinge the consideration howof to your discretion, I remitt you to God. Mannsffilde, the 14 of maye 1600

Your unfortunate brother in lawe Monntagu Wood

To the worshipfull my approved good sister in law Mrs. Albigall Willughby at Sutton Cofilde

LETTER 2 ON THE SAME PAPER, FOLDED OVER[491]

Sister Abigall I writt you a letter from London, wherein I tolde you I was in good hope, that your sister Fraunces had forsaken her hauntinge of taverns, espetiallye with her wanted companions, but when I came home I founde the contrarye, for she was at that instant, withe and of them at an Inn, and she is growen thor[...] intisement to be altogether carelesse, of her owne honestye and my creditt, I have binn at home these three weekes, and have used bothe geutle perswations to winn her, and theateninge speaches to restrayne her, from bad places and worse companye, but neither will provayle with her, and she dowttinge that I woulde have kept her with indoores, hathe taken her apparrell and [...] and hath setled her selfe to live at a poore ladyes howse whoe livethe of devotion of her freinds, and here consumethe all she hathe, sence withe departure of hers, I have binn often with her intreatinge her, to live at home, or if she will goe to anye of her freinds, I meane her sisters, I have offered her that I will send her withe men and horses but she regardethe not either of these motions, I would have sent you worde sooner of these accidents, but that I herde that Mr Percivall Wyllughby woulde have binn at Wollaton at the assises, to whome I ment to have made these matters knowen, thoughe they be allreadye too mutch knowen, for the whole countree was possessed [?] therewithe before my cumminge home, and for that he hath sumtyme seemed to wishe her good, it

---

[491] Mi, C 29. There is a brief abstract in *HMC Middleton*, 170.

maye be he wanted advise her nowe [...] to sutche a course, as might be of lesse scandall to her, then her present behaviour is and of late hathe biin, it is wofull to thinke of and to fowle to write the particulars thereof, and thoughe he hathe herd before chalenged [?] with harde usage her, without iust cause yet I dare refer this, to him or anye honest minde to sensure, and for that I woulde save her creditt as mulche as I maye, I am content to forget all the ill past upon her promise to shun sutche companye as now the countree cryethe shame of, I thought good to advertise you of this beinge her best freinde, to the ende if sum of her friends will worke amendement in her by good perswation, I shall be glad hereof, and if upon returne of this messenger, I perceave not a likelihood, that som of them will doe som good indevour herein, I will geive over howse and remove my selfe from thence. Herefore I earnestlye intreate you, to be a meanes, to som well disposed freinde of yours, herein, and soe I leave you. Mannffilde this 11 of July 1600.

Your most unfortunate brother in lawe Mountagu Wood

It appears by an old writing that the mannor and Lordship of Lamly did belong to Sir Francis Willughby who left it to his Lady (after Lady Wharton) for her life; at her death [in 1621] it descended to the six Daughters as co=heirs of Sir Francis Willughby. The sixth part of that estate which fell to Brigit, who was Sir Percivall Willoughbys Lady, and Sir Francis Willughby's eldest Daughter her Son Edward sold; Henry Hastings sold his sixth part of the wood and wast grown [ground?] to John Wood. The Lord Spencer sold his sixth part to Edward Willoughby his Brother=in=law, which with his own sixth part went to Edward his Grandson. William Pargiter sold his sixth part, with the wood and wast grownd to severall persons.

Montiegue Wood Esquire and Frances his Wife conveyed [f. 195] their sixth part of this mannor and Lordship of Lamly to Francis Hacker Esquire and George Lacock Gentleman to the use of Henry Wood, Mary Wood, Abigail Wood, John Wood, Frances Wood, Elizabeth Wood and Edward Wood, the Children of Mountague and Francis [*sic*] Wood. This writing shews that Wilsey Wright, of Lamly, married Mary Wood, and purchased the parts of Henry Wood and John Wood, her Brothers and that Abigail Wood (since the Lady Darcy) conveyed her part to Elizabeth her Sister, who sold the same together with her own 6th part to Lawrence Palmer Clerk, and the wood and wast ground she sold to John Wood Esquire.

By this conveyence of the estate it appears that Francis [*sic*] Wood by Mountague Wood, her Husband, had three Sons and four

Daughters[492] and that the mannor and Lordship of Lamly was not the Woods estate, but the Willughbys, and his being called Wood of Lamly must be from his living upon that part of his Wives estate, and 'tis very probable his own estate was very small.

[f. 196] Having finished what account I could find (from the old papers in the Library at Wollaton) of Sir Francis Willughbys five younger Daughters, before I return to Sir Percivall Willoughby and his Lady, and their perplexed affairs, I think it will be proper here to set down what account I have been able to find of the Willoughbys of Willoughby and Eresby in Lincolnshire, that being the family from whence Sir Percivall Willoughby was descended.

1. The pedigree of the Willoughbys of Willoughby in Lincolnshire begins with William who was Lord of the mannor of Willoughby in

2. Lincolnshire, and by it, it appears that his Son was William and also his Grandson, and that this third William Willoughby was

3. the Father of Hugh and Robert

The first which Dugdale mentioned of this family was Ralph de Wileghby of Wileghby near Alford[493] in Lincolnshire, whose lands he says were seised for his adherence to the rebellious barons, about the end of King John's reign. But in the first of Henry the third making his peace he obtained the Kings precept to the Sherif of that County for the restitution of them. Dugdale makes this Ralph, to be the Father of Hugh and Robert and both he and the pedigree, agree that Hugh married one of the Daughters and coheirs of William de Cokerinton by Berta, his Wife, the Daughter and coheir of Lambert de Scotenai (a great man in Lincolnshire). Dugdale writes this Lady's name, Frethesend, but the pedigree spells her name Frideswold. This Lady brought to Hugh the inheritance of lands in Cumberworth, and Thorpe, and I believe something in Horn=Castle, because the pedigree calls him Willoughby of Horn=Castle.

---

[492] In the Lambley parish registers the following children are listed: John, son of Mountague Wood, generosus, bapt. 23 Sept. 1599; Elizabeth, dau. of Montague Wood, gener[osus], bapt. 10 July 1612; Edward, son of Mountague Wood, gener[osus], bapt. 10 October 1615; John, son of Mountague Wood gener[osus], buried [...] September 1599. Montague Wood was buried 6 Oct. 1635. T.M. Blagg (ed.), 'Extracts from the parish registers of Lambley and Woodborough, Notts.', *A Miscellany of Notts. Records*, TSRS, XI (Nottingham, 1945), 139.

[493] For the most part, Cassandra follows Dugdale's account. See Sir William Dugdale, *The Baronage of England* (London, 1675–1676), 82–83.

4. This Hugh left no Children, his Brother Robert married the second Daughter and coheir of John Oreby. Oreby's eldest Daughter married John de Somervill. It is very probable that this Somervill might be the Grandson of that Sir Gualtier de Somervile [f. 197] a Norman [d. 1036], that William the Conquerour gave the mannors of Barton and Whichnor in Staffordshire to. And tis likely that Alice the Daughter of Roger Somervill who married Edmund Willughby of Nottinghamshire, as the 2^d page of this book shews,[494] might be of the same family.

Hugh Willoughby dying without issue.

5. William the Son of Robert Willoughby by [blank] the Daughter of John Oreby became heir to both his Uncle and Father; and in the 44th year of Henry the 3^d, upon the death of Frideswold, the widow of Hugh Willoughby his uncle, had the lands of her inheritance. Dugdale gives this account of Robert the Father of this William Willoughby, that in the 48th year of Henry the 3^d he taking part with the rebellious barons, was so domineering in Yorkshire, that the Sherif of that County could not execute his office there for the King. William the Son of this Robert was in the 54th year of Henry the 3^d signed with the cross, together with many others who then accompanied Prince Edward to the Holy Land.

He married Alice the eldest Daughter and coheir of John Beck, Lord of Eresby in Lincolnshire. Her other Sister married Richard de Harecourt.

This William Willoughby by Alice his Wife had two Sons and a Daughter. Margaret his Daughter married Walter, the Son of Walter Licanby Knight. Thomas the eldest Son of William married Margaret [blank] but dyed without issue, which made Robert the second Son heir of the family.

There remains no further account of this William but that he dyed An: D: 1306.

6. Robert, Lord and Baron Willoughby of Eresby, in right of his Mother, who was the eldest Daughter and coheir of John Beck, Lord of Eresby. This Robert Willoughby in the 25th of Edward the first was in that expedition, then made into Gascoine, and in the 28th of Edward the first, he was in the Scotish wars. In the 33th of Edward the first he obtained a charter for free warren, in all his demesn=lands at Eresby and Willoughby in Lincolnshire. In the 34th of Edward the first, he was again in the wars of Scotland, and likewise in the fourth of Edward the second.

---

[494] Not included in this edition.

[f. 198] Upon the accession of lands which came to him by descent (upon the death of Anthony Beck, Bishop of Durham, who was the Brother of John Beck, his Mothers Father) he being before possessed of a very ample estate, and having been very servicable to the King in his wars with France and Scotland, Dugdale says he was then in the 7th year of the reign of Edward the second summoned to Parliament amongst the Barons of this Realm; he being at that time about forty years of age. Dugdale also says that he was again in armes, in the eighth of Edward the second, to restrain the incursions of [the?][lxxviii] Scots. He gives an account of very many Lordship[s][lxxix] that this Robert Willoughby was then possessed off [of], in th[e][lxxx] Counties of Lincoln, Northampton, and Derby, one of which was the mannor of Willoughby and part of Scryvelty in Lincolnshire, and that he shared with Edmund de Somervill the mannor of Oreby etc.

He married Margaret the Daughter of Edmund, Lord Deyncourt. There is no account of his having any Child besides John, his Son and heir. He dyed An: D: 1316.

His Wife survived him, and had for her dowrie an assignation of the mannor of Willoughby, with certain lands in Ulseby and Dierthrope, as also the mannor of Wyspington, and certain land[s] in Wythalle and Serquelby [?] Langton, Thymelby, Foletby, Levethon, Boston, and Braytoft, all in Lincolnshire.

Endnotes

[i] The word 'him' inserted with caret.
[ii] Corrected in the manuscript by overwriting see on she.
[iii] The original is smudged on the the second 'a' in 'appartaining'.
[iv] The word 'from' inserted via caret.
[v] The words 'such a' inserted via caret.
[vi] The misspelled word 'govening' corrected with letter 'r' placed above 'e^{r}n'.
[vii] In all instances, Cassandra spelled haste as 'hast'.
[viii] The words 'the copy of' inserted via caret.
[ix] Corrected to 1564 from 1464?
[x] The word 'then' is inserted via caret.
[xi] Cassandra wrote 'portion' twice and crossed out the second one.
[xii] 'be' inserted above the line with a caret.
[xiii] Corrected in the MS from Willughby to Willoughby by superscript, Will^{o}ughby.
[xiv] 'Willughby' in the MS, although it is probably Willoughby.
[xv] Original reads 'mind——For'. Cassandra often uses a long line in the middle of text, which seems to indicate a full stop.
[xvi] Cassandra wrote 'of the meanest sort of the meanest sort of servants' in the original MS.
[xvii] In the original, 'serving of ——' with no full stop.
[xviii] The manuscript is splotched right here and the word illegible; 'in' makes the most sense.
[xix] 'and suppers' is crossed out.

xx It is unclear in the original if this is a 6 or an 8, since a correction was made in the original. There is less ink indicating an 8.
xxi Beginning here, Cassandra drew a table instead of relying on dashes.
xxii The word 'to' inserted via caret.
xxiii No period or capitalization after closing parenthesis in original.
xxiv Although Cassandra uses a dash here, the meaning is more clearly a comma than a full stop.
xxv The word 'was' inserted by caret.
xxvi The word 'chiefly' inserted by caret.
xxvii The word "writ" inserted by caret.
xxviii Word "journey" begun on bottom of f. 105 as "jour=" and then restated as "journey" at the top of f. 106.
xxix The word 'y^t' inserted by caret.
xxx Blank with line in original.
xxxi The letter 'u' inserted by caret.
xxxii The word 'as' inserted by caret.
xxxiii The words 'dated June the 9th 1585' inserted by caret.
xxxiv Phrase in parentheses is marginalia inserted by caret at # mark.
xxxv The word 'from' inserted by caret. There is no punctuation before or after the word 'from,' and it is written in lower case.
xxxvi Crossed out in original.
xxxvii Crossed out in original.
xxxviii There is an unreadable word crossed out here.
xxxix The ending 'ing' added by caret.
xl 'in their' is inserted by caret.
xli 'had' inserted by caret.
xlii The words 'ye time' inserted by caret.
xliii Cassandra wrote the name twice: 'In which time J: Barrows+' and then turned the page ninety degrees counterclockwise and coninued in the margin '+J: Bartowes weding dinner …' In the *Derbyshire Parish Register, Marriages: Derbyshire XIII, Marriages at Morley, 1540–1837*, Vol. 1 (1540–1735) [which, according to the note accompanying the transcription, might be incomplete due to damage], a ley [lay] marriage is recorded in 1590 between 'Robert Burrowes and Annes Ardey.' On the same page, a marriage is recorded between 'Sir Henry Sacheverell, knt., & Dame Margery.'
xliv The words "tis probable' inserted by caret.
xlv The word 'y^e' inserted by caret.
xlvi The words 'she is' inserted by caret.
xlvii The words 'painted in' inserted by caret.
xlviii The word 'the' inserted by caret.
xlix The word 'security' inserted by caret.
l The word 'the' inserted by caret.
li Cassandra has used a hash mark '#' to indicate where items were to be inserted in the text. There is such a mark at the top of this folio but no corresponding place in the text.
lii The words 'the copy of' inserted by caret.
liii The word 'had' inserted by caret.
liv The underlining is in the original.
lv The word 'Lady' inserted by caret.
lvi There appears to be a word missing here.
lvii The word 'nothing' inserted by caret.
lviii Whmbrok in original.
lix The words 'be so bold as to' inserted by caret.

[lx] The word 'you' inserted by caret.
[lxi] The letters 'able' inserted by caret to complete the word unreason.
[lxii] Cassandra began the word and, on the next page, wrote the entire word.
[lxiii] The words and numerals 'May ye 15th' inserted by caret without full stop. The word 'in' that begins the following sentence is not capitalized in the original.
[lxiv] The word 'at' is inserted above the line.
[lxv] 'such' is written twice.
[lxvi] The word 'then' inserted by caret.
[lxvii] No closing parenthesis in original.
[lxviii] The word 'he'.
[lxix] Second 'a' inserted by caret.
[lxx] Another 'they could' crossed out.
[lxxi] The word 'the' inserted by caret.
[lxxii] Originally Cassandra seems to have written 'was'.
[lxxiii] The word 'Mother' inserted by caret.
[lxxiv] The sentence ends with a comma.
[lxxv] The words 'Sr Percivall Willoughby' inserted by caret.
[lxxvi] The words 'one may believe' inserted by caret.
[lxxvii] The word 'are' inserted by caret.
[lxxviii] The MS is damaged here. Dugdale has 'the'.
[lxxix] Damaged MS.
[lxxx] Damaged MS.

SELECT BIBLIOGRAPHY

Primary Sources

Manuscripts

British Library, London
    Lansdowne 46, 101, 12 and 49.
Folger Library, Washington DC, USA
    STC 10443
    X.d.428 (126).
Nottingham University Library, Nottingham
    Middleton Collection
        Mi 1–7   Papers of the Willoughby Family of Wollaton, Nottinghamshire, Middleton, Warwickshire and Birdsall, Yorkshire, including, title deeds, estate records, family papers, legal and manorial records; c.1175–1835
        A 31, 32   Medley Account books
        A 5, 42, 60/2, 69/1–2, 70
        A 57   Account Book
        Ac 49; C 8/2, 10, 11b, 14, 17, 18, 25, 29, 142/248/23; D 4804
        F 1/5, 6/5, 7, 10, 15; I 1/2, 5, 17/1/1, 36, 37; L 3/ 1 & 2
        LM 13   Memoirs and observations taken out of old muniments, genealogical material
        LM 26   Cassandra Willoughby, 'An Account of the Willughby's of Wollaton', referred to as the Account
        LM 27   Cassandra Willoughby, 'An Account of the Willughby's of Wollaton', 2
        LP 1–10; M 145/6; O 2, 16; X 2/5.
London Metropolitan Archives
    Parish Register for St Giles Cripplegate, London, covering 1596.
National Archives, Kew, London
    C   Chancery
            C 2 Eliz./F4/49
            C 2/Eliz/I1/20
            C 2/Eliz/Z1/12
            C 3/294/13
            C 781591.
    PROB   Probate registers
            Prob. 11.

Shakespeare Birthplace Trust Record Office, Stratford-upon-Avon
   DR18/20/21/1   Stoneleigh MSS, Gloucestershire Papers 20–21, Travel journals.
Huntington Library, San Marino, CA, USA
   Stowe Temple Brydges Collection, Boxes 1 and 2.

Published Primary Sources

Abstracts of the Inquisitiones Post Mortem and other Inquisitions relating to Nottinghamshire, II, ed. J. Standish, Thoroton Society Record Series (TSRS), 4 (Nottingham, 1914).
Acts of the Privy Council of England, New Series, ed. J.R. Dasent, 46 vols (London, 1890–1964).
An Inventory of the Historical Monuments in Dorset, IV: North (London, 1972).
Baker, Richard, *Chronicle of the Kings of England* (London, 1670).
Bess of Hardwick's Letters: The Complete Correspondence c.1550–1608, https://www.bessofhardwick.org/home.jsp
Blagg, T.M. (ed.), 'Extracts from the parish registers of Lambley and Woodborough, Notts.', in Blagg, T.M. (ed.), *A Miscellany of Notts. Records*, TSRS, XI (Nottingham, 1945), 135–146.
Boulton, Helen E. (ed.), *The Sherwood Forest Book*, TSRS, 23 (Nottingham, 1965).
Bowler, H. (ed.), *Recusant Roll No. 2 (1593–1594)*, Catholic Record Society, 57 (1965).
Boyd, Percival, https://www.findmypast.co.uk/articles/world-records/full-list-of-united-kingdom-records/life-events-bmds/boyds-marriage-index-1538-1840.
Calendar of Proceedings in Chancery in the reign of Queen Elizabeth, ed. J.W. Bayley, Vol. III (London, 1832).
Calendar of the Fine Rolls, Vol. XX: *Henry VII, 1485–1509* (London, 1962).
Calendar of the Patent Rolls preserved in the Public Record Office: Henry VII, 1485–1509, 2 vols (London, 1914–1916).
Calendar of the Patent Rolls preserved in the Public Record Office: Elizabeth, 1558–[1582], 9 vols (London, 1939–).
Camden, William, *The Visitation of the County of Warwick in the Year 1619: Taken by William Camden, Clarencieux King of Arms*, ed. John Fetherston (London, 1877).
Chandos, Cassandra, Duchess of, *The Continuation of the History of the Willoughby Family, being Vol. II of the Manuscript*, ed. A.C. Wood (Eton, 1958).
Collins, Francis (ed.), *Feet of Fines of the Tudor Period*, III: 1583–1594, Yorkshire Archaeological Society Record Series, VII (London, 1889).
Crisp, Frederick Arthur, *Registers of Shipbourne, Co. Kent* ([London?], 1921).
Dugdale, Sir William, *The Antiquities of Warwickshire* (London, 1656).
Dugdale, Sir William, *The Baronage of England* (London, 1675–1676).
Farrer, W., *Honors and Knights' Fees*, 3 vols (London and Manchester, 1923–1925).
Fetherston, John (ed.), *The Visitation of the County of Warwick in the Year 1619*, Harleian Society, 12 (London, 1877).
Foster, E R. (ed.), *Acts of Proceedings in Parliament 1610*, Vol. II (New Haven, CT, 1966).
Foster, Joseph, *Alumni Oxonienses: The Members of the University of Oxford, 1500–1714* (Oxford, 1891).
Fry, E.A. and G.S. Fry (eds), *Abstracts of Dorset Inquisitions Post Mortem at the Time of Charles I* (London, 1894).

Goldring, Elizabeth, Faith Eales, Elizabeth Clarke, Jayne Elizabeth Archer, Gabriel Heaton, and Sarah Knight (eds), *John Nichols's The Progresses and Public Processions of Queen Elizabeth I: A New Edition of the Early Modern Sources*, Vol. I (Oxford, 2014).

Hakluyt, Richard, *The Principall Navigations, Voyages, Traffiques, and Discoveries of the English Nation*, ed. Edmund Goldschmid, Vol. III, Pt 2 (Edinburgh, 1886).

Howell, Esq., James, *A French and English Dictionary Composed by Mr Randle Cotgrave and another in French and English* (London, 1673).

Leadam, I.S. (ed.), *The Domesday of Inclosures for Nottinghamshire, from the returns to the Inclosure Commissioners of 1517 in the Public Record Office*, TSRS, 2 (Nottingham, 1904).

Marshall, George (ed.), *The Visitations of the County of Nottingham in the Years 1569 and 1614*, Harleian Society, 4 (London, 1871).

Meyrick, Sir Samuel Rush (ed.), *The Heraldic Visitations of Wales and Part of the Marches between the Years 1586 and 1613, under the Authority of Clarencieux and Norry*, Vol. I (London, 1846).

Munk, William (ed.), *The Roll of the Royal College of Physicians of London* (London, 1878).

Nichols, John, *The Progresses and Public Processions of Queen Elizabeth* (London, 1823).

North Country Wills: Being Abstracts of Wills Relating to York, Nottingham, Northumberland, Cumberland, and Westmoreland, 1383 to 1558, Vol. I, Surtees Society 116 (London and Durham, 1908).

O'Day, Rosemary (ed.), *Cassandra Brydges (1670–1735), First Duchess of Chandos: Life and Letters* (Woodbridge, 2007).

Phillimore, W.P.W. and T.M. Blagg (eds), *Nottinghamshire Parish Registers: Marriages*, Vol. VIII (London, 1905).

Quaritch, B., *Introduction to Select Cases in the Court of Requests, 1497–1569* (London, 1898).

Ray, John, *A Complete Collection of English Proverbs* (1768; rev. edn, London, 1813).

Seddon, P.R. (ed.), *Letters of John Holles, 1587–1637*, Vol. I, TSRS, 31 (Nottingham, 1975).

Stevenson, W.H. (ed.), *Historical Manuscripts Commission Report on the Manuscripts of Lord Middleton* (London, 1911).

Stretton, Tim (ed.), *Marital Litigation in the Court of Requests 1542–1642*, Royal Historical Society, Camden 5th Series, 32 (Cambridge, 2008).

Testamenta Eboracensia, or, Wills Registered at York, Vol. VI, Surtees Society, 106 (Durham, 1902).

The good Huswifes Handmaide for the Kitchin (London, 1595).

Thoroton, Robert, *The Antiquities of Nottinghamshire* (London, 1677); ed. and repr. with large additions by John Thoresby as Thoroton's History of Nottinghamshire, 3 vols (Nottingham, 1790).

Welch, Mary A. (ed.), 'Willoughby letters of the first half of the sixteenth century', *TTS*, 24 (1967), 1–98.

Willoughby, Sir Francis, *The Lute Book of Francis Willoughby, c.1575*, facs. edn (Kilkenny, 1978).

Wood, A.C. (ed.), *The Continuation of the History of the Willoughby Family by Cassandra, Duchess of Chandos, being Vol. II of the Manuscript* (Eton, 1958).

Secondary Sources

Published Secondary Sources

Adams, Simon, *Leicester and the Court: Essays on Elizabethan Politics* (Manchester, 2002).
Airs, Malcolm, *The Tudor and Jacobean Country House: A Building History* (Stroud, 1995).
Akrigg, G.P.V., *Shakespeare and the Earl of Southampton* (Cambridge, MA, 1968).
Baddeley, John James, *The Aldermen of Cripplegate Ward from A.D. 1276 to A.D. 1900, together with some account of the office of Alderman, Alderman's Deputy, and Common Councilman of the City of London* (1900; London, 2016).
Baker, John, *The Oxford History of the Laws of England, VI 1483–1558* (Oxford, 2003).
Baldwin, T.W., *William Shakespeare's Small Latine and Lesse Greeke* (Urbana, IL, 1944).
Barnes, Patricia M. & C.F. Slade (eds), *A Medieval Miscellany for Doris Mary Stenton*, Pipe Roll Society, NS 36 (London, 1962).
Bearman, Peter S., *Relations into Rhetoric: Local Elite Social Structure in Norfolk, 1540–1640*, (Rutgers, NJ, 1993).
Bell, Henry Nugent, *The Huntingdon Peerage* (London, 1821).
Bindoff, S.T., *A History of Parliament: The House of Commons, 1509–1558*, Vol. II (London, 1982).
Birkhead, Tim (ed.), *Virtuoso by Nature: The Scientific Worlds of Francis Willughby, FRS (1635–1672)* (Leiden, 2016).
Bridenbaugh, Carl, *Vexed and Troubled Englishmen, 1580–1642* (Oxford, 1968).
Bridgeman, George Fanshaw (ed.), *Memorials of a Warwickshire Family* (London, 1906).
Briscoe, J. Potter, *Bypaths of Nottinghamshire History* (Nottingham, 1905).
Brown, Carleton, *Poems by Sir John Salusbury and Robert Chester* (Bryn Mawr, 1913).
Bryson, Alan, 'Order and disorder: John Proctor's history of Wyatt's Rebellion (1554)', in Mike Pincombe and Cathy Shrank (eds), *The Oxford Handbook of Tudor Literature: 1485–1603* (Oxford, 2009), 323–336.
Cameron, Alan, 'Sir Henry Willoughby of Wollaton', *TTS*, 74 (1970), 10–21.
Cameron, Alan, 'Some social consequences of the dissolution of the monasteries in Nottinghamshire', *TTS*, 79 (1975), 50–59.
Chalfant, Fran C., *Ben Jonson's London: A Jacobean Placename Dictionary* (Atlanta, GA, 2008).
Chambers, E.K., *The Elizabethan Stage*, Vol. II (Oxford, 1923).
Charmantier, Isabelle, Dorothy Johnston, and Paul J. Smith, 'The legacies of Francis Willughby', in Tim Birkhead (ed.), *Virtuoso by Nature: The Scientific Worlds of Francis Willughby, FRS (1635–1672)* (Leiden, 2016), 360–385.
Cioni, Maria, *Women and Law in Elizabethan England with Particular Reference to the Court of Chancery* (New York, 1985).
Cobbing, Beryl and Pamela Priestland, *Sir Thomas Stanhope of Shelford: Local Life in Elizabethan Times* (Radcliffe-on-Trent, 2003).
Cole, Mary Hill, *The Portable Queen: Elizabeth I and the Politics of Ceremony* (Amherst, MA, 1999).
Cook, Ann Jennalie, *Making a Match: Courtship in Shakespeare and his Society* (Princeton, NJ, 1991)
Cooke, W.G., 'Queen Elizabeth never slept here: Cassandra, Duchess of Chandos as an authority for royal progresses', *REED [Records of Early English Drama] Newsletter*, 14:1 (1989), 18–20.

Cooper, J.P., 'Patterns of inheritance and settlement by great landowners from the 15th to the 18th centuries', in J. Goody, J. Thirsk, and E.P. Thompson (eds), *Family and Inheritance: Rural Society in Western Europe, 1200–1800* (Cambridge, 1976), 192–327.
Cressy, David, *Dangerous Talk: Scandalous, Seditious, and Treasonable Speech in Pre-Modern England* (Oxford, 2014).
Crisp, Frederick Arthur (ed.), *Visitation of England and Wales*, Vol. IX (London, 1911).
Cross, Claire, *The Puritan Earl: The Life of Henry Hastings, Third Earl of Huntingdon* (London, 1966).
Curry, Patrick, *Prophecy and Power: Astrology in Early Modern England* (Princeton, NJ, 1989).
Dawson, Giles E., 'Problems in editing sixteenth- and seventeenth-century letters', in Dale B.J. Randall (ed.), *Medieval and Renaissance Studies: Proceedings of the Southeastern Institute of Medieval and Renaissance Studies (1974)* (Durham, NC, 1976), 87–103.
Daybell, James, *Women Letter-Writers in Tudor England* (Oxford, 2006).
Daybell, James and Gordon, Andrew (eds), *Cultures of Correspondence in Early Modern Britain* (Philadelphia, PA, 2016).
Doyle, James William Edmund, *The Official Baronage of England* (London, 1886).
Dunham, W.H., *Lord Hastings' Indentured Retainers, 1461–1483* (New Haven, CT, 1955).
Enis, Cathryn, 'The Dudleys, Sir Christopher Hatton and the justices of Elizabethan Warwickshire', *Midland History*, 39 (2014), 1–35.
Erickson, Amy Louise, *Women and Property in Early Modern England* (London and New York, 1993).
Erickson, Amy, 'Mistresses and marriage, or a short history of Mrs.', *History Workshop Journal*, 78 (2014), 39–57.
Farrer, William and J. Brownbill (eds), *A History of the County of Lancaster: IV*, VCH (London, 1911).
Finch, M.E., *The Wealth of Five Northamptonshire Families, 1540–1640*, Northamptonshire Record Society, XIX (1956).
Fletcher, Anthony and Diarmaid MacCulloch, *Tudor Rebellions*, 6th edn (London, 2016).
Friedman, Alice T., *House and Household in Elizabethan England: Wollaton Hall and the Willoughby Family* (Chicago, 1989).
Friedman, Alice, 'Portrait of a marriage: The Willoughby letters of 1585–1586', *Signs*, 11 (1986), 542–553.
Gibson, Marion, *Possession, Puritanism and Print: Darrell, Harsnett, Shakespeare and the Elizabethan Exorcism Controversy* (New York, 2015).
Girouard, Mark, *Life in an English Country House* (New Haven, CT, 1978).
Girouard, Mark, *Robert Smythson and the Architecture of the Elizabethan Era* (London, 1966).
Godfrey, John T. (ed.), *Notes on the Parish Registers of St. Mary's Nottingham, 1566 to 1812* (Nottingham, 1901).
Godfrey, John Thomas, *The Court and the Honour of Peverel: In the Counties of Nottingham and Derby* (Nottingham, 1882).
Goodrick, Alfred Thomas [Scrope], 'The original Marmion', *Blackwood's Magazine*, 193 (March 1913), 390–399.
Gordon, Eleanora C., 'The fate of Sir Hugh Willoughby and his companions: A new conjecture', *The Geographical Journal*, 152 (July 1986), 243–247.

Gowing, Laura, review of Bernard Capp, *When Gossips Meet: Women, Family and Neighbourhood in Early Modern England* (Oxford, 2003), in Reviews in History, Institute of Historical Research (November 2003), http://www.history.ac.uk/reviews/review/365.

Gray, H.L., 'Incomes from land in England in 1436', *English Historical Review*, 49 (1934), 607–639.

Greaves, Richard, *Society and Religion in Elizabethan England* (Minneapolis, MN, 1981).

Green, Ian, *Humanism and Protestantism in Early Modern English Education* (Farnham, 2009).

Griffiths, Paul and Simon Devereaux (eds), *Penal Practice and Culture, 1500–1900: Punishing the English* (London, 2004).

Guy, John, *Elizabeth: The Forgotten Years* (New York, 2016).

Hanna, Ralph and Thorlac Turville-Petre (eds), *The Wollaton Medieval Manuscripts: Texts, Owners and Readers* (York, 2010).

Harris, Barbara J., *English Aristocratic Women, 1450–1550* (Oxford, 2002).

Hasler, P.W. (ed.), *The History of Parliament: The House of Commons 1558–1603* (London, 1981).

Hasted, Edward, *The History and Topographical Survey of the County of Kent*, Vol. VIII (Canterbury, 1799).

Hembry, Phyllis May, *The English Spa 1560–1815: A Social History* (London, 1990).

Hinckle, William G., *A History of Bridewell Prison, 1553–1700* (London, 2006).

Hobson, J.H., 'The Wollaton Estate and the Civil War, 1643–1647' in J.H. Hobson, P.A. Kennedy, and V.W. Walker (eds), *A Nottinghamshire Miscellany*, TSRS, 21 (Nottingham, 1962), 3–15.

Hodson, J.H., 'The first Wollaton Hall', *TTS*, 72 (1968), 59–67.

Innes, Joanna, 'Prisons for the poor: English Bridewells, 1555–1800', in F. Snyder and D. Hay (eds), *Labour, Law and Crime: An Historical Perspective* (London, 1987), 42–122.

Ives, Eric, *Lady Jane Grey: A Tudor Mystery* (London, 2011).

Johnson, Joan, *Excellent Cassandra: The Life and Times of the Duchess of Chandos* (Gloucester, 1981).

Johnston, Alexandra F., 'Sir Francis Knollys and his progeny: Court and country in the Thames valley', in Norman J. Jones and Daniel Woolf (eds), *Local Identities in Late Medieval and Early Modern England* (New York, 2007).

Johnston, Dorothy, 'The life and domestic context of Francis Willughby', in Tim Birkhead (ed.), *Virtuoso by Nature: The Scientific Worlds of Francis Willughby, FRS (1635–1572)*, (Leiden, 2016), 1–43.

Jones, Norman, *The Birth of the Elizabethan Age: England in the 1560s* (Oxford, 1993).

Jones, Norman, *Governing by Virtue: Lord Burghley and the Management of Elizabethan England* (Oxford, 2015).

Jones, Norman J. and Daniel Woolf (eds), *Local Identities in Late Medieval and Early Modern England* (New York, 2007).

Kenneth Charlton, *Education in Renaissance England* (London, 1965).

Kerry, Charles, 'Notes to the pedigree of the Strelleys of Strelley, Oakerthorpe and Hazlebach', *Journal of the Derbyshire Archaeological and Natural History Society*, 14 (1892), 92–118.

Kilbourne, Payne Kenyon, *The History and Antiquities of the Name and Family of Kilbourn (in its Varied Orthography)* (New Haven, CT, 1846).

Kinney, Arthur F. and Jane A. Lawson (eds), *Titled Elizabethans: A Directory of Elizabethan State and Church Officers and Knights, with Peers of England, Scotland, and Ireland, 1558–1603*, expanded edn (New York, 2014).

Lancashire, Ian, *Dramatic Texts and Records of Britain: A Chronological Topography to 1558* (Cambridge, 1984).

Land, Stephen K., *Kett's Rebellion: The Norfolk Rising of 1549* (Ipswich, 1977).

Langham, Mike and Colin Wells, *The Baths at Buxton Spa* (Leek, 2005).

Lee, J.M. and R.A. McKinley (eds), *A History of the County of Leicester: V*, VCH (London, 1964).

Levin, Carole, *Propaganda in the English Reformation: Heroic and Villainous Images of King John* (Lewiston, NY, 1988).

Levin, Carole, *The Heart and Stomach of a King: Elizabeth I and the Politics of Sex and Power* (Philadelphia, PA, 1994).

Lisle, Leanda de, *The Sisters Who Would Be Queen: Mary, Katherine, and Lady Jane Grey* (New York, 2008).

Loades, D.M., *Two Tudor Conspiracies* (Cambridge, 1965).

MacCaffrey, Wallace, 'Talbot and Stanhope: An episode in Elizabethan politics', *The Bulletin of the Institute of Historical Research*, 33 (1960), 73–85.

Macfarlane, Alan, *Marriage and Love in England: Modes of Reproduction, 1300–1840* (Oxford, 1986).

Mack, Peter, *Elizabethan Rhetoric: Theory and Practice* (Cambridge, 2002).

Malden, H.E. (ed.), *County History of Surrey: III*, VCH (London, 1911).

Markham, David Frederick, *A History of the Markham Family* (London, 1954).

Marshall, Pamela, *Wollaton Hall and the Willoughby Family* (Nottingham, 1999).

Mayhew, N.J., 'Population, money supply and the velocity of circulation in England, 1300–1700', *Economic History Review*, 2nd ser., 48 (1995), 238–257.

Moran, J.H., *The Growth of English Schooling, 1350–1540* (Princeton, NJ, 1985).

Morey, Adrian, *The Catholic Subjects of Elizabeth I* (London and Boston, and Totowa, NJ, 1978).

Morris, A.J.H., *The Quatercentenary of Sir Walter Raleigh's Trial* (Brisbane, 2003).

Morris, Norval, and David J. Rothman, *The Oxford History of the Prison: The Practice of Punishment in Western Society* (Oxford, 1998).

Nicholls, Mark, 'Treason's reward: The punishment of conspirators in the Bye Plot of 1603', *The Historical Journal*, 38 (1995), 821–842.

O'Callaghan, Michelle, ' "An Uncivill Scurrilous Letter", "Womanish Brabb[l]es", and the Letter of Affront', in James Daybell and Andrew Gordon (eds), *Cultures of Correspondence in Early Modern Britain* (Philadelphia, PA, 2016), 169–185.

O'Day, Rosemary, 'Family galleries: Women and art in the seventeenth and eighteenth centuries', *Huntington Library Quarterly*, 71 (2008), 323–349.

O'Day, Rosemary, *Women's Agency in Early Modern Britain and the American Colonies* (Abingdon, 2007).

O'Hara, Diana, *Courtship and Constraint: Rethinking the Making of Marriage in Tudor England* (Manchester, 2000).

Orange, James *History and Antiquities of Nottingham*, Vol. II (Nottingham, 1840).

Orme, Nicholas, *English Schools in the Middle Ages* (London, 1973).

Owen, H.G., 'A nursery of Elizabethan nonconformity, 1567–1572', *Journal of Ecclesiastical History*, 17 (1966), 65–76.

Page, William and J. Horace Round (eds), *A History of the County of Essex: II*, VCH (London, 1907).

Palliser, D.M., *The Age of Elizabeth: England under the Later Tudors 1547–1603*, 2nd edn (New York, 1992).

Payling, Simon, *Political Society in Lancastrian England: The Greater Gentry of Nottinghamshire* (Oxford, 1991).

Peck, D.C., 'The earl of Leicester and the riot at Drayton Park, 1578', *Notes and Queries*, NS 27 (April 1980), 131–135.

Pelham, R.A., 'The establishment of the Willoughby ironworks in north Warwickshire in the sixteenth century', *University of Birmingham Historical Journal*, 4 (1953–1954), 18–29.

Pevsner, Nikolaus, 'Double profile: A reconsideration of the Elizabethan style as seen at Wollaton', *The Architectural Review*, 107 (1950), 147–158.

Poole, William, 'The Willughby Library at the time of Francis the Naturalist', in Tim Birkhead (ed.), *Virtuoso by Nature: The Scientific Worlds of Francis Willughby, FRS (1635–1672)* (Leiden, 2016), 227–243.

Questier, Michael C., *Catholicism and Community in Early Modern England: Politics, Aristocratic Patronage and Religion, c.1550–1640* (Cambridge, 2006).

Reaney, P.H. and R.M. Wilson, *A Dictionary of English Surnames* (London, 1991).

Salisbury, Edward Eldridge and Evelyn McCurdy Salisbury, *Family Histories and Genealogies*, Vol. 1, Pt 2 (New Haven, CT, 1892).

Salzman, L.F. (ed.), *A History of the County of Warwick: IV*, VCH (London, 1947).

Scott, S.D., '"A booke of orders and rules" of Anthony Viscount Montague in 1595', *Sussex Archaeological Collections*, 7 (1854), 173–212.

Sim, Alison, *Masters and Servants in Tudor England* (Stroud, 2006).

Skillington, S.H., 'Medieval Cossington', *Transactions of the Leicestershire Archaeological and Historical Society*, 19 (1936–1937), 275–292.

Smith, Richard S., 'A woad growing project at Wollaton in the 1580s', *TTS*, 65 (1961), 27–46.

Smith, Richard S., *Early Coal-Mining around Nottingham 1500–1650* (Nottingham, 1989).

Smith, Richard S., 'Huntington Beaumont: Adventurer in coal mines', *Renaissance and Modern Studies*, 1 (1957), 115–153.

Smith, Richard S., *Sir Francis Willoughby of Wollaton Hall* (Nottingham, 1988).

Smith, Richard S., 'Sir Francis Willoughby's ironworks, 1570–1610', *Renaissance and Modern Studies*, 11 (1967), 90–140.

Snook, Edith, *Women, Beauty and Power in Early Modern England: A Feminist Literary History* (London, 2011).

Southworth, John, *Fools and Jesters at the English Court* (Stroud, 1998).

Stephens, W.B. (ed.), *A History of the County of Warwick: VII*, VCH (London, 1964).

Stone, Lawrence, *The Crisis of the Aristocracy, 1558–1641* (Oxford, 1967).

Stretton, Tim, *Women Waging Law in Elizabethan England* (Cambridge, 1998).

Stretton, Tim and Krista J. Kesselring (eds), *Married Women and the Law: Coverture in England and the Common Law World* (London, 2013), 163–191.

Taylor Jr, James D., *Sir Thomas Wyatt the Younger, c.1521–1554, and Wyatt's Rebellion* (New York, 2013).

Thomason, Laura E., *The Matrimonial Trap* (Lewisburg, PA, 2014).

Thrush, Andrew and John P. Ferris (eds), *The History of Parliament: The House of Commons 1604–1629* (Cambridge, 2010).

Tighe, W.J., 'A Nottinghamshire gentleman in court and country: The career of Thomas Markham of Ollerton (1530–1607)', *TTS*, 90 (1986), 30–45.
Tittler, Robert, *Nicholas Bacon: The Making of a Tudor Statesman* (Athens, OH, 1976).
Todd, Barbara J., 'Written in her heart: Married women's separate allegiance in English law', in Tim Stretton and Krista J. Kesselring (eds), *Married Women and the Law: Coverture in England and the Common Law World* (London, 2013), 163–191.
Tomlinson, Edward Murray, *History of the Minories* (1907; London, 2014).
Venn, John, *The Biographical History of Gonville and Caius College 1349–1897*, Vol. I (Cambridge, 1897).
Vines, Alice Gilmore, *Neither Fire nor Steel: Sir Christopher Hatton* (Chicago, 1978).
Walker, J. Holland, 'An itinerary of Nottingham', *TTS*, 39 (1935), 1–20.
Walsham, Alexandra, *The Reformation of the Landscape* (Oxford, 2011).
Whittle, Jane, 'Lords and tenants in Kett's Rebellion 1549', *Past & Present*, 207 (2010), 3–52.
Williams, Elijah, *Early Holborn and the Legal Quarter of London*, Vol. I (London, 1927).
Wood, Andy, *The 1549 Rebellions and the Making of Early Modern England* (Cambridge, 2007).
Wood, Thomas, *An Institute of the Laws of England*, 4th edn (London, 1724).

Unpublished Secondary Sources

Bloom, Michael R., 'The careers of Sir Richard II de Wiloughby and Sir Richard III de Willoughby, chief justice of the king's bench (1338–1340); and the rise of the Willoughbys of Nottinghamshire', DPhil thesis, University of Oxford, 1985.
Goldsmith, Joan Greenbaum, 'All the queen's women: The changing place and perception of aristocratic women in Elizabethan England, 1558–1620', PhD thesis, Northwestern University, 1987.
Hayden, John Kelly, 'Sir Francis Willoughby of Wollaton, 1547–1596', PhD thesis, University of Virginia, 1991.
Holder, Nick, 'The medieval friaries of London: A topographic and archaeological history, before and after the dissolution', PhD thesis, University of London, 2011.
House, A.P., 'The city of London and the problem of the liberties, c.1540–c.1640', DPhil thesis, University of Oxford, 2006.
Rossell, P.E., 'The building of Wollaton Hall, 1580–1588', 2 vols, MA thesis, University of Sheffield, 1957.
Smith, Richard S., 'The Willoughbys of Wollaton 1500–1643 with special reference to early mining in Nottinghamshire, 1500–1643', PhD thesis, University of Nottingham, 1964.
Smith, Robert Frederick William, 'John Trussell: A life (1575–1648)', PhD thesis, University of Southampton, 2013.
Tonks, J.M.J., 'The Lyttletons of Frankley', MLitt thesis, University of Oxford, 1978.

INDEX

abuse: *by husbands* 11, 18–19, 40, 45, 47, 56–57, 59, 62, 211, 245, 251; Montague Wood 18–19, 215, 251; by Elizabeth Willoughby 57, 174–175, 181n, 240, 249–250; by father 194; *suffered by*: Frediswith Willoughby Adams 19, 153n; Dorothy Willoughby Hastings 204–220; Juliana Stanhope Hotham 103n
Adams, Frediswith (Phridelwide/Frediswide), née Willoughby (b. *c*.1575) 19, 153n
Adams, John (b.1560) 14, 15n, 47n, 153, 171, 172n, 173n, 195
adultery (infidelity) 16, 46–47, 55n, 57n, 125, 140n, 158; alleged of women 59, 105, 120, 158
Agard, William of Bromley Regis, Staffs. (*c*.1585) 190
agates (aggetts) 192
Aldridge, Robert, rector of Wollaton (d.1616) 131
Aleppo, Syria, consul of 248
alimony 46n; *see also* maintenance
alms, almes, almsgiving 24, 41, 112
alternative spellings of family names: Danet 75n; Goodere/Goodrich 148n, 191n; Littleton 86n and *passim*; Willoughby 4n, 22, 116–117 and *passim*
Althorp, manor of, Notts. 236
America, North 4n, 51, 101n, 250n
Ancaster, Lancs. quarry 164
Anderson, Sir Richard 236
apothecary (druggist/drugster) 244, 249
arms and armour 80, 82, 116, 124, 155n, 232, 256
Arundell, Margaret, *see* Willoughby, Margaret, Lady Arundell
Arundell, Mary née Wriothesley 138n
Arundell, Sir Matthew 32n, 37, 38–39, 53, 55n, 80, 88, 92–95, 99
Arundell, Sir Thomas, of Wardour Castle (*c*.1502–1552) 88n, 95n
Arundell, Thomas, 1st Baron Arundell of Wardour (*c*.1560–1639) 138n

Arundell, William (d.1591) 139
Aspley Hall, formerly Lenton Priory (monastic house) 26, 98n
assizes 241, 252
Assurance, the, written agreement between Sir Francis and Sir Percival Willoughby 7, 183
astrology 146
astronomy 31n, 103
Atkinson, John (physician) 193–194
Atkinson, William, apostate priest and spy 197n

Bacon, Francis, lord chancellor (1561–1626) 100n; bribery of 50, 185n, 199
Bacon, Sir Nicholas, lord keeper (1510–1579) 100n, 131n
Bacon, Richard 171
Baker, Richard (*c*.1670) 21, 68, 137–138, 169, 176n
baptism 16, 46n, 103n, 122n, 153n, 158n; children in parish registers 10n, 231n, 254n
Barnard, Emma 4
Barons' revolt of 1264–1267 12n, 20
Barton Stacy, manor of, Hants. 244–245
Barwyke (Berwyke), Gabriel (executor) 28, 32, 51, 69–71, 80, 88n
bath, *see* spa
Baynham, Sir George 165n
beacons, firing of 170
Beardmore, Joahn 125; *see also* Joahn/Johan
Beaumont, Huntingdon (*c*.1560–1624) 124, 129
Beaumont, Nicholas 124n, 139n
believability of Cassandra's Account 10–21
Belvoir Castle 162
Berkswell, Warks. 45, 120n, 128n
Bestwood Park 227
betrothal, *see* troth, proposal, marriage settlements
biliment 246n
Birdsall House 22n
Bloxworth, Dorset 138n

INDEX

Blyth, servant 141–142, 155
board, costs of 13, 28–32, 36, 71, 74–79, 82–85, 92, 96n, 100, 100, 129, 168–169, 248; at school or university 13, 28, 30–32, 77–78, 84; boarding at Frankley 36, 94, 96n; boarding at Wollaton 248; *see also* education, Minories, Tilty, travel, wages, Bridget Willoughby's wedding
Boleyn, Anne 88n, 182
Boleyn, Mary 32, 137n
books and reading (not account books) 7–8, 30, 31, 42, 50–52, 92, 105, 117n, 119, 121, 141, 202, 242; *see also* literacy
Bore Place, Kent 4n, 106n, 116n, 136, 140n, 141, 144, 148, 153, 173, 195, 102n, 238n; stripping of by Mary Weston 195, 241
Boughton, Edward (*c.*1545–1628) 122–123
Boughton, Elizabeth, née Catesby 122n
Bradgate House, Leics. 26–28, 70
Brereton Hall, Cheshire 213
Brereton, William, 1st Baron Brereton (1550–1631) 213
Brickhill, Bucks. 140
Bricknell, Luce (Lucy) 233
Bridewell 99n, 100n; bridewells (eponym) 14–15 100–101, 172
Bromley, Thomas, lord chancellor (1530–1587) 131n
Brydges, Cassandra Willoughby, duchess of Chandos: Account *passim*, accuracy of transcription 10–16, as transcriber and editor 3–23; biographical background 4–5; concerns regarding women 19; disregarded as an author 20; draws conclusions 16–19; interests 6–7, 19–20; letter writing 193n, 218; many roles of 5–16; obedience 17; requesting information 193n; self-effacing 9
Brydges, Henrietta 68n
Brydges, James, duke of Chandos 8–9, 69n, 193n
Brydges, Sir John 76n
Bugge, Ralph (d. *c.*1250) 22–23
Bugge, Richard 22–23
Burghley, William Cecil, Lord (1520–1598), lord high treasurer 15, 43, 46, 48, 57n, 104n, 156n, 171n, 198–199, 202n
butler and under butler (household offices) 110–113
buttery 112–114
Buxton: spa also waters, baths at Buxton: 43, 96n, 107–109, 117

Bye Plot (Watson's Plot) and Main Plot, *see* conspiracies

cabal of servants 41, 101–102, 105, 150, 156
cabinet of specimens 7
Caius College, Cambridge 55, 221–227
Calvinism 3, 55
Cambridge 28–29, 72, 75n, 135n
Cambridge, University of 28n, 32, 55, 107n, 135n
Camden, William 20, 215n
Caine's Farm (Cane, manor of), Dorset 210–211
Cannons, Middx, built by the duke of Chandos 193n
Canon (Chanon) Row, London 132
capitalism, early, *see* enclosures, tree cutting, money, South Sea Company, wages
Carey, Harry, 1st Baron Hunsdon 138n
Carey, Mary, *see* Mary Boleyn
Carlton (estate) 194
Carrolton (estate) 194
Castle, the, inn in Holborn 37n, 73n, 84; *see also* Holborn
Catcher, John (d.1638), alderman 14, 17, 172–174
Catesby, Anne, née Throckmorton 103n
Catesby, Elizabeth 101n, 122n
Catesby, Sir Richard (d.1553/4) 101n, 105n
Catesby, Robert 101n
Catesby family 54, 105n
Catesby, servant 101–102, 105, 129
Catesby, Sir William 93n, 101n, 105n
Catholics 3, 24, 26, 38, 52n, 53–55, 72n, 80n, 87n, 88n, 96n, 97n, 101n, 107n, 138n, 142n, 221n, 230–231; investigation of 118n; Henry Willoughby (1451–1528) 26; Sir John Willoughby 25–26; *see also* recusants
Cecil, Robert, 1st earl of Salisbury 197n, 221n
Cecil, William, 1st Baron Burghley, lord high treasurer (1520–1598), *see* Burghley
chancery court (equity court) 44n, 49, 124n, 134n, 149n, 181n, 184n, 191, 196, 198n, 201n, 202n, 213n, 219n, 250n
Chantry, the 24; location 168–169, 175–176, 177
chapman (occupation) 179
Charleton, Elizabeth 165n
Child, Sir Josiah 4

INDEX

childbearing and childbirth 15n, 17–18, 40, 45, 46, 49, 87n, 97, 106, 127–128, 130, 136, 169n, 174, 177–178, 185n, 193–194, 198, 204, 219–220, 242; *see also* pregnancy

childbearing age 136

childhood, Willoughby orphans 3, 27–33, 68–87, 89

Christmas 100, 120–121, 168, 173, 202n, 215, 234

Church of England 3, 88n, 97n, 115; *see also* Protestant Reformation

church attendance/management 19n, 57, 116n, 131n, 153n, 198n, 219, 245; non-attendance 53; *see also* recusancy

churches 24, 27, 69, 126n, 131, 163–164

Clare Hall, Nottingham 166n; *see also* Thurland Hall

Clifton, Sir Gervase (1516–1588) 153n

Clifton, Sir Gervase, 1st Bt (1587/8–1666) 164n

Clifton, Winifred (m. 1565) 165

Clinton, Edward Fiennes de, 1st earl of Lincoln (1512–1584/5) 96n, 137n, 145n

clothing 13, 28, 70, 79, 85, 88 107, 109, 127, 129, 141, 167n, 173n, 182, 192–193, 238; *see also* fashion

Cludd, J., servant 124–126, 149–151, 155, 181, 183–184, 186, 188–189, 205; plot to kidnap and marry away Bridget Willoughby 188–189, 205; *see also* Fisher, Bridget Willoughby

co-heirs/heiresses 26, 205, 253

coal (cole) 14, 21, 23, 25–26, 36, 41, 50n, 80, 81n, 86, 87n, 96n, 98n, 103n, 124, 138n, 139, 141–142, 202n; metaphor 143; traded for stone 164

coin, shortage of; debasement of 69n, 172n; coins 139; *see also* currency

Cokayne, Sir Thomas of Ashburn, Derbys. (1520–1592) 118

Coke, James, servant 115

Colby/Coleby, Thomas 49n, 184, 185n, 193

Coleorton (Collarton), Leics. 124, 131

Commission of Peace 100–101

common law 44n, 45n, 198n; and allegiance to the monarch 123

Conquest, the 12n

Conrados, Francis (servant to Sir Percival Willoughby) 149–155, 230n

conscience 133, 154, 159–160, 232

conspiracies to bring Lady Jane Grey to the throne (1553) 23, 29–30, 69n, 73–74, 167n; Wyatt's Rebellion (1554) 29–30, 72n, 74n, 75n, 76n, 77n, 82n, 96n; Bye Plot (Watson's Plot) (1603) 55n, 56n, 221n; and Main Plot 55n; Gunpowder Plot (1605) 38n, 54, 90n, 101n

Conway (Conuay), Elene, née Greville, (1545–1590) 192n

Conway (Conuay), Sir John (1535–1603) 192n

Cossall, Notts. 23, 49, 82n, 98–99, 100n, 178–180, 183, 196, 198n, 200, 247

court of Elizabeth I 2, 32–33, 37, 47, 53, 82n, 88n, 91–97, 99, 106n, 130, 133, 135–137, 163, 169; at Tybballs (Theobalds?) 234; at Hampton Court 138, 139, 169; at Kenilworth 93–94; York 97; *see also* Elizabeth I, progresses

court of Edward VI 72

court of Mary I 33, 47, 53, 72, 77n, 79–80, 82n, 46n

court of requests (equity court) 45n, 133n

court of Peverell (Peveril, Derbys.) 83n

courtesy (curtisie) 70n, 146, 186, 190, 224–228, 239

courtship 35n, 36–38, 48, 184, 205–208, 220–235, 237–241

Coventry, Warks. 24n, 25, 45, 110, 120–121, 125–128, 150; Carmelite order at 24n; mayor of 45, 126–128

Cranewell, Isley 184

credit/discredit 12n, 15n, 59–62, 105, 107–108, 113–114, 123, 130, 133–134, 145, 151, 153–154, 158, 161n, 167, 172n, 177, 206n, 208–209, 226, 230, 252–253

creditors/credit 15n, 62, 171n, 172n, 206, 209n

criminal justice system 14–15, 100n, 165n; ideology 52, 158n; *see also* bridewells, Fleet prison, highwaymen, imprisonment, justice of the peace (office), Michael Moleyns, commission of peace, prisoners, recusancy, (high) sheriff (office), Star Chamber, vagrancy, Warwick Gaol, whipping

Croft, James, comptroller of the household 132n

currency 69n, 139n, 171n, 172n

Curzon, Cicely of Billesly 86n

custos rotulorum (office) 54, 67n

Danet, John 75n, 76
Danet, née Lenton, Elizabeth 75n

Danet, Mary, previously Lenton, (m. George Medelye) 75n, 82, 88n
Dannett or Danet, Thomas 29, 76nn
Darnell, John 131n
Darnley, Henry Stuart, duke of Albany 96n
Davantry, Northants 248
death, causes of: battle 27, 68–69, 109n; carbon monoxide poisoning 81n; childbirth 168n; execution 24, 29–30, 37n, 38n, 54, 72n, 74–75, 76n, 77, 88n, 104n; falling from a horse 245; heat stroke 84; in infancy 185n; *see also* murder, poison
death of: Margaret Willoughby Arundell 163n; Dorothy Willoughby Hastings 167; Elizabeth, Lady Willoughby 47, 180, 181n; Francis Willoughby (1578–1580), son of Sir Francis Willoughby 136; Sir Francis Willoughby 49, 185n, 197; Margaret Willoughby Spencer 169n; Henry Willoughby 27, 68–69, 109n; Thomas Willoughby of Bore Place 106, 194–195; mother of Sir Percival Willoughby 143n; Lady Jane Grey 29–30; Henry Grey 29–30; John Grey 37n, Thomas Grey 29–30, John Lyttleton 173n
death threats, *see* threats
debt 9, 38n, 47, 48–50, 57, 81, 86, 99n, 100n, 119n, 124n, 129n, 134n, 139n, 159–161, 164, 165n, 167n, 170n, 171–172, 179, 199, 201–202, 203n, 206, 209, 219, 226, 235–236, 241, 242–244, 247
debtors' prison 57, 99n, 100n, 171n, 203n, 241–243; *see also* imprisonment
defamation 40, 102, 105, 155; *see also* credit/discredit
Derby, William, servant 116
Derbyshire 22, 24, 43n, 56n, 86n, 107n, 118n, 165n, 176n, 184n, 206n
Devereux, Robert, 2nd earl of Essex 221n
Deverell, Katherine 46, 158n
diamonds 120, 247
Diana, Princess of Wales 237n
diaper and damask 246
diet/dyet/dyat 45, 76, 85, 102n, 107–108, 126, 168; *see also* dining, food
Dilke, Anne, née Fisher 186n
Dilke, Thomas of Maxstock 186
dining 112–114, 163, 165; dining chamber 112–114; dining table 42, 71, 88, 110, 112–114, 149, 165n; linen for table (diaper) 246

disinheriting 140n; Winifrid Willoughby 241
dishonesty and honesty 11, 18, 37n, 41, 46, 59–63, 72, 82, 99–100, 105, 117, 124, 134, 146n, 152, 154, 157–158, 184, 188, 204, 207, 212, 228, 251–252
disobedience, *see* obedience and disobedience
disowning 44, 57, 121, 140n
divorce 140n, 158; alimony 46n
doctors (phisitians) 7, 41, 52, 72, 106–107, 178, 185, 193, 239, 245, 249
dogs 41, 94, 111, 180; use like a dog 56, 215; proverb 93, 226
Dorset, marquis of *see* Grey, Henry
dowries 24, 25n, 36–37, 38–39, 47–48, 176n, 256; *see also* marriage settlements
Drake, Bernard 250n
Drake, John Esq. 56, 250
Draycot, George 246
Draycot (Draicott, Draycott, Dracot) Henry, servant 120n, 121–122, 125–126, 150, 171n, 188–189, 205; in the 'cabal' 41, 102
Drayton Bassett, Staffs. 129n
Dudley Ambrose, 3rd earl of Warwick 96n, 97n, 105n
Dudley, Anne, née Russell, countess of Warwick (1548–1604) 105n
Dudley, Anne, née Seymour (1538/9–1588) 105n
Dudley, Guildford 29, 74n
Dudley, Henry 77n, 78n
Dudley, John, 1st duke of Northumberland 74n, 105n, 129n
Dudley, Robert, 1st earl of Leicester (c.1533–1588) 37, 42n, 45, 87n, 93, 94, 97n, 105n, 122n, 128n, 133–135, 137, 141–142, 191n
Dudley Castle 134n
Dugdale, William 20, 22, 68, 89, 90n, 91n, 254, 255–256
Dun, John, servant 116
Duport, Thomas (c.1513–1592) 130
duty: to husband 42, 62, 108–109, 132, 143, 145; to monarch 123; to parents 250n; to father and father-in-law 121, 138, 144, 149, 154, 190, 211, 233, 239; to mother 156, 230–231; to wife 132, 143, 189–190; to God 250n; to Sir Francis Willoughby 182; to Cassandra 193n; to Lady Mollyns 193; to Lord

INDEX

John Grey of Pirgo 91; to brother-in-law 214; *see also* conscience

East India Company 4n
East Indies 244
ecclesiastical courts 36n, 46n, 57, 250n
economist (oeconomist) 202
editing 12n, 64n
education 1, 3, 13, 28, 30–32, 37, 77, 79, 84–85, 88, 91, 101n, 131, 135n, 203, 249; humanist 31; of women 30, 31n, 37, 88, 91–92, 103, 131; *see also* school
Edward VI, king of England 25, 28, 69n, 70, 71, 72n, 75, 76n, 81, 96n, 99n, 145n, 167n; death of 75
Egerton, John 23n
Eikle, perhaps Eccles parish, Shropham, Norfolk 231–233
Elizabeth I, queen of England 3, 14, 23, 30n, 32, 41, 43, 44–46, 49n, 77, 79n, 80, 83, 85, 87n, 93–94, 97, 99, 101n, 102–103, 106, 107, 109–110, 123, 127, 131n, 133, 135–137, 138n, 142n, 145n, 152n, 164, 170–172, 176n, 185, 190n, 198; allegiance to 44, 123; appeal to 101n, 133, 135–136; Middleton/Wollaton visit 43, 109–110, 164; progresses of 43, 93–94, 97, 103, 105, 109–110, 135–136, 145n, 183, 201; *see also* court of
elopement 232n, 239–240
enclosures 15, 24, 27, 68–69, 76n
entertainment 43, 66, 87, 90, 94, 110, 111–114, 117n, 143, 162n, 168, 184, 212; *see also* courtship, hunting, hospitality, theatre
Eresby, Willoughbys of 116–117, 136, 140n, 190n, 193n, 204n, 254–255; *see also* alternative spellings of names, Thomas Willoughby of Bore Place
Essex Rebellion (1601) 89n, 101n
Essex, Robert Devereux, 2nd earl of 221n
executions, *see* death, Wyatt's Rebellion
exile from the realm 29, 33, 54, 55n, 77n, 220n
exorcism 131n

Fanshaw, Thomas, remembrancer of the exchequer (1533–1601) 122n, 206
fashion 43n, 106, 182, 202
fines 14, 40, 55n, 98, 139, 142, 172, 180n, 209, 236; 'pass the fines' 118

fire: at Wollaton Hall 1, 7n, 174n; Hastings barn fire 218; metaphor 131
fish 42, 166, 213, 241; fishponds 167n; fishing rights 22; metaphor 188
Fisher, servant 156, 181–183, 186; defended by Sir Francis Willoughby 186; *see also* 'cabal'
Fisher, Clement (*c.*1539–1619) 117n, 122–124, 140, 181n, 186–189, 205, 234, 247
Fisher, Mary, née Repington 117n, 118n, 122n, 181n, 187
Flanders, attack on 137
Flanders lace 92
Fleet Prison 14, 172, 176n, 185n, 197n, 202n, 213; *see also* Michael Mollyns
folk healing/old wives' remedy 218
food and drink 71, 84n, 106, 110–117, 162–163, 180; *see also* diet
food preservation 180
fool: epithet 17, 134, 153, 173; occupation 43, 115, 117n, 118; sarcasm 43, 118; self-effacing 226; sex implied 251
fool, Mary the 43, 115n, 118
foolishness 108n, 159, 231
foreigners (strangers) 111
Fox, servant 111, 116, 182, 192
Fox, George Willoughby, illegitimate son of Edward Willoughby, *see* Willoughby, George
France 23, 136–138, 144, 148, 256
Francis II, king of France 137n
Francis, duke of Alençon, later duke of Anjou (Hercule François, 1555–1584) 137
furniture: lack of at Wollaton Hall 168–169, at Thomas Willoughby's London house 177; of horse litter 177n

garden, physic (medicinal) 7
garnets 246
gender relations 58n
genealogical materials 1, 8n, 20, 22n, 68
genealogies 5, 142n, 167n, 238, 245–247, 247–249, 253–254
gentlemen servants 31n, 40n, 103, 203; Catesby 129; Conrados 149; Marmion 101n; Trussel 86n
gentry 2, 16n, 2–23, 33n, 38n, 40n, 41n, 86n, 97n, 88n, 129n, 132n, 162n; upper gentry 2, 16n, 22–23, 38n, 41n, 88n; income and spending 38n, 41–42
Gerard SJ, John 221n

274   INDEX

Germany, *see* Hamburg, Würtemberg
glass manufacturing 21
gold 138n, 167n, 170n, 172n, 182–183, 218; coins 138; embroidery 182; buttons 183, 'old gold' 183
Goodere/Godier (Goodrich), Henry (1534–1595) 170n, 191n; *see also* alternative spellings of family names
gossip: talk 2, 102–103; as women (gosseps) 127–128
Grange: Willoughby house, Lincoln's Inn 140 Tilty 70n, 71n; Wolvey 177
Great Brickhill, Bucks. 140
Great Seal 100–101; *see also* Francis Bacon, lord keeper
Great Sweat 28–29, 75n
Green: friend of Sir Percival Willoughby 184, Sir Francis Willoughby's servant 124; tenant family 184n
green: clothes 167n; cloaks or coats (livery) 240
Greetworth House 247
Greville, Elizabeth Willoughby, 3rd Baroness Willoughby de Broke (d.1562) 82n, 122n, 153n, 191n
Greville, Fulke (d.1569) 153n
Greville, Fulke (1536–1606) 82, 93, 122–123, 129, 135, 232n
Greville, Fulke, 1st Baron de Broke (1554–1628) 44, 82n, 93, 122–123, 129, 135, 232n, 241n
Greville, Robert (b. *c.*1540) 153n
Grey, Lady Anne, daughter of Viscount Lisle 25–26
Grey, Lady Anne, sister of 3rd marquis of Dorset, m. Henry Willoughby, parents of Willoughby orphans, *see* Willoughby
Grey, Lady Catherine 72, 73, 88n
Grey, Edward, Viscount Lisle 25
Grey, Lady Frances Brandon 71, 72n, 77n, 79, 80
Grey, Lord Henry, 7th Baron Codnor 25
Grey, Henry, 3rd marquis of Dorset, duke of Suffolk 26, 27–30, 35n, 37, 69–73, 74n, 77n, 81n, 132n; wardship of Willoughby orphans 27–28, 29–30; executed 30
Grey, John of Pirgo 30n, 36–37, 72n, 71–73, 76, 81, 87–89, 91
Grey, Lady Jane 23, 29–30, 69n, 70n, 72–73, 75n, 167n

Grey, Margaret Wotton 27n, 70n, 71n, 72n, 74n
Grey, Lady Mary 72, 73, 79n, 129n
Grey, Thomas, 1st marquis of Dorset 26, 78n
Grey, Thomas, 2nd marquis of Dorset 26, 27n, 69n, 72n, 73n
Grey, Lord Thomas, 71, 73n, 74n, 75n, 76n
Grey family 23, 25–27, 28, 30, 37, 54, 69n, 70n, 71, 72, 73, 76n, 82n, 83, 86, 87, 88n, 130n, 231n
groom (household office) 111–112
guardian/guardianship 13, 28, 30, 32; *see also* George Medley
Guildford, Mary Wotton (*c* 1500–1558) 78n
Guildford, Henry (d.1532) 78n
Gum, George, servant 115
Gunpowder Plot 38n, 54, 90n, 101n; *see also* conspiracies

Haddam's wife, *see* Hotham, Juliana Stanhope
hairstyles 182
Hakluyt, Richard 51, 81n
Halesowen (estate) 36
Halesowen (town) 184n
Hall, John 27
Hamburg, Germany 244, 248
Hampton Court 138, 169
handwriting 10, 27n, 45n, 60–61, 133n, 171n, 216–217
Hannam, Major 244
Hardwick, Bess of, Elizabeth Talbot, née Hardwick, countess of Shrewsbury (d.1608) 102n, 107n, 152n, 177n, 187
Hart, Percival of Lullingstone Court, Kent 106n
Hastings, Dorothy, née Port 206n
Hastings, Francis 206–207
Hastings, George 93, 162, 175, 176, 206–207
Hastings, Henry (Harry), m. Dorothy Willoughby 19, 48n, 56, 93n, 166–167, 175n, 176, 190, 202n, 204–220, 236, 253; abuse of Dorothy Willoughby Hastings 215, 218–220; character questioned 207
Hastings, Henry, 3rd earl of Huntingdon (*c.*1536–1595) 19, 41, 56, 97n, 117n, 167, 170, 177, 185–196, 190–191, 204–215; earldom restrained 206; honesty questioned 206

INDEX

Hastings, George 93, 162, 166–167, 175–176, 206–207
Hastings, Katherine, dowager countess of Huntingdon 206
Hatton (Haddon), Christopher, lord chancellor (1540–1591) 101n, 122n, 142, 206n
health and illness 9, 11, 18–19, 40, 42–44, 47, 49, 57, 62–63, 84, 95, 105–110, 136, 137, 157–158, 163, 177–178, 180, 185, 191, 197, 218–220, 239, 242, 245, 249; health care for the poor 107n; sea air 110; *see also* Buxton, spa
Henry II, king of France 137n
Henry VII, king of England 20, 24; supported by Henry Willoughby 24
Henry VIII, king of England 24–25, 26n, 28, 68, 72n, 73n, 78n, 86, 97n
heraldry 44, 122
Herbert, William, earl of Pembroke (1506/7–1570) 93–94, 95n, 97n
Heyman, Peter 142n
Heyman, Ralph 142
Hicks, Michael Sir 46
highway robbery/highwaymen 86n
Hinton, Hants 212
Holborn (Holbourn) 84, 140
Holland lace 182
Holles, Denzel (1538–1590) 109n
Holles, Eleanor, née Sheffield 109
Holles (Hollis), Sir John, later earl of Clare/earl of Clare 3n, 166n
Homer, *The Iliad* and *The Odyssey* 223
horses 28, 41n, 36, 41–42, 70, 72n, 84, 92, 106, 109, 121, 126, 141, 177n, 178, 185, 232n, 236; accident 236; gelding 80, 88, 128, 132, 178, 199, 232; mare 94, 219
hospitality 16, 41, 119, 111–113, 119, 166n; *see also* entertaining, dining
Hotham, John 41, 103–105
Hotham, Juliana Stanhope (Mistress Haddam) 41, 103–105
household accounts 1, 8, 14, 20, 30–31, 33, 39n, 41, 68, 69n, 78, 86n, 95n, 101n, 111, 114–115, 125n, 141–142, 161–163, 165, 168; building Wollaton Hall 21, 165
housekeeping (household management) 2, 39, 57, 73–75, 111–116, 125–126; Cassandra 7–8; Abigail Willughby Pargiter 57, 181, 245–246; royal household 32, 137n; servants (Draycot and Cludd) 121, 126

Hoxton, Shoreditch (Hogsden) 156
human nature 154
hunting 54, 84, 93, 106, 167n, 185
Huntingdon, Henry, *see* Hastings, Henry, 3rd earl of Huntingdon
husbands 3, 17, 21: allegations of abuse 18–19, 214, 218–220, 247; duty to wives 132, 143; allusion to sexual assault 212; protection of 124, 173; *see also* obedience
hypocoristic 144, 229

illness (sickness): cost of treating 41, 108, 178; Dorothy Willoughby Hastings 215; miasma theory of illness 107–108, 110; *see* health and illness
imprisonment 14–15, 172; for debt 57, 97n, 171n, 202n, 213; of Edward Willoughby 57, 241–243, of Sir Percival Willoughby 202n, 203n, 213; for suspicion of treason 30; for treason 76n, 82n, 90n; of daughters 57, 240–242; threatened 240; of Mary, Queen of Scots 102n, 150n; of wives in the house 2, 19n, 47, 56–67, 62, 151n, 218–219; Lady Jane Grey 74n; *see also* Tower of London, Fleet prison, marriage, Warwick Gaol
income, sources of 8, 24–26, 39, 101n, 111, 139, 140–141, 164n, 200–202, 209n; to build Wollaton Hall 142n; wealth-building marriage 22–23, 26, 36, 87n, 152n, 203; fines, rents, hereditaments, interest, manufacturing, coal receipts, investments, sale of land, sale of personal property *passim*
income, monetary crisis 171n, 172n
indebtedness crisis 171n; *see also* debt, debtors' prison
industrialization, early, *see* coal, mining, iron manufacturing, paper mill, River Trent, tree cutting, Wollaton wagonway
inflation 48, 69n, 171–172
inns 37n, 45, 73n, 84, 125, 126, 140, 252
Inns of Court: Lincoln's Inn 28n, 29, 106n, 174n, 195n, 221n; Grey's Inn 49n, 124
Inquisitions *post mortem* 49n, 56n, 84n, 120n; of Francis Willoughby 49n, 56n, 197n, 235n
intestate 17, 197n
Ireland 221n, 248, 249

INDEX

iron manufacturing 21, 50, 139, 183, 196, 200–201, 214
irony 86n, 158n
Italian: language 103, 149; script 31
Italian stone 164
Italy 164, 244
Ithell: name 86n 102–105

Jamaica 4n
James I, king of England 55n, 82n, 117n, 122n, 149, 169, 176n, 220, 221n, 242
Jane, queen of England, *see* Grey, Lady Jane
Jesuits 118n, 221n
Jesus College, Cambridge 32n
jewellery 120–121, 144, 182–183, 185n, 192n, 197n; *see also* agates, diamonds, garnets, gold, pearls, rubies
Joahn, servant 11–12, 44–45 125
Joane, servant 86n
jointure 19, 36, 49, 80n, 92, 98, 186, 190–191, 204n, 206
Jonson, Ben 235n
justice, theory of 52–53, 133n, 158n; 'law and order' 52
justice of the peace (office) 24, 33, 47n, 52–53, 101n, 122n, 158n, 188; and prosecuting adultery 158n; chief justice of the king's bench 22

Kearney, Dr John, of Kildare 68
Kearney family 68
Kenilworth (Kenningworth, Killingworth, Kellemyale) 43, 93–94, 97n, 110n, 109; *see also* court of Elizabeth I
Kett's Rebellion 27, 68–69, 109n
Keyes, Elizabeth and Henry Sacheverell, sons of 175–176, 257
Kingsbury Hall, Warks. 43–44, 100, 110, 118, 121–124, 132, 135, 139, 178–180, 183, 196, 200; settlement on Bridget and Sir Percival Willoughby 178–180, 196, 200
Kirby Bellars Priory 227n, 229–230, 234
knavery 102, 154–155, 167n, 177, 188–189, 226; exposed 188
knighted 37, 43, 92–93, 101n, 110n, 117n, 134n, 196; Sir Matthew Arundell 37; Sir William Catesby 101n; Sir John Lyttleton 92–93; Sir Francis Willoughby 43, 92–93, 101n, 110n; Sir Percival Willoughby 37n, 17n, 149

knights 22–23, 26, 37n, 38, 93, 137–138, 198, 236, 255
Knollys, Elizabeth 32–33
Knollys, Sir Francis (1512–1596) 25n, 32–33, 43, 54, 83n, 91n, 109–110
Knollys, Lettice 88n
Knoyle, Wilts. 193

labourers 164, 198n; wages 164
Lady Day (24 March), quarter day and beginning of legal year: rents 215, 218
Lambley (Lamly, Lamley) Manor 18, 169n, 194, 218, 251, 253–254
Langton, manors of 142, 170n, 256
laundress (household office) 115, 129
lawyers 37n, 49n, 81–83, 84n, 95, 98, 130n, 134n, 170–171, 179; fees 81–3, 84n; *see also* Inns of Court, George Medley
lead mine 22
Leicestershire 22, 70n, 71, 167n, 179n, 248
Lenton Priory (monastic house), later Aspley Hall 26, 98n
Lenton Fair 165
Lenton, [Mary] Mrs or Mistress (governess) 28, 30–31, 70, 74–75, 76, 82, 85–86
letter writing 1–21, 25–28, 33–63 *passim*, 87, 185, 215; conventions Figures 4, 5, 6, 7, 220; falsifying letters 218; open letters 229–231; perusing before sending 160; seal broken 215; vituperative 1, 117, 187–188; *see also* seals
Lewes family 185
Lincoln's Inn Fields (the Grange) 140, 181
Lincolnshire 22, 24, 98, 136, 164, 254–256
linen 113, 155, 192–193, 195, 246n
literacy and illiteracy 1, 3; female literacy 3, 215, 218n
litigation (complaint, sue, sute) 14, 38, 39, 45n, 59, 81n, 83n, 84n, 90, 95n, 99, 109, 121n, 133, 165n, 172, 179, 185n, 198, 200–202, 203n, 244; marital 133; divorce 59, 140n, 158; *see also* Paramour, suit of
litigiousness 165n
Littleton (Lyttleton), Gilbert 38, 53, 90, 121n, 173n
livery 109, 203; of Edward and Winifrid Willoughby 238
livestock 24n, 27, 69, 110, 165, 178; *see also* enclosures
loans 41, 50, 164n; interest 41, 49–50, 170n, 179, 200–202, 209, 236; *see also* money borrowed

INDEX

London 11, 13, 16n, 17, 18, 28, 29–30, 32n, 40, 41–42, 45, 49, 62, 70, 72, 76n, 77–79, 83–85, 89, 92, 94, 99, 100n, 103, 105–107, 110, 120, 121, 125–127, 129n, 131–132, 139–141, 144n, 150, 156, 158–161, 168n, 172n, 174, 177, 179, 183–185, 187, 191, 194–195, 206n, 207, 218, 223, 225, 231, 236, 240, 246, 251–252
Lord Chamberlain's Men 137n
lottery 249
Loughborough, Notts. 208
Lucy, Thomas Sir 93
lutes 50, 107, 134n, 208; strings 92, 208
luxury 42, 166
lying 52, 59–63, 102, 104, 130, 135, 154–156, 158, 160, 175; Dorothy Willoughby Hastings 215; *see also* cabal, Conrados, servants, intrigue
Lyttleton (Littleton), Elizabeth, *see* Elizabeth Littleton Willoughby
Lyttleton (Littleton), Gilbert, *see* Gilbert Littleton
Lyttleton (Littleton), Sir John 11, 33n, 37–39, 42–44, 53–54, 87–90, 92–95, 101–102, 108, 118–122, 125–128, 131, 133, 173; as untrustworthy 38–40, 88–90, 95; complaint to Francis Willoughby 101–102; lawsuits 38n, 39n, 90, 121n
Lyttleton (Littleton) family of Frankley 3, 33, 36, 87–94, 118n

Magdalen College, Oxford 29n, 174n
maintenance (while separated) 46, 97n, 104n, 108, 127–128, 136, 218, 241
malice 15, 16n, 59–63, 157–158, 189; and Catcher and Skinner, aldermen 14, 172, 173n; *see also* misogyny
Man, Dr Thomas (*c*.1655–1690) 7
Manners, Eleanor, née Paston 165
Manners, Elizabeth, née Charleton 165
Manners, John, 4th earl of Rutland (*c*.1551/9–1588) 163n, 165, 168
Manners, Theodosia, née Newton 165n
Manners, Thomas 'Lusty' (1537–1591) 162, 165, 175
Manners family, earls of Rutland 41, 162–163, 165, 168, 175
Manor Abbey Farm 184n
Mansfield, Notts. 152n, 205, 252
manufacturing 20–21, *see also* iron; paper mill; glass

Markham, Anne, née Roos, m. Griffin Markham 55n, 221n
Markham, Anne Stanhope, née Strelley 152n
Markham, Sir Griffin 55–56 152n, 153n, 220–234
Markham, Margaret 23n, 235
Markham, John, of Cotham 27n, 152n
Markham, Mary, née Griffin 228
Markham, Robert 23, 152, 208, 221
Markham, Thomas (*c*.1523–1607) 53, 56, 134n, 152, 152–155, 161, 166n, 175n, 206n, 220–221, 227n, 228–229
Markham family 23, 53, 54–56, 102, 123, 152–154, 220–229
Marmion, Gabriel, servant 161n, 205n, 206n
Marmion, Henry, servant 86n, 101–102, 133
Marmion, Henry, executor 27n, 86n
Marmion, William 86n, 101–102, 115, 149–155, 152n, 191, 183–184; 'an ill man' 150
Marmion (Marmyon) family 12n, 69n, 86n, 101–102, 133, 149n, 152n
marriage: *companionate* 2, 58, 141–148, 235–243; *happy*: Abigail Willoughby to William Pargiter 57, 247–249; Bridget Willoughby to Sir Percival Willoughby 58, 136, 141–149; Margaret Willoughby courted by Griffin Markham 35–36, 220–235; Margaret Willoughby to Robert Spencer 56, 220, 235; Winifrid Willoughby to Edward Willoughby 57, 237–240; *in upper classes* 37n; *love match, see* Margaret Willoughby and Robert Spencer, Winifrid and Edward Willoughby; *marrying age* 36n; *obedience of wife* 2, 11, 17–18, 46–47, 58, 62, 129, 159, 177; *of equals* 58; *of* Francis Willoughby to Elizabeth Lyttleton *passim*, 2, 33–47, 33–35, 36n, 37, 38–40, 42–47, 59–63, 86–180; *of* Francis Willoughby to Dorothy Colby Tamworth 48–49, 184–186, 191–194, 197; *of* Margaret Willoughby to Matthew Arundell 53, 80, 88n; *of* Thomas Willoughby to Mary Weston 106n, 195; *opposition to*: Francis Willoughby and Elizabeth Lyttleton 38–40, 43, 88–91; Margaret Willoughby and Griffin Markham 54–56, 227–235; Winifrid Willoughby

and Edward Willoughby 238–241; *and religion* 53–55; *see also* Margaret Willoughby and Griffin Markham; *servants meddling in* 102–105, 124–126: *see also under individual names*; unhappy Bess of Hardwick and George Talbot, 6th earl of Shrewsbury 102n; Francis and Elizabeth Willoughby 87–180; Frances Willoughby and Montague Wood 18–19, 57, 249–254; Juliana Stanhope and John Hotham 103n–104n; Dorothy Willoughby and Henry Hastings 56, 166–167, 205–208; *wealth-building* 22–25; *see also* abuse, adultery, divorce, dowries, duty, elopement, husbands, illegitimacy, marriage settlements, reconciliation, scandal, submission to husbands, proposal, unwanted suitors, weddings

marriage settlements (agreements) 3, 8, 26n, 36–39, 42, 47, 47–49, 56n, 58, 86n, 88, 103n, 118, 144n, 168n, 206n, 221n; excessive nature of 36n; lack of 49; Bridget Willoughby and Francis Willoughby 144n; Dorothy Willoughby and Henry Hastings 48n; Francis Willoughby and Elizabeth Lyttleton 36–39, 42, 88n, 90; Margaret Willoughby and Griffin Markham 221n; Margaret Willoughby and Robert Spencer 56, 221n

Marrow, Margaret, née Littleton 120, 129

Marrow, Samuel, Berkswell, Warks. 120n, 128n

Mary I, queen of England (Mary Tudor) 29, 33, 53, 54, 70, 72–80, 87n, 137n

Mary, Queen of Scots (Mary Stuart) 43n, 96, 107n, 137n, 102n, 152n

meat for horses 41, 140, 141

Medbourne Manor House, Leics. 179n

medicine: study of 9, 51–52; practice of 7, 41, 51–52, 74, 106–107, 178, 185, 193, 245, 249; medication 178

Medley (Medelye), George (d.1562/3) 13, 27–32, 33n, 69–73, 75, 78n, 81, 82n, 84, 85; accounts 13, 27–29, 30–31, 33, 69–70, 72n, 75–86; under suspicion 30, 76

mental health 11–12, 108–109, 125, 133, 143, 145, 155, 157, 220; Dorothy Hastings 218; Henry Hastings 167n; Winifrid Willoughby 214, 237

Meringe, Elizabeth 115n, 123–124

Meringe, William: will of 123n

Meringe/Mearing family 115n, 123n

Michaelmas 138

Middleton Hall, Warks. 4–5, 8n, 23, 28, 36–37, 40n, 42–45, 51, 69n, 70, 76, 79, 80, 83, 84n, 86, 88, 93n, 96, 101n, 106, 107–110, 117n, 118, 139, 149, 162, 170n, 174n, 178–180, 183–184, 186, 188–189, 196, 198, 200–201, 212–213, 227; force Sir Percival Willoughby from 190–194; troops to take possession from Bridget Willoughby 194

Middleton, Baron (1672–1729), *see* Thomas Willoughby

military revolution (1560–1660): Major Hannam in the King's service 244

mines 14n, 22, 23, 36n, 87n, 98n, 102n, 119n, 124n, 139n, 184n, 188, 210n; flooding 42n, 52n; *see also* coal (cole)

Minoresses of St Mary of the Order of St. Clare 28n; *see also* Minories

Minories 28, 29, 78n, 79, 82

miscarriage 15n, 40, 87n, 99, 127, 193n; *see also* pregnancy

misogyny 15n, 89, 150, 172, 215, 250–251

modesty 252

Moleyns, Elizabeth, née Gilbert 185, 191n, 193, 213

Moleyns, Sir Michael (Molins, Mollyns, Mullins, Murrin) (d.1615) 15, 16n, 185, 181, 196, 197–199

monasteries, dissolution of 26, 69n, 71n, 73n, 88n, 98n, 99n, 132n; *see also under individual names*; monastic houses

monastic houses 24, 26; Willoughby's Chantry 24, 168–169, 175–176, 178: abbeys 13, 24 26, 28–29, 70–73, 76–76, 78, 85–86, 89, 97n, 124n, 137n, 184n; friary 24, 132n, 227n; priories 98n, 137n, 227n; *see also* monasteries, dissolution of

money 22n, 30, 39, 48–49, 57, 76, 78, 80–82, 86, 87, 91, 95–96, 98, 101n, 110, 121, 128–130, 139–142, 148, 155, 161, 169–172, 175, 179, 194, 196–197, 199–202, 206, 209–210, 211n, 218–219, 236–238, 242, 247; abuse, monetary 215, 218–219; allowance 45, 47, 102n, 115, 127–128, 130, 133, 243; borrowed 48, 82, 132, 142, 167n, 169, 170, 172, 209; ready 30, 57, 78, 82, 101n, 115,

126, 130, 238; scarcity 117n–172; and servants' conspiracy 150, 181–183, 194; for Dorothy Colby Tamworth Willoughby 49–50, 192–197; amount Sir Percival Willoughby owed 197, 200–201

Moscow 81

moving house (removed to) 4, 8, 13, 28, 29, 70–61, 76, 79, 96, 110, 162

murder 44, 90, 96, 124, 155, 170; poison 49, 56, 185n, 197, 215, 218; threatened 240

music 9, 31–32, 41–42, 50, 91n, 116, 135n, 187; *see also* lutes; virginal

musicians 9, 41, 43, 116, 141

nationalism 76n; *see also* Wyatt's Rebellion

Newnam surname 14, 172

noblesse oblige 107n

Northamptonshire (county) 56, 57, 169n, 237, 247–249

North-East Passage 81n

Northern Rebellion (1569) 96–97

Nottingham 1, 22, 42, 103, 104n, 118, 131n 155, 163–166, 168, 175, 176, 193, 196, 237; borough 24

Nottingham Castle, constable of 165n

Nottingham, University of vii, ix, xix, 1

Nottinghamshire 3, 4, 6 (Figure 1), 14n, 16n, 21–26, 46n, 47n, 53n, 71n, 81n, 83n, 98–101, 103n, 119n, 123n, 124, 134n, 152n, 158n, 165n, 197n, 198n, 200, 210, 238n, 255; high sheriff of 24, 47n, 152n, 238

Nuneaton House, Wolvey Grange 170, 177n

nurse (household office) 40n, 129

nursery 114, 116

obedience and disobedience 2, 170n; in marriage 2, 11, 15, 17–18, 46n, 47, 59–63, 108–109, 123, 129, 141, 161, 177–78; to parents 2, 17–18, 55, 202–232, 242, 228, 247, 250n; to the Queen 172n

old wives' remedy/folk healing 218

one-hundred-year lease 214

Order of the Garter 169

Oxford, University of 94, 174n, 211n, 245

Paget (Padget) family 29, 38, 54, 80, 82–83

palimpsest 209n, 217 (Figure 7)

paper mill, considering construction of 21n

paper, cost of 41, 143

Paramour lawsuit 129–130, 191n

Pargiter, William of Nottinghamshire 57, 202n, 245–249

Paris, University of 13, 29, 82

Parry, Robert 250n

patriarchal justice 133n

patriarchy, navigating 58; Dorothy Colby Tamworth Willoughby stripping the estate 181–197; Margaret Willoughby and Markham engagement 231–232; 'Gods will to plague [...] with vile men' 215, 251; Winifrid Willoughby eloped to escape mother 240n; Frances Willoughby Wood and female sexuality 57, 249–253; Mary Weston and Bore Place, Kent 195

Payne, Robert: conspiracy against Sir Francis Willoughby 170–171; woad cultivation 171n

Payne, Robert of Basingstoke (m. dau. Winifrid Willoughby) 254; *see also* Barton Stacy

Payne, Thomas (d. aft. 1591) 179

Payne, William (d.1615) 177n

pearls 182–183, 192, 246

Peckham, Bridget Willoughby (*c*.1600) 10

Peckham, George 215n, 219

Peckham, Katherine, née Trussell 215

peerage 23, 48

Penne, John, servant 113, 116, 124

Penruddock, (Penruddoke) 36n, 39n, 95n

personal property: *see* clothing; diaper and damask, gold, jewels; lace, linen, plate, clock [246]

Peverell, Honour (Peverell Fee) 83, 99n

physician (phisitian) 7, 52, 74, 106–107, 178, 185, 193, 247, 250; *see also* medicine

Pickerell, John, gent. of Shipbourne, Kent 154

Piers, John, archbishop of York (1522/3–1594) 175n

plague: bubonic 242; the Great Sweat 23, 28n, 29, 75n

plate 80, 113, 120, 185n, 200, 202n

Plunket, Hon. Randle 68n

poetry and poets 8, 78n, 82n, 86n, 94n, 249n, 235n, 250n

poison 49, 56, 185n, 197, 215, 218

Poker, Joahn 125n

Polesworth Hall, Warks 170n

Port, John of Etwall, Derbs. 204

portraits 2n, 8, 9, 36n; of Elizabeth Willoughby 35 (Figure 3); of Francis Willoughby 34 (Figure 2)

pregnancy: hazards 134; of Dorothy Willoughby Hastings 208; of Mrs. Nevill, Lady Latimer 15n; of Capt. Nunames wife 15n; of Abigail Willoughby Pargiter 242; of Dorothy Hastings Ryves Tregonwell 219–220; of Bridget Willoughby 188, 194; of Dorothy Colby Tamworth Willoughby 49, 185n, 193, 194n, 198, 204; of Elizabeth Willoughby 17–18, 40, 45, 47, 87n, 99, 106, 127; of Frances Willoughby Wood 247; *see also* childbearing, miscarriage
Prestwood (Lyttleton estate) 108, 121, 128
prison 14–15, 30, 41, 47, 57, 74n, 76n, 82n, 90n, 99, 100n, 105n, 170n, 185n, 197n, 202n, 203n, 214, 240, 244: Sir Percival Willoughby debtor's prison 202n, 203n, 214; Edward (Ned) Willoughby debtor's prison 242–243; *see also* Bridewell, debtors' prison, Fleet prison, imprisonment, Warwick Gaol, Edward Willoughby
privacy, no expectation 158–159
privy chambers 79n, 100n, 176n
Privy Council 14–15, 32, 53, 95n, 129n, 170–171
privy seal 45n; lord privy seal 85, 133n
proposal (of marriage) 37n, 134, 235, 238; Dorothy Willoughby Hastings 208; Margaret Willoughby Spencer 228, 235; Dorothy Colby Tamworth Willoughby 184; Sir Percival Willoughby 146; Winifrid Willoughby 234
prostitution 120n
Protestant Reformation in England 3, 26, 32–33, 53–54, 87n, 107n, 142n 167n; *see also* Calvinism; Catholics; Henry Hastings, 3rd earl of Huntingdon; individualism; Puritanism; recusants
public nature of marriage troubles 44, 59–63, 102–104, 118, 120–121, 122–123, 130–131, 135–136, 158
Puddletown Manor, Dorset 205n
Pudsey, Richard 239
pumps (mining) 41n, 50n
Puritanism 16–17, 37n, 49n, 52, 55, 131n, 132, 154, 159–160, 230, 232, 246, 253; *see also* Henry Hastings, 3rd earl of Huntingdon; Protestant Reformation
pursuivant (office) 129, 141
Pyrford Manor 137

Queen Elizabeth I, *see* Elizabeth I, queen of England

rape: Henry Hastings 215, 218; Montague Wood 18, 251
Rawson, Ann (Stanhope) 103–104, 134n
Ray, John 4
reconciliation: attempts at 59–63, 118–119, 122–123, 127, 130–131, 136, 156; Elizabeth Willoughby not reconciled to Margaret Arundell 122; Francis and Elizabeth Willoughby reconciled 61, 172–178; Sir Francis and Sir Percival Willoughby reconciled 153–154, 178–179; Winifred Willoughby not reconciled to parents 243; Frances Willoughby Wood to Montague Wood 253–254
recusant families, *see* Arundell, Catesby, Lyttleton (Littleton), Markham, Paget, Wriothesley
recusants 37n, 53–56, 73n, 80n, 88n, 129n, 152n, 165n, 219n; George Willoughby Fox 37n, 73n; *see also* Catholics
rent 23, 41, 69n, 83n, 95n, 132, 166n, 176n, 183, 200, 205n, 209, 210, 211, 212n, 215, 218, 251; quit rent 200; *see also* Lady Day rents
Repington, Francis 98n
Repington, Mary (m. Clement Fisher) 122n, 181n
Repington, Maud, née Cotton (m. George Willoughby Fox) 73n, 98
Repington, Richard 37n, 98, 122n, 181n
reputation 16, 30n, 61, 95n, 108, 111, 151, 153, 156, 234, 248, 250; and spending/debt 48, 167, 235–236; Sir Percival Willoughby and Thomas Markham 130–155, 161; and Frances Willoughby Wood 250, 251
Richard III, king of England 24
Ridgeway, Cassandra 19
riot: Coventry 25; Drayton Park (Paramour) 130n
Robinson, Thomas (*c.*1578) 129n; *see also* Paramour
Rouen, siege of 221n
rubies 183n, 246
rumour 59–63, 102, 103–104, 135, 152, 158, 187; *see also* reputation
Russell, William, servant 49n, 184, 190–191, 192, 235, 246; wife of and jewels 183

Ryves, John of Damay Court, Dorset (d.1624/5), m. dau. of Dorothy Willoughby Hastings 218

Sacheverell, Henry (c.1548–1620) 175–176
Sacheverell, Jane, née Bradburn (1559–1621) 176n
Sackville, Robert, 2nd earl of Dorset (1561–1609) 181
St Anthony's School, London, see schools
St Giles Cripplegate parish cemetery 49, 185n, 197n, 198n
Sandys, Edwin, archbishop of York (1516–1588) 175n
Savage, John (1554–1615) 191–192
scandal: Dudley 87n, 88n; Stanhope 104n; Sir Percival Willoughby 150–153; Frances Willoughby Wood 252–253; see also gossip, rumour, reputation
schools: Saffron Walden Grammar School, Essex 30, 84; St Anthony's, London 13, 30–31, 77, 84; Westminster School 249
seals, personal: Dorothy Hastings 215; John Lyttleton 90; Thomas Markham 229; Thomas Willoughby 13, 82; resealed 215; sealed box of gold 218; sealed with the heart 130; Bridget Willoughby 215, 247; Elizabeth Willoughby 160; Sir Percival Willoughby 247
seminarians 118n
seneschal (office) 26
separation of Elizabeth and Francis Willoughby (1578–1588) 46, 86n, 127–174
sermons 31, 50, 53n, 54, 119, 202
servants of Francis Willoughby, menservants 2–3, 10, 16–17, 27n, 29, 36, 40–41, 44–45, 55n, 70, 72, 75–77, 78–98, 86, 92, 100, 101–105, 109, 110, 114, 15–116, 118, 119–122, 123, 124, 125–126, 127, 129, 132, 134, 135, 138, 139, 148–154, 160–161, 163, 168–169, 170n, 171n, 177, 181–183, 186–187, 194, 203, 218, 231, 248; complaints about 44–45, 47, 101–102, 132, 150, 177, 192; in defense of Fisher against Percival Willoughby 186; enrichment as motivation to interfere 150, 181–183, 194, 203; at Frankley 36, 92, 100; as gentlemen 40n, 101n, 116, 202–203; interfere in Margaret Willoughby Spencer's marriage 235–236; left in charge 45, 124–126, 148; lists of instructions 47, 111–114; 125–126; living arrangements 149; outwitted 203; payments to 31, 41, 70, 75, 77, 78–79, 84n, 110, 115–116, 129, 168–169, 218, 421, 248; servant to Elizabeth Willoughby 123–124; Dorothy Colby Tamworth Willoughby 49n, 186, 203: outwitted by 203; and Elizabeth Willoughby: attack on 124–125, separation from 45, 125, 134, plot to defame 43–44, 99–103, 117–120; Mearing (lady's maid) 123–124; scribe 134; Percival Willoughby, plots against 147–153, 184–186, 201; see also under individual names: Blyth, Catesby, Cludd, Conrados, Draycot, Dun, Fisher, Fox, Gum, Ithell, Joahn/Joane, Marmion (father and son), Penne, Rigley, Russell, Mearing, Shaw, Squire, Trussell, Willoughby (Henry)
servants of Francis Willoughby, maidservants 28, 68, 75, 121–122, 127, 172, 238, of Edward Willoughby 236; Winifrid Willughby as maid to Elizabeth Willoughby 237; see also household offices, butler, housekeeper, laundress, keeper of the horse, panter, usher; see also [Mary] Lenton, governess
Sewell, William, the younger, mayor of Coventry (1542–1624) 124–126
sexual intercourse 57, 95, 172, 248n
Seymour, Edward, duke of Somerset 25–26, 73n, 104n, 105n
Seymour, Jane 12, 68
Shaftesbury Abbey, Dorset 95, 96n, 149
Shakespeare, William 137n, 138n, 155n
Shakespearean language 155n, 207
Shaw, Thomas, servant 113
Shawe, Thomas 41, 114n
Sheffield, Edmund, 1st Baron Sheffield (d.1549) 109n, 137
sheriff (office) 24, 33n, 47n, 87n, 106n, 122n 152n, 172n, 176n, 128
Sherwood Forest 52n, 150n, 227n
ships 81n, 171
Skinner, Thomas, alderman and lord mayor of London (d.1596) 14, 172
slander 11, 59–60, 102, 104n, 152–154, 158, 187; see also rumour, lying, reputation
smallpox 78–79, 234

INDEX

Smallwood Manor 81, 83, 213n
Smith, Richard, MD (d. *c.*1599) 107, 185
Smythson, Robert (*c.*1533/7–1614) 164n
soldiering 25, 55n, 57n, 77n, 165n; king's service 236–237, 244; *see also* Sir Griffin Markham
South Sea Company 9
spa 43, 96, 107–109, 117, 239; *see also* Buxton
Spain 139, 171, 178n; *see also* war with Spain, Spanish Armada, and France
Spanish Armada 171
Spencer, John 49, 235–236
Spencer, Robert, 1st Baron Spencer of Wormleighton (1570–1627) 48n, 50n, 56, 153n, 168–169, 173, 176, 180, 220, 234–37; broken marriage contract with Margaret Markham 234–237; marriage to Margaret Willoughby 51–52, 217, 234–237
Spencer family 48n, 49, 56, 101n, 102n, 169
spices 42, 166; *see also* luxury
spying 11, 59–60, 78n, 136n, 138n, 197n, 221n; Griffin Markham 221n; on Elizabeth Willoughby 11, 59–600
Squire, John, servant 10, 86n, 102–105; as spy for Elizabeth Willoughby 103
Stanhope, Anne, née Rawson 103–104
Stanhope, Edward 134
Stanhope, Juliana, *see* Hotham [Haddam]
Stanhope, Margaret, née Port 120n, 206
Stanhope, Michael 103n
Stanhope, Thomas, of Shelford 16n, 53, 103, 104n, 120–121, 134–135, 162, 175
Stanhope family 16n, 24, 41, 102n, 103n, 104n, 129, 134–135, 152n, 206
Stanhope–Markham dispute 134n, 153; *see also* Conrados
Star Chamber 129–130, 170–171, 185, 203n
Steeple Hall, Essex 179
stepmothers 16n, 194–196, 198; stepson 37n, 98n; stepfather 4, 15, 19, 185n
Strelley, Anthony (1528–1591) 102–103
Strelley, Sir Anthony Sir (1528–*c.*1596) 102–103, 165
Strelley, Joan, née Baynham 165n
Strelley family 83n, 101n, 102–103, 117n, 152n, 165n, 219n
strong room 3, 12n; *see also* muniments room
Stuart, Arabella 169n, 221n
Stuart, Mary, *see* Mary, Queen of Scots
sub-feudal estates 212n

submission to husbands 45, 47, 122–123, 124, 130, 131–132; *see also* duty, wives to husbands
sugar 30, 42, 166
suicide: threatened 12, 45, 125
suitors: unwanted 19
suspicion 11, 16, 38–40, 49, 55, 59, 70n, 89, 143, 151, 157–158, 160, 170, 185n, 197, 211, 215, 226, 229, 230; of switching children 198; under suspicion 29, 30, 76n, 78n, 82n, 138n
Sutton Passeys, Notts. 82n, 98, 101n, 194, 200
Sutton Coldfield (Co(l)filde), Warks. 98n, 101n, 252
Sutton, Edward, 5th Baron Dudley 134
swords, *see* arms and armour

tailor (occupation) 129, 141
Talbot, George, 6th earl of Shrewsbury 102n, 107n, 152, 177n
Tamworth, John of Leake 49n
tenants 69n, 76n, 86, 184n, 188, 200, 214–215, 218: *see also* rent
tenements 92n, 132n
theatre (players) 24, 42, 72, 94n, 137n
Thoresby Hall 8n
threats and threatening behaviour 17 (to curtail freedom), 47, 57 (to imprison at home); *by:* Cludd to Elizabeth Willoughby 124; Henry Hastings to Dorothy Willoughby 218; Elizabeth Willoughby to Edward Willoughby 240; Elizabeth Willoughby to Sir Francis Willoughby 133; Elizabeth Willoughby to kill herself 12, 45, 125; Clement Fisher to Bridget Willoughby 117n, 187; Bridget Willoughby and Fisher 187–189; Francis Willoughby to Sir Percival Willoughby 185, 189; Percival Willoughby to Thomas Markham 153; of Spanish invasion 139n; to Percival Willoughby to go to Star Chamber 185
three-life estate 41n, 49, 190, 196n, 200, 210, 211n
Thurland Hall, Nottingham 166, 168, 175
Thurland, Thomas, mayor of Nottingham 166
Thynne, Thomas, 1st viscount Weymouth (bap. 1640–1714) 193n
Tilty Abbey (Tyltey, Tylty) 13, 28–29, 70–73, 75–76, 78, 84n, 85–86, 89

timber, *see* tree cutting
Topcliffe, Jane Willoughby (*c*.1525–*c*.1571) 97n, 98
Topcliffe, Richard 97
topography 9
torture 76n, 97n
touring 9
Tower of London 29, 69n, 74, 76n, 167n
travel, international 13–14, 37n, 82, 136–137, 145–149, 169, 244
treason 54n, 72n, 86n, 168; *see also* conspiracies
tree cutting (wood, timber) 41, 49, 86, 96, 138–139, 194, 196, 218
Tregonwell, Dorothy Hastings Ryves 218–220
Tregonwell, Thomas 219n
Trent, River 22, 96, 134n, 166n
troops 29, 194; raising of by the Queen 198, 236
troth 146, 208; *see also* betrothal
Trowell, Notts. 49, 178, 179, 183, 196, 198n, 200, 247
Trussell, Henry, servant 102n, 133, 136, 176–177; son of John Trussell 101n
Trussell, John of Billesley, bailiff at Wollaton (*c*.1515–1582) 70n, 86, 215n
Trussell family 86n, 101n, 133n, 215n
trustworthiness of the Account of Cassandra, duchess of Chandos 9–16
tuberculosis (consumption) 164n
Tudor, Mary, *see* Mary, Queen of England
Tyrone, earl of: plot to poison 197n

universities, *see* Cambridge, Oxford, Paris
usher (household office) 111–113, 141; gentleman usher 78
usury 129n
Valence 176n, also Thomas (*c*.1595) 195n
Vane, Sir George 234
varlet (verlet) 62, 103, 158, 160
venison 106
virginal (instrument) 30n, 31, 187

Wadley Manor/House, Littleworth, Berks. 209
wages 41, 68n, 108, 113–114, 127; as maintenance for wives 113, 216; board wages 166–167; labourers 162; *see also* servants
Wales, Welsh 92n, 101n
Walpole, Horace 8n

Walsingham, Francis, lord privy seal (*c*.1532–1590) 26, 45, 83, 99n, 131, 133
Wars of the Roses 20, 24
war with Spain 234; *see also* Spain, Spanish Armada
Wardour Castle 36n, 86n; *see also* Matthew Arundell
wardship of Willughby orphans 25, 27–33, 66–85, 89, 107n; of Frances Willoughby, dau. of Dorothy Colby Tamworth 15–16, 19–197, 248n
Ware Park, and manor of, Herts. 206
Warwick Gaol 239
Warwickshire 4, 23–24, 36, 43, 45, 53n, 67n, 84n, 87, 98–99, 101n, 121n, 133, 140n, 167, 198, 208, 219, 234, 246, 247; *see also* sheriff, Middleton, Wormleighton
Watson's Conspiracy, *see* Bye Plot
wedding gloves 184
weddings 19, 48, 166–167, 169, 206; Bridget Willoughby 136–140, 142; Dorothy Willoughby Hastings 166–167; Margaret Willoughby Spencer 169
Westminster 95n, 130, 221, 241; Westminster Abbey 135n
Weston, Mary 104n
Whalley, Ralph 178n
Wharton, Dorothy Colby Tamworth Willoughby 15, 48, 49, 182–202, 234n
Wharton, Philip, 3rd Baron Wharton (1555–1625) 183n
whipping 14–15
White Friars, London 129–130
Whmbrok 208
whore, as insult 11–12, 44, 123, 195; as designation of class/caste of women 14, 118n, 170
widowhood (both sexes) 15, 19, 41, 48, 49, 67n, 75, 85, 86n, 96n, 115n, 121n, 147n, 150n, 182–183, 197–200, 202, 233n, 253
Willoughby (Willughby), Abigail 18, 57, 179, 181n, 190–191, 199n, 200n, 243–247, 248n
Willoughby, Ambrose 169
Willoughby, Lady Anne, née Grey (d.1547/8) 26, 27, 67n, 81n
Willoughby (Willughby), Bridget 2–4, 10, 19, 21, 48n, 49, 56–58, 101n, 104n, 120n 115n, 134, 139, 141–154, 172n, 176, 178–179, 180–181, 184–187, 189, 190–191, 194n, 195n, 196n, 198–200, 201–202, 203, 207n, 214–215, 218n,

230n, 235, 238, 239–240, 243, 248n 253; companionate marriage 2, 58, 141–154; correspondence about missing heirlooms 190–191, 199–201; correspondence with husband Sir Percival 141–147; correspondence with sisters 214–215, 235, 238, 239–240, 243, 253; friendship with father-in-law 153; heiress 144; and plot to be kidnapped by servants and wed to Clement Fisher 184–188, 203; wedding 136–40; *see also* Sir Percival Willoughby

Willoughby, Bridget, née Read (1485–1558) 140n, 232n

Willoughby, Charles, 2nd Baron Willoughby of Parnham 171n

Willoughby, Sir Christopher, 10th Baron de Eresby (1453–1488/9) 136, 140, 193n

Willoughby (Willughby), Dorothy (1512–*c.*1555) 140n

Willoughby (Willughby), Dorothy 19, 48n, 56, 93n, 117n, 134n, 138, 149, 166–167, 170n, 177, 202n, Figures 6–7; marriage to Henry Hastings 204–220, 251

Willoughby (Willughby), Dorothy Colby Tamworth; *see also* Wharton, Dorothy Colby Tamworth Willughby 15, 49, 169n, 184–203

Willoughby, Edward (d.1541) 12, 25–26, 73n, 93n, 97n, 98, 131, 140n

Willoughby, Edward (Ned) of Bore Place, Kent 14, 57, 172–173, 175, 190, 196n, 201n, 214n, 237–244; in debtors' prison 57, 241–242

Willoughby (Willughby), Elizabeth, née Lyttelton/Littleton *passim*; clothing of 182–183; death of 47, 180, 181n; *and Francis Willoughby*: correspondence (1585–1588) 59–63, 126–127, 129–130, 132–133, 136, 157–161; marriage 2, 33–47, 87–91, reunification 173–174; separation 45–47, 125–173; and 'froward humour' 17, 40, 42–43, 100, 119, 159; judgement of character 17, 119–121; listed with servants 115; maintenance 45–46, 127–128, 136; portrait of 35, Figure 3; threatened by servants 124, 150; *see also* health and illness

Willoughby (Willughby), Frances 18–19, 49, 57, 119n, 181n, 201n, 202n, 214, 249–253; and cruelty from Elizabeth Willoughby 58, 249–250; independence of 250–251; marriage to Montague Wood 57, 251

Willoughby (Willughby), Frances (daughter of Dorothy Colby Tamworth) 49, 183n, 191; died in infancy 183n, 191

Willoughby (Willughby), Sir Francis (the builder) *passim*; adultery 11–12, 16–17, 44, 46, 46n, 123, 156n; as justice of the peace 47n, 52–53, 158n; as high sheriff of Nottinghamshire 47n; and the building of Wollaton Hall 161–173; childhood and education 4, 27–33, 68–87, 89, 91, 107n, 109n; *and Elizabeth Willoughby*: *passim*: correspondence (1585–1588) 59–63, 156–161, date of marriage 2, 87, reunification 173–174; separation 46, 125–142; death 49, 185n, 197–198; estate encumbered 48–50, 198–202; judgement of character 16, 50, 119; inquisition *post mortem* 197n; portrait of 34, Figure 2; second marriage to Dorothy Colby Tamworth Willoughby 49, 184–197

Willoughby, Sir Francis (1588–1665), son of Bridget and Percival 19

Willoughby, Francis (the naturalist) father of Cassandra 4; friendship with John Ray 4

Willoughby, Sir Francis, 1st Bt (1668–1688), older brother of Cassandra 4, 7, 19

Willoughby, Frediswith/Phridelwide/Frediswide 19, 153n

Willoughby, George, illegitimate son of Edward Willoughby, aka Fox 37, 42, 73, 84n, 89, 91, 98, 111n, 117n, 122n, 169, 181, 183, 203; recusant 37n

Willoughby, Helen Egerton 23n

Willoughby, Sir Henry (1451–1528) 23–25

Willoughby, Sir Henry (d.1549) 13, 26–27

Willoughby, Henry (6th Baron Middleton) 3

Willoughby, Henry de Eresby (1540–1606) 116–117n; 204n

Willoughby, Henry, unidentified 115, 116–117n

Willoughby, Hugh (the Navigator; d.1554) 25, 38n, 81, 83, 86, 116–117

Willoughby, Joanna (Jane), née Strelley 115n 155n

Willoughby, John (*c.*1537) 12, 25–27

Willoughby, Katherine, née Hart 104n

Willoughby, Lettice (dau. of Bridget) 19
Willoughby, Margaret, née Markham 22n
Willoughby (Willughby), Margaret, Lady Arundell (1536–1587) 4n, 10, 12, 13, 27–33, 36, 37–40, 53, 55n, 67–68, 72–78, 80, 86n, 87–102, 122–124, 128, 131–136, 143, 147, 156n, 161, 234n; childhood 27–33, 36, 37, 53, 55n, 68, 72–78, 80, 101n; death 161; education 30–31, 101n; marriage 36n, 78, 86n; and reaction to Francis Willoughby's marriage 37n, 38–40, 43, 45, 87–89, 90, 99–100, 131–133; room at Wollaton 156n
Willoughby (Willughby), Margaret 48n, 55–56, 152–153, 169, 220–237
Willoughby, Michael, 13th Baron Middleton 206n
Willoughby, Sir Percival (de Eresby) of Middleton and Wollaton 1, 2, 4, 7, 10, 14–17, 21, 33n, 40, 47n, 48n, 49–50, 5658, 101n, 104, 114n, 115, 120n, 129, 134–137, 141–154, 160–161, 166–174, 176–185, 187–189, 192–203, 208, 210–212, 216, 218, 226, 210–212, 216, 218, 226, 228, 230, 235–237, 240–241, 243, 245–246, 248, 250–252; debtor's prison 201n; encumbered estate 40–50, 198–200; European travel 13–14, 37n, 80, 132, 134–135, 137, 142–147; bound to Francis Willoughby's debts 49–50, 177–178, 198–200; as heir 16, 49, 176–178; lawsuits 194, 196n, 201n, 248n; knighted 147; wedding 137–139; Thomas Markham's plot (Conrados) 147–153, 177; *see also* Bridget Willoughby, Middleton Hall
Willoughby, Richard de (d. *c.*1362/3) 22, 23n; *see also* Bugge, Ralph
Willoughby, Robert (b.1565) 138n
Willoughby, Robert de Eresby (1511–*c.*1555) 138n
Willoughby, spelling of 21–22, 114–115
Willoughby, Thomas de Eresby (1486–1555) 140n
Willoughby, Thomas (of Bore Place, Kent) 40, 48n, 105–106, 116n, 134n, 136–137, 140–141, 144, 148–149, 150, 154–155, 169–170, 172, 181, 194–195, 202n, 237–238, 241
Willoughby (Willughby), Thomas (*c.*1541–1559), older brother of Francis Willoughby 13, 25, 27–30, 32n, 69, 71–72, 73n, 74–75, 76n 80n, 81–84; death 30, 32, 83–84
Willoughby, Sir Thomas, 1st Baron Middleton (1672–1729), younger brother of Cassandra 4, 7 19n, 68
Willoughby (Willughby), William Deverell (1584–1634?), illegitimate son of Francis Willoughby (Willughby) 46, 158n
Willoughby, William of Normanton and Nuneaton (d.1587) 170
Willoughby (Willughby), Winifrid 57, 237–244; abuse of 57, 239–240; elopement 57, 240; mental health 214, 237n; *see also* Edward (Ned) Willoughby
Willoughby family background 21–27
Willoughby-on-the-Wolds 22
wills 5, 36n, 93n, of Matthew Arundell 88n; of Richard Catesby 101n; of James Jeffrey 139n; of John Lyttleton 173n; of Thomas Man 7; of George Medley 69n; of William Meringe 123n; of Anthony Strelley 103n, 163n; of Bridget Willoughby 232n; of Francis (Willughby) Willoughby, the builder, intestate 16–17, 197n; of Henry Willoughby 25, 37n; of John Willoughby 26n; of Robert Willoughby 232n; of Thomas Willoughby 140n
Wilton [Abbey] House, Wilts. 94, 97
wine 24, 42, 113n, 148, 178, 244
wives *passim*; *see also* abuse, banishment, divorce, duty, marriage
woad 21, 47n, 171n
Wollaton 7–8, 10, 21, 23, 27–28, 42–43, 49, 70, 80, 82n, 83, 84n, 96n, 98, 101n, 102n, 110–111, 117n, 118, 139, 149–151, 161, 163–169, 171, 173n 176–178, 179–85 189–190, 194, 196, 198, 220, 230, 232, 235, 235n, 237–238, 245–248, 250n, 252; absence from Wollaton 42, 46,183–184, 218; Chantry at, *see* Chantry; Church 131; coal mining at 23, 25, 41n; and Dorothy Colby Tamworth Willoughby 185, 193; as inheritance 178–180, 183, 196, 198n, 200; Christmas at 234; clothing in wardrobe 182–183, 192; escape by Frances 57, 250n; escape by Winifrid 237–238; iron works at 200; library at 8, 51, 53n, 71, 79–80, 85, 89, 95, 106, 108, 118–119, 124–125, 128, 139, 157,

169, 170, 179, 181–182, 199–200, 221, 233–235, 240, 247, 249, 254; visit by Winifrid and Edward Willoughby 241

Wollaton Hall 1, 2n, 4, 6, Figure 1, 7, 21, 36n, 51–52, 162, 164, 174n; building of 47–48, 156, 162n, 163–164, 168–169, 236; financing of 49, 142n, 169, 238; Old Hall, 28n, 36, 42, 158n, 163–164

Wollaton Wagonway 124n

Wolvey Grange, Warks. 177n

women *passim*; *see also* abuse, education, co-heirs, duty, marriage, female sexuality; individual names

wood sales, *see* trees

Wood, A.C. 1; disparagement of Cassandra, duchess of Chandos 20

Wood, Montague, of Lambley, *see* Frances Willoughby

Woodland (estate) 56, 93, 94, 98, 167, 177n, 190, 209–215, 218–219; *see also* Henry Hastings, Dorothy (Willughby) Willoughby

wool 22, 79

Wriothesley, Henry, 2nd earl of Southampton 138n

Wriothesley, Mary 138n

Wriothesley, Thomas, 1st earl of Southampton (recusant) 80n

Württemberg, or Wirtemberg, Germany 169

Wyatt's Rebellion 29, 30n, 72n, 74n, 75n, 76n, 77n, 82n, 81n, 96n

yeoman: household office 111–113, 141; social class 198n

York, archbishopric 158n, 175